W9-AUK-746

PetSpeak

PetSpeak

Share Your Pet's Secret Language!

You're Closer Than You Think to a GREAT Relationship with Your Dog or Cat!

By the Editors of Pets part of the family™

Pets: Part of the Family public television series is generously underwritten by PETsMART and PETsMART.com.

Notice

This book is intended as a reference volume only, not as a medical manual. The information given here is designed to help you make informed decisions about your pet's behavior. It is not intended as a substitute for any treatment that may have been recommended by your veterinarian. If you suspect that your pet has a serious behavior problem, we urge you to seek competent help.

Printed in the United States of America on acid-free ∞, recycled paper 

Library of Congress Cataloging-in-Publication Data

Petspeak : you're closer than you think to a great reationship with your dog or cat! / by the editors of Pets, part of the family.
p. cm.
Includes index.
ISBN 1–57954–077–5 hardcover
ISBN 1–57954–337–5 paperback
1. Dogs—Behavior. 2. Cats—Behavior. 3. Human-animal communication. 4. Human-animal relationships. I. Title: Pet speak. II. Pets, part of the family (Firm)
SF433 .P47 2000
636.088'7'019—dc21 00–009290

Distributed to the book trade by St. Martin's Press

2 4 6 8 10 9 7 5 3 1 hardcover
2 4 6 8 10 9 7 5 3 1 paperback

Visit us on the Web at www.rodalestore.com, or call us toll-free at (800) 848-4735.

OUR PURPOSE

To explore, celebrate, and stand in awe before the special relationship between us and the animals who share our lives.

PetSpeak Staff

MANAGING EDITOR: Ellen Phillips
EDITOR: Matthew Hoffman
WRITERS: Selene Yeager with Mariska van Aalst; Brett Bara; Alisa Bauman; Rick Chillot; Karen Commings; Susan Easterly; Tony Farrell; Leah Flickinger; Linda Formichelli; Mark Giuliucci; Lucinda Hahn; Bill Holton; Joanne Howl, D.V.M.; Jordan Matus; Susan McCullough; Arden Moore; Jana Murphy; Kristine Napier; Margo Trott; Winnie Yu
ART DIRECTOR: Darlene Schneck
INTERIOR AND COVER DESIGNER: Christina Gaugler
PHOTO EDITOR: James A. Gallucci
COVER PHOTOGRAPHER: Dennis Mosner
ILLUSTRATOR: Wendy Wray
INFORMATION GRAPHICS: Christina Gaugler
ASSISTANT RESEARCH MANAGER: Leah Flickinger
ASSISTANT FREELANCE RESEARCH MANAGER: Sandra Salera Lloyd
BOOK PROJECT RESEARCHER: Lois Guarino Hazel
EDITORIAL RESEARCHERS: Karen Jacobs, Rebecca Kleinwaks, Mary S. Mesaros, Elizabeth B. Price
SENIOR COPY EDITORS: Karen Neely, Jane Sherman
EDITORIAL PRODUCTION MANAGER: Marilyn Hauptly
LAYOUT DESIGNER: Daniel MacBride
ASSOCIATE STUDIO MANAGER: Thomas P. Aczel
MANUFACTURING COORDINATORS: Brenda Miller, Jodi Schaffer, Patrick Smith

Rodale Active Living Books

VICE PRESIDENT AND PUBLISHER: Neil Wertheimer
EXECUTIVE EDITOR: Susan Clarey
EDITORIAL DIRECTOR: Michael Ward
MARKETING DIRECTOR: Janine Slaughter
PRODUCT MARKETING MANAGER: Kris Siessmayer
BOOK MANUFACTURING DIRECTOR: Helen Clogston
MANUFACTURING MANAGERS: Eileen Bauder, Mark Krahforst
RESEARCH MANAGER: Ann Gossy Yermish
COPY MANAGER: Lisa D. Andruscavage
PRODUCTION MANAGER: Robert V. Anderson Jr.
OFFICE MANAGER: Jacqueline Dornblaser
OFFICE STAFF: Susan B. Dorschutz, Julie Kehs Minnix, Tara Schrantz, Catherine E. Strouse

Board of Advisors

C. A. Tony Buffington, D.V.M., Ph.D., professor of veterinary clinical sciences at the Ohio State University in Columbus

Karen L. Campbell, D.V.M., professor of dermatology and endocrinology at the University of Illinois College of Veterinary Medicine at Urbana–Champaign

Liz Palika, a columnist for *Dog Fancy* magazine; owner of the Dog Training with Liz obedience school in Oceanside, California; and author of *All Dogs Need Some Training*

Allen M. Schoen, D.V.M., affiliate faculty member in the department of clinical sciences at Colorado State University in Fort Collins; director of the Veterinary Institute for Therapeutic Alternatives in Sherman, Connecticut; and author of *Love, Miracles, and Animal Healing*

John C. Wright, Ph.D., a certified applied animal behaviorist; professor of psychology at Mercer University in Macon, Georgia; and author of *The Dog Who Would Be King* and *Is Your Cat Crazy?*

Contents

Introduction 1

PART 1

The Amazing Senses of Dogs and Cats

CHAPTER 1
Vision 11

CHAPTER 2
Hearing 21

CHAPTER 3
Smell 28

CHAPTER 4
Touch 35

CHAPTER 5
Taste 41

CHAPTER 6
The Sixth Sense 47

PART 2

From Whiskers to Tails—A Complete Guide to Body Language

CHAPTER 7
Whiskers 55

CHAPTER 8
Eyes 59

CHAPTER 9
Ears 65

CHAPTER 10
Facial Expressions 73

CHAPTER 11
Tails 82

CHAPTER 12
Posture 91

PART 3

Speak!

CHAPTER 13
What Your Dog Is Telling You 103

CHAPTER 14
What Your Cat Is Telling You 110

CHAPTER 15
How You Can Talk Back 115

PART 4

How Your Pets Read You

CHAPTER 16
What Your Body Is Telling Them 123

CHAPTER 17
The Problem with Height 133

CHAPTER 18
The Etiquette of Eye Contact 140

CHAPTER 19
Watch Your Tone of Voice 147

CHAPTER 20
Make Your Hands Safe Instead of Scary 152

CHAPTER 21
Talking with Scents 159

CHAPTER 22
When Affection Isn't a Favor 168

PART 5
Putting It Together

CHAPTER 23
Choosing the Right Puppy....................177

CHAPTER 24
Choosing the Right Kitten....................184

CHAPTER 25
Picking a Good Older Pet 189

CHAPTER 26
Choosing and Using Names 196

CHAPTER 27
Teaching Commands 200

CHAPTER 28
10 Step-by-Step Training Lessons for Dogs 206

CHAPTER 29
Four Step-by-Step Training Lessons for Cats....................216

CHAPTER 30
Fun and Games 222

CHAPTER 31
You're in Charge....................229

PART 6
When Communication Breaks Down

CHAPTER 32
Aggression toward People 237

CHAPTER 33
Attacking Feet or Hands....................243

CHAPTER 34
Attacking Paper 248

CHAPTER 35
Barking and Meowing 252

CHAPTER 36
Begging 259

CHAPTER 37
Biting 263

CHAPTER 38
Chasing Cats 267

CHAPTER 39
Chewing..............................272

CHAPTER 40
Crowding............................278

CHAPTER 41
Digging...............................282

CHAPTER 42
Drinking from the Toilet....................289

CHAPTER 43
Dung Eating.......................293

CHAPTER 44
Early-Morning Awakening 297

CHAPTER 45
Eating Grass and Plants...........................300

CHAPTER 46
Eating Objects 306

CHAPTER 47
Fear of Being Alone 310

CHAPTER 48
Fear of Noises....................316

CHAPTER 49
Fear of Strangers..............321

CHAPTER 50
Fighting with Other Pets..................326

CHAPTER 51
Finicky Eating....................331

CHAPTER 52
Food Stealing.....................338

CHAPTER 53
Hiding.................................345

CHAPTER 54
Hogging the Bed................348

CHAPTER 55
House Soiling.....................352

CHAPTER 56
Howling and Yowling 358

CHAPTER 57
Humping.............................363

CHAPTER 58
Jealousy 368

CHAPTER 59
Jumping On Counters.......................372

CHAPTER 60
Jumping Up........................376

CHAPTER 61
Killing Mice 380

CHAPTER 62
Kneading
and Nursing 384

CHAPTER 63
Leash Pulling.......................388

CHAPTER 64
Licking 394

CHAPTER 65
Nighttime Activity.............399

CHAPTER 66
Overexcitement..................403

CHAPTER 67
Possessiveness
with Toys 408

CHAPTER 68
Rolling in
Smelly Things.....................414

CHAPTER 69
Rubbing 418

CHAPTER 70
Scratching
Furniture 422

CHAPTER 71
Sneaking onto
Furniture 428

CHAPTER 72
Sniffing 433

CHAPTER 73
Spraying
and Marking.......................437

CHAPTER 74
Throwing Up 444

CHAPTER 75
Travel Phobia 449

CHAPTER 76
Wool Sucking 454

CHAPTER 77
Yawning 458

Index......................................463

Talking With Dogs and Cats

"Don't eat me!"

These could have been the first words a young wolf pup tried to say to a human. Historians believe that ancient people may have occasionally considered wolves as cuisine more than as companions. But at some point around 100,000 B.C., a little potential pot roast must have rolled over, wagged her tail, and flashed her big brown eyes, causing the Mesolithic mothers in the tribe to spare her from the soup pot and welcome her into the family.

"The wolves that humans found the most adorable, and the most useful, were likely the ones allowed into the fold," explains Bruce Fogle, D.V.M., a veterinarian in London and author of *Know Your Cat* and *Know Your Dog*. "They kept the ones who said, 'Hey, I can bark at intruders!' and 'Hey, I can help with hunts!' and 'Keep me around, and I'll be a faithful, trusty companion.'"

About 9,000 years later, the first domestic cats were sending messages of their own. Dropping gifts of dead mice and rats in front of the ancient Egyptians, these sleek, feline predators proved that they could protect the precious grain supplies from local rodents. Eternally grateful, the Egyptians welcomed them into their homes and worshipped them as deities, too.

Those were the days when "petspeak" was simple.

From Workmates to Roommates

Since then, dogs and cats have traveled with us across the globe, and life has gotten easier in many ways. Food is plentiful. Shelter is available. And we know each other pretty well. But in some ways, life has gotten tougher. Dogs and cats have gone from busily working with their people to spending most of the time alone, locked up in houses and apartments, with few opportunities to roam outside. As a result, behavior problems have become more of an issue than ever before.

"The root of many modern problems between pets and people is that we no longer ask them to do the jobs they were originally domesticated to do," says Stephen Zawistowski, Ph.D., a certified applied animal behaviorist and a senior vice president of animal services and science advisor for the American Society for the Prevention of Cruelty to Animals in New York City. "Our pets don't always understand what we expect from them. We don't always understand what they're trying to tell us. And so we get into trouble."

Knowing how to talk to pets and understanding what they're saying is more important today than it has ever been. Fortunately for us, animal behaviorists and veterinarians have spent years studying how pets and people communicate. So learning "petspeak" can be as simple as learning "humanspeak." You just have to be willing to spend a day in their paws.

WHAT WE SAY, WHAT THEY HEAR

You probably don't realize it, but you send signals to your pets all the time, even when you're not saying a word. Every move you make sends a message about how you're feeling and what you're up to—and how it's going to affect them.

"You are the most important thing in your pets' lives," says Dr. Zawistowski. "They look to you for food, shelter, and companionship. It is in their best interest to be completely in tune with every message you send out." This means more than just listening when you call their names. It means analyzing the heaviness of your footsteps, the tension in your face, the smell of your body, and the tone of your voice when you walk through the door. "Our pets use all five of their senses to interpret their world," he says. "They can literally smell when you've had a bad day because you give off a different scent when you're angry."

Dogs and cats also understand more human language than we give them credit for. They probably comprehend dozens of words, says Dr. Fogle. Some dogs can understand as many as 300. "Heck, they even catch on to us when we try to spell things out, like 'b-a-l-l,'" he adds.

Common Faux Paws

Even though pets are attuned to every message that we send, they interpret meanings with their canine and feline brains. Here are six classic misunderstandings: the differences between what people say and what their pets understand.

You Say or Do	They Think	Try This Instead
Wave your hands and yell "Stop that!" when your dog is rooting through the trash.	"Wow! The way she's yelling and jumping around, she must want to play in the trash, too!"	Lower your voice the same way dogs do when they're telling other dogs that they mean business.
Yell at your cat when she's on the kitchen counter.	"That person is a lunatic! I'm going to run and hide whenever she comes into the room."	Set up a noisemaker, like a Snappy Trainer. The noise will startle your cat, but she won't think you had anything to do with it.
Stand tall while telling your dog to come.	"Holy cow. She looks so tall and scary, I'd better run the other way."	Crouch down with your body in an open position and call out in a friendly, welcoming voice.
Continue stroking your cat as her purrs increase.	"All of this physical attention is really winding me up. One more stroke, and I'm gonna have to use my claws."	Some cats enjoy a lot of stroking, but it's not as comforting as people imagine. Purring is a sound of arousal, not just of affection. So limit your strokes to a few at a time.
Put out your hand for a strange dog to sniff.	"This strange person is going to grab or whack me with that outstretched hand. I better nip it."	Keep your hands by your sides and let the dog approach you just as she would another dog.
Coaxing a shy cat to you by bending down with your arms out.	"Who is this big, scary creature, and why is she threatening me?"	Turn to the side and act nonchalant. Cats often feel threatened by big displays of attention.

NAME: Man Ray and Battina
OCCUPATION: Photographer's models

William Wegman's famous weimaraners look almost human when they're draped with flowing wigs, Victorian dresses, and fancy suits. But it's the very fact that they're *not* human that has allowed William, one of the country's best-known photographers, to create such stunning images of his beautiful gray dogs.

"Dogs have many expressions that parallel human looks," says William, who is the creator of the best-selling book of images, *Man's Best Friend*. "They cock their heads, they yawn, and they smile. But often these expressions don't indicate the same emotions in dogs as they do in humans. Yawning can mean they're nervous or anxious, for example. And smiling can be a sign of overexcitement. For me to capture the right expressions, I have to understand what all of their expressions really mean and how to evoke them."

William has worked with many weimaraners, starting with Man Ray in 1970. Battina is one of his current models. The magic of his photographs depends on his ability to find exactly the right words to elicit certain expressions from his cooperative dogs. Man Ray, for example, would cock his head whenever William said "George." "That was my father's name, and he loved my father," he explains. "Battina gives interested expressions to 'dog' and 'baseball.' It takes some experimentation to find the words the dogs like best, but talking to them always works better than food."

The dogs never seem to get tired of posing, he adds. "Weimaraners like games a lot, and they see photography and film as an interactive game. They take their work seriously, but they also love it."

THE ANIMALS TALK TO YOU

If you were to watch your pets as closely as they watch you, you'd see that they're not only listening to you much of the time, they're "talking" to you, too.

Most of these messages, of course, aren't verbal. Up to 80 percent of a dog's communications are through scents and body language. Every wag of a tail and twitch of an ear is telling a story, whether we know it or not.

Cats also like to let us know how they're feeling. Like dogs, they communicate through body posture and behavior as well as with an intricate vocabulary of more than 20 distinct meows, purrs, chirps, and other sounds. "Cats probably view us as mother figures," explains Benjamin Hart, D.V.M., Ph.D., professor of physiology and behavior at the University of California, Davis, School of Veterinary Medicine and author of *The Perfect Puppy: How to Choose Your Dog by Its Behavior*. "We're more important to them than any other cat, and they spend a lot of time trying to tell us how they feel as well as what they want and need."

Even though our pets send us dozens of messages each day, we're often oblivious to what they're saying. "So much of our pets' body language is subtle," says Dr. Fogle. "Little things like a flick of a tail, the drop of a gaze, and the smallest dilation in pupils can speak volumes, but we may never know it. And that's exactly where many behavior problems begin."

If you don't hear your pet when she tries to tell you that she's bored, anxious, threatened, or sick, she'll "speak" a little louder—by chewing your best Italian shoes or pooping 10 feet from the litter box. "Once you understand some of the more subtle signals that your pet is having trouble, you can take the appropriate steps to avoid larger, more troublesome behavior problems," says Dr. Fogle.

PETSPEAK ISN'T UNIVERSAL

The language we use with dogs (and the language they use with us) is much different from the language we share with cats. They're different species, after all. But dogs also vary quite a bit in what they understand and the ways in which they communicate. One glance at a Rottweiler standing next to a poodle makes it pretty

Acting Out

Here are a few of the most common behavior problems that might be prevented if you really understood what your pets were saying.

What Pets Do	What We Think It Means	What It May Really Mean
Destroying shoes when you're gone.	She's angry or afraid.	She's fearful about being alone. Dogs soothe themselves by mouthing something that smells like you.
Scratching the furniture.	She's destructive.	She needs something (like a quality scratching post) to call her own. Cats are territorial, and scratching lets the world know that something belongs to them.
Incessant barking.	She must see or hear something.	She's anxious or bored and needs more excitement in order to let off steam.
Pooping outside the litter box.	She's being spiteful.	The litter box is a mess. Or another cat is invading her bathroom space.
Howling.	She hears something scary, or something is hurting her ears.	Dogs often get lonely when they're by themselves, and howling is their way of making contact with others. Or it could be that she simply likes to sing.
Tearing around the house like a cat possessed.	She's possessed.	She is probably bored and needs a ball or a stuffed mouse to chase and pounce on.

clear that while dogs are members of one species, they're worlds apart when it comes to breeds. We have spent thousands of years breeding dogs for specific purposes, from rounding up livestock to warming our laps. These dogs do speak a common language, but the ways they communicate are anything but universal.

"Dogs have undergone all sorts of anatomical and behavior changes that have made them less able to communicate with one another as well as with us," says James Serpell, Ph.D., director of the Center for the Interaction of Animals and Society at the University of Pennsylvania in Philadelphia. "Adaptations like floppy ears, shaggy fur, and curly tails all can conceal their expressions," he explains.

Differences in temperament also influence how pets communicate. "Traditional guard dogs like Chows are going to have more aggressive tendencies than companion working dogs like golden retrievers," says Dr. Zawistowski. "You need to use different communication tactics with different dogs." Prolonged eye contact with a golden retriever, for example, isn't going to get much of a reaction at all. If anything, she'll just figure you're in the mood for some loving and will climb on your lap. Do the same thing with a strange German shepherd, and she may take it as a direct threat.

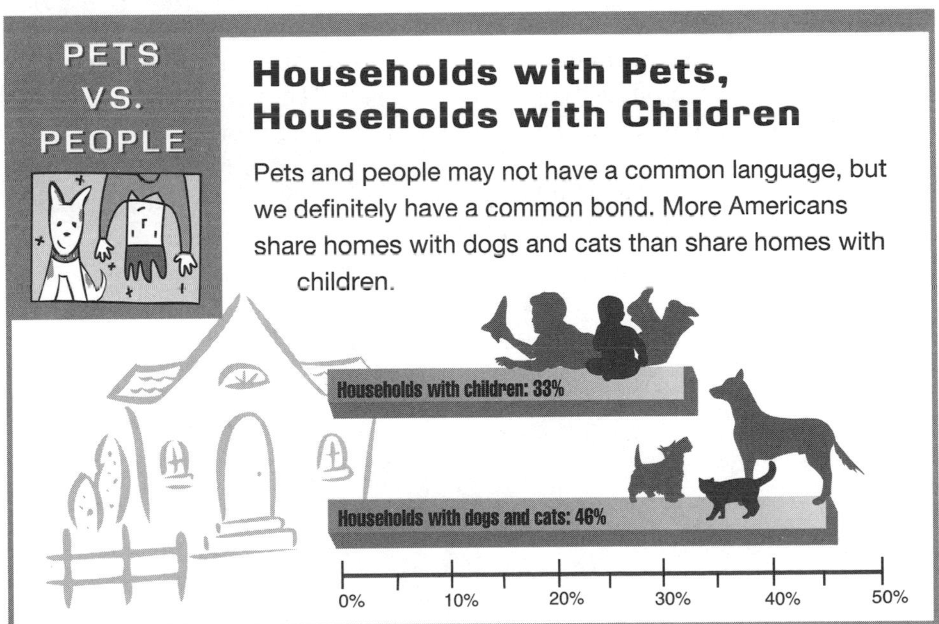

"You really have to know your pet to establish the most meaningful communication," says Dr. Zawistowski. "Trainers will tell you that you need to maintain alpha status by never letting your dog sleep with you or walk through a door ahead of you or sit on the couch with you. But that's not true with every dog. Sure, it could lead to behavior problems with a very dominant or aggressive breed. But it's only cheating you out of having a lot of fun with your Labrador. It's important to know the difference."

In a World of Their Own

People are inclined to believe that everything their pets do is a signal to them. That's usually not the case, however. Dogs and cats do a lot of things that are natural for them, such as digging in the yard or howling at the moon. "Sometimes they're just following their animal instincts," says Dr. Fogle. "If your dog was bred to dig out moles, she's going to want to dig out moles."

Cats also possess quite a bundle of instinctive behaviors, Dr. Fogle adds. "It's perfectly natural for one cat to get upset when another cat comes into her territory. There are things you can do to make the transition easier, but the hissing and urine marking are normal reactions, not bad behavior that you need to punish."

Understanding the world as pets see it, and seeing how they interact with everything that surrounds them, is the first step to understanding them fully. Dogs and cats are not children, even though we often treat them that way. "They're a whole other species that can see, hear, smell, and sense things we can only imagine," Dr. Zawistowski says. "They've been bred to perform incredible tasks of all kinds. Once we understand them, we can begin to give them the kind of environment and lifestyle that they need to be truly happy."

PART 1

The Amazing Senses of Dogs and Cats

CHAPTER 1

Vision

The typical domestic dog has 20/75 vision, about the same as the typical domestic 90-year-old human. He can't tell a red fire hydrant from a chartreuse one. And he sometimes has trouble finding objects sitting an inch in front of his face.

Then there's the average domestic cat. If he were human, he'd need glasses just to read a billboard. He can't tell a bluebird from a blackbird, and he probably couldn't see a Meow Mix commercial on TV if his acting career depended on it.

But before you start shopping for glasses, consider things from their point of view. Dogs and cats really don't see worse than humans. They see differently—and, in many ways, far better.

"Pets live in a world that we can't even imagine," says Gregory Bogard, D.V.M., a veterinarian in Tomball, Texas. "Our perception of the world is based primarily on our vision. For them, it's just one tool that complements the other senses."

These are important differences to keep in mind when communicating with pets visually. Whether you're teaching them obedience or playing a game of catch, taking advantage of their visual strengths can make a big difference in building a healthy, happy relationship.

How Dogs See

Ever since their days as pack hunters, dogs have been trackers. To survive in the wild, it was critical for your dog's ancestors to be able to detect motion, no matter how slight or how far away it occurred. And they had to do so in the low light of dawn and dusk, when their prey was out and moving about. Sharp vision wasn't critical, but the ability to see in dim light was.

A dog's corneas are somewhat flatter than those of humans. This allows them to gather more light, but at the expense of visual sharpness. Your dog's world might seem somewhat blurry, but you'd be amazed how well he can see in the dark.

NAME: Cap
OCCUPATION: Herder

When one of Alasdair MacRae's barnyard animals gets out of line, he calls on Cap to give it "The Stare."

"He just has a way of looking at animals and making them do whatever he wants," Alasdair says about Cap, a Border collie who works on Alasdair's farm near Charlottesville, Virginia.

A typical day for Cap involves herding sheep and pigs, although he's been known to round up ducks, cats, and even people who go too far afield. Cap's instincts are typical of his breed, which was created to tend flocks along the border region of England and Scotland.

Eyesight plays a key role in Cap's work. Although he's trained to react to whistles and shouts, his superior vision helps him locate wayward animals from amazing distances. Alasdair says that Cap can spot a sheep more than a mile away, run it down, and bring it back in a matter of minutes.

Of course, finding an animal is one thing and getting it to move in the right direction is another. That's where Cap's stare comes in handy. Like most Border collies, Cap has bright, close-set eyes that can absolutely mesmerize livestock. Many Border collies have one brown eye and one blue eye, which enhances their piercing gazes.

"Sheep react to different things about dogs: movement, speed, a little meanness," Alasdair says. "But the eyes can make a very big difference. I think the sheep see that crazy look and figure they'd better do what they're told. I know I would."

Dogs don't see color as well as we do, either. Again, it's a tradeoff. Human eyes contain millions of color-sensitive structures called cones. Dogs have some cones, and research has shown that they can distinguish some colors, usually in the blue and violet ranges. But most of their vision comes from structures called rod receptors. Rods are only sensitive to black and white, but they are ultrasensitive to light.

Perhaps the biggest difference between human and canine vision is the width and depth of field. Because their eyes are set farther apart than ours, dogs take in a wider view. They don't need to turn their heads very far to see something moving. The problem with the eyes being so far apart, though, is that they don't share much information. This means that dogs don't have good binocular vision, which limits their ability to see clearly directly in front of them or to judge the distance of a nearby object.

Your dog's vision isn't determined only by nature. Over countless generations, breeders have sought to improve different aspects of vision. In some breeds, for example, long-distance vision is prized, which is why herding dogs, such as sheepdogs, may be able to see hand signals from a human more than a half-mile away. Terriers, on the other hand, were bred to have their eyes closer together. This gives them a narrower field of vision, perfect for chasing—and catching—small, burrow-dwelling animals. And many dogs, such as Afghans, have been bred to have their eyes very close together, giving them a loving, almost humanlike appearance.

HOW CATS SEE

Like dogs, cats are renowned for their hunting skills. But unlike dogs, who depend on speed and stamina to catch their prey, cats use more of a stalking, silent approach and have developed the necessary vision to help them do it.

Cats hunt small animals and pounce from close range, so they need better focusing skills than dogs. This is why their eyes are placed much closer together. Their binocular vision is terrific, almost as good as that of humans. Binocular vision gives them decent depth of field, which means that they don't pounce 7 feet for a mouse that is 8 feet away. Dogs, who evolved to hunt prey larger than themselves, don't need that kind of precision.

Cats have very large eyes relative to the size of their heads, which is part of what makes them so attractive to humans. More important, at least from a predator's point of view, is that their big eyes admit lots of light at night. "The animals that cats hunt come out at night, so they need to capture every little bit of light possible," says Gwen Bohnenkamp, owner of Perfect Paws, a dog and cat training center in the San Francisco Bay area, and author of *From the Cat's Point of View*.

To enhance their nighttime vision even more, cats' retinas are coated with a reflective layer called the tapetum fibrosum, which boosts the amount of light they take in. (Reflections from this layer are what cause cats' eyes to glow in passing headlights.) In fact, cats can see in one-sixth of the light that humans need. Finally, cats have a wider field of view than most people.

As always, along with these superior skills come some trade-offs. Cats have poor color vision. And they don't see terribly well in bright light because their eyes are designed to see best in the dark. During the day, your cat's pupils narrow to slits to keep out the light.

Most breeds of cats have similar types of vision. The only exception is the Siamese cat, which has little, if any, binocular vision. When hunting, Siamese cats can only guess at the exact distance of their prey.

SEEING EYE-TO-EYE WITH YOUR PETS

Since humans and pets see in different ways, they must find some middle ground in order to communicate effectively with eyesight. Dogs and cats use their other senses to complement vision to a greater degree than humans do, says Dr. Bogard. While eyesight is our best sense, smell is equally or more important to dogs. And both cats and dogs use hearing at least as much as vision. So when you're communicating with your pets, you'll have the best results when you combine visual cues and signals with cues that incorporate their other senses.

Since cats don't focus well on objects that are very close or too far away, it's best to stay within their optimal visual range when you're trying to communicate, Bohnenkamp says. If you're too far away, your cat will barely see you, and if you're too close, it will make him a little uncomfortable because he won't be able to read the subtle clues of facial expression and body language, she explains.

Dogs don't focus especially well at any distance, so it's less important where you stand. But it's usually a good idea to stay a few feet away when teaching obedience or giving discipline, says Andy Bunn, a trainer in Charlotte, North Carolina. Getting too close and going nose-to-nose with dogs is often intimidating to them because most dogs are a lot smaller than we are. A large human face looming inches away, combined with a stern voice, will cause some dogs to cower and others to become aggressive, he says. In either case, your dog will lose his concentration and will be less likely to respond to whatever it is you're trying to say.

You always want your pets to look you in the eye when you're trying to get their attention, but you don't want to turn it into a staring contest. "If you want to get into a fight with a dog you don't know, just look him square in the eye," Dr. Bogard says. The reason for this is that dogs originally lived in packs, and only the leader of the pack is permitted to stare at the others. A stare from a "lesser" dog may be perceived as a challenge, he explains.

The Appearance of Fun

There's an old saying among anglers: "Pretty-colored lures don't catch more fish, but they sure catch more fishermen."

It's the same with cats and their owners. Pet supply stores are packed with colorful cat toys—neon orange balls, lime green mice, and fuchsia-feathered mobiles. These bright-looking toys catch the attention of plenty of cat owners, but the cats couldn't care less. All they want is a toy that reminds them of prey.

"If you really want to bond with your cat, pick a toy that has lots of motion," says Gwen Bohnenkamp, owner of Perfect Paws, a dog and cat training center in the San Francisco Bay area, and author of *From the Cat's Point of View*. "Cats are geared to spotting and pouncing on things that move, and the color doesn't make a bit of difference." They also respond to shapes, so toys that resemble mice, voles, chipmunks, birds, or other animals make the best gifts.

This doesn't mean that you have to throw out that hot pink, squeaky rubber toad just because it's brighter than a 200-watt bulb. If it's the right shape and moves the right way, your cat will still enjoy it. "Besides, colors are good for at least one thing," Bohnenkamp says. "They make it easier for you to find the toy when it falls behind the sofa."

If you run across an unfamiliar dog and are worried about his intentions, don't try to intimidate him by making prolonged eye contact. It's better to turn sideways and look at him out of the corner of your eye. Among dogs, this signals peaceable intentions and could save you from a chomp on the leg, Bunn says.

With family pets, usually it's fine to look them in the eye. For one thing, you're supposed to be the acknowledged leader in the family, and this won't be perceived as a threat. Also, says Bunn, many dogs enjoy calm, up-close eye contact with their owners, and there's no harm in it at all as long as everyone knows his role. The rules change, however, if your dog is sometimes aggressive. In that case, you'll want to avoid prolonged eye contact until you can get some advice from your veterinarian or a professional trainer.

Eye contact is a mixed bag with cats. Sometimes a cat will view it as a threat, sometimes as affection. "It varies widely from cat to cat, so I'm not sure there's any basic rule," Bohnenkamp says. One exception to this is when you're disciplining your cat, in which case eye contact could be a problem, she adds. For example, staring and yelling at your cat when he jumps on the counter will only make him fearful, and he probably won't understand why you're angry. A better approach is to stand where he can't see you and give him a quick spray with a water pistol. Your cat will learn that jumping on the counter results in getting wet, but the message won't be delivered with the type of threatening stare that could make him distrust you in the future.

THE RIGHT BODY LANGUAGE

Because they see things differently, dogs and cats don't respond in the same way to exuberant body language, so you have to tailor it to each pet. Dogs notice movement and may get excited by it. So when you're "talking" with your dog, don't hesitate to wave your arms, jump up and down, and generally make a fool of yourself. The same is true when you're teaching your dog to respond to hand signals. You'll want to exaggerate them at first so that he can clearly understand what you're trying to communicate, Dr. Bogard says.

Try any slapstick stuff on a cat, however, and he'll probably look at you like you've had one too many cups of coffee—if he looks at you at all. Cats don't respond well to dramatic hand and

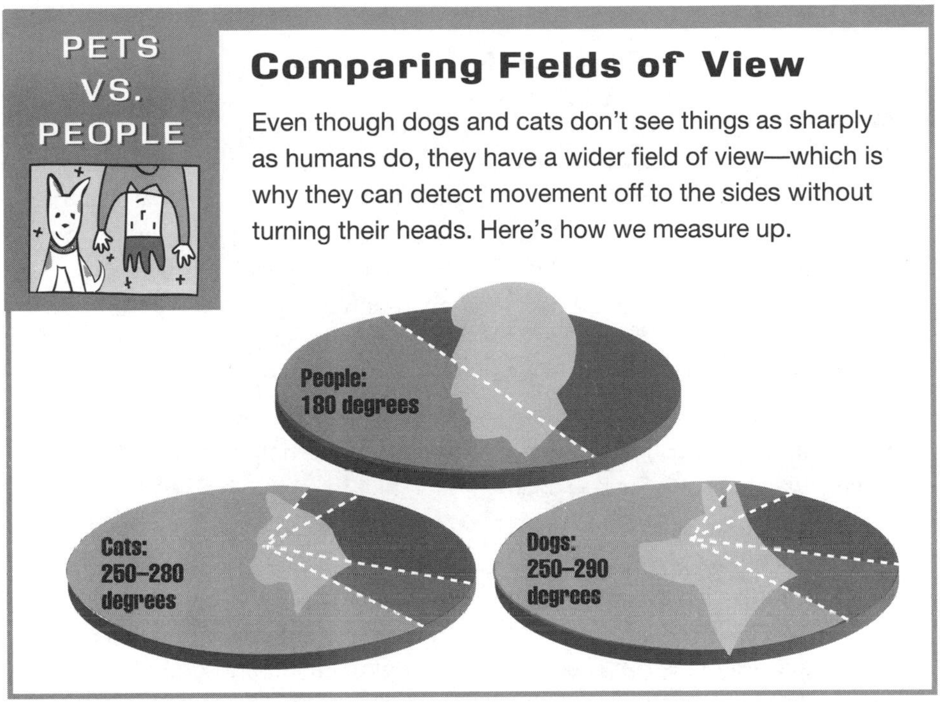

body gestures. "It's like they're saying, 'I can see you, already. Let's have a little dignity here,'" Bohnenkamp says. A better way to get your cat's attention is with subtle movements—a slight wiggle or twitch of a favorite toy, for example. He'll get your meaning right away. Whether or not he'll play, however, depends entirely on his mood. "If he wants to respond to the movement, he will," she says.

It's also important to be honest with your body language. Cats are absolute experts at picking up visual clues. "It's very tough to fool cats by saying one thing while you're feeling something else," Bohnenkamp says. "They can pick up on the smallest of details: how you're standing, what your posture is like, the look on your face. All the sweet talk in the world isn't going to work if your cat decides you're up to no good."

When it's time to take him to the vet, for example, act like you're going to the vet, Bohnenkamp says. Bend over, pick him up, and get going. All the smiley-faced, I-love-you-snookums, now-get-in-the-box stuff will just be wasted. Worse, it will probably make your cat more nervous because he'll know there's some serious deception going on.

Fun with Frisbees

Tired of the tuggy sock? Bored with the Booda Bones? A great way to energize your relationship with your dog is to teach him a new game that takes advantage of his natural vision skills: Frisbee catching.

"It's not as hard as it looks," says Andy Bunn, a trainer in Charlotte, North Carolina, whose late dog, Kiesha, was the state Frisbee champion and a world-ranked competitor. "Almost any dog can be taught to catch a Frisbee within a short time. And he'll be having a great time with you for the rest of his life." Bunn offers the following tips for teaching dogs to go airborne.

1. Start with the basics by teaching your dog to retrieve. Put him on a 30-foot lead and toss a ball or stick for him to chase. When he picks up the object, tell him to "come" or "bring it," and gently guide him back to you with the lead.
2. Once he knows how to retrieve, teach him to "catch it." Have him sit in front of you while you toss small food treats. Say "catch it" as you release the treat, and praise him lavishly when he takes it cleanly in his mouth.
3. To get him used to a Frisbee, kneel on the ground and roll the Frisbee on its side. Allow your dog to chase and catch it, which will get him used to putting it in his mouth. After he masters some ground control, hold the Frisbee above his head and say "catch it," while encouraging him to jump up and take it from your hand. This will get him used to placing the disc in his mouth. Next, hold the Frisbee a little highter above his head and say "catch it" until he jumps up and takes it from your hand. Then, jog away from your dog while holding the Frisbee in front of him, which will help him learn to grab the disc as it flies in the air.
4. Finally, take him somewhere he can run and begin throwing the Frisbee, starting with short throws that are easy for him to grab.

"You'll probably need more practice throwing than your dog will catching," Bunn says.

It doesn't really matter what model of Frisbee you use, although Bunn recommends choosing one that is lightweight and easy to toss. After playing, take a few moments to smooth the rough edges caused by teeth marks by rubbing a piece of fabric around the edges. This will keep your dog from cutting his gums the next time you play.

Dogs are a little easier to sucker with sweet talk and a smile, but they're still adept at reading body language. "Dogs can tell when something's up just by looking at the way you carry yourself," Dr. Bogard says. "If you're trying to act happy when you're really upset at something they just did, dogs will often respond warily." Again, it's best to act naturally. When you're taking your dog to the vet, a matter-of-fact wave and a "Come here, boy" is usually the best approach.

HOW VISION CHANGES

It's normal for dogs and cats to lose some of their vision as they get older. Many pets develop a condition called nuclear sclerosis, in which fibrous tissue grows on the lenses of the eyes, making vision a little cloudy. Some pets develop cataracts as well.

In humans, a slight loss of vision can be a serious problem. In dogs and cats, however, it's less critical because they're able to memorize how to get places and because they rely on their other senses. They can make up for their foggy eyes by using their superior senses of hearing, smell, and touch. "Pets are so good at feeling their way that people often don't realize that their eyes aren't what they used to be until pretty late in the game," says Dr. Bogard.

But even though dogs and cats get along fine with weak vision, it does make it harder for the two of you to communicate. You may have to work with your pet's other senses in order to keep the lines of communication open.

Suppose, for example, your pet always came running when you held up his food bowl, but lately he can't see well enough to know it's suppertime. You can get his attention by shaking the bowl to rattle the kibble or tapping the bowl with a spoon, says Dr. Bogard. You can use the same trick to keep older pets active and entertained—by getting toys that rattle, jiggle, or squeak. Noisy toys will get his attention, and he'll be able to find them even when he can't see exactly where they are.

Take advantage of scents as well as sounds, says Bunn. Dogs and cats sometimes get disoriented when their eyes start to go, which can lead to painful and possibly dangerous accidents, like walking face-first into the sharp corner of a coffee table.

Dr. Bogard recommends spraying table legs and potential

danger spots with perfume. The smell will alert your pet before he walks into danger. It's a good idea, though,especially if you have wood furniture, to try this out first on an inconspicuous part, such as underneath or on the back of a leg, to make sure that the perfume does not damage the finish.

When praising or disciplining your pet, verbal cues become invaluable as his eyesight wanes. Even if your dog was trained to respond to hand signals, you'll probably need to start using voice commands as well. Basic verbal commands like "sit," "stay," and "come" can help avoid confusion—and possibly keep your dog out of danger when he can't see trouble up ahead, says Dr. Bogard.

Finally, don't forget about the amazing power of touch. Dogs and cats appreciate human touch, and nothing gives more comfort than a pat on the head, a belly rub, or a scratch under the chin. Even when your pet can't see the love and affection on your face, he'll certainly feel it in your hands.

CHAPTER 2

Hearing

Orchestra conductors have incredible hearing. Even when they're surrounded by 70 or more instruments, they can tell when a single instrument hits a note that's a half-tone off pitch. But despite their well-trained ears, they wouldn't begin to impress a cat napping in the balcony.

Consider this: Each whole tone that's discernible to human ears is heard as 10 distinct tones by cats. They can hear pitches that humans can't, like the ultrasonic squeak of a mouse under the stage. And while skilled conductors can distinguish where a sound is coming from—for example, the sound of an error from the third violin—cats could tell whether the clinker originated from the violin's bridge or neck, which are approximately 3 inches apart.

Dogs don't hear quite as well as cats, but they hear a lot better than people. They can perceive sounds that are twice as high as those humans can detect. They have great distance hearing, too. A sound that a human can barely pick up from 25 yards will, for dogs, come in loud and clear at 250 yards.

Different breeds of dogs have different hearing skills. Small dogs, for example, have tiny ears that excel at amplifying the highest frequency waves. This means that a tiny Pomeranian can hear high-frequency sounds almost as well as a cat. Large dogs with large heads, on the other hand, have ears that are best suited for amplifying low sounds, which is why Saint Bernards can detect the low rumbles of shifting snow that precede an avalanche.

Despite the fact that dogs and cats can hear many things we can't, they're very much attuned to human sounds, which is why communicating with pets is as easy as it is. "Our speaking range is easily heard by pets," says Lisa Smith, a pet-behavior consultant and veterinary hospital manager in Severn, Maryland. And their meows and woofs are within the frequency ranges that humans hear best.

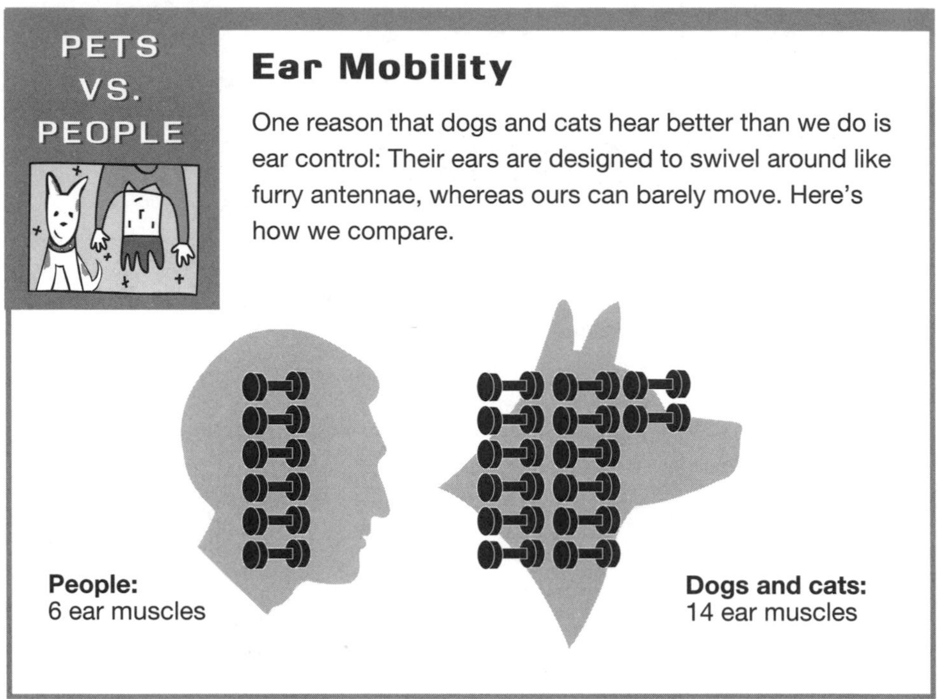

WHY THEY HEAR SO WELL

At some time in the distant past, human hearing was a lot better than it is today. One reason it's not as sharp anymore is that we came to depend on our pets' senses when we welcomed them into our lives. "Dogs have acted as alarm systems and hunting aids for humans for more than 10,000 years," says Colin Groves, Ph.D., a teacher and researcher in biological anthropology at the Australian National University in Canberra. "We've relied on canine ears for so long that we've lost the need for supersensitive hearing."

Research has shown, in fact, that human brains have shrunk by about 10 percent, mainly in the regions that control the senses, during the time we have been living with dogs. Dogs, on the other hand, have lost about 30 percent of their brain size, mainly in the higher-thinking regions, during the same time.

While humans were losing some of their hearing, dogs and cats were sharpening theirs. There was good reason for this. Even though ancient pets hung out with people, our ancestors didn't always keep them well-fed. Dogs and cats had to hunt for lunch, and lunch wasn't likely to cooperate. The only way to hunt successfully was with stealth and sharp senses.

Dogs and cats developed different types of hearing because they hunted for dissimilar prey. Cats specialized in small game, such as mice and birds, and their ears evolved to detect the high squeaks of mouse chatter and the flutter of bird wings. Dogs needed bigger game to fill their bellies, and large animals make noises in the lower frequencies—frequencies that dogs are adept at hearing.

Pets today catch most of their meals from food bowls. They don't really need keen ears to survive, but they retain the ability just the same. They keep in practice by listening for the rattle of biscuit boxes or the squeak of the refrigerator door. They also use

Long-Distance Hearing

Matt Shumaker always gets a great homecoming. Every day after work, his two dogs—Wendy, a bearded collie, and Yeti, a Great Pyrenees—greet him at the gate. His arrival is the high point of their day, and they're always at the gate long before he arrives.

"No matter what time of day my husband decides to show up, Wendy and Yeti always tell me when he's getting close to home," says Matt's wife, Kathleen. It doesn't take special talent to hear the throaty rumble of Matt's Dodge diesel truck pulling into the driveway—even the people in the family can hear that. But the dogs start getting excited a few minutes before the truck actually pulls up, Kathleen says. And they never get misled by the sounds of the four other Dodge diesels in the neighborhood, including the one that drives up the street at about the same time as Matt comes home. "It's just uncanny," she says. "The trucks all sound identical, at least to me."

Yeti's and Wendy's hearing, however, is apparently more discriminating. "I wonder if the dogs are picking up the sound of a unique front-end squeak," says Steve Brassell, service manager at Danneman's Auto Service in Laurel, Maryland. "People don't have a chance of hearing that."

Whatever it is that Wendy and Yeti actually hear, they're never late to the gate. Kathleen suspects that what they're really hearing isn't the truck at all, but, in their eager imaginations, their master's welcoming voice. For dogs, that's well worth waiting for.

their hearing, and their voices, to endear themselves to people, especially around mealtimes.

HOW PETS HEAR

When you toss a pebble in a pond and watch the waves roll away, you're getting a perfect picture of how sound travels. Sound waves are very tiny. Those created by a human voice at normal volume, for example, are about a millionth of an inch high. You can't see them, but dogs and cats have no trouble "trapping" the waves. Their ears are much more complex than ours. Here's how they work.

- The earflaps, or pinnae, act like satellite dishes. They literally catch sound waves and funnel them into deeper parts of the ear.
- The sound waves travel down the long, L-shaped ear canal to the snail-like hearing apparatus called the organ of Corti, which by itself has 7,500 different parts.
- As sound waves enter the ears, they're divided into hundreds of subfrequencies, each of which is amplified more than 800 times. Then they're transformed into electrical energy.
- The electrical energy pulses through miles of nerves as it travels to the brain.

Hearing is a complex process, but it happens very fast. From the time you speak, it only takes about a second for dogs and cats to hear and identify the sound and to react according to what they hear.

LEARNING TO HEAR

It's paradoxical that animals with such great hearing are born with their ears sealed shut. Puppies and kittens are deaf to their mother's voice for about 2 weeks, until the ear canals open. But they can hear other sounds before then. "Sound waves travel through the body, too," says George Strain, D.V.M., professor of neuroscience at Louisiana State University School of Veterinary Medicine in Baton Rouge. When a newborn cuddles against her mother, she feels and hears her heartbeat. When you talk to a puppy or kitten while holding her against your chest, she'll hear—or at least feel—your voice and learn to love it from the start.

NAME: Tar
OCCUPATION: Sheep Rescuer

The summer morning breeze blew gently in the Canadian mountains, carrying the faint bleat of a young lamb in distress. The sound was so faint that Meaghan Thacker, owner of a sheep ranch in British Columbia, Canada, wasn't sure that's what it was. It could have been a sheep. Or it could have been the echo of the wind coming off the steep mountain walls.

"The sound was so faint that I wasn't at all certain that it was real," Meaghan says. But her dog, a black-and-tan kelpie named Tar, knew exactly what it was: the sound of trouble.

He cocked his head from side to side, paced slowly from one spot to the next, then stared at one spot in the dense field. When Meaghan walked over, she saw a large hollow log. She looked inside the log, and there was a baby lamb. Its feet had broken through the rotted wood, and it was trapped.

Tar watched intently as Meaghan freed the woolly captive and set her down. When the lamb seemed to be unhurt, Tar was satisfied and trotted back to his flock.

"Learning to hear is a process," says Dr. Strain. "There's no one day when a young animal suddenly hears like an adult. The ear canals open a tiny bit each day, and the brain slowly gets used to handling sound." By 4 weeks of age, the ear canals are fully open, and the youngsters' brains can handle sound almost as well as adults' do.

Hearing at Home

Dogs and cats have such sharp hearing that it's often impossible to open a can of tuna without a cat wrapping itself around your legs, or to enjoy a potato chip without having to look at a few uninvited sets of eyes. It's not that dogs and cats are perpetual mooches, although some certainly are. It's their nature to listen closely to what's happening in their daily lives and to focus on things that mean the most to them.

You can take advantage of the way dogs and cats hear to communicate a little more clearly with your pets.

- Using high-pitched sounds like kissing noises invariably gets the attention of cats because their ears are most attuned to high pitches, Smith says. "We tend to talk in a lower range that just isn't that interesting to them."
- Cats pay more attention to people when they hear sounds that start with "s," "f," "sh," "ch," or "h" sounds. These consonants are always spoken in a higher pitch than vowels or other consonants, and cats find these sounds appealing.
- Pets' ears are designed to detect vibrational changes. When they ignore their owners, it's often because the words—especially the tone and pitch—sound like everything else they've been hearing. "If you want to keep a pet's attention, give her something new to listen to," suggests Smith. Add acoustic variety by whispering, then talking normally, then talking more loudly, and so on. Or deliberately vary your pitch. The more your voice changes, the closer attention your pet will pay to what you're saying.

Because dogs and cats hear things people can't, you can take advantage of their skills every day by trying to hear—or at least notice—all the things they're picking up. Here are a few examples.

Intruders. Anthropologists believe that our ancestors first invited pets into their camps because they could hear danger long before the humans could. "To understand what dogs are hearing, you just need to watch how they listen," says Joanne Hibbs, D.V.M., a veterinarian in Knoxville, Tennessee. "They'll generally bark when they hear something new. A wagging tail means a friend is in the yard, but rising hackles usually mean danger."

Mice. Mice are shy, retiring creatures, and by the time you know they're in the house, there are probably a lot of them. Cats, on the other hand, spot them right away. When your cat is acting fascinated by a wall, you can be pretty sure it's time to break out the mousetraps.

Insects. Cats can even detect the almost-silent wanderings of insects such as termites. Watching your cat when she listens, and investigating when she's showing a lot of interest in a particular spot, can help you head off architectural reconstruction jobs in progress.

CHAPTER 3

Smell

To understand what smell means to cats and dogs, stop thinking like a human for a minute.

Poop isn't a smelly pile on the grass—it's a personalized business card. That fire hydrant on the corner isn't a public rest room for pooches—it's the society page of the *Pet Times*, full of the comings and goings of the local population. And that new laundry soap doesn't leave a fresh, clean scent—it leaves a warning to your cat that something or someone strange may have entered the house.

"We will never fully understand what smell does for dogs and cats," says Dan Carey, D.V.M., a veterinarian at the Paul F. Iams Technical Center in Dayton, Ohio. "Their sense of smell is so much more powerful than ours, and it means so many more things to them. Without the ability to smell, pets would really be at a loss to 'see' the world around them."

When it comes to pure nose power, no mammal matches the dog. In fact, only certain varieties of eels and butterflies are better at smelling their surroundings. It's been estimated that dogs can catch a whiff of something that's 100 times less concentrated than what humans can detect. You can smell a loaf of bread baking in the oven; your dog can smell a week-old crumb under the refrigerator. It's no wonder that humans rely on dogs for everything from finding truffles a foot underground to finding lost humans buried under an avalanche.

Not that cats are scent slouches. The average cat has about five times more smell-detecting nerve endings than a typical human. And cats use smell for everything from greeting each other to knowing when a female is in heat, not to mention deciding whether their supper has the right stuff or should be rejected.

Knowing how pets use their sense of smell can make a big difference in how humans get along with them. Allowing your dog or cat to take full advantage of his best tool will keep him happier and healthier, even if it leaves you scratching your head once in a while.

SEEING WITH SMELL

From the moment they enter the world, dogs and cats rely on smell for survival. They're born blind and must rely primarily on smell and touch to find food and protection. They quickly learn how to use their powerful noses. In fact, a newborn kitten can detect his favorite feeding nipple on his mother by smell alone.

Even after kittens and puppies open their eyes, smell remains their primary means of interaction with the outside world. Senses like vision and taste, while important, serve mainly to supplement smell. "In humans, sight is the dominant sense most of the time," Dr. Carey says. "To us, smell is not nearly the most important sense. In dogs especially, and also in cats, it's just the opposite. Smell is simply more important to them than it is to us."

Because smelling is so vital, cats and dogs have not one, but two organs to detect odors. The first, of course, is the nose. In both dogs and cats, the basic structure is the same as it is in hu-

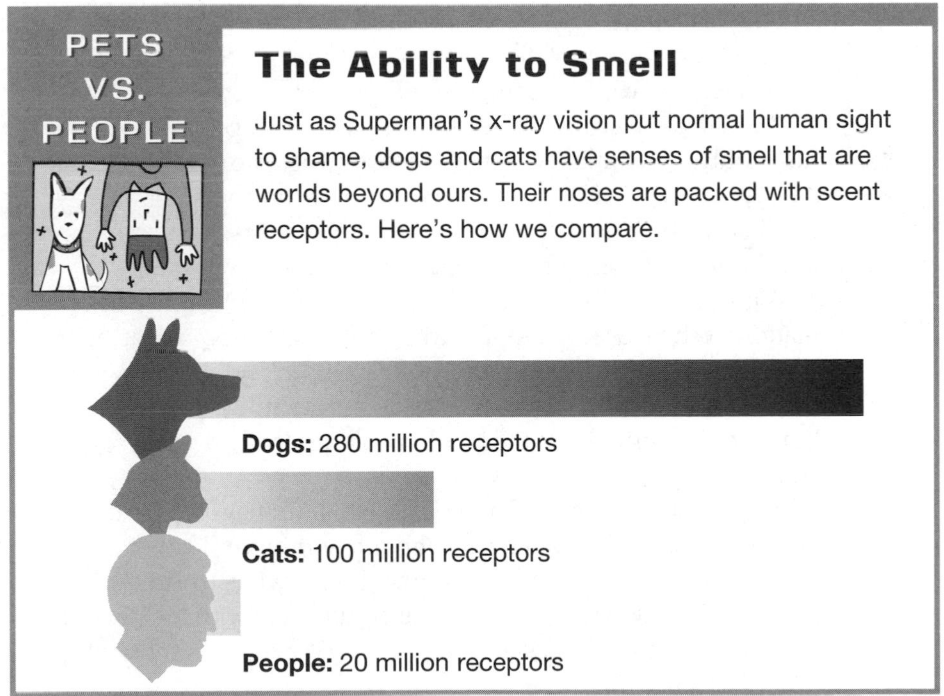

mans. Once air enters the nostrils, it is warmed and moistened. Some of the air then gets funneled through an area of thin folds called the olfactory mucosa. This is where all those millions of scent receptors are located. To get an idea of the difference between pets and people, consider that this area takes up about ½ square inch in humans, but up to 6 square inches in cats and nearly 20 square inches in some dog breeds. It's no wonder that dogs have developed long noses—they need to hold on to all those smells.

Smelling is also the reason for a dog's wet nose. Moisture helps trap the molecules of smell that drift inward, making it easier to collect and interpret them. Licking the nose helps keep it moist and wipes away old smells.

In addition to their powerful noses, dogs and cats have another smelling tool—a tube located in the nasal septum (which is paired with nerve endings on the roof of the mouth) called the Jacobson's organ. While cells in the nose detect all odors, the Jacobson's organ pays attention only to odors linked to food and sex. When a pet picks up on these smells, the Jacobson's organ fires off a signal to the hypothalamus, the part of the brain responsible for controlling appetite and sex drive.

The Jacobson's organ is responsible for one of the strangest (from a human point of view) of all cat behaviors, flehmen. When a cat catches a whiff of something especially interesting, he will arch his neck, elevate his head, curl back his top lip, and open his mouth. This makes him look as though he's stupefied or angry, but he's simply concentrating hard on the smell. Many smells will stimulate flehmen, but this behavior is most common in tomcats who detect nearby females in heat.

What do pets do with all of this smell power? Gather information: Who's been passing through the territory? What have they been eating or rolling in? Is this food okay to eat? Which way did that pretty kitty go? Mmm, is that an 80 percent lean burger on the grill down the block, cooking slowly over mesquite chips?

It's probably just as well that humans don't have a pet's sense of smell. Unless we zipped through a few thousand generations of evolution, we probably wouldn't know what to do with it anyway. "I think people would go absolutely crazy trying to cope with all the smells," Dr. Carey says. "We couldn't possibly

Healing Smells

Aromatherapy has arrived in the pet world. Practitioners say that the right mix of fragrant essential oils can do remarkable things for pets, including heal wounds, repel fleas and ticks, and even calm the emotions.

The oils in certain plants appear to contain natural chemicals that stimulate (or calm) the central nervous system. "This isn't New Age, silly stuff," says Christina Chambreau, D.V.M., a holistic veterinarian in Sparks, Maryland, and educational chairperson for the Academy of Veterinary Homeopathy. "It's a healing art that's used around the world with great success."

There are dozens of essential oils, which can be used alone or in combination to achieve many different results. Dr. Chambreau recommends starting out with lavender. Dilute 15 drops of human-strength lavender oil with about ½ ounce of vegetable oil. Using a dropper, apply 3 or 4 drops to the fur around the neck and chest, where your pet won't be able to lick it off. The scent of lavender oil is very soothing and can be used any time pets are upset, she says. Most will start feeling better within a few minutes, and the treatments can be used several times a day.

Cats are much more sensitive to oils than dogs are, so you'll want to talk to an expert in aromatherapy before using the oils at home, she adds.

process it all." It would be like being able to see individual atoms all of a sudden—we couldn't see the forest for all the trees.

NOSE NEWS IS GOOD NEWS

We can't hope to truly understand our pets' sense of smell. What we can do is help them use it in ways that make them happier and more comfortable in their human environments.

Encourage them to "chat." Dogs are social animals, which is why dogs on leashes seem perfectly happy to displace a few neck bones in order to reach a fellow canine on the other side of the street. Our impulse is to rear back on the choke chain and bring them to heel. But it might be better to let them have their way sometimes.

"It's fine to let your dog greet another dog," says Dawn Hoppe, a trainer and breeder in Barberville, Florida. "It gives him a chance to learn more about the other dog and to be calm in public places."

In fact, humans are usually the ones making the biggest stink in these situations. Most people are uncomfortable with all the sniff-this, smell-that stuff that dogs do. "They're just doing what comes naturally to them," Hoppe says. "Their behavior is similar to two humans shaking hands." While we gather information about people by the strength of their grips and the looks in their eyes, dogs pick up the same information by sniffing each other's front and rear ends.

This isn't to say that you have to stop for every dog who passes, Hoppe says. But if you allow your dog some interaction, he will be happier on the whole and less likely to misbehave when he's on a leash. Obviously, you have to be cautious. Some dogs are aggressive toward other dogs, so you'll want to ask owners if it's okay for the dogs to meet. Sometimes, perfectly sane-looking dogs are poorly socialized and just itching for a fight.

Invite the big sniff. Dogs and cats greet new humans the same way they greet their peers—nose-first. The polite way to introduce yourself is to allow them to give you the once-over with their snouts, Hoppe says. This little ritual doesn't take long, and it allows pets to get a read on you quickly.

Stop and smell the flowers—and the hydrants. Even when there aren't other dogs and cats around, pets use smell to understand their surroundings.

They need smell breaks once in a while, says Andy Bunn, a trainer in Charlotte, North Carolina. It doesn't always have to be a lamppost. Pets can pick up a lot of information by smelling storm drains, grass, even a seemingly empty patch of sidewalk. We'll never know what they're smelling, but if the odor is important enough to make them freeze in place, it's worth letting them take it in.

Cats don't rely on smells as much as dogs do, but they need opportunities to breathe deeply, too. At the very least, leave windows open so that they can sample outside air and all the intriguing odors it contains.

Put your scent where you want them to be. Dogs and cats are intensely attracted to human smells. You can take advantage of this to change their behavior. Suppose you're having trouble keeping your dog off the couch. While some pets sit on furniture because it's soft, many others do it because that's where their owners' scents are strongest, Hoppe says. You can coax them to sit elsewhere by using a piece of you—a T-shirt you've recently

Teaching Dogs to Track

If you've ever wondered how bloodhounds manage to track people over incredible distances, it goes something like this.

Every human has an individual smell, just as we have individual fingerprints. Tracking dogs are trained to focus on that smell, which comes mainly from the evaporation of sweat. Once dogs are introduced to the smell (usually from an article of clothing), they're able to remember it because they store the scent molecules in their multifolded nose cells.

The truly amazing thing isn't that they can find the smell, but that they can figure out which way the person is going. Dogs are able to do this by comparing memory of the original scent stored in their brains to the current scent they smell in the air. They detect minute changes that occur as scents lose some of their ingredients to the air over time. They track by constantly seeking out "fresher" smells and heading in that direction.

Every dog can learn to track. Here's how.

- Toss your dog's favorite toy a few times and let him retrieve it.
- Hide the toy in an obvious spot, somewhere he can see and smell it. Reward him profusely when he finds it.
- Start hiding the toy in more difficult locations—out of sight behind a door or under a bush outside. Once he's consistently tracking the toy, it's time for you to become the trackee.
- Carry the toy with you and wander off within an enclosed area. Once you've been gone for a few minutes, have someone let your dog loose, suggests Liz Palika, a trainer in Oceanside, California. If he has the heart of a tracker, he'll come after you—or actually, after the toy you're carrying.

You may think it's cheating to use a toy, but it's not. It's the way real search-and-rescue dogs are trained. In fact, at real rescue scenes, handlers sometimes have to hide with the toys to keep the dogs motivated. Once dogs find their handlers, they feel great and are ready to keep doing their real work.

worn (but not washed), for example—as a beacon. "When you're not around, pets feel closest when they're sitting in a place where they can smell you best," she says.

Let them smell the real you. Pets love people *au naturel*. That's why they sometimes act uneasy when their people use perfumes or hand creams. "You just don't smell like you, and that can throw them off," Bunn says. This is especially true for cats, who dislike strong, perfumed smells.

Put more smells in their lives. Dogs and cats love toys, smells or no smells. But they really get excited when people add tantalizing scents to their favorite gizmo. If your dog loves those bouncy, hollowed-out rubber toys, smear a little peanut butter on the inside. The smell will drive him crazy as he tries to reach the food, Hoppe says. You can do the same thing with cats, using prescented toys or rubbing a little catnip over them.

Cook for smell. Cats are notoriously finicky eaters, but their balky behavior sometimes has less to do with taste than with smell. Before they take a bite of food, cats sniff it to make sure it meets their standards. "Cats won't take a nibble of anything that smells like it might be harmful to them," says Dr. Carey. In fact, if they can't get a good whiff of something, they'll always err on the side of caution and walk away from a perfectly good meal.

Dr. Carey suggests warming their food just a little. This gets the food molecules moving faster, which makes scents more distinctive.

CHAPTER 4

Touch

It's hard to believe, but a national survey found that 4 percent of pet owners don't touch their dogs or cats during the course of an average week. If they only knew what they were missing, they'd join the other 96 percent in a heartbeat.

Research has shown that petting pets can instantly lower blood pressure and make people breathe deeper and more slowly. It's like a glass of warm milk: soothing, relaxing, and available anytime you want it. But enough about humans.

"Touch is extremely important to animals," says Betsy Lipscomb, a cat-behavior consultant and president of the Wisconsin Cat Club in Milwaukee. "It provides them with information about the world around them, stuff they can't pick up in any other way." From feeling the breeze made by passing prey to detecting minute vibrations before an earthquake hits, pets' sense of touch gives them more information than humans can possibly imagine.

Being touched by people makes most pets feel good, too. Researchers have discovered that being petted by humans has basically the same effect for cats and dogs as it does for us: their heart rates slow down and their blood pressure levels drop. It reduces stress and makes them feel loved. Touch, in other words, is a wonderful way for people to communicate with their pets.

A Touching Story

Dogs and cats have developed very complex systems for reading the world through touch. These kick in right at birth, or even in the womb in the case of cats. Whiskers are the first hairs to grow within the uterus, so they're ready to work as soon as kittens emerge into the outside world. Since dogs and cats are born blind, they depend on touch (and smell) to find mother and her milk.

Most mammals, including dogs, cats, and humans, use touch to recognize five different sensations: hot, cold, pain, gentle pressure, and firm pressure. We all do this with the aid of nerve endings located near the surface of the skin and at the base of hair follicles, says Gregory Bogard, D.V.M., a veterinarian in Tomball, Texas.

Without these nerve endings, pets and people would have tremendous trouble feeling much of anything—the ground beneath our feet, the bite of a mosquito, or the heat from a hot stove.

Not surprisingly, pets leave humans groping when it comes to touch. Both dogs and cats, for instance, have supersensitive receptors called Pacinian corpuscles in the pads of their paws. These receptors are so good at picking up vibrations that some pets may be able to sense the minute rumblings of an earthquake 10 to 15 minutes before we thick-skinned humans can.

To get a sense of what they're standing on or what's around them, dogs and cats often engage in a tapping ritual. They'll use their paws to gently tap the ground or an object and sense the vibrations. They'll keep hitting it, a little harder each time, until they have all the information they need, says Lipscomb. It's similar to the way humans feel the ground in front of them with their feet to make sure that it's firm enough to support them.

Dogs and cats aren't quite the same when it comes to touch. Dogs depend far more on their sense of smell. Cats, however, depend largely on touch. They're superb hunters and stalkers, and they have a mind-boggling array of touch tools that aid them in their lethal business.

Nose nerves. In addition to their exquisitely sensitive paw pads, cats have a rich supply of nerve endings in their noses. This

Some Like It Hot

Cats love warm places. In fact, they love them a little too much. Veterinarians treat a lot of cats who lounged too long on radiators, car engines, and hot stoves, getting nasty burns in the process.

Cats aren't very sensitive to heat. Their skin stays comfortable when they're exposed to higher temperatures than human skin can handle. This can be a real problem because temperatures that feel comfortable may be hot enough to damage the skin. This also explains why cats often get burned by candles or other open flames. The warmth from the flame feels so good that they keep moving closer. That's about when their fur or whiskers suddenly incinerate.

is why cats often greet people and pets nose-first, Lipscomb says. "In addition to getting a whiff of each other, they're literally getting a feel for the visitor."

Guard hairs. In addition to the usual fur, cats are well-supplied with body hairs that are designed to detect the slightest changes in their environments. Guard hairs are among the most important. Most cat hairs grow in clusters, but the guard hairs grow singly, one to a follicle. Bigger and thicker than regular hairs, the guard hairs are located all over the body. When the hairs brush against things, nerve impulses shoot information to the brain, alerting cats to things around them and to changes in their environments.

Whiskers. Far more important than guard hairs are whiskers. Whiskers can reach several inches in length, and they're deeply rooted in the skin—about three times deeper than guard hairs. They're so sensitive that they trigger nerve impulses when they move as little as 1/2,000th the width of a human hair. The slightest breeze from a passing mouse moves the whiskers and sends an instant message: Dinner is just a pounce away.

Cats' main whiskers are located on either side of the nose. Smaller whiskers grow on the cheeks, above the eyes, and under the chin. Cats are able to move rows of whiskers back and forth to "read" things around them, Dr. Bogard says. Whiskers also serve as protection for the eyes. When the whiskers touch something while cats are prowling at night, the eyes automatically blink to keep sharp objects from hitting them.

Finally, whiskers tell cats whether they can fit through a narrow opening. Generally speaking, if the tips of the whiskers touch the sides of the opening, it's a no-go. That's why it's very rare to see cats getting stuck between fence posts. Their whiskers are just too sensitive to let it happen.

Dogs also have whiskers, but they're not as prominent or as sensitive as cats', and ultimately, they're not as important, Dr. Bogard says. This is why you'll occasionally see an overly eager dog trapped between a rock and a hard place.

Touch That Talks

All of this touchy-feely stuff is impressive, but it doesn't help modern pets very much. Apart from indulging in recreational mouse hunts, they don't need touch nearly as much as they used to. With one exception: Pets crave touch as part of their bonding with people—and with each other.

Studies of both dogs and cats have shown that pets who are touched a lot when they're young feel closer to people. The first few weeks are especially important. In fact, people who are buying pets from breeders should always ask how much the pets have been handled, Lipscomb says. "If they just leave the pets alone for the first 2 to 7 weeks, they'll grow up less likely to enjoy human contact," she says.

Dogs and cats depend equally on the emotional power of touch. But they respond to touch in different ways, and they have different likes and dislikes. Let's look at cats first.

A LITTLE IS BETTER THAN A LOT

"There is nothing more appealing to a cat than being petted," Lipscomb says. "Most cats absolutely live for human touch. They find it comforting, partly because it reminds them of their days as kittens touching their mothers."

The Healing Touch

Pets just don't plan ahead. They see a squirrel and—boom!—it's zero to 60 in 1.2 seconds. Or they merrily bound up to the highest place in the house, never thinking about how long a leap it's going to take to get back down.

"That kind of stuff can hurt," says Jim Durant, who practices pet massage in West Hartford, Connecticut. "They often get pulled muscles and injured joints. You'd think they'd learn to stretch a little first."

Veterinarians have traditionally treated muscle and joint pain with anti-inflammatory drugs. But an increasing number of experts now recommend therapeutic massage, which can break up old scar tissue and reduce pain and swelling. "It's just wonderful to see how much good massage can do," he says. "They just give you that look, and you know they're thankful for it."

Pet massage isn't anywhere near as common as its human counterpart, Durant adds. There isn't a certification process, so anyone can claim to be a pet masseuse, even people with no real experience. So if your pet is hurting and you want to try some natural pain relief, ask your veterinarian to recommend a qualified expert in your area.

But enough is enough. Even though cats adore human contact, they get uncomfortable when it continues for too long. "Think of how good it feels when a hairdresser combs your hair," Lipscomb says. "That's what it's like being petted. But imagine how awful it would be if the hairdresser never stopped combing. It would stop feeling good and start hurting."

Cats aren't shy about letting people know when they've had enough touching. Their usual strategy is to roll over on their backs. It looks like they're inviting a belly rub, but what they're really doing is getting their claws into position. People who keep stroking at this point usually get nailed.

Cats are happiest when you rub their heads. Focus on the ears, cheeks, temple, and chin. Most cats enjoy long strokes down their backs—you'll know you're doing it right when they arch their backs and raise their bottoms. Don't waste time petting the paws, however. They're really too sensitive to withstand much touching, and most cats prefer having them left alone.

MORE, MORE

Dogs are much easier to please than cats. Rub them for a few minutes, and they'll turn into furry heaps of Jell-O—then roll over and sleep for 14 hours.

Actually, it's more complex than this. Dogs interpret and respond to touching quite differently than people do. Unlike cats, who evolved as solitary creatures, dogs used to spend their days in the company of other dogs. They were very physical with one another, and they sent a lot of messages with touch. Many of the messages were loving, but some were assertive or aggressive. Dogs understand that people aren't dogs, of course, and they accept touches from us that they'd never accept from their peers. But rubbing them the wrong way can still be a source of tension, so it's worth understanding what they do and don't like.

Scratch under the chin. When you really want to put a dog at ease, rub her gently under the chin. Among dogs, this is a sign of respect and love, and it's the way puppies greet adults. It feels good, and it's totally nonthreatening, says Janet Wall, a therapy dog handler in San Diego.

Rub the chest and back. Dogs enjoy long strokes just as much as cats do, and they adore having their chests rubbed, Wall says.

Go south. The base of the tail is a high pleasure spot for most dogs. You won't see them arch their hind ends as much as cats do, but you may notice them doing a little side-to-side dance with their backsides. Pulling the tail, however, even when you do it gently, can be somewhat painful, Wall adds.

Stay off the top. It's natural for people to rub the tops of dogs' heads, if only because it's the easiest spot for them to reach when standing up. Most dogs have learned to accept top-of-the-head rubs as a sign of human affection, but their natural instinct is to dislike it because that's the way dominant or aggressive dogs show their superiority. When you have a new dog in the family or are greeting a dog on the street, rubbing the top of the head sends an unmistakable signal of authority, and that's not the best way to start a relationship.

Spend time on the belly. Many cats are reluctant to have their bellies rubbed, and generally, they set limits on how much touching they'll tolerate. But dogs adore belly rubs, and once they're under your spell, they'll let you—actually, they'll demand it—rub them for as long as you're willing.

CHAPTER 5

Taste

De *gustibus non disputandum.*

No one knows who coined this famous little phrase, but one thing seems pretty certain. Whoever first said, "There's no accounting for taste" must have been watching dogs and cats eating supper.

As far back as human beings have used trash cans, dogs have been picking through them for treats. And as long as people have been feeding cats, they've been holding their noses at the delicacies that their finicky friends prefer.

How can pets stand this stuff, let alone insist upon it? As usual, their behavior goes back to evolution and survival. When it comes to food, dogs aren't worried about subtle flavors. They're just looking for something to fill their bellies. And while cats are somewhat more discriminating than their canine counterparts, they mainly care about finding meat that won't kill them.

"Pets and people can taste pretty much the same things," says Benjamin Hart, D.V.M., Ph.D., professor of physiology and behavior at the University of California, Davis, School of Veterinary Medicine and author of *The Perfect Puppy: How to Choose Your Dog by Its Behavior*. "The difference is that pets are mainly concerned about finding food that's edible. Humans are the ones who are concerned about niceties and table manners."

Of all their senses, taste is probably the least important to dogs and cats. But that doesn't mean you can't communicate better by learning to pamper your pet's palate. For starters, you can figure out which foods your pets enjoy most and then give them what they want. You can also use taste treats to teach pets proper behavior. And you can figure out what pets are saying when they turn their noses up at dinnertime. It could be that they've had too much of a good thing. Or maybe something's bothering them so much that they can't bring themselves to chew.

Meals and Variations

Since dogs and cats love to eat so much, it's always surprising when they refuse to finish their suppers. The reasons are usually pretty simple.

Their food isn't fresh. Food that's been stored open in a refrigerator just doesn't taste as good as fresh-from-the-can stuff. Dry food that's more than a month old will lose zip, too.

They're under too much stress. People tend to eat a lot when they're tense or anxious, but many pets do the opposite. "Stress often kills appetite," says C. A. Tony Buffington, D.V.M., Ph.D., professor of veterinary clinical sciences at the Ohio State University in Columbus. "If your dog or cat refuses to eat, you may want to look around and see if something's bothering him." Sometimes it's company at the house or the strain of moving or a misplaced litter box. Once things calm down, pets usually start eating normally again.

They feel ill. A very common reason for lost appetite is illness, especially when accompanied by fever, says Benjamin Hart, D.V.M., Ph.D., professor of physiology and behavior at the University of California, Davis, School of Veterinary Medicine. Cats who stop eating for more than 24 hours and dogs who don't eat for 48 hours need to see a veterinarian because they could have a serious illness.

They aren't hungry. Dogs and cats vary tremendously in the amounts of food they need. Some are light eaters, while others pack it in like linebackers. Pets who are getting extra treats generally spend less time at the food bowl. Appetites also change during the year, often dropping off in summer, then picking up again when things turn cold.

Facts about Flavor

In dogs, cats, humans, and most other mammals, the sensation of flavor comes from two areas: the tongue (taste) and the nose (aroma). Each species has tastebuds, those tiny, supersensitive bundles of cells located on the tongue. As food passes along the tongue, pieces fall into little pits where the buds are located. Receptors on the outside of the buds react with the food particles and send nerve impulses to the brain. These impulses tell us whether something tastes salty, sweet, bitter, or sour. We recognize a food's specific flavor by the combination of receptors it sets off. For instance, chocolate will cause more sweet receptors to fire than salty ones, while pork rinds will do just the opposite.

Although the basic systems are the same, humans are a bit more discriminating than pets. We can tell the difference between, say, broiled lobster and grilled shrimp, while our pets' tastebuds can only manage something like, "Hot, salty, meaty stuff that makes me want to beg real bad."

Of course, anyone who's ever had a head cold knows that tastebuds aren't worth a hoot without smell. This is where pets blow people away. A dog's sense of smell is hundreds of thousands of times more sensitive than ours—so much so that they can actually "taste" scent molecules. Cats are also blessed with a keen sense of smell. So while humans can smell broiled lobster, a cat can smell something like "broiled Maine lobster shipped in brine," while a dog might add, "cooked for 7 minutes in a Kenmore oven."

Despite their incredible sensitivity, pets—especially dogs—aren't too concerned about taste. We seek culinary perfection, but dogs and cats are mainly interested in whether the stuff they're

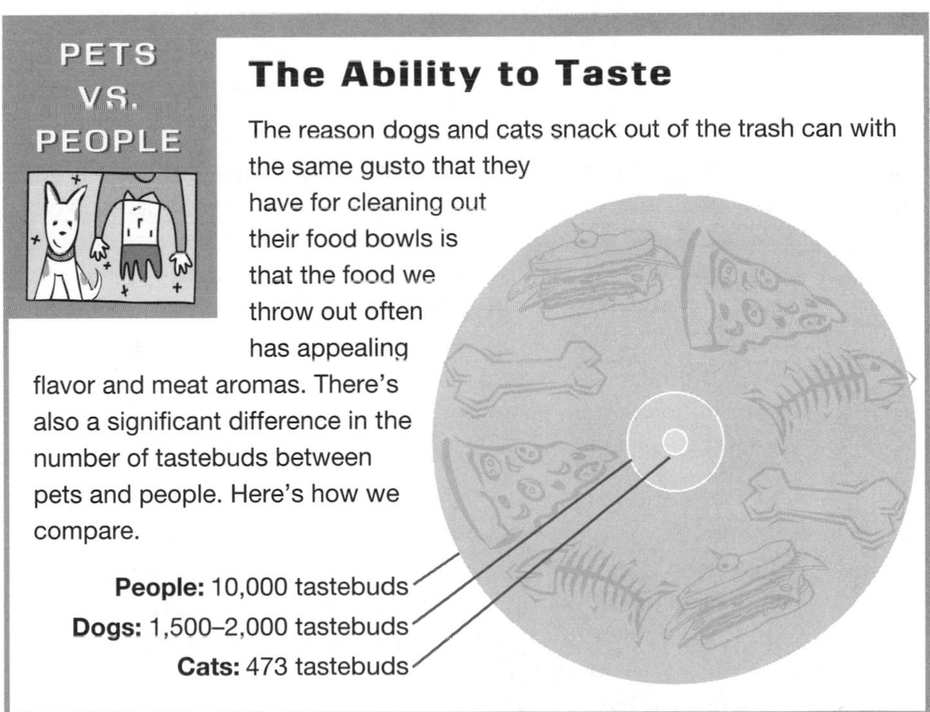

PETS VS. PEOPLE

The Ability to Taste

The reason dogs and cats snack out of the trash can with the same gusto that they have for cleaning out their food bowls is that the food we throw out often has appealing flavor and meat aromas. There's also a significant difference in the number of tastebuds between pets and people. Here's how we compare.

People: 10,000 tastebuds

Dogs: 1,500–2,000 tastebuds

Cats: 473 tastebuds

about to eat is nutritious or dangerous. Dogs have a very long history of scrounging for food. They'll taste just about anything: plants, animals, animal droppings, and whatever else they run across during the course of the day. Taste is just a way of telling whether what they're about to wolf down is okay. Even so, it's not a sense they really depend on. "To tell you the truth, I'd say that many dogs basically have no clue what they're shoveling in," says Dan Carey, D.V.M., a veterinarian at the Paul F. Iams Technical Center in Dayton, Ohio.

Cats tend to be more picky than dogs. One reason for this is that they're carnivores, and spoiled meat is best left behind for scavengers. Another reason is that they're, well, cats, and cats are generally more particular about life than dogs. Because they care more about what they put in their mouths, it's tougher to slip them day-old food or extras like medicine.

Cats do seem to have one blind spot when it comes to taste: They have a very limited ability to identify sweets. While most animals prefer food with sucrose in it, cats don't seem to notice it. In fact, researchers in the 1950s found that cats could not tell the difference between sugar water and plain water, even when the sugar level was so high that it was potentially dangerous. Cats apparently can't taste artificial sweeteners either.

TRICKS WITH TASTE

Although flavor isn't the most important thing to pets, food certainly is. It gives them a sense of comfort and well-being even as it satisfies their appetites. And it can be a powerful tool for communication as well. "If you give a pet food that he really likes, you'll get his attention in a hurry," says Kevin Simonson, cofounder of the Bone Appetit Bakery chain of pet-treat stores, based in Omaha, Nebraska.

Since food is such an emotional issue—for pets as well as their owners—veterinarians recommend following a few basic rules.

• Dogs and cats are creatures of habit, which means they're most comfortable when they're in familiar surroundings, with familiar people and familiar tastes. "Just because people want to try different foods all the time doesn't mean that dogs and cats do," says C. A. Tony Buffington, D.V.M., Ph.D., professor of veterinary clinical sciences at the Ohio State University in Columbus.

It's fine to change foods periodically, he adds. Some pets—cats

NAME: Angel

OCCUPATION: Food Taster

For Angel, life was a little slice of heaven. All she had to do was show some taste, and all her meals were free.

A domestic shorthaired cat, Angel worked as a taste tester at the Iams Animal Care Center in Dayton, Ohio. Her job was to help Iams technicians decide which foods would appeal most to cats around the country. "The best food in the world isn't any good if a pet won't eat it," says Dan Carey, D.V.M., a veterinarian at the Paul F. Iams Technical Center in Dayton.

Along with more than 350 fellow taste testers, Angel always followed the same routine. She would sit quietly while technicians placed two bowls containing different foods in front of her. She was trained to sniff each food before taking a bite—which is not the easiest thing for hungry cats and dogs to do.

Then the fun began. She would take a bite from one bowl or the other, while a watchful technician noted her "first-bite preference"—the food that was most appealing to the nose. After this, she was free to eat from either bowl, and she would continue eating until one bowl was completely empty or 30 minutes had passed. That food was considered to have the most "staying power" with the tastebuds.

Angel has since passed on, but she left her legacy at Iams: a litter of snow white kittens—Betty, Leuk, Cruiser, and Lily—who have carried on the family's culinary tradition.

especially—may get bored with the same food after a few months and will crave a new flavor. Let them have it. But make the change slowly by mixing some of the new food in with the old for a few days. This will help prevent diarrhea or other digestive problems that may occur when pets suddenly start eating something new.

• Warming food slightly is a great way to indulge your pet's tastebuds. Make it just warm enough that it gives off some aroma—that's what makes the meal for dogs and cats.

• Nothing says "listen up" better than the rattle of the treat tin. You can use this to your advantage when you're trying to communicate with dogs and cats, says Andy Bunn, a trainer in Charlotte, North Carolina. You can use treats as rewards for obedience training, house training, litter-box training, or any other kind of training you can think of.

"Don't give a pet treats 125 times a day," Bunn adds. "That devalues treats. If you give a treat only when pets have done something exceptional, it will mean more to them."

"I haven't seen a dog yet who won't devour peanut butter," Simonson adds. Dogs also swoon for flavors such as chicken and Parmesan cheese. Cats are much less predictable, although they usually will go for high-scent, meat-based treats.

• Watch what they forage, because pets, especially dogs, will eat and drink most anything they can get their paws on. In nature, this wasn't too much of a problem because there weren't many attractive poisons lying around. In today's world, however, man-made products such as antifreeze can be a real problem. In fact, more than 100,000 pets are poisoned each year by sweet-tasting antifreeze, and more than 75 percent don't recover due to kidney failure. Antifreeze is so toxic, and pets like the taste so much, that Dr. Hart recommends switching to an antifreeze such as Sierra, which contains a less harmful active ingredient.

CHAPTER 6

The Sixth Sense

In February 1996, Ellen Ottenburg checked into a hospital in West Hills, California, to give birth to a baby girl. While mother and child were recuperating, the family's three Doberman pinschers mysteriously disappeared from home. Ed, Ellen's husband, was frantic. He drove around the city for hours looking for the dogs, with no luck.

Late that night, Ellen looked out the window of her third-floor hospital room. What she saw amazed her: Sitting on the sidewalk, no worse for wear after traveling miles across busy city streets and highways, were all three dogs, looking patiently up at her window.

Not only had the dogs managed to find the hospital, they knew which room she was in. And once the three musketeers saw Ellen in the window and realized that she was fine, they willingly went home with Ed. How they got there—and why they thought they had to come—no one was able to say

Amazing Tales

Scientists have learned a lot about the sensory abilities of dogs and cats, and new stories continue to appear that seem to defy rational explanations. The Ottenburgs' dogs are a case in point, but their story is just one of thousands. As long as people have owned pets, they've suspected that their animals have extrasensory powers. As far back as 2000 B.C., the ancient Egyptians believed that cats possessed mysterious powers to bring health, wealth, and happiness. Cats were so highly regarded for these unique capabilities that they were revered as religious icons and protected by priests.

Pets aren't seen as deities anymore, but there are still a lot of unanswered questions about their sensory—or extrasensory—abilities. A cat named Shoo-Shoo, for example, had the uncanny ability to alert nurses in a Dickinson, North Dakota, nursing home minutes before the clients had seizures. Then there was Redsy, an Irish setter who refused to let her master board his fishing boat one morning, an hour before a hurricane ripped down the coast. And J. T., a dog in England who dazzled researchers by predicting when his owner was getting ready to leave the office. J. T. would move to the French doors of his home and settle down for a proper greeting whenever the faraway master headed for his car. Scientists found that J. T.'s predictions were accurate 85 percent of the time.

"We can't scientifically know how this is done," says Marty Becker, D.V.M., a veterinarian in Bonners Ferry, Idaho, and coauthor of *Chicken Soup for the Pet Lover's Soul*. "It simply transcends our current scientific logic."

WITHIN THE SENSES

Many of the seemingly inexplicable things that pets do may be explained by the unique ways in which they perceive the world. For example, dogs and cats are intensely attuned to body language. They don't have the language skills that people do, so they depend on body language to communicate with people and other pets, says Rolan Tripp, D.V.M., affiliate professor of applied animal behavior at Colorado State University Veterinary School in Fort Collins and author of *Pet Perception Management*. They can tell at a glance, by looking at your posture, muscle tension, and the way you walk, whether you've had a good or a bad day. They can even tell what you're going to do next—which is why they mysteriously disappear minutes before their owners have a chance to pack them up and take them to the vet.

People don't depend on body language as much as pets do, so they aren't always aware of the signals they're sending out. Some signals, in fact, are so subtle that we couldn't see them even if we tried. But pets, dogs especially, always see these signals because at one time their survival depended on their powers of observation.

In the days when dogs lived in tight-knit groups called packs, it was essential for each dog to know how the other dogs were feeling or what they were about to do. Dogs who were observant had an advantage in the struggle to survive. Dogs today haven't lost touch with their ancient heritage. What often seems like mind reading may in fact be exceptionally keen observation. "Pets are very sensitive to our feelings and moods," says Roger Reep, Ph.D., associate professor in the department of physiological sciences at the University of Florida College of Veterinary Medicine in Gainesville.

A PH.D. IN SMELL

In addition to good powers of observation, dogs and cats have exceptional senses. Their sense of smell, for example, is vastly superior to that of humans. Researchers believe that dogs and cats smell odors that we don't even know exist, such as those caused by subtle shifts in our bodies' chemistry when we're feeling happy or sad. There's also some evidence that dogs can detect faint chemical scents caused by a variety of illnesses.

In a letter published in a British medical journal, doctors describe a case in which a 44-year-old woman decided to have a mole examined because her dog wouldn't quit sniffing it. Tests revealed that the mole was cancerous, suggesting that some tumors give off a faint aroma dogs can detect. In one study, a nurse covered herself with bandages and placed a cancer sample beneath one of them. A schnauzer named George was able to pinpoint the sample nearly every time.

Dogs' sense of smell also allows them to follow scent trails that humans are oblivious to. This may be what enables them to occasionally find their way home—or to find their owners—over dozens or even hundreds of miles. "Pets live in a whole different sensory world than we do," Dr. Tripp says. "We really can't even imagine what it would be like to be able to get that much information from just a sniff."

It's not only their sense of smell that allows dogs and cats to do things that seem to be impossible. Their other senses also give them an edge. For example:

• Cats' whiskers are connected to nerves that transmit messages to the brain. The whiskers can detect slight changes in air currents, which is what allows them to find their way in pitch darkness. Dogs may also use their whiskers to navigate, but they're nowhere near as sensitive as cats'.

• Dogs and cats have incredible hearing. For example, a sound that would be inaudible to humans from 30 yards would be clearly heard by a dog more than 100 yards away. Dogs and cats

NAME: Willie
OCCUPATION: Seizure-Alert Dog

There are jobs that pay the rent, and there are jobs that change lives. Willie, a 5-year-old golden retriever, is lucky enough to have the latter, and he's made a real difference in the life of Joanne Weber of Grand Blanc, Michigan.

Joanne has epilepsy, and she depends on Willie to keep her safe from seizures. Joanne can't always tell when seizures are coming, but Willie can, usually 5 to 10 minutes ahead of time. "He nudges me and acts agitated before it's going to start," she says. The advance warning allows her to take precautions such as taking medication, turning off a hot stove or iron, or getting to a safe place where she can lie down until the seizure passes. When seizures are severe, Willie can press an emergency button to call for help.

Willie didn't come by his talents entirely on his own. He worked with the Michigan-based nonprofit group PAWS with a Cause, which trains seizure-response dogs. But even within this select group, Willie was a star, says Michael Sapp, the group's chief operating officer. Willie started alerting Joanne to seizures after he'd lived with her for 11 months. Most dogs require 3 to 5 years before reaching that skill level.

As proof of Willie's skills, Joanne recalls the time when she was on a dock taking pictures and Willie was on the shore nearly 150 feet away. "He was acting strange, kind of agitated, and someone pointed out that he was directing his behavior at me," Joanne says. "The camp director knows us, and she told someone to come and get me." By the time Joanne reached the shore, the seizure had begun.

can also hear frequencies we can't, such as the shifting of snow preceding an avalanche or the ultrasonic squeak of a mouse.

• While our eyes are set closely together, dogs' and cats' eyes are farther apart. They have great peripheral vision, which is why they often can detect movements that originate almost from behind them.

The combination of great senses and an inherent desire to know what's happening around them allows dogs and cats to be aware of all sorts of "invisible" things. This can help explain why they suddenly jump up and look at you expectantly just when you're *thinking* of going for a walk or filling the food bowl. They're not reading your mind, scientists say. They're just seeing things that you don't. "The way a dog or cat puts it all together is completely different from the way we do it," says Dr. Reep.

AT YOUR SERVICE

Even though experts can't explain how dogs and cats do many of the things they do, this hasn't stopped people from taking advantage of their unique capabilities. In some parts of the world, for example, dogs are part of an informal earthquake-alert system because they'll sometimes start barking when they sense the slightest tremor in the Earth's crust. In this country, an increasing number of dogs are being used by people with epilepsy to help them detect oncoming seizures. Dr. Reep decided to test the skills of family pets at responding to seizures. He found that about 5 percent of pets living with people who had frequent seizures were able to detect them before they occurred.

Dr. Reep suspects that these pets have the ability to detect a unique scent that precedes a full-blown seizure. But they also appear to have abilities that extend beyond the usual five senses. "There were a lot of stories of pets getting up and going into the next room to alert their owners to a seizure," he says. "They obviously weren't responding to a body-language cue or even an electromagnetic cue, because they weren't nearby."

THE DEEPEST BOND

While most scientists believe that the "extrasensory" powers of dogs and cats are, in fact, totally sensory, some veterinarians are convinced that dogs and cats read minds every day and that it's possible for us to read theirs as well. Telepathy isn't some otherworldly power, says Laurel Davis, D.V.M., a veterinarian in Asheville, North Carolina. She believes that everyone has the ability to communicate telepathically, although this ability tends to be neglected as we get older.

She tells the story of a woman who attended an animal-communication seminar. After it was over, the woman saw a man in the driver's seat of a parked car, and a big dog was in the passenger seat next to him. The woman decided to try some of the things she had learned at the workshop. She stood still in the parking lot and for 10 minutes spoke mentally with the dog. Then she walked over to the car. The dog greeted her warmly, much to the amazement of the dog's owner, who explained that this was a dog with a history of extreme aggressiveness who had never before let anyone near the car.

Scientists may never know for sure whether or not dogs and cats have a sixth—or seventh or eighth—sense, but pets certainly have a gift that's no less impressive: the ability to bond totally and without reservation with their owners. "There have been times when I've done everything I can medically for a pet and have exhausted every option," Dr. Becker says. "And yet, pets who were so sick that I thought they were going to die were bouncing around in their cages, ready to go home." He suspects that many so-called miracle cures are stimulated by nothing more than the intense psychic bond between pets and their people. It's as though pets are saying, "Hey, I'm going home—I'm needed there."

PART 2

From Whiskers to Tails–

A Complete Guide to Body Language

CHAPTER 7

Whiskers

If you were to put your cat in a darkened maze, she'd confidently stroll all the way through without knocking into the sides or bumping into a wall. Cover her eyes, and she'd still be able to locate a mouse in a field. Even if you covered her ears and nose as well as her eyes and then tried to sneak up on her, she'd probably be aware of you before you got close.

Are cats psychic? Lots of people think so. But scientists have found that cats' rather astonishing powers of perception are due less to mental wizardry than to the wonders of the whiskers.

Cats use their whiskers constantly. The whiskers act almost like sonar, telling cats how close they are to objects around them. Cats also use their whiskers to communicate. Depending on the position, whiskers tell other cats when to stay away and when to approach.

Dogs have whiskers, too, growing from their muzzles and eyebrows. They don't rely on them the way that cats do, says Liz Palika, a trainer in Oceanside, California. A dog's whiskers mainly act as protective "feelers" to protect the eyes. When dogs run through brush and a branch flicks the whiskers, they automatically blink. "But dogs don't really use their whiskers to communicate," says Palika. In fact, many breeders trim a dog's whiskers to make them look good, something you'd never do with a cat.

"Cats rely on their whiskers to pick up information from their surroundings," says John C. Wright, Ph.D., a certified applied animal behaviorist; professor of psychology at Mercer University in Macon, Georgia; and author of *The Dog Who Would Be King* and *Is Your Cat Crazy?* "Once you understand just how your cat's whiskers work, you can use that information to improve your relationship."

Wired to Her World

When you look at cats head-on, you'll get a pretty good view of their intricate whisker systems. You'll see a vast collection of long hairs, known as vibrissae, sprouting above their eyes, at the base of their ears, along their cheeks, and under their chins. There are also whiskers on the backs of the front legs, an inch or so above the paws. Whiskers grow from special follicles that are located about three times deeper in the skin than fur follicles and are much larger.

Your cat's whiskers are sensitive enough to detect even the slightest changes in air currents and air pressure. This means that they can use their whiskers much like bats use sonar to find their way in the dark. By sensing changes in air currents, they can literally feel how close they are to walls or other objects. Some whiskers are specialized, and each set does a different job.

On the cheeks: Being the most prominent whiskers on cats, these sprout from behind the nose and extend slightly beyond the body on either side. They make it possible for cats to gauge when an opening is too small for them to sneak through.

Over the eyes: As cats negotiate their way through bushes and brush, these whiskers help them avoid injury by triggering a blink reflex when something brushes against them.

Under the chin: These whiskers help cats find morsels of food when they're eating in the dark.

In a very real sense, whiskers are like several extra sets of eyes. They allow cats to see the world in greater detail. In fact, cats who lose their sight may develop whiskers that are longer and thicker than usual. They learn to swivel these whiskers constantly to detect slight changes in air current, temperature, and air pressure, which allows them to get around without the benefit of vision.

Reading Whiskers

Because the whiskers have a hot line to the brain, they provide unique insights into your pet's moods and actions. You can tell when she is contented, irritated, or ready to play. "Just by watching a cat's whiskers, you can predict when she is going to bite about 50 percent of the time," notes Dr. Wright. "Cats will often broadcast what their next behavior will be with movement of their whiskers."

Whiskers straight out to the sides. Cats normally hold their whiskers out to the sides in a relaxed, natural position. This means that nothing is stimulating their curiosity or distracting them. They're just happy and content.

Whiskers flattened. When the whiskers shoot straight back from the nose and lie flattened against the cheeks, you can be pretty sure that your cat is afraid of something. Cats normally assume this whisker position when they're feeling defensive, such as during confrontations with dogs or other cats.

Whiskers fanning and swiveling. Cats who are curious about something in their environment use their whiskers almost like antennae. They swivel them about in order to read subtle changes in the air. Something as simple as a door opening will put the whiskers in motion. Even an impending storm may cause them to move.

Whiskers spread out and angled forward. When a cat points her whiskers straight out in front of her face, watch out. "This is the face of a cat who is likely to bite," says Dr. Wright. "When a cat sticks those whiskers out forward like that, she is putting her sensors ahead of her to feel what she is going to bite."

What Whiskers Can Tell You

Reading your cat's whiskers is an easy way to tell what mood she's in, or if she's going to bite. (If her whiskers are pointed forward, look out!)

Working with Whiskers

Because the whiskers are extraordinarily sensitive, they require special handling on the parts of owners, says Dr. Wright.

Watch the waist-whisker ratio. Unlike their wild kin, house cats aren't locked in day-to-day struggles for survival that require their senses to be in top condition. But just as you wouldn't intentionally hamper your cat's ability to hear, you shouldn't hamper her ability to use her whiskers by letting her get too heavy, says Dr. Wright. The whiskers on the upper lip should stick out just a bit farther than the widest part of the body. Cats are aware that when their whiskers fit through an opening, the rest of their bodies will, too. When their bodies get wider than the whiskers, however, they're in danger of getting stuck in a hole in a fence, for example, or between the couch and the wall. For the sake of your cat's safety as well as her health, you want to make sure that she doesn't become overweight, Dr. Wright advises.

Leave them alone. Cats vary in the amount of petting they enjoy. Some like it a lot. Others don't care to be handled. But all cats dislike having their whiskers touched too much. Because the whiskers are so sensitive, petting or stroking them is the equivalent of shouting in your cat's ear or shining a bright light in her eyes. "It's a good idea to let children know not to tug or pull on a cat's whiskers," adds Dr. Wright.

Make her an eight-stroke cat. Some cats dislike a lot of physical contact and will scratch or bite when they've had enough. "We call it the petting-and-biting syndrome," says Dr. Wright. "You pet them a couple of times, and they seem to enjoy it. Then, after one or two more strokes, they turn around and attack your hand."

You can use your knowledge of whisker movements to encourage cats to be more tolerant of physical affection, says Dr. Wright. "When your cat is lying down calmly, begin to stroke her, keeping count of the strokes and keeping an eye on her face. When you see her eyes dilate and her whiskers shoot forward—usually after three or four strokes—stop petting her. Let her whiskers stop flaring and return to their normal position. Then begin again. If you do this a couple of times a day, within several weeks you may be able to turn your cat from a three-stroke cat into an eight-stroke cat, or maybe more."

CHAPTER 8

Eyes

The ancient Egyptians fashioned cat's-eye amulets called utchats, which were used for good luck. People kept them around the house to protect against accidents and disease. They hung them above doors to repel vandals and thieves. They even gave them as wedding presents to ensure that the newlyweds would be blessed with many children.

Cat's-eye charms are no longer given a special place above our hearths, but real cats' eyes, along with their canine counterparts, continue to hold a special place in our hearts. "Eyes have always been very special to people because we use our eyes more than any other sense to figure out our world," says Patricia Simonet, Ph.D., a certified applied animal behaviorist and assistant professor in the science and humanities departments at Sierra Nevada College in Lake Tahoe, Nevada, where she teaches and conducts research in animal behavior, animal communication, and animal intelligence and cognition. "Since we don't speak the same language as our animals, we try to understand what they're thinking or how they're feeling by the way they look at us."

Glances Full of Meaning

People who spend a lot of time around animals can tell when they're happy, worried, healthy, or ill just by looking at their eyes. The glances that pets give are full of messages, but unless you're intimately familiar with a dog or cat, it's not always easy to read them correctly, says Alex Brooks, director of Alex Brooks School of Dog Training in Des Plaines, Illinois. "People misinterpret their pets' expressions all the time," he says. "They think those sad puppy eyes mean that their dog is feeling remorseful about eating the couch, when what his eyes are really saying is, 'Wow, you look pretty scary right now. Maybe you won't hurt me if I look down at the floor.'"

One reason there's so much confusion about the messages

Out of the Blue

Many Siamese cats have stunning blue eyes. This color is rare in other breeds, however, which is a good thing. Non-Siamese cats with blue eyes and white coats have a high risk of being born deaf. The same genes that control eye color also play a role in hearing.

It's not very common, but some cats are "odd-eyed"—meaning that they have one blue eye and one gold eye. In the strange logic of genetics, these cats are sometimes deaf on the blue-eyed side.

given by eyes is that people attribute certain moods or characteristics to pets' facial expressions, says D. Caroline Coile, Ph.D., a researcher specializing in canine senses, who raises and shows salukis near Tallahassee, Florida. Unlike cats, whose faces are really quite similar to others in their species, dogs have a lot more variation. Some breeds have droopy eyes and heavy jowls, while others have tight facial skin and alert expressions. It's easy to confuse a dog's natural look with his personality.

For example, boxers, pugs, and bulldogs have large, prominent eyes that can make them look perpetually frightened or threatening. Old English sheepdogs look very nonthreatening, in part because their eyes are nearly concealed beneath curtains of hair. Even when they give a threatening stare, other dogs and people can't see it.

But despite a few differences among breeds, all dogs and cats use their eyes in similar ways. The messages they give, however, are sometimes a little different. Here are the main signals you're likely to see.

Wide open. People often see this look when they take their pets to the veterinarian for a checkup. Opening the eyes as wide as they'll go allows cats and dogs to take in as much of their surroundings as possible. In cats especially, the pupils signal fear by dilating dramatically, expanding to nearly the size of the entire eye, says Barbara S. Simpson, Ph.D., D.V.M., a board-certified veterinary behaviorist and a certified applied animal behaviorist in Southern Pines, North Carolina.

Cats are a little different from dogs in that their eyes also dilate when they're ready to lash out in self-defense, says John C. Wright, Ph.D., a certified applied animal behaviorist; professor

NAME: Oscar
OCCUPATION: Hypnotist

Gaze into Oscar's big brown eyes for more than 20 seconds, and *you'll* be the one doing tricks. This is because Oscar, who looks like any other sweet, lovable Labrador, is actually HypnoDog, the sidekick of professional hypnotist Hugh Lennon of Yorkshire, England.

"I read this story about a farmer who claimed he had a dog who could hypnotize people, so I had to go and see him," Hugh says. "Oscar was only 10 months old at the time. He had the oddest eyes I'd ever seen, and he stared so intently at people. I bought him on the spot."

Hugh wanted Oscar as a pet, but he soon discovered that the pup was a real show-stealer. "I used to take him to shows for companionship," he says. "But then one night, I brought him on stage with me. He started staring at this girl, and she fell into hypnosis—without me doing a thing." At that moment, Oscar became Oscar the HypnoDog.

Though Hugh has been a hypnotist for a long time, he can't explain how Oscar performs his magic. Not everyone "goes under" Oscar's unrelenting stare, but those who do slip into a hypnotic state quickly. One of the most remarkable moments in Oscar's career was when he was wandering through the audience, as he often does after his show, and came upon a man eating potato chips.

"Being a dog, of course, he sat right in front of the chap and stared at him while he crunched away," Hugh says. "Before you knew it, there was a whole lot of excited commotion. The man crumpled over in his chair—completely hypnotized."

of psychology at Mercer University in Macon, Georgia; and author of *The Dog Who Would Be King* and *Is Your Cat Crazy?* "When you see your cat's eyes suddenly widen, it's best to back off."

Narrow and dilated. When a cat is just feeling a little steamed, his eyes will probably narrow a bit, just as people's do, says Scott Line, D.V.M., Ph.D., a board-certified veterinary behaviorist in Winston-Salem, North Carolina. In the moments before a cat decides he's truly angry, his pupils dilate, his eyes narrow, and his ears go back, he says.

Long, slow blinks. Cats who are calm and relaxed will invariably look at their owners through long, slow blinks, an expression known as a kitty kiss.

Eyes shut. A cat with his eyes closed is a picture of unadulterated, contented bliss. "Closed eyes are the sign of absolute contentment," says Steve Aiken, an animal-behavior consultant in Wichita, Kansas.

Frequent blinks. Blinks mean something different in dogs than in cats. While cats blink languorously when they're happy, dogs tend to blink more when they're feeling stressed. Liz Palika, a trainer in Oceanside, California, sees a lot of blinking during classes, when dogs are under pressure. Along with yawns, blinks are known as calming signals, she explains. "Dogs who are blinking a lot are saying, 'Please, let's just take a break and relax!'"

Down and away. On the playground of life, dogs have learned that the best way to avoid conflicts with bigger, meaner dogs is

Just Back Off!

Your cat's never too subtle about letting you know when he's mad. If his ears go back and he half-closes his eyes but the pupils are dilated, stop petting him, picking him up, or otherwise getting in his way. And if his eyes widen with the pupils still dilated, back off: He's ready to strike.

The Eyes Have It

When a dog looks at you, he's definitely trying to tell you something. If your dog looks away as if he's ashamed when you're fussing, he's really begging for mercy. A happy, alert stare from your own dog means that he's asking for play, attention, or (frequently) dinner. If a strange dog looks you in the eyes, however, it's often a sign of aggression.

Aggressive stare: I'm top dog

to look away rather than make eye contact. They carry this lesson over to their relationships with people. When their owners are angry or scolding, dogs will look away, says Dr. Simpson. It's their way of saying, "I'm no threat, so please don't hurt me."

Straight at you. Dogs know that when they want attention or instructions about what to do, the quickest way to get results is to look people right in the eye. They've learned over thousands of years that people respond best to direct eye contact. Their own instincts, however, tell them never to stare because it's considered aggressive, or at least rude, says Dr. Coile. This is why a direct stare from your own dog is friendly, while a stare from a strange dog is probably a threat.

"Dogs who stare are saying, 'I'm top dog,' and they are daring the other dog, or the person, to either put up their dukes or back down," she explains. "Unfortunately, many people don't realize this and are bitten while trying to show their sincerity by staring into an aggressive dog's eyes."

While dogs may use stares as challenges, cats usually stare when they're concentrating and trying to figure things out, says Benjamin Hart, D.V.M., Ph.D., professor of physiology and behavior at the University of California, Davis, School of Veterinary Medicine and author of *The Perfect Puppy: How to Choose Your Dog by Its Behavior*. "Cats stare at whatever they're interested in," he says. "If your cat is looking at you, he's probably just waiting to see what you'll do next. And he probably won't mind if you stare back."

Strange Glances

Dogs and cats don't see all that well compared to people. Even though they can spot the tiniest flash of movement from the corners of their eyes, sometimes they have trouble seeing what's right in front of them. So they do the dog and cat equivalents of furrowing their brows and staring harder.

"You may find that your own dog barks and glares at you madly when you're standing on the front porch and he's inside," says Dr. Simonet. "It seems like it should be obvious to him that it's you, but he probably can't see you very well. Once you start moving and talking, he'll recognize you and calm down."

Similar things happen with cats, Dr. Wright adds. "They get information from how we move. So your cat may stop 15 feet away and look at you intently, making you think that something's wrong. But he's really just bringing you into focus and assessing what you're going to do next," he says.

CHAPTER 9

Ears

Humans use their ears only for hearing. Fixed tightly to the sides of our heads, our ears are pretty inexpressive. Sure, we can adorn them with silver hoops or diamond studs, and some people can even wiggle them a bit. But that's about it. We can't tell what people are feeling by looking at their ears or communicate messages by moving our own.

Among our four-legged companions, however, the ears are much more versatile. Attached to their heads with up to 20 fully functional muscles, the ears are fully mobile. Dogs and cats can twist their ears to pinpoint the origins of sounds, and they move them around to express a variety of thoughts and emotions.

"Understanding the subtle ways in which our pets communicate with us, like the way they have their ears set, makes living with them easier," says Stephen Zawistowski, Ph.D., a certified applied animal behaviorist and a senior vice president of animal services and science advisor for the American Society for the Prevention of Cruelty to Animals in New York City. "We don't have to speak the same language because we can interpret one another's body positions."

Charles Darwin, the originator of the concept "survival of the fittest," pondered why dogs and cats have such mobile ears. He believed that animals that fought with their teeth had to be able to pull their ears back to prevent adversaries from grabbing these convenient tooth-holds. This may explain why, when pets are angry, their ears pull back.

But Darwin's theory explains only part of the story. Watch dogs or cats in different situations. You'll see that they don't just pull their ears back. Depending on the breed and what they're trying to say, they may thrust them forward, drop them down, perk them up, or lay them perfectly flat against the head.

"Our pets use body language to convey every emotion they feel," says Patricia Simonet, Ph.D., a certified applied animal behaviorist and assistant professor in the science and humanities departments at Sierra Nevada College in Lake Tahoe, Nevada, where she teaches and conducts research in animal behavior, animal communication, and animal intelligence and cognition. "Try spending a day watching how your dog's or cat's ears change position when he's happy, worried, afraid, or interested. You'll be surprised how many changes you notice."

Of course, dogs and cats use every part of their bodies, from the

Ears and Evolution

Just as your hair color, build, and skin tone reveal something about your family history and heritage, your dog's ears reveal something about his. Dogs started out with pointed ears that stood straight up, like wolves'. "The dogs that you see today have been modified over thousands of years of selective breeding to have just the right characteristics for what man needed them for," says Benjamin Hart, D.V.M., Ph.D., professor of physiology and behavior at the University of California, Davis, School of Veterinary Medicine and author of *The Perfect Puppy: How to Choose Your Dog by Its Behavior*.

Common ear shapes include:

Pricked or semi-pricked ears. Collies, huskies, shepherds, and most terriers have ears that stand straight up on top of their heads. (Semi-pricked ears flap down slightly at the tips.) Huskies and Samoyeds have this ear shape because they're genetically quite similar to their ancestor, the wolf. Terriers and collies, on the other hand, have been bred for this ear shape because it provides superior hearing. Bred for hunting small game, terriers need to be alert to the slight rustle of a rabbit or fox in the brush. Collies, bred for herding,

Pricked ears

Semi-pricked ears

head to the toes, to convey emotions and desires. But you can tell volumes just by "reading" their ears. Let's take a look at dogs first.

READING YOUR DOG'S EARS

Dogs' ears come in a wide array of shapes and sizes, and they're one of the most expressive parts of the body. You have to

Drop ears

Cropped ears

need to hear the call of their masters, who may be many fields away.

Drop, or pendant, ears. Also called floppy-eared, these dogs include Labradors, golden retrievers, whippets, and hounds. Dogs may have been bred for floppy ears in order to slightly muffle their supersensitive hearing. This might heighten their other senses, like smell and sight, and lessen distraction from every little rustle around them.

Retrievers, for instance, need keen sight in order to track birds in the sky, see where they fall, and then sniff them out to retrieve them. Wolfhounds and whippets, sometimes called sight hounds, rely on their excellent vision to track wolves and deer. And for bloodhounds, bred to sniff a scented trail, sensitive hearing would only be a distraction.

Cropped ears. When people buy a guard dog, they want him to look mean, and floppy ears just don't cut it. But ears that stand straight up can be quite intimidating. Guard dogs like Doberman pinschers and Great Danes haven't been bred to have special ears. Instead, the ears are cropped, or surgically altered, so they stand up. This gives dogs a daunting look and helps prevent the ears from getting damaged in a scuffle. Cropping, however, is gradually falling out of favor.

look closely to read them correctly, however. Positions that look almost the same can mean entirely different things.

Raised slightly. Dogs who are happy and comfortable will raise their ears slightly, as though they're saying, "I'm happy, and I'm paying attention. Just tell me what to do," says Emily Weiss, Ph.D., curator of behavior and research at the Sedgwick County Zoo in Wichita, Kansas. "When your dog is relaxed, with his tail low and the ears pricked slightly and a little forward, that's the sign of a happy, confident, alert dog."

Raised high. Dogs raise and rotate their ears to locate and identify sounds. When your dog finds something to be particularly excited about, like the sound of footsteps coming up the front walk, he'll prick his ears high and point them forward in the direction of the sound. This is a sign that he's alert and ready for action.

"When he raises his hackles (the fur on the back of the neck) as well as his ears, then he's also feeling threatened," says Liz Palika, a trainer in Oceanside, California. "A dog who wants to say, 'Back off! This is my territory!' will try to make himself as big as possible. This includes lifting his ears as high as he can and raising his hackles, which makes his head look larger than life."

Relaxed, slightly down, and back. When nothing exciting is going on, which is most of the time, dogs keep their ears in a relaxed position. This is what you'll often see when you're petting your dog or rubbing his head. It means he's not particularly excited, just relaxed and content. He may draw his ears back a bit, leaving you plenty of room to rub the top of his head.

Flat and back. Just as dogs try to make themselves look larger when they're feeling aggressive, they shrink a bit when they're nervous. When your dog lays his ears flat against his head, and his tail is low and between his legs, you'll know he's afraid and is perfectly willing to back down from whatever is threatening him. "Submissive dogs usually put their ears back and flat against the skull when they're faced with an aggressive dog or person," explains Palika.

Ears that are flat and back aren't always a sign of submission. Dogs who assume this position, along with other "fighting postures" such as snarling or growling, may be getting ready to attack. Moving the ears back helps ensure that they don't get bitten in the scuffle.

Sweeping back and forth. As with humans, dogs sometimes

Ear Interpretations

You can read your dog's ears like signal flags. From happy and alert to curious, relaxed, afraid, or even confused, it's all there in his ears' positions.

have mixed emotions and aren't sure exactly how they feel. This ambivalence is often expressed in the way they move their ears. "You might see your dog's ears wavering back and forth when you reprimand him and he doesn't really like what he's hearing," says Palika. "It's his way of saying, 'I accept your reprimand . . . reluctantly.'"

READING YOUR CAT'S EARS

Cats have smaller ears than dogs, and there's less variation in size and shape among different breeds. As a result, their ears often seem less expressive than dogs'. "We also tend to pay less attention to cats' body language because we don't spend as much time training them as we do dogs," says Dr. Simonet. "But cats have similar body-language responses."

Perked up and slightly forward. This is the classic look of a happy cat: His ears are perked up and slightly forward, and his whiskers are relaxed. Cats who are confident and interested in what's going on around them will also put their ears up. When your cat comes toward you with his ears up and forward, he's giving you a greeting and is ready to hear what you have to say—or at least is prepared to get a little bit of attention.

Straight back. As with dogs, cats will move their ears back when they're anticipating trouble. At the same time, they'll move their whiskers forward to get a better sense of whatever it is that's aggravating them. When your cat's ears are in this position, it's a sign that he's really upset, and you'd best keep your hands out of the way.

Flat against the head. Unlike an angry cat, who will pull his ears straight back, cats who are frightened flatten their ears against the sides of their heads. They lay their whiskers down as well. No one's sure why cats do this, since flattening the ears muffles their sense of hearing and would seem to make them more vulnerable.

Some experts theorize that cats flatten their ears in order to seem as small and unthreatening as possible. Cats who flatten their ears and crouch low to the ground seem to be saying, "Don't worry about me; I'm not here." Another theory is that by flattening their ears, cats are intentionally blocking sounds they find threatening, which allows them to hold perfectly still without

Cat Ear Signals

Reading your cat's ears is the easiest way to tell what he's thinking. It's also the best way to avoid being bitten when Fluffy decides he's had enough.

panicking until the threat passes by. And, of course, clamping the ears against the head means that they are less likely to get chomped should a battle ensue.

Swiveling to the outside. Cats have an astonishingly well-developed sense of hearing and can locate and identify the slightest sound, such as a mouse in a wall across the room. Part of what enables them to pinpoint the source of a sound with such accuracy is their ability to turn and point their conical ears toward the sound. When you see your cat swiveling one or both ears to face outward, you'll know that he is interested in something he hears.

WHAT'S MY PET SAYING?

Behavior
Walking on Ledges

What It Means
"I'm Looking for Prey"

Cats love high places. Countertops, window ledges, and the tops of bookcases have an almost irresistible allure. The higher the place, the more cats are tempted to explore it.

They don't go high just to indulge their natural derring-do. Cats are hunters, and the higher they climb, the better their view of potential prey down below. And since cats are better climbers than some of *their* predators, high places make them feel safe and secure.

The problem with their attitude about altitude is that many high places are precariously narrow, and small missteps can result in big falls. Nature planned for this by providing mammals with a special structure in the inner ear called the vestibular apparatus. Consisting of a series of canals, fluid, and tiny hairs, this structure gives cats an extraordinary sense of balance, allowing them to maneuver smoothly and gracefully over almost tightrope conditions. The sight of Socks casually sauntering on a shelf near the ceiling might make you nervous, but you can be sure he's pretty secure. On the rare occasions when cats do take a false step, their keen sight, muscle reflexes, and sense of balance help them do what cats do best—land on their feet.

"You might be talking to your cat, and it looks like he's really concentrating on what you're saying," says John C. Wright, Ph.D., a certified applied animal behaviorist; professor of psychology at Mercer University in Macon, Georgia; and author of *The Dog Who Would Be King* and *Is Your Cat Crazy?* "Then you'll see the right pinna, or outer ear, swivel away in the other direction, and you'll know he's just tuned you out for something more interesting."

CHAPTER 10

Facial Expressions

There's a good reason we can tell a lot about people's moods and personalities from their expressions. Lying beneath the human complexion are 44 intricately interwoven muscles, which can contract and loosen into about 5,000 expressions. This facial versatility may be a problem at the poker table, but it allows us to communicate with each other without saying a word, and at great distances. You can tell if a person standing 100 yards away is happy or preoccupied, angry or focused. You know, or at least can suspect, if an approaching stranger is friendly or not.

In his book *The Expression of the Emotions in Man and Animals*, Charles Darwin theorized that people couldn't survive without their rich facial vocabularies. Facial expressions allow us, even as babies, to convey our needs so that others can understand. And no matter where you travel in this world, facial expressions are remarkably similar. They truly are a universal language.

Dogs and cats also depend on facial expressions to communicate not only with each other but also with their people, says Patricia Simonet, Ph.D., a certified applied animal behaviorist and assistant professor in the science and humanities departments at Sierra Nevada College in Lake Tahoe, Nevada, where she teaches and conducts research in animal behavior, animal communication, and animal intelligence and cognition. In the evolutionary scheme of things, facial expressions may have been more important for them than for us. Animals with sharp claws and strong teeth need to be able to give each other signals like "Back off" and "I'm not looking for trouble" without getting too close. "And if you look carefully, you'll notice that their expressions really aren't all that different from our own," says Dr. Simonet.

WHAT'S MY PET SAYING?

Behavior
Smiling

What It Means
"I'm Imitating My People"

Not so long ago, scientists were convinced that either dogs and cats had no emotions at all or their emotions were totally different from ours. People with pets knew better, of course, and today many experts in animal behavior believe that pets have emotional lives that are no less rich and exciting than our own. They've even found that pets—especially dogs, since they've been bred to work closely with people—have picked up some of our mannerisms, including smiles.

"Historically, dogs have not smiled at one another because it's not a canine mannerism," says Myrna Milani, D.V.M., a veterinarian in Charlestown, New Hampshire, and author of *CatSmart* and *DogSmart*. "They may have given submissive grins to each other, but that's more of a tense, worried look than a friendly one."

In today's world, however, dogs spend their entire lives with people, and their facial expressions possibly have evolved to reflect that. "The beguiling smile with the pulled-back lips and the subtle 'Hey, look at this!' body language is something they may have learned from hanging out with people all of these years," says Dr. Milani. "It's an expression they reserve just for people, and sometimes only very special people."

A Practical Tool

Most facial expressions happen involuntarily. We feel an emotion, and our facial muscles respond. "Dogs and cats have facial muscles very similar to our own, so their faces respond much in the same way," says Dr. Simonet. "When they're surprised, their eyebrows go up. When they're angry, their lips curl. We don't always notice their expressions because their faces are covered with fur and shaped differently from our own. But they're there."

We think of facial expressions mainly as being a communications tool, but for dogs and cats, they also have practical purposes, says Steve Aiken, an animal-behavior consultant in Wichita, Kansas. "Opening their eyes wide when they're scared helps dogs and cats scout out as much of their environment as possible," he explains. "And baring teeth when they're angry puts them in the ready position to bite if they need to."

Learning your pets' expressions will allow you to recognize and predict their feelings and desires. You can also tell from facial expressions how pets are getting along with other pets and with the people in their lives.

"Just be aware that some dog breeds are able to express themselves more, or less, fully than others," says D. Caroline Coile, Ph.D., a researcher specializing in canine senses, who raises and shows salukis near Tallahassee, Florida. "Old English sheepdogs obviously can't communicate as much with their eyes as other dogs. And many dogs have been bred to have features like very dark eyes, heavy facial wrinkles, or tiny ears, which can limit their ability to express themselves. So you always have to look at the whole animal to figure out for sure what they're saying."

The Game Face

Athletes put on what they call a game face when they're preparing to face competition. Despite the name, this expression is pretty serious. Dogs and cats, on the other hand, have a more literal game face—one that's a lot more silly than somber. Also

If your dog "bows" to you and starts grinning, he's ready to play

called a play face, it's the expression they have when they're feeling playful and want someone to join them.

The game face looks a whole lot like an open-mouthed grin. The lips are pulled back, the ears shift back and forth, and the eyes are constantly shifting from direct stares to exaggerated looks away. Dogs, puppies especially, usually put on their game faces right after they've assumed a posture called a play bow, in which they stick out their front paws and lower their front ends while putting their rears high in the air, says Barbara S. Simpson, Ph.D., D.V.M., a board-certified veterinary behaviorist and a certified applied animal behaviorist in Southern Pines, North Carolina.

Cats are a little less exuberant with their play faces. They don't pounce wildly or run around like dogs do. Instead, they'll sit and look directly at each other. Their ears will move forward, their eyes will narrow, their pupils will dilate, and they'll lean forward slightly, waiting to see who's going to make the first move—which is usually a fast pat to the face. Then the games will begin.

The Aggressive Face

Dogs and cats (and people) rarely have to resort to physical violence because certain facial expressions are so intimidating that they tell the whole story: "Move outta my way, or you're hamburger." Pets who aren't looking for trouble will gladly step aside when they encounter the aggressive face. All dogs and cats will occasionally assume this expression, but pets who are naturally dominant are masters of these shriveling stares.

A dog who's feeling aggressive will move his ears up and for-

It's hard to mistake what this expression is telling you: "Back off, or I'll bite!"

ward. His eyes will be set in a direct, fixed stare. And if he's really feeling mean, his upper lip may be raised, showing some teeth. This is the face of a dog who's seriously considering an attack, says Dr. Simpson.

Cats are equally expressive in their anger, says Aiken. "The first thing you'll see when cats are angry are pupils that have shut to narrow slits," he says. The whiskers will usually jut forward, and they may open their mouths, baring some teeth. Cats who are seriously considering an attack will pull their ears back slightly while at the same time rotating them outward so they flatten to the sides. This looks rather silly, but it's very practical. When cats do decide to dive in and attack, rotating and flattening the ears allows them to move them out of harm's way.

THE DEFENSIVE FACE

Sometimes the best defense is a good offense—and sometimes it's wiser to duck and cover. When it comes to facing down bullies, cats seem to prefer the former, while dogs often go belly-up with the latter. Regardless of how they respond to real or imagined threats, both dogs and cats show their fear with a defensive face—an expression that means they just want to be left alone.

In some ways, cats who are frightened look a lot like cats who are aggressive. If you look closely, however, you'll see that all the

The classic "hangdog look." He's not really ashamed—he just doesn't want to be hurt.

expressions are reversed. "Instead of the pupils constricting, they'll dilate wide. This allows cats to expand their peripheral vision so they can see if anything is coming at them from the sides," says Larry Lachman, Ph.D., an animal-behavior consultant based in Carmel, California, and author of *Dogs on the Couch* and *Cats on the Counter*. Cats will also flatten their ears and pull their heads and whiskers back. They'll often hiss as well.

Unless dogs are looking for a fight, they won't put on the theatrical display of a frightened cat. Rather, they'll whimper and try to make themselves as small and as little of a threat as possible. They'll duck their heads, fold their ears back, and look down or away. Their whole center of gravity will shift downward as they shrink inward and low to the ground. "These expressions are very puppylike," says Dr. Lachman. "When your dog makes them, he's hoping the attacker treats him like a puppy and doesn't hurt him."

THE CONFUSED FACE

Imagine a classroom filled with sophomores on the first day of physics class, and you'll have a pretty good idea of what dogs and cats look like when they're confused. You're talking, but it's obvious that the message isn't getting through. They'll give you pleading looks that say, "Say that again, this time in my language."

"You are the most important creature in your dog's life, and

A cocked head is a plea for clear communication. He's trying to say "Huh?!"

when you talk, he desperately wants to understand," says Aiken. "When he understands what you're saying, he'll respond with an action. When he doesn't understand, it's just as obvious. He'll sit there, eyes wide, ears perked up, and mouth closed. He'll probably be cocking his head from one side to the other."

Cats don't worry as much as dogs about what you're saying. Their confusion usually arises when they can't figure out something that has their curiosity piqued. "If they think you're holding something they'd like to have, like a catnip mouse or a treat, cats can give the most insistent stares until they figure out what they want to know," says Dr. Simonet. Not wanting to miss a thing, the ears will perk up and move toward you, and the eyes will be bright and alert. They won't shift their gaze until their curiosity is satisfied, she says.

THE SAD FACE

No one's sure whether dogs and cats feel sadness in the same way that people do, but they unmistakably are familiar with the emotion—and they have a distinct expression that tells you when they're feeling blue. "They get visibly upset when they know we're not happy with them," says Alex Brooks, director of Alex Brooks School of Dog Training in Des Plaines, Illinois. "What you are seeing is actually a look of submission." In other words, your

Your dog may look sad if you're ignoring him or he knows that he's made you angry.

pet doesn't want you to be mad anymore, so he shrinks down and makes himself look small and helpless.

Dogs who seem sad will close their eyes slightly, and they'll look a little sulky. In some breeds, the ears will hang listlessly at the sides of the head, and the facial muscles will droop a little, says Dr. Coile.

Cats aren't as focused on pleasing humans the way dogs are, so you're less likely to see them with sad expressions. "If a cat's eyes are droopy and listless and he doesn't have much muscle tone in his face, chances are that he has a health problem, and you should see the vet," Aiken says.

The Happy Face

There's no mistaking the look of contentment on dogs' and cats' faces when they're feeling well-loved and well-fed and are generally happy all over. "Pets who are calm, collected, and content just radiate bliss," says Aiken.

Cats who are thoroughly content will shut their eyes—if not completely, almost all the way, and their ears and whiskers will sit in a relaxed, neutral position. The only way to tell if a cat is happy or merely asleep is to look at his face. Happy cats will curl their mouths up just slightly, giving a hint of a smile.

A happy cat is the picture of contentment.

Dogs in a state of bliss look similarly relaxed. The dog's entire body, including his ears and face, looks almost devoid of muscle tone, says Liz Palika, a trainer in Oceanside, California. "The mouth will be loose or maybe hanging open slightly," she says. "The ears will be up slightly, but not perked up or forward. And the eyes will be relaxed and slowly blinking. If you give your dog regular exercise, this should be a common expression."

Nothing says"I'm happy" like a big doggy smile.

CHAPTER 11

Tails

Back in the days before daily newspapers and CNN, some folks believed that they could predict bad news by watching their dogs' tails. When dogs were sleeping with their tails out straight and their paws upturned, that meant bad news was on the way. The direction the tail was pointed told from which direction bad tidings would come.

Dogs' tails are no more effective than tea leaves for foretelling the future, of course, but that doesn't mean they don't have a lot to say. Dogs and cats use their tails as much as—and probably more than—their voices to send each other messages. Since we don't have tails of our own, we're basically illiterate when it comes to "tailspeak." So we make a lot of mistakes, such as assuming that dogs whose tails are wagging are feeling friendly—which is about as accurate as predicting the weather by watching how sleeping dogs lie.

In order to understand the tales tails tell, it helps to understand why dogs and cats have these expressive appendages and what they're really used for. Tail movements and positions tell a lot about what pets are thinking. Even the shapes of tails have something to say.

Form and Function

Cats who live in the wild use their tails largely for balance. When a cheetah rockets after a gazelle, she uses her tail like a gyroscope. It allows her to whip around at full speed without falling over. House cats don't hit speeds of 65 (or more) miles an hour. But they use their tails in much the same way—to maintain their balance while making fast turns or while walking along high, narrow surfaces. Dogs also use their tails for balance, but because they don't leap from tree branch to tree branch or from banister to piano top, their tails come less into play.

Apart from adding ballast for balance, tails provide a conve-

WHAT'S MY PET SAYING?

Behavior
Tail Chasing

What It Means
"Whee! This Is Fun!"

Dogs and cats don't think of their tails as being serious or profound. They see them as nearly perfect toys. Tails hide for a long time, then suddenly spring into sight, prompting a dizzying, circular chase as pets try mightily to catch them.

"Some dogs and cats chase their tails just a few times when they're very young, but for others, the game never gets old," says John C. Wright, Ph.D., a certified applied animal behaviorist; professor of psychology at Mercer University in Macon, Georgia; and author of *The Dog Who Would Be King* and *Is Your Cat Crazy?* "Pets who continue this game are usually very excitable and playful. Once they start chasing their tails, they get so worked up that they don't even recognize them as their own."

Some pets, however, get a little too involved in tail chasing—they'll do it compulsively, and sometimes nonstop. Pets who seem driven to chase their tails and don't seem to be taking any pleasure from it need to be seen by a veterinarian.

nient means of communication. Since they typically fly high above the animal, dogs and cats use their tails like flags to send messages from a distance. And because the tails are highly mobile, dogs and cats have developed a rich vocabulary of language based on positioning and movement.

"Our pets can speak volumes by just moving their tails back and forth," says D. Caroline Coile, Ph.D., a researcher specializing in canine senses, who raises and shows salukis near Tallahassee, Florida. "How fast the tail wags and how high or low it is all mean different things."

Among dogs, things have gotten a little complicated because they've been bred to have certain tail shapes and characteristics, says Myrna Milani, D.V.M., a veterinarian in Charlestown, New Hampshire, and author of *DogSmart* and *CatSmart*. Things get even more confusing because some dogs have their tails docked, or cut short. Still, most dogs communicate with their tails in similar ways.

CANINE WAGS

Probably the most obvious, and most misunderstood, form of tail language is the wag. Even people who have spent their entire lives around dogs assume that full-throttle wags mean a dog is saying "hi" with all her might. But tail wagging can't be interpreted this easily because dogs who are aggressive and are preparing to attack will also wag their tails.

"A wagging tail means nothing more than that a dog is feeling excited about something," says Scott Line, D.V.M., Ph.D., a board-certified veterinary behaviorist in Winston-Salem, North Carolina. "Sometimes the excitement is positive, and sometimes it is negative. You have to look at the dog more closely to figure out which is which."

High, stiff, and wagging. A tail that's upright like a mast doesn't necessarily mean that a dog is feeling aggressive, but she's certainly being assertive, says Larry Lachman, Ph.D., an animal-behavior consultant based in Carmel, California, and author of *Dogs on the Couch* and *Cats on the Counter*. "Many people get bitten because they misinterpret stiffly wagging tails. A tail held high and wagging stiffly is the sign of a dominant dog, and it could mean that the dog is ready to attack."

Low, fast wags and short sweeps. When a meek dog is approached by a more assertive dog—one with her tail up and stiffly wagging—she has only one reasonable response: to show the bossy dog that she isn't a threat. "Dogs who are fearful or submissive often will respond to another dog's approach by holding their tails low and wagging them just slightly," says Dr. Coile. "This means, 'Hey, I'm friendly and no threat at all.'"

Low, slow wags and large sweeps. Sometimes a wag is really just a wag. "You'll know your dog is wagging because she's happy to see you and wants to play when her tail is low or even with her body and is wagging a little slowly, but in wide sweeps back and forth," says Dr. Coile. "Usually, her whole butt will be wiggling as well."

Dogs don't speak only with their tails, of course, and the only way to accurately interpret tail movements is to know something about the breed. "Some hunting dogs, like spaniels, have been bred to wag their tails constantly while pursuing quarry," says Dr. Milani. "To signal that they've found their game, they stop wag-

Tail Talk

A wagging tail isn't always a sign of a friendly dog. In fact, if the wagging tail is held upright, it's a sign of dominance. Play it safe: Don't pet a strange dog if you don't want to be bitten.

ging and hold their tails stiffly up in the air. On the other hand, herding dogs are bred to have less tail movements so that their wagging tails don't distract or excite the animals that they're trying to herd. If you didn't know that about these animals, you might think one was overly excited while the other was overly staid, when it's really just the way they were bred."

Feline Twitches

Although cats have long, expressive tails, you won't catch them wagging them. "Cats do more of what we call tail twitching, where just the tip of the tail moves," says Steve Aiken, an animal-behavior consultant in Wichita, Kansas. "And it rarely means they're feeling happy when they do it."

Fast-twitching tip. Cats who are agitated or irritated seem to channel all of their energy into the top 2 inches of their tails, which will briskly twitch back and forth. "Some cats will also twitch their tails when you pet them, right before they turn around and give you a playful bat on the hand," says Dr. Line. "It's just a sign of excitement."

Tail lashing. A cat who's slightly irritated will twitch her tail. A cat who's *very* irritated is more likely to lash it back and forth. That's when it's time to really back off, Aiken says.

Slow-twitching tip. People who are comfortable and relaxed sometimes gently tap their feet. Happy cats do a similar thing by slowly twitching and rolling the tips of their tails. If you're not sure if what you're seeing is a fast or slow twitch, look at the rest of the cat: A cat who is content will also relax her whiskers, and her body will be downright limp.

Tail high and quivering. Even though cats don't wag their tails the way dogs do, sometimes they're so happy that their entire tails go into a bit of a quiver. When a cat is facing you and the tail is erect and quivering all along its length, you're being told, "You're the best thing in the whole world."

Feeling Up or Down?

The real beauty of tails is that you can sometimes tell at a glance how pets are feeling at the moment. Even when tails aren't moving, the positions—up or down, tucked or straight—are direct reflections of their emotions.

"If you watch closely, you can see your pet's mood change by

Cat Tails

Cats' tails tell tales about how they're feeling—you just need to know how to read them. Once you know the signs, you'll be able to decipher a cat's tail movements as easily as a dog's. What's your cat trying to tell you today?

watching the tail," says Dr. Coile. "When a shy dog meets someone for the first time, she might start with her tail so far down between her legs that you can't even see it. But as she warms up, you'll see it begin to emerge and become obvious." The same is true for cats. Their tails will raise, lower, fluff up, curl down, or stick straight up depending on how they're feeling.

Between the legs. When someone feels bad because he's done something wrong, we say he has his "tail between his legs"—an expression we definitely took from our dogs. "Dogs who are feeling afraid and submissive will crouch low and tuck their tails between their legs," says Liz Palika, a trainer in Oceanside, California. "It's as though they're saying, 'Don't hurt me.'"

Cats respond in a similar fashion. As peace-loving animals, their first inclination is to avoid confrontations. They do this by trying to look as small and nonthreatening as possible. "Since it's hard to do that with your tail sticking straight up in the air, the first thing cats will do is tuck it low between their legs," says Aiken. Cats with their tails tucked are invariably nervous or worried, he explains.

Straight up. A jaunty, high tail is a sign of a happy cat. Among dogs, however, a high tail is a sign of full alert. Whether they're happy or not, a high tail means they're feeling dominant and in charge—or at least they're trying to convince you (or other dogs) that they feel that way. "When they want to look aggressive, they'll stick their tails so straight up that they look like they're growing out of the tops of their heads," says Dr. Coile. "When other dogs see that, they know it's best to back down."

Down and even. While happy cats hold their tails high, happy, relaxed dogs let them droop down. "When your dog's tail is hanging even with her body, she's feeling at ease," Palika says.

U-shaped. Just as people curl their index fingers when they want someone to approach, cats curl their tails over their backs—it means they want another cat (or a person) to come and play.

Fluffed up. It's hard to look threatening when you're small, cute, and furry. But cats are masters of disguise. When they want to look meaner and tougher, they instantly make themselves look bigger by sticking their tails up and fluffing them out. At the same time, they'll rise on their toes to make themselves look really big. The message is unmistakable: "Back off—or else." Some dogs also raise their tail fur in confrontations, but they're more likely to raise their hackles, the hairs on top of the neck.

Man-Made Confusion

Even though nature has equipped dogs with this fast, effective means of communication, humans have spent thousands of years trying to botch it up, says Dr. Coile. "Because we've been

The Tail Tells All

You can tell your pet's mood—and his emotional state—by watching her tail. A jaunty tail is a sign of a happy cat but a dominant dog, while holding the tail between the legs tells a sorry tale for both species.

breeding dogs to have specific tail characteristics, and because we've been docking the tails of various breeds, we've really made it tough for many dogs to communicate clearly with other dogs," she says. Unlike dogs, cats haven't been bred to perform certain jobs, so their tails have remained basically unchanged.

Italian greyhounds, for instance, have been bred so that their tails are perpetually held low or tucked between their legs. "To other dogs, they look like they're always scared or submissive," Dr. Coile explains. Alaskan malamutes, on the other hand, have been bred to have their tails up all the time. This means they sometimes get into scuffles because other dogs think they're trying to be dominant. "Though tail docking is popular in certain breeds, it means dogs lose much of their ability to communicate with their tails," she says.

CHAPTER 12

Posture

A dog is standing in front of you. His teeth are showing, and his tail is waving back and forth. Is he: (a) relaxed; (b) telling you he's happy you're home; or (c) preparing to attack?

As you may have guessed, this is a trick question. No matter which answer you chose, you were potentially right. Looked at another way, no matter which answer you chose, you were potentially wrong. And being wrong if the actual answer were "c" would be really bad news.

The point of this quiz is to show that even though dogs and cats give very clear signals with their heads, tails, and facial expressions, you can't read any of these signals in isolation. You have to look at the whole animal, top to bottom, to really understand what he's trying to say. The context matters, too: Are you a stranger? A friend? The giver of discipline?

"Wagging tails are a perfect example," says John C. Wright, Ph.D., a certified applied animal behaviorist; professor of psychology at Mercer University in Macon, Georgia; and author of *The Dog Who Would Be King* and *Is Your Cat Crazy?* "Most people interpret tail movement as a positive, friendly signal. But some dogs swish their tails back and forth when they're agitated or aggressive. If you don't pay attention to what the rest of the dog is doing, you can find yourself in trouble. The same is true when you're trying to read cats. Things like how the animal is standing, how he holds his ears, and how tense or relaxed his muscle tone appears all play important roles in what he's trying to say."

The Unspoken Word

Animals developed an intricate language of body positions in order to survive in the wild. Dogs especially, as highly social animals, had to develop a system that allowed them to communicate with other dogs in their group. They used various postures to show who's boss, signal an attack, avoid confrontation, and initiate play. They could convey some of these messages vocally by barking, growling, whining, and howling, but making lots of noise wasn't always a good idea since it could scare off potential prey or alert predators to their presence.

Cats also use body language to communicate, but they tend to rely more on their intricate vocal language, which consists of a variety of chirps and meows. "Cats didn't live in big social groups like canines did, so they didn't have to communicate with one another constantly," says Scott Line, D.V.M., Ph.D., a board-certified veterinary behaviorist in Winston-Salem, North Carolina. "Cats use their body language only when they have to."

While their ancestral roots are quite different, both dogs and cats use body language, with varying degrees of success, to communicate with humans, says Dr. Line. "Because they're so dependent on us and we don't speak the same language, they have to be able to tell us what they need in as many ways as they can."

Pets have much simpler lives than humans, so they don't require a huge range of social signals. Nearly all of their body language is used to communicate basic emotions and intentions, such as "Let's play," "I'm tougher than you," or "I wish you'd leave me alone." As with human body language, however, even slight shifts in position can convey entirely different messages. Here are the main messages you're likely to see.

It's Playtime

Along with eating and sleeping, playing is what young pets do best. It's not only fun but also an important part of their development and social conditioning. By romping with one another (and with us), they improve their motor skills, sharpen their senses, and get some much-needed exercise. Some historians believe it was dogs' love of play that encouraged cave dwellers, who originally brought dogs into their settlements some 20,000 years ago, to keep these furry creatures as companions.

It doesn't take a lot of encouragement for pets to run after a tennis ball or chase a catnip mouse. Getting people motivated, however, is considerably more difficult, and dogs and cats have developed a variety of signals to get our attention and indicate their willingness to have some fun.

Bowing. Among dogs, the most enthusiastic play signal is the

WHAT'S MY PET SAYING?

Behavior
Rolling on His Back

What It Means
"Look What I Found!"

Dogs love being outside. The freedom. The sights. And especially the smells. They get so excited that sometimes they'll throw themselves on the ground and wiggle around on their backs, feet flailing in the air. It's obvious they're having a great time.

This position signals more than wild exuberance, however. "When dogs roll over on their backs and start wiggling around like that, they're actually trying to cover themselves with a scent on the ground that they find exciting and want to share with others," says Stephen Zawistowski, Ph.D., a certified applied animal behaviorist and a senior vice president of animal services and science advisor for the American Society for the Prevention of Cruelty to Animals in New York City. "When they lived in packs, one dog might go out and find some fresh elk droppings. To let the others know, he'd roll around in it and go back to the pack so the others could smell what he'd found."

But as often occurs, messages intended for other dogs are interpreted entirely differently by people. Your dog might be saying, "Look what I found!" but the message you're getting is, "This guy needs a bath!"

play bow, in which they lower their front ends and raise their bottoms, tails up and wagging, says Marc Bekoff, Ph.D., a canine researcher and professor of environmental, population, and organismic biology at the University of Colorado in Boulder. This posture always means that a dog is eager to romp, although there may be ulterior motives. Dogs who have done something wrong, such as knocking over a lamp because they were overly rambunctious, will sometimes give a play bow just to let you know that they didn't mean any harm and only wanted to play, he says.

Pouncing. Cats are usually less aggressive in soliciting play than dogs, but they have their own ways of getting your attention. "Instead of jumping around and play bowing, a cat will crouch low, several feet away, and wait for just the right moment before pouncing," says Stephen Zawistowski, Ph.D., a certified applied animal behaviorist and a senior vice president of animal services and science advisor for the American Society for the Prevention of Cruelty to Animals in New York City. "It's his way of saying, 'I'm here to play.'"

Of course, cats preparing to pounce may be motivated by things other than play, like the sight of a mouse. You can tell the difference by looking at their faces. Cats who are pouncing for fun will usually be wearing their "play face," in which the pupils are dilated and the ears are facing forward.

Bottom wagging. Dogs use their tails to convey all kinds of messages, from "Let's play" to "Stand back, or I'll bite." So you can't assume a wagging tail is a plea for fun. A wagging bottom, on the other hand, is an unmistakable sign. "A dog who wants to play will be standing before you with his tail dropped low and his ears relaxed or back," says Dr. Wright. And his whole back end, not just the tail, will be wagging fairly quickly.

Belly up. When a dog interacts with other dogs, he may roll over on his back and expose his belly. It's his way of showing that he's feeling submissive and doesn't want any trouble. "Dogs have learned that when they use this posture with humans, it usually gets them a belly rub and some playful attention," says Liz Palika, a trainer in Oceanside, California. "They start doing it when they feel happy, loved, and playful."

Cats also roll over when they're feeling playful, adds Dr. Wright. But because this position puts their paws and claws up and at the ready, it's usually a signal that they want an aggressive kind of play.

I'm Okay, You're Okay

Wild animals usually respond to humans with one of two types of body language—those signaling fear and the desire to run, and those signaling their intention to fight. Dogs and cats, on the other hand, despite their wild backgrounds, enjoy the benefits of domestication. They're able to spend their lives relaxed and content inside safe, comfortable homes. As a result, they have developed postures that signal nothing more than their love and trust.

"Whether your dog is lying at your feet, sitting down, or just

Playful Postures

Dogs and cats use their whole bodies to tell you when it's time to play. When you see any of these postures, you know it's time for fun!

standing around, you can tell he's content just by looking at his posture and muscle tone," Palika says. His ears will hang loose, his lips will be drooping slightly, and his tail will be slightly down and relaxed.

Cats have a similarly relaxed appearance when they're content, says Dr. Zawistowski. "Cats smile with their whole bodies—lying down, muscle tone completely relaxed, eyes closed. You can just see they're happy."

Cats also show contentment in their walks, says Dr. Wright. "Happy, relaxed cats will approach you with their tails high in the air and with very relaxed muscle tone, so they just swish and sway with every paw step," he says. "Their ears will be straight up and relaxed, and their pupils won't be dilated. They'll just prance along."

Cats have another, slightly unusual way of showing their contentment with life: They'll butt you with their heads. Cats see their human companions as mother figures, and that's the same signal kittens use when they're happy and comfortable, says Steve Aiken, an animal-behavior consultant in Wichita, Kansas. "Cats will come toward you with their heads and ears a little down and forward, tails up in a friendly way, and then just ram their heads into you."

You can make your cat especially happy by holding out your fist when he approaches, Aiken adds. Your fist resembles a cat's head, and cats love making head-to-head contact.

Who's in Charge?

Life in the wild was just one big territorial struggle. Because they lived in packs, canines had to constantly establish their place in the group. As lone hunters, cats had to tell other feline predators to stay away from their turf. Even though modern life is a lot cushier, dogs and cats still have instinctive urges to establish their positions within the family, especially when there are other pets in the house. They have developed a rich body-language vocabulary that shows how they see themselves in the family hierarchy.

It's not true that every dog and cat wants to be "top dog"—many don't, says Dr. Wright. And it's not uncommon for dogs to perceive themselves as dominant in one situation and subordinate in another. But since displays of dominance can be quite dramatic, we'll look at those first.

Talking in Their Sleep

Dogs and cats spend about half of their days sleeping. Even when they're sawing the wood, however, they say a lot with their body language.

"Boy, am I relaxed. Or maybe it's hot in here." Dogs love sleeping on their backs, but they only do it when they're feeling totally safe and relaxed. Cats occasionally sleep on their backs, too—not because they're feeling safe, but because they're a little warm, and sleeping belly up is cooler than sleeping belly down.

"Brrr." Cats look peaceful and content when they sleep curled up, but they're probably just cold, and pulling themselves into a ball helps conserve body heat. Dogs also like to sleep curled up, and they'll often tuck in against someone or something for added comfort. It's their way of saying, "I like a little extra security when I nap."

Bigger and badder. "Whenever an animal wants to show how tough he is, he'll make himself look as big as possible," says Larry Lachman, Ph.D., an animal-behavior consultant based in Carmel, California, and author of *Dogs on the Couch* and *Cats on the Counter*. "A lion fluffs up his mane. A bear stands up on his hind legs. And your pets use the same body-language tricks."

Dogs who are serious about establishing their territory will stretch their height as much as they can while leaning forward a little, with their hackles (the hair on the neck) raised. The tail will go straight up, and they'll point their ears and lips forward. "This is a dog who doesn't want to be messed with," says Dr. Lachman.

Cats are also concerned about status, but they don't make the big displays that dogs do, Aiken says. They're more likely to display body language that disrupts their usual social codes. For example, cats generally stay 4 to 6 feet away from other cats in the same household, unless they happen to be playing. A cat who's trying to establish dominance will walk right up to another cat, sit stiffly, and stare. "Eventually, the other cat will get the idea and pack up and go," Aiken says.

The T-posture. Whenever two dogs get together, whether they live in the same family or are meeting for the first time, they take a moment to establish (or reestablish) their respective social rankings. "If there is one dog who is more assertive than the other, he will come up and put his chin over the other dog's shoulder,

Leader of the Pack

Dogs have a lot to say when it comes to showing who's boss. They don't even have to bark or growl to put another dog in her place—the body language says it all.

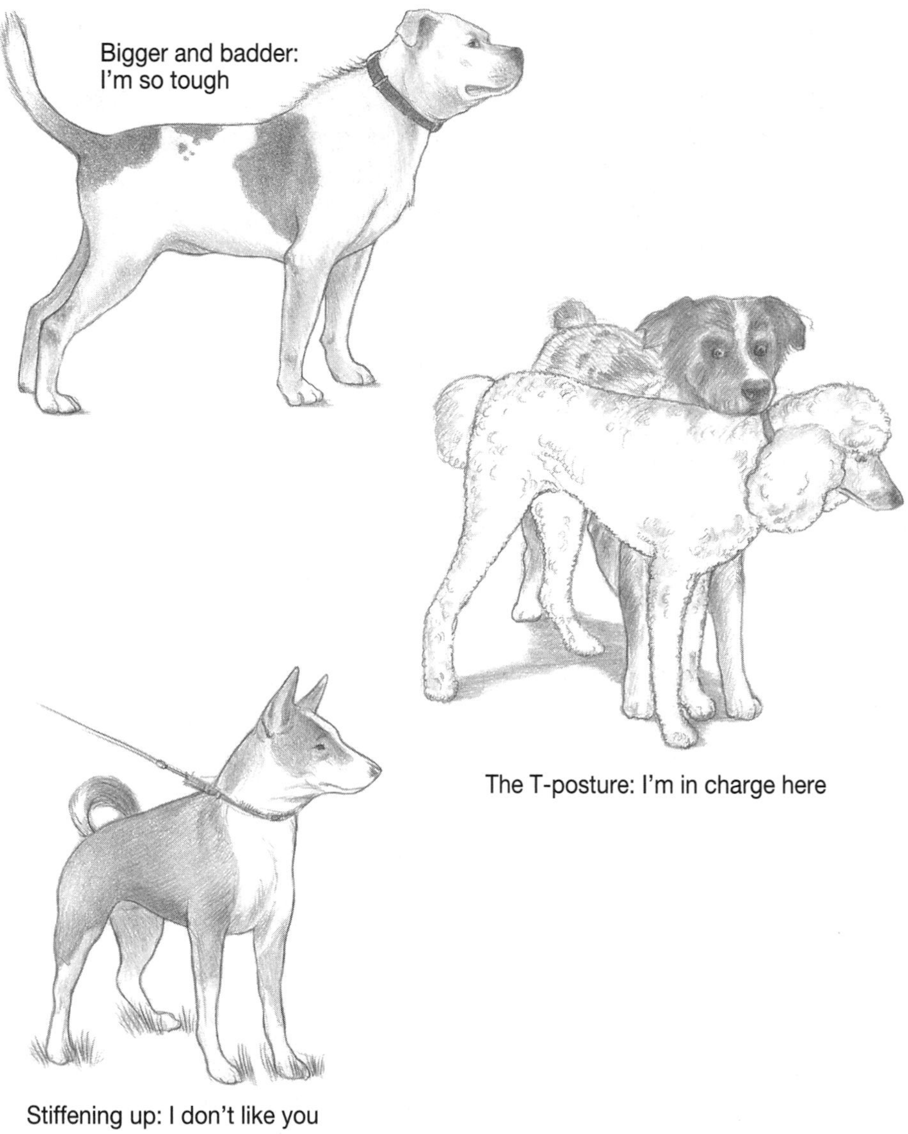

Bigger and badder: I'm so tough

The T-posture: I'm in charge here

Stiffening up: I don't like you

making a T with their bodies," says Dr. Wright. "Dogs are aware that it means that the dog on top is in charge."

Stiffening up. When someone you don't like or are nervous about steps into your personal space, your body stiffens, and your facial features become rigid. Pets undergo similar changes, says Dr. Wright. "The first sign that animals are unhappy about something is a stiffening in their muscle tone." You'll see this in several places: The ears will stand up more than usual, the tail will be high and alert, and the face will look hard and rigid.

ATTACK

Sometimes scowl comes to growl between animals, and there's the threat of a fight. When things heat up, one pet will usually go into an attack mode, while the other prepares for defense. Confrontations usually don't go any further than posturing, which is scary enough. But sometimes posturing leads to fighting, so it's important to know what to look for.

Dogs who are preparing to attack bring many postures into play. They'll stand tall, raise their hackles, raise their ears, and stiffen their faces. They'll also face you straight on while making direct eye contact. "This is a very threatening posture," Dr. Lachman says.

Cats preparing to attack will also stare and face the object of their anger. Their whiskers will point forward as well. In some cases, they'll raise their hips much higher than the rest of their body, which gives the impression they're about to charge.

"Though you don't have to worry much about attacks from strange cats, you do have to be rather cautious around strange dogs," says Ira B. Perelle, Ph.D., a certified applied animal behaviorist and chairperson of the development committee for the Animal Behavior Society in Bloomington, Indiana. If you ever encounter a dog showing an attack posture, you may be able to defuse the situation by assuming the *opposite* posture: Turn to the side, look away, and make your body look as loose as possible. Once a dog believes you're not a threat, he'll be much less likely to attack, says Dr. Perelle.

While cats will occasionally assume attack positions, it's more common for them to give signals of defense. They do this by making themselves look as big and scary as they can, launching what behaviorists call a defensive threat, says Dr. Wright. "This is the classic Halloween-cat pose," he explains. "He wants to look big and mean because he hopes it will make the offender think he shouldn't mess with him."

DON'T HURT ME

Most dogs and cats will do everything possible to avoid confrontations. Their usual technique is to make themselves look as innocent and defenseless as possible—not just when they're confronted by other pets, but any time they're feeling nervous and insecure.

"Dogs and cats will try to make themselves appear as small as possible when they want to avoid an attack," says Dr. Lachman. "They'll crouch down with their bellies low to the ground, their tails tucked low between their legs, and their ears back in a way that says, 'Hey, no threat here. I'm just a small, defenseless animal.'"

It's common for puppies to try to make themselves disappear when they're first being leash-trained, adds Myrna M. Milani, D.V.M., a veterinarian in Charlestown, New Hampshire, and author of *DogSmart* and *CatSmart*. "They'll flatten themselves against the ground and won't budge," she says. "Their owners will give them a command, and they'll get even flatter. It's not stubbornness—it's fear. They're trying to avoid confrontation."

When a confrontation is really heating up, dogs will sometimes decide that crouching on their bellies isn't making them appear submissive enough. So they'll flip over and lie on their backs. "It's a completely submissive display, like throwing up the white flag and saying, 'Hey, I'm unarmed,'" Aiken says.

This signal isn't quite as clear-cut with cats because they'll often lie on their backs in order to have their claws ready to repel an attacker. But they may use this position to signal submission as well, says Katherine Houpt, V.M.D., Ph.D., a board-certified veterinary behaviorist, professor of physiology, and director of the behavior clinic at Cornell University College of Veterinary Medicine in Ithaca, New York. "Young male cats, in particular, will do this with older male cats to show their submission," she says.

PART 3

Speak!

CHAPTER 13

What Your Dog Is Telling You

Several years ago, executives at the Thompson's Pasta Plus pet food company in Kansas City, Missouri, launched a contest to find the dog who could say "pasta" with the greatest clarity, diction, and style. A good Italian accent, they added, would be a plus.

Out of the ranks of more than 100 would-be spokesdogs, Melbourne, an Australian shepherd mix from Cheektowaga, New York, won paws down. His reward, which his owner appreciated more than he did, was a trip for two to Italy.

People have always wondered about their pets' capacity for conversation and their grasp of the spoken word. Despite Melbourne's impressive videotaped demonstration, most experts believe that dogs will never be able to speak English or any other human language, says John C. Wright, Ph.D., a certified applied animal behaviorist; professor of psychology at Mercer University in Macon, Georgia; and author of *The Dog Who Would Be King* and *Is Your Cat Crazy?* "Dogs who 'mumble' at their owners have probably tried out a vocal behavior at some point and gotten a favorable response," he says. "Then the dog feels, 'Oh, that was great! They liked it. I'll do it again.'" And conversation, as we like to call it, begins.

Why Talk at All?

We don't think of dogs as being great conversationalists, but they depended on vocal communication long before they lived with humans. Dogs learned their communication skills from wolf ancestors. Humans saw the value of those skills when the dogs began warning them of impending danger. Through selective breeding, humans were able to increase their dogs' ability to communicate.

Dogs also engage in the type of barking chain made famous in Disney's *101 Dalmatians*. When dogs in packs wanted to keep in touch with each other, they would howl, and other dogs would pass on the signal, says Judith Halliburton, an animal-behavior consultant and trainer in Albuquerque, New Mexico, and author of *Raising Rover*. The barking chain probably wasn't meant to deliver a specific message, she adds. "It's a general alert, like a siren, and not a public-address announcement."

While today's dogs may think that they have important information to pass along, there's no practical reason for them to form barking choruses. But they do it anyway, if only because the ancient instincts are still there.

FOR OUR EARS ONLY

Dogs aren't all that talkative with other dogs, but they've learned that barking—or whining, howling, or whimpering—gets responses from their owners. It doesn't take a canine Einstein to figure out that subtle signals like body language and scent usually go over their owners' heads, while a resounding woof invariably gets a quick response of breaking out the biscuits, for example, or opening the back door so they can run outside. Dogs are adept at figuring out what sounds people respond to, and they'll vary their vocalizations accordingly. If a loud woof usually gets your attention, there's going to be a lot of woofing in the family. If you're more likely to respond to a whine, your canine thespian will start sounding as pitiful as Oliver Twist.

Whining, incidentally, is a sound that dogs rarely make in the wild. It's a sound associated with puppies, and few adult dogs want to be perceived by their peers as being childish or submissive, says Dr. Wright. In the human family, however, these sounds get people's attention, making them closer to "peoplespeak" than to actual "dogspeak."

Even the garden-variety bark is a fairly new development, Halliburton says. In the days when dogs depended on stealth to catch their dinners, barking was useless—or worse. Dogs today don't depend on silence for their dinners, and barking invariably gets them some attention. So they do a lot of it. Even when dogs are alone, they'll sometimes bark, either because they're lonesome or because it's a way to pass the time, she says.

Beyond the basic barks and whines, dogs make about 11 different sounds. Most of us will never hear all of these sounds because dogs tend to make them only when they're with other dogs. In their dealings with humans, dogs generally limit themselves to 4 basic sounds: barking, whining, growling, and howling. Each means different things, so it's worth learning the difference, says Dr. Wright.

Barking

Dogs understand people a lot better than we understand them. Experts have found that dogs can respond to as many as 300 words. Most people, on the other hand, can't distinguish one bark from another. Even though there are quite a few different barks, they usually mean one of two things: "Go away" or "Please notice me."

• Among dogs, high-pitched barks are considered submissive, or at least immature. Dogs who want something from their human "parents" often ask for it in a polite, pleading sort of way. A high-pitched bark may be their way of saying, "Thank goodness you're home!" or "Won't someone come and play with me?"

• Nearly identical to the high-pitched, attention-getting bark is the "hurry up" bark. This is the eager sound dogs make when you've held on to the tennis ball too long or you're too slow lacing up your sneakers while they're holding the leash in their mouths.

• Dogs who are barking for the benefit of other dogs, especially dogs who they feel are intruding on their space, usually give a low-pitched bark, says Dr. Wright. Used to convey authority and perhaps a touch of menace, these "sentry" barks are considered to be powerful warnings. Some dogs give this type of bark only when a person or another dog is threatening their peace of mind. Others, however, feel compelled to defend their territory against just about anything, from a squirrel running up a tree to a branch falling off a tree.

Whining

Whining is generally a sign of immaturity, in dogs as well as in people. The only reason adult dogs whine is that they've learned it always gets a response from dear old Mom, which is

NAME: Scruffy

OCCUPATION: Actor

"Wonder dog" is a tough name to live up to, but Scruffy, a mixed breed in Belton, Missouri, certainly does his best. Ever since he was rescued from an animal shelter in Kansas City, Missouri, Scruffy has been throwing himself into his career as an actor, spokesdog, and Hallmark calendar model. And his success, which has been considerable, is largely due to his voice.

Scruffy, who played Ruff in a touring production of *Dennis the Menace*, is prized for his ability to bark (loudly or softly) and growl on command, says Michael Reynolds, his owner and trainer. Actually, he admits that Scruffy is a bit reluctant to growl. The best way to get him to let loose is to bring Thor, a Rottweiler that Michael also represents, onto the set. "Scruffy is as calm and loving a dog as you could ever meet, but Thor just brings out his growls," he says. "I guess it's professional rivalry."

While barking, growling, and yawning on command are pretty impressive, it's Scruffy's ability to bark quietly—to "whisper," as Michael puts it—that gets the attention of dog owners, who wish they could teach their own dogs to turn down the volume. But for a dog who understands about 100 different commands, barking softly is just another day's work.

how they perceive the people in their families. Whining is a way of saying, "I'm submissive, and I'd humbly like to ask you something," says Dr. Wright.

Whining isn't always puppyish petulance, he adds. It has a variety of meanings depending on the social situation in which it occurs. For example:

"I'd really like to come close to you, and won't you let me?" Whether dogs are interacting with dogs or people, they're constantly aware of social rankings. A dog who's naturally shy and retiring will be nervous about approaching a higher-status dog—especially a dog who's shown signs of being aggressive. A dog who's feeling submissive may be similarly nervous about approaching a person. A whine is their way of acknowledging their subordinate status and announcing that they're not a threat.

"Would you please help me out?" Dogs are much more patient than people. With the possible exception of food, they'll usually ask for things in the politest way possible—by looking excited, wagging their tails, or running back and forth. When you start to hear whining, it's probably a message of last resort: "I've looked in the window, sat outside the door, barked at you, and tried everything I know. Won't you please, please open the door?"

"Ouch." Dogs who are hurting will often complain with a plaintive whine, says Dr. Wright. That's why you should call your vet if your dog is suddenly whining more than he used to, he advises.

Just as some people complain all the time, some dogs whine all the time. They don't necessarily need attention, a veterinary checkup, or anything else, says Dr. Wright. It may simply mean that they're darned good actors who have learned that whining convinces people that they're in desperate need—even though all they really want is a scratch behind the ears.

GROWLING

If a bark is a warning, a growl is the threat that follows. Some happy-go-lucky dogs will go their entire lives without growling, while others feel it's necessary to intimidate the mail carrier on a daily basis. Growling dogs want to be, and should be, taken seriously.

"I tell my clients that every growl means 'I'm going to bite you—maybe not right this minute, but you're pushing me,'" says Sheila McCullough, D.V.M., clinical assistant professor of small animal medicine at the University of Illinois College of Veterinary Medicine at Urbana–Champaign. Growls are often idle threats, but unless you comprehend dogspeak extremely well, it's best to assume that the dog means business. Dogs should never growl at their owners, she adds. If you're hearing a lot of growls at home, be sure to talk to your vet. Your dog may have a physical problem that's making him cranky, or more likely, he needs a little social refresher course from a professional trainer or behaviorist.

HOWLING

In the wild, howls are like long-distance telephone calls. They allow dogs to keep in touch even when they're far apart—an instinct that continues in today's neighborhood canine gangs. A long, loud "Arroo!" usually means "Give me your coordinates" or "Is anybody out there?" Sometimes it means nothing more than "I have a lovely voice, don't you think?"

Howls that sound truly mournful are usually caused by separation anxiety, a condition in which dogs feel desperately lonely when their owners are gone. Dogs with separation anxiety will

Oh, the Sound!

Judith Halliburton, an animal-behavior consultant and trainer in Albuquerque, New Mexico, and author of *Raising Rover*, has seen a lot of strange behavior, but she still talks about the Border collie who loved to jump in the shower stall when it wasn't in use and howl at the top of his lungs. His owner was understandably a little worried as well as annoyed at all the ruckus. So she asked Halliburton to come over and see what was causing it—and what could be done to stop it.

It didn't take Halliburton long to figure out that the dog was just fine. In fact, he felt so good about life that he had to sing about it. "That dog was howling in the shower because he liked the acoustics," she explains. "He was just singing his heart out."

sometimes howl for hours. And since it only happens when the dogs are alone, their owners may be unaware that there's a problem until the neighbors come knocking.

INDIVIDUAL DIFFERENCES

Dogs go through their most vocal stages during adolescence. Eventually, they settle into quieter patterns of vocalization as adults. When dogs suddenly start barking, moaning, howling, or growling, you need to pay attention. "When dogs who weren't vocal before become vocal, they're under some kind of stress," Halliburton says. "Whether it's a physical or behavioral issue, they're doing everything they can to communicate it."

While some dogs are born talkers who appear to love the sounds of their own voices, others rarely let out a peep. The biggest factor that determines how much dogs talk is breeding. At one time, breeders deliberately bred dogs to be vocal because people were interested in having watchdogs. In addition, they bred dogs to be more subservient and puppyish, and additional barking came along with the package, says Dr. Wright.

You can predict whether dogs are likely to be talkers just by considering the breed. For example:

- Herding dogs such as collies tend to be very vocal because they were bred to use their voices to gather wayward sheep and move the herd.
- Miniature breeds such as Pomeranians are often big barkers because it's the only weapon they have for scaring off other dogs, says Halliburton.

While some dogs were bred to bark, others were prized for their silent natures. Basenjis, for example, were originally bred in Africa to guide hunters and warn them of dangerous animals ahead. They were bred to silently "go on point" in response to looming threats. Rhodesian Ridgebacks are also quiet dogs because they were bred to hunt lions, and a quiet nature was an undeniable advantage.

When these or other "silent" breeds start barking, you want to pay attention, Halliburton says. Their instinct not to bark is so strong that they only do it when there's a pressing need. Quiet dogs are not known for crying wolf, she explains.

CHAPTER 14

What Your Cat Is Telling You

People have been wanting to put words in cats' mouths almost since the beginning of time. People around the world, from Native Americans to the ancient Egyptians, believed that cats harbored great knowledge and power but were mysteriously silent in sharing it. Perhaps the most famously enigmatic feline is the Cheshire Cat in *Alice's Adventures in Wonderland*. He smiles and looks entirely assured, but the darned cat won't tell Alice which way to go. Of course he knows, but he's not telling.

It's obvious why cats acquired a reputation for silence. Unlike dogs, who lived in packs and needed to communicate with each other, wild cats were (and are) solitary hunters who depended on stealth and quiet cunning. Apart from vocalizing during mating rituals and while raising kittens, cats didn't have a lot to talk about before humans came along.

Once cats started living with people, however, their mouths went into motion. In part this was because breeders hoped that chatty cats would make better companions and watchcats. But a lot of the change was due to the cats themselves. Intelligent cats quickly realized that making a little noise was the only way to communicate with their powerful but apparently dim two-legged companions, who didn't have a clue about body language or scent markings. "It's almost as though they were thinking, 'Okay, dummy, I guess I'm just going to have to say it,'" says Pam Johnson-Bennett, a feline-behavior consultant in Nashville and author of *Twisted Whiskers* and *Psycho Kitty?*

"One of the strategies that cats use when a need is not being met is vocalization," adds John C. Wright, Ph.D., a certified applied animal behaviorist; professor of psychology at Mercer University in Macon, Georgia; and author of *The Dog Who Would Be*

Chatty Cats

Cats are known for being vocally reserved, but some are so talkative that it's almost impossible to make them quit. Siamese, Tonkinese, Himalayans, Javanese, Oriental longhairs, Cornish rex, and Sphynx cats have all been bred, recently or in the past, to be talkative and outgoing.

"When someone tells me that a Siamese or a Tonkinese cat is too vocal, unfortunately, I just have to tell them to live with it," says Pam Johnson-Bennett, a feline-behavior consultant in Nashville and author of *Twisted Whiskers* and *Psycho Kitty?*

King and *Is Your Cat Crazy?* Whether the message is, "My box is dirty," "I'm hungry," or "I want to go outside," once cats discover that saying it gets results, then say it they will.

The most common form of cat chat, the meow, is unique to domesticated cats, Dr. Wright adds. Cats who have been socialized and introduced to people at an early age tend to be more vocal than those who've had to go it alone.

More Than Meows

Apart from their deep, rumbling purrs and the occasional yowl, house cats usually communicate with drawn-out, slightly plaintive-sounding meows. Their vocabulary can seem pretty limited, but apparently they keep things simple for our sakes. Cats have been found to make at least 20 distinct sounds, says Bonnie Beaver, D.V.M., a board-certified veterinary behaviorist, certified applied animal behaviorist, professor of animal behavior at Texas A&M University College of Veterinary Medicine in College Station, and author of *Feline Behavior: A Guide for Veterinarians*. Their vocal range is extensive, ranging from a barely perceptible purr of contentment to the can't-miss-it mating howl.

Scientists have divided all the various cat sounds into three groups: vowels (such as "meow"), purring sounds, and strained intensity sounds such as hisses and screams, says Dr. Beaver. Cats who live in the wild have at least as much, and possibly more, of a working vocabulary than dogs. Much of their vocabulary, however, is devoted to attracting mates, mating, and raising kittens. When you factor these activities, along with the task of guarding property, out of the lives of spayed or neutered house cats, the need for a large vocabulary disappears. Cats end up using just a few sounds to express their basic needs to their owners, their peers, or other pets in the neighborhood.

ONE WORD SAYS IT ALL

Cats may be creatures of few words, but they're masters of using tone, volume, and inflection to change the meaning of a meow. Depending on how it's pronounced, cats use "meow" to express such things as "Where *have* you been?" or "Sorry, would you say that again" or "Get your lazy self out of bed this very minute and feed me—I'm wasting away before your very eyes."

Cats have distinctive voices just as people do, and most owners learn to distinguish their pets' particular wants and needs just by the volume and inflection of their voices. But all cats use the meow in similar ways. Here are some examples.

"Mro-o-o-ow." The loud, reverberating, drawn-out meow is called a demand meow. When cats don't get what they want—food, attention, an open door—they'll keep insisting, getting a little louder each time, says Dr. Wright. Basically this sound means, "What is taking so long?"

"Mew." A short, clipped, soft-spoken meow is a greeting or acknowledgment. It's basically the meow cats use in polite conversation, with no demands or requests attached. Some cats use this sound every time their owners walk in the room. Some only use it when they've been asked a question, and some forgo civility altogether and never "mew" at all.

"Mrowo-o-o-ow." Similar to the demand meow, the complaint meow is the sound cats make when something isn't to their liking. It roughly translates as, "Why haven't you given me this yet?'" says Dr. Wright. Most cats begin with the demand meow to see what happens. When they don't get what they want, they'll move on to complaints.

PURRING

The purr is the most singular sound in the feline vocabulary. Unlike meows, which people can mimic reasonably well, purrs simply can't be produced by the human mouth and vocal cords. The whirring sound occurs as air passes over the larynx when cats inhale and exhale. They purr as effortlessly

WHAT'S MY PET SAYING?

Behavior
Teeth Chattering

What It Means
"I'm Practicing My Bite"

Cats are born hunters, which means they're also born killers. Mother Nature has been kind in giving them a fast, fairly painless mechanism for subduing their prey. Cats, from the smallest domestic shorthair to the roaring lion, have a specialized bite designed just for killing. In addition, cats are able to locate the precise spot on their prey's neck to administer the bite, killing prey by cutting the spinal cord. This protects the cat since the killing bite is so accurate that the animal can't turn around and fight back.

When a cat sits at the window and spies potential prey outside, he is as still as a statue. But inside his body, every nerve is piqued for the hunt, and his teeth may give an unmistakable chatter. Part of this is sheer excitement, but it may also give cats the opportunity to practice the mighty bite they'd use if they were only able to get outside.

as they breathe, and they could keep it up indefinitely if they wanted to.

The purr is probably the most misunderstood form of cat chat. More than a few people have continued stroking a cat who they thought was purring with contentment, only to receive a knuckle full of claws for their misunderstanding. Cats do purr when they're happy, says Dr. Wright. But they also may purr when they're in pain (purring during labor isn't uncommon) or uncomfortable. A cat who suddenly ratchets up his purr and is moving his whiskers forward or to the sides is probably irritated and getting ready to bite or scratch.

"Cats don't purr as a way of telling us things," says Dr. Wright. "It's only a reflection of their emotional state." Most of the time, of course, that emotional state is one of security and contentment. It's the sound cats make when they're feeling the same kind of warm coziness they felt when they were with their mothers. Cats happily purr when they're with people or other cats. They purr just as happily when they're alone, he says.

HISSES, CRIES, AND GROWLS

There are few sounds as haunting as those made by an angry, emotionally charged cat. Many a large dog has frozen in his tracks at the hiss of a 10-pound kitty. Known as strained intensity sounds, hisses, cries, and growls are reserved for extreme situations, and most of them originated in the ferocious spirits of cats' wild ancestors.

According to Desmond Morris, a cat expert and author of *Catwatching*, it's not a coincidence that a cat's hiss is very similar to the hiss of a snake. It's possible that cats, aware of the healthy fear and respect their predators had for snakes, learned how to mimic the reptilian *Sss*. When combined with other warning signals, like bared incisors, pasted-back ears, and spitting, hissing gives the unmistakable message, "I wouldn't if I were you."

Cats have an entire vocabulary of strained intensity sounds, all of which sound slightly spooky.

- Caterwauls are probably the most annoying sounds that cats make. Females in heat call almost nonstop for males, and the males loudly fight among themselves as they vie for her acceptance.
- Screams are the most intense and neighborhood-jarring of feline sounds, and they only occur when cats are mating. As part of an excitation response, female cats often let loose with a high-pitched, furious scream.
- Growls can be whisper-quiet, but for people who own cats, they're jarring, frightening sounds that mean something's about to happen. If you haven't heard growls before, it's possible to mistake them for purrs, says Johnson-Bennett. It's not a mistake people make more than once, though, because cats who are growling are intending to launch an attack.

SILENT SPEECH

Cats will occasionally open their mouths and make a meow-like motion—but not a sound will come out. Experts still haven't figured out why cats mime these meows, says Dr. Wright. One theory is that cats, like people, are sometimes indecisive and will open their mouths to speak, then change their minds. Since cats sometimes make these motions when they're hunting or stalking prey, it's possible that they're unconsciously practicing their bite. Or perhaps the "silent" meow is a perfectly good meow after all, but humans have such poor hearing that they can't hear it.

CHAPTER 15

How You Can Talk Back

A survey conducted by the American Animal Hospital Association found that 89 percent of people with dogs or cats believe that their pets understand all or some of what they have to say. Our pets will never have the same extensive spoken vocabularies as people, but it's obvious that they're capable of learning dozens, or even hundreds, of words. More important, they love to interact with us. Our talking with pets gives them the opportunity to be part of our world and to feel closer to us.

Take Moonie. A Siamese cat belonging to Gerald and Loretta Hausman of Bokeelia, Florida, Moonie isn't content just to lie in their laps and purr. He wants conversation, and when they aren't talking enough, he'll stand on his hind legs and put his paws on their lips. "He demands that we speak to him," says Gerald Hausman, a researcher and coauthor of *The Mythology of Cats*.

Most dogs and cats aren't this overt, but all pets crave the sounds of their owners' voices. It gives them the chance to bask in the attention that comes from being spoken to. Unless you're giving specific commands, it doesn't matter all that much what you say to your pets, says Gary Landsberg, D.V.M., a board-certified veterinary behaviorist in Thornhill, Ontario, Canada, and coauthor of *Handbook of Behaviour Problems of the Dog and Cat*. The rhythms of conversation are naturally soothing, and pets don't have any trouble detecting the love and affection in your voice, he explains.

Every pet is capable of learning more human language, although some breeds are more adept than others, adds Patricia McConnell, Ph.D., a certified applied animal behaviorist and assistant adjunct professor in the department of zoology at the University of Wisconsin at Madison. "Dogs who were bred to work as part of a team with humans, such as herding dogs, some of the retrievers, and German shepherds, tend to be good listeners who pick up more language," she says. Setters and pointers, on the other hand, were bred to pick up scents or visual cues. Hearing wasn't as important to them, so they're less attuned to their owners' voices.

TALKING IN WAYS THEY UNDERSTAND

Researchers have found that people change their voices when they talk to dogs and cats, just as they change their voices when talking to children. And they use similarly simple words. There's nothing wrong with speaking simply, and pets do respond differently to various tones and inflections. But there's no reason to restrict your vocabulary too much. They're very good at understanding what you're saying.

That's not to say that they automatically understand words. Just as children spend years in school learning the fine points of vocabulary, dogs and cats need a little coaching to understand what we're saying. Here are a few tips you may want to try.

Talk up to them. Short, simple words are the easiest for dogs and cats to learn, but don't limit yourself to using a childish vocabulary. Pets who are spoken to often and exposed to a wide variety of words and sentences will naturally expand their vocabularies and comprehend more of the nuances in your voice, says Dr. Landsberg.

"Dogs especially can make associations, or pairings, between your words and the events that follow," he explains. That's why most dogs perk up when they hear "happy" words, like *dinner* or *walk*. They learn that these words precede very nice events, and they remember them later. Of course, the opposite is also true. "If your dog loves to ride in the car and knows the word *car*, that's great," Dr. Landsberg says. "But if he hates it, he may hear you say 'car' and go dive under the bed."

Use the same words. Since dogs and cats will never understand the intricacies of language as well as people do, they need to hear the same words and phrases over and over before learning them for good. Telling your cat "come," "come here," and "please come here" may get his attention, but he won't have a clue what you're trying to say. "You need to use the same term every time and follow it up with the same event or action," says Suzanne Hetts, Ph.D., a certified applied animal behaviorist in Littleton, Colorado.

WHAT'S MY PET SAYING?

Behavior
Ignoring Commands to Stay

What It Means
"Didn't You Mean the Opposite?"

On the first day of obedience school, trainers are accustomed to the sight of owners milling around after their dogs, saying "Stay, stay, stay, stay." The dogs, of course, have no intention of staying. The more they're told to stay, the more they move around.

There's a reason this happens, and it all goes back to puppyhood, says Patricia McConnell, Ph.D., a certified applied animal behaviorist and assistant adjunct professor in the department of zoology at the University of Wisconsin at Madison. Researchers have recorded the sounds that mother dogs make when they're telling their pups to do something. When they want them to quit being rambunctious, they make a long sound that drops in pitch at the end. If they spoke English, it would sound something like "Sta-a-ay." On the other hand, when they want their pups to do something active, they use short, repeated sounds and a higher-pitched voice.

Those puppies in puppy school aren't deliberately disobeying. It's just that the sound they're hearing—"Stay, stay, stay, stay"—sounds an awful lot like Mom telling them to hurry up and do something. So they keep running around.

The best way to make a dog stop what he's doing is to give a brief, low-pitched command, letting your voice drop at the end: "Sta-a-ay." If he doesn't stop, don't keep repeating the command. Step in front of him like a traffic cop and put your palm in front of his face. Combining the command with the signal helps him get the message that he missed the first time around.

Say their names first. It sounds conceited, but dogs and cats (and people) have one word that they like best: their own names. "When you go to a restaurant and wait in a crowded room for your name to be called, you won't even hear the first 20 names the maître d' calls. You *will* hear it when he calls yours," says Judith Halliburton, an animal-behavior consultant and trainer in

Albuquerque, New Mexico, and author of *Raising Rover*. Using your pet's name before you start talking will get his attention right away and let him know that he needs to pay attention, she explains.

Once you get that attention, though, you have to do something with it, says Brandy Oliver, a dog-behavior consultant based in Seffner, Florida. "Sometimes our pets are doing something we don't like, and we say their names a few times, usually in an irritated tone," she says. If pets hear their names and look up, and then nothing happens, they will start to tune out after a while. They'll still recognize their names, but they won't realize that they're supposed to be doing something, says Oliver.

Speak in a higher voice to get them moving. Dr. McConnell has done research on the tones of voice pets respond to. She has found that dogs and cats, along with such fellow mammals as camels, buffalo, and horses, get excited when they hear voices that rise at the end. This tone sounds friendly, and they want to respond and come closer. That's why phrases expressed as questions—such as "Hey, Sparky, how ya' doin'?"—will quickly bring them to their feet and encourage them to come to you.

Lower your voice to calm them down. Whereas a voice that rises at the end gets tails wagging, a lower-pitched, drawn-out phrase that drops at the end signals a warning or a correction. This is the tone you want to use to bring activity to a halt.

"People run into problems when they try to calm their pets or get them to settle down by letting their voices drift upward," says Dr. Hetts. Pets respond to this tone with excitement, not calm. So their owners, naturally enough, keep repeating the command, and each time, their pets get more and more excited.

TALKING WITH YOUR BODY

Dogs and cats pay attention to words, but they pay more attention to body language. In fact, when you speak and get their attention, the first thing they notice is your body language. Only afterward do they take note of the tone of your voice. Vocabulary comes dead last, says Dr. Hetts.

What this means is that dogs and cats will have a hard time understanding you unless you speak with your body even more than with your words. When you're using gestures, they can either help your pet nail down what you're saying or totally throw him off course. Here are a few things you'll want to try.

Combine hand signals with spoken commands. There's nothing wrong with speaking to pets without moving your body, but combining words with specific gestures can be very helpful, says Dr. McConnell. For one thing, this gives pets two different signals that mean the same thing—it doubles the chance that they'll understand what you're saying. A bonus is that pets will respond to hand signals even when they can't hear your voice—when you're on a noisy street, for example, and you want your dog to sit before stepping into the crosswalk.

Use body language that makes sense. Just as universal symbols—like the slash through a cigarette—can be understood by anyone, certain gestures are easiest for pets to learn. When you want your pet to come toward you, for example, move your hand toward your body or bend down and pat your knees. When you want pets to stop, give the palm-out signal while standing still yourself.

Make eye contact. Dogs and cats are exquisitely attuned to eyes. They can detect even minute changes, like the widening or narrowing of the pupils. Catching your pet's eye is probably the best way to get his attention. He'll know that there's something you want him to do, and he'll wait expectantly until you tell him what it is, Oliver says.

Teach them to listen. "I've taught every dog I've ever trained to know how to listen," Oliver says. "It helps them pay attention when I have something to say. You can also use it to get them to be quiet for a few minutes."

It's an easy command to teach, she adds. See what causes your pet to perk up his ears—the rattle of the treat box is always a safe bet. When his ears go up, tell him "listen." Keep practicing until his ears come up every time you say the word.

Talk in the moment. No matter how clever dogs and cats are, they'll never learn enough language to understand things that aren't happening at the moment. "When you shake your finger and scold your dog for something he did 10 minutes—or 6 hours—ago, he'll have no idea what you're talking about," says Halliburton. Communication only works when pets can see exactly what you're talking about. "They just can't follow you back to events in the past," she says. "They don't know how."

SPEAKING THEIR LANGUAGE

People who go to France try to speak French. People who want to talk to dogs and cats try to speak *their* language. In either case, the result is more likely to be confusion than communication.

"I always tell people not to bother growling or barking at their dogs," Halliburton says. "You can try, but your dog is probably thinking, 'Bless her heart, I can't understand a word she says with that accent.'"

With cats, however, it's a little different. "I think the best way to communicate with your cat is probably to imitate the way he communicates," says Dr. McConnell. "When you want a cat to relax, purr. When you want to greet a cat, turn sideways, don't stare, and blink your eyes slowly. Among cats, these gestures add up to a peaceful greeting."

When mother cats bring food to their litters, they make a little trilling sound, Dr. McConnell adds. Hearing a similar sound will make cats feel all warm and welcoming. This probably explains why people the world over ask cats to come by repeating the same word several times, like "Kitty, kitty, kitty." It resembles a trill. "It seems that everyone has figured out that that's the best way to call a cat," she says.

PART 4

How Your Pets Read You

CHAPTER 16

What Your Body Is Telling Them

People used to think that animals were dumb. Then a horse named Clever Hans came to town. An Arabian stallion from Russia, Clever was purchased by a retired German schoolmaster, Wilhelm von Osten, in 1900. After giving Clever much instruction, Osten believed that he had taught the horse not only to count but also to solve higher mathematical equations. On a chalkboard, Osten would write calculations, some including square roots, and Clever would tap out the right answers with his hoof.

Audiences around the world were astounded—until one skeptical scientist challenged Clever by writing an equation on the board that only Clever and no one else could see. Clever failed that test and similar ones that followed. But he succeeded in one way that no one had considered: He was reading body language.

Experts realized that Clever was "solving" problems by detecting almost imperceptible shifts in his owner's body language as he approached the right answer. "If that isn't brilliant, I don't know what is," says Myrna Milani, D.V.M., a veterinarian in Charlestown, New Hampshire, and author of *DogSmart* and *CatSmart*. "The moral of the Clever story is that animals are not dumb in the least. They're smart in ways we can barely comprehend."

Dogs and cats are just as capable as horses at reading their owners' body language, Dr. Milani adds. That's why they can suddenly turn up missing when you're getting ready to go to the vet, or why they look dejected when you're planning to take a vacation without them. They're masters of the unspoken word.

"Humans tend to neglect this whole area of body language because we're so dependent on our complex spoken vocabulary," says Steve Aiken, an animal-behavior consultant in Wichita, Kansas. "We get into the habit of thinking that our animals put as much emphasis on our words as we do, but that's far from the truth. Dogs and cats can pick up the most subtle changes in muscle tension, vocal tones, facial expressions, and body movements. Then they add up all these signs and figure out exactly what's going on. If you want to really communicate with your dog or cat, you have to learn to see yourself just as they do."

The moment you walk through the door, the assessment begins: How heavy are your footsteps? How tense is your face? Did you glance at the biscuit box? Dogs and cats notice every action. "They've been bred for thousands of years to be hyper-responsive to our every move," says Wayne Hunthausen, D.V.M., an animal-behavior consultant in Westwood, Kansas, and coauthor of *Handbook of Behaviour Problems of the Dog and Cat*. "Their existence is highly dependent upon what we do next, so you'd better believe they pay attention."

Face-to-Face

It doesn't take more than the hint of a smile or a shift of your eyes for a dog or cat to jump up next to you on the sofa or to grab the leash and make a beeline for the door. Pets are very face-oriented, says Stephen Zawistowski, Ph.D., a certified applied animal behaviorist and a senior vice president of animal services and science advisor for the American Society for the Prevention of Cruelty to Animals in New York City. They're especially attuned to facial expressions that indicate they're going to get something good, like a walk or a snack.

"It's not that dogs and cats innately understand the difference between a smile and a frown," says Benjamin Hart, D.V.M., Ph.D., professor of physiology and behavior at the University of California, Davis, School of Veterinary Medicine and author of *The Perfect Puppy: How to Choose Your Dog by Its Behavior*. "But they learn very quickly what your facial expressions mean."

Dogs and cats use facial expressions of their own to communicate with one another, says Dr. Hunthausen. But expressions that mean one thing to them can mean something entirely different to people. Once you learn to interpret your pets' facial expressions—and discover how they interpret yours—you'll see why words alone don't begin to tell the whole story.

Staring. In the animal world, nothing is quite as threatening as a direct stare. Dogs especially use eye-to-eye contact when

NAME: Echo and Escort

OCCUPATION: Guide Dogs

Jaywalking is illegal in most major cities—and pretty dangerous. Yet Ed and Toni Eames of Fresno, California, can't tell for sure whether or not they're stepping into harm's way, even at crosswalks. Since both Ed and Toni are blind, they trust their golden retriever guide dogs, Echo and Escort, to watch out for them in situations when they cannot.

"Our dogs look at the way we stand at intersections," says Toni, coauthor, with her husband, of *Partners in Independence*. "If they see that we're not facing the proper direction, they'll straighten us out." They'll also refuse to let them cross the street when it's unsafe. "It's definitely teamwork," says Ed. "The dogs learn to read our body language, and we learn to read theirs. I listen for traffic, and when I think it's safe, I tell Echo 'Forward.' If I feel that he's not budging, I know there are cars coming."

As with all guide dogs, Echo and Escort also have been trained to believe they're twice as big as they really are. "That way, when the dogs maneuver through crowded areas like malls and restaurants, they're sure that we will fit through the same spaces that they can," Toni says. "When we have to move through a particularly tight space, Echo will slow to a crawl until I get the hint and move behind him," Ed adds. "Then we walk through single file."

Though Escort and Echo are working dogs, there are times when they are off-duty. "Our sign to them that they can take a break is to remove their harnesses," Ed says. "Then they become like every other pet dog, bringing us balls to throw and pestering us to play."

they're issuing a challenge or threatening to attack. Among humans, on the other hand, direct eye contact is perceived as friendly. What usually happens is that dogs who are somewhat timid get unnerved when their owners come home and "confront" them by looking straight at them. Things get more serious when people stare at strange dogs. If the dog is bold or aggressive enough, he may consider a stare to be a prelude to a fight.

"This doesn't mean you can't look at your pet," says Emily Weiss, Ph.D., curator of behavior and research at the Sedgwick County Zoo in Wichita, Kansas. "But instead of staring, glance at him, then avert your gaze so that he sees the whites of your eyes. This way, you'll show interest in him without showing any threat."

Yawning. The next time you're in your veterinarian's waiting room, take a look at the dogs waiting their turn—they'll be yawning more than a roomful of students at an 8 o'clock class. You'll also see a lot of yawning among dogs in obedience classes. "It often doesn't mean they're tired," says Liz Palika, a trainer in Oceanside, California. "It means they're feeling stressed and want a time-out."

Yawns are known as calming signals, signs that pets need a break from whatever's going on around them. Cats sometimes yawn when they're upset, but it's much more common in dogs. A dog who yawns once is probably sleepy; a dog who keeps yawning is telling you that something isn't to his liking, Palika explains. You can use the same cue to tell your dog that *you* need a break. "When your dog is being overly persistent in trying to get you to pay attention to him, try yawning and turning away from him," she suggests. "It doesn't work all the time, but sometimes it does."

Raised eyebrows. When dogs and cats see something that catches their attention, they raise their eyebrows and open their eyes as wide as they can to take it all in, says Aiken. "When you're talking to your pet, try raising your eyebrows and making your eyes a little bigger," he suggests. "Chances are, your pet will do the same, and you'll have his attention."

Smiling. The smiles we share with each other can be completely unnerving for dogs and cats, especially when they don't know who you are. The reason for this is that showing teeth may send the message that you're more interested in eating them than greeting them. "Human smiles can actually be quite frightening to animals because they look a lot more like a fierce growl than a happy hello," Dr. Weiss says.

There's absolutely nothing wrong with smiling at your own pets, because they know your expressions and what they mean. Pets who don't know you, however, have no choice but to interpret your expressions according to their own experience. "Strange cats or dogs may not react so well to you leaning over them and pulling your lips back and baring your teeth," says Dr. Weiss. "In fact, if you do that to an aggressive dog, you could end up in a fight."

A BODY OF LANGUAGE

Dogs and cats can establish their territory, signal an attack, or initiate play with their friends, all without making a sound. They do it with posture. Even slight changes in posture can convey totally different meanings. Pets who stand tall and approach each other straight-on are saying, "Back off," while those who duck their heads slightly and approach from the side are saying, "I hope you don't mind if I come closer."

Just as dogs and cats learn to interpret our words and facial expressions, they also watch and interpret our body language. "Whether or not you're aware of it, your pet is reading your body posture, trying to determine what you're going to do next," Aiken says.

Because dogs and cats are so sensitive to body language, the slightest shifts in posture may send messages that we don't intend. When you stand up on your toes and arch your back, for example, you may be doing nothing more than stretching. But pets will sometimes view your exaggerated height as a sign of aggression. Learning how they interpret our various postures is one of the best ways to put dogs and cats at ease, Aiken says. And you can use this knowledge to communicate a little more clearly.

Approach them sideways. People face each other directly when they're trying to project confidence or friendship, but pets see things differently. When one dog or cat wants to challenge another, he'll approach straight-on, as though to say, "So, what're you gonna do now?"

Approaching pets sideways is considered good manners.

"Your pets can have the same reaction when you approach them head-on," says Scott Line, D.V.M., Ph.D., a board-certified veterinary behaviorist in Winston-Salem, North Carolina. "Walking straight toward them can look pretty threatening, especially since this is how we usually approach our pets when they've done something wrong. And if you're approaching an animal other than your own, it can look especially intimidating."

It's helpful to approach dogs and cats by turning your body slightly to the side, Dr. Line says. This is how pets with good intentions approach each other, and they'll respond favorably to what they perceive as a socially correct approach. "You'll instantly appear more friendly," he says.

Roll over and play. Whenever pets play, one or the other will invariably wind up lying on the floor belly up. "This is the least

Lying on your back with your belly up is a clear signal that you're feeling relaxed, friendly, and willing to play.

threatening position possible because you're totally exposed," says Aiken. "To show your complete trust and willingness to play with your pet, you can take the same pose." Cats especially like it when people lie on their backs. They're so used to people looming over them and scooping them up that seeing a person with his belly up is a welcome change.

If you're lying on your back merely to have a quiet moment together, you're likely to be disappointed, Aiken adds. Belly-up is considered a play position, and sooner or later your pet is going to start licking, nose-nudging, and head-butting you. "You should only do this if you really want their attention," he says.

Bend at the knees, not the waist. The one human posture pets probably like the least is the one many of us do the most—bending over them to say hello. Given the height differences between people and pets, bending over makes sense to us. But dogs and cats don't see it that way. In their world, only pets who are trying to push them around will voluntarily loom over them. "It's something people do all the time," says Katherine Houpt, V.M.D., Ph.D., a board-certified veterinary behaviorist, professor of physiology, and director of the behavior clinic at Cornell University College of Veterinary Medicine in Ithaca, New York. "It can be pretty scary, especially for dogs."

The reason dogs don't like it is that they have their own position, called the T-posture, which is somewhat similar—and is considered very pushy. A dog who wants to assert his dominance will sometimes rest his chin on another dog's shoulder so that their bodies assume a T shape. Cats don't like people bending over them either, but they're less bothered by it than dogs are because the T-posture isn't part of the cat vocabulary.

Since pets learn from experience, pets in your family won't assume the worst every time you bend over to scratch them between the ears. But they'll be much more comfortable if you greet them by crouching or sitting down rather than bending, says Dr. Houpt.

Crouch when you call. One of the most common and frustrating experiences is telling your pet to come, then waiting helplessly while he hightails it the other way. Training (or the lack of it) is largely responsible for this lack of responsiveness, but your posture may also be involved since pets perceive an upright stance as being a threat, says Larry Lachman, Ph.D., an animal-

Crouching and calling out in a high, friendly voice is the best way to get dogs to come in a hurry.

behavior consultant based in Carmel, California, and author of *Dogs on the Couch* and *Cats on the Counter*. "When we stand tall and bellow for our pets to come, our body language is contradicting what we're saying," he explains.

The most effective way to encourage pets to come on command is to squat down low, turn slightly to the side, and call out in a high, friendly voice—preferably without making direct eye contact. "You'll be surprised how much more willing they'll be to come," Dr. Lachman says.

Take a bow. Just as dogs assume different postures depending on their moods, they also have distinctive body positions that indicate they want to play. One of the most common is a pouncy posture called a play bow. A dog who wants another dog (or cat) to play will often stick his front feet way in front, lower his head,

A position called a play bow is an unmistakable signal that dogs—or their people—want to play.

WHAT'S MY PET SAYING?

Behavior
Approaching People Who Don't Like Animals

What It Means
"I Like Their Body Language"

"Dogs and cats often fawn over the people in the room who don't like them because they have the least aggressive body language," explains Steve Aiken, an animal-behavior consultant in Wichita, Kansas. "Instead of coming at them head-on or bending over the way animal lovers do, these folks are usually looking away and are turned off to the side in a very nonthreatening way. So they're your pet's natural choices as the first people to come up and greet."

and push his bottom up in the air. It's a signal that's universally understood among dogs, Dr. Lachman explains.

"If you want to get your dog really excited—preferably outside if you have breakable furnishings—you can do it yourself," he adds. "Just get down on all fours, hit the ground with your forearms, stick your butt in the air, and wait for your dog to start pouncing around in circles."

The Meanings of Movements

Dogs and cats evolved as hunters and trackers, so they're highly attuned to movement. This is what enables them to detect the twitch of a mouse's tail in high grass or to spy a bird falling from the sky. It also makes it possible for them to "read" people or other pets.

"Anyone who lives with pets can see how carefully they watch every move," says Dr. Zawistowski. "All you need to do is uncross your legs in your chair, and all eyes are on you, waiting to see if you're off to get some food or do something fun."

This level of attentiveness makes life easier in some ways because it provides a useful tool for communicating with dogs and cats. But it can also make things harder because our pets not only notice every move we make, they also look for messages where, in many cases, none were intended.

Dogs are more attuned to movements than cats because they evolved in highly structured societies called packs. Their survival depended on knowing what other dogs in the pack were up to, so they watched them very closely. Today, they continue to take their cues from their pack members, the human family, says Dr. Zawistowski. When you're calm, they'll be calm, too. But if you're wired up and running around, they'll be highly strung as well.

This can be a real problem in families with energetic young children. Although children and dogs can be the best of friends, children are the family members most likely to be bitten by dogs, says Dr. Houpt. "Dogs were bred to respond to movement, so when a small child starts running around and waving his hands in the air, dogs think 'Rabbit!' and start chasing."

CHAPTER 17

The Problem with Height

There's a natural pecking order among people. Adults rule the roost, and older siblings boss the younger ones. In the neighborhood, the biggest kids get the most respect—out of fear, if nothing else.

This pattern doesn't change much as we get older, as any 6-foot-5 bodyguard can attest. Dogs and cats have a similar "height hierarchy." They're somewhat skittish about size and a little wary about people until they get to know them. It makes sense because we're so much bigger than they are. Even when they know us, our height can be an issue during training or disciplining. Not only do we tower over them, but our faces are too far away for them to see clearly. Without meaning to, we can appear as rather ominous, overshadowing figures to their upturned eyes.

"The mere fact that we're so tall and walk around on two legs sends the signal that we're in charge—it makes us look potentially aggressive to our animals," says Emily Weiss, Ph.D., curator of behavior and research at the Sedgwick County Zoo in Wichita, Kansas. "That's one of the reasons that men generally have an immediate edge when it comes to training, and why pets frequently don't listen as well to children. Men are generally the biggest members of the house, while children are the smallest."

Dogs, especially puppies, are often a little skittish around very tall people, says John C. Wright, Ph.D., a certified applied animal behaviorist; professor of psychology at Mercer University in Macon, Georgia; and author of *The Dog Who Would Be King* and *Is Your Cat Crazy?* "Researchers have found that wolf pups won't even approach tall flagpoles that are put in front of them. Large, looming objects are simply intimidating."

PETS VS. PEOPLE

Size Variations

People and cats have one thing in common: They're roughly the same average height as others in their species. Among people, 5-foot-4 is nearly average for American women and 5-foot-9 is average for American men. Among cats, 9 to 10 inches is the usual height. Dogs, however, have tremendous size variations depending on the breed. In fact, the largest dog is more than 130 times heavier than the smallest. There's a lot of difference in height as well. Here's how they stand.

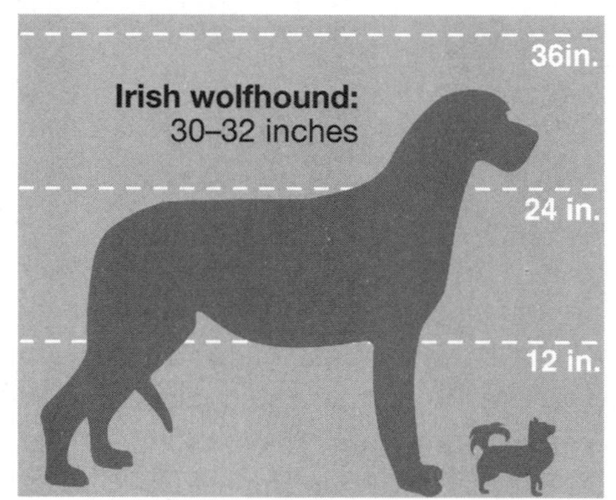

Chihuahua:
5–6 inches

Big and Scary

Large people (or objects) are often intimidating to dogs and cats because size plays such a big role in their own lives. It's one of the main factors in determining how pets get along.

Among dogs, the toughest one in the bunch is usually the biggest—or at least the one who can act the biggest. When a dog wants to tell other dogs that he's king of the hill, he'll try to make himself look as big as possible. He'll stiffen his legs and stand tall. He'll hold his tail and ears high, and he may raise his hackles (the fur on the back of the neck) when he really wants to make a point. Less assertive dogs respond to these "large" displays by tucking their tails between their legs, crouching low, flattening their ears, or rolling over—anything it takes to say, "See, I'm just a small weakling. No threat at all."

Cats also use their size to intimidate. They'll arch their backs and thrust their tails high in the air, striking a classic Halloween-cat pose. Researchers have noted that cats, and especially kittens, appear to play with their height. They'll face each other, stand up on their hind legs, and stick out their paws. Then they'll swat and bite at each other. It's all in play, but it gives them practice in dealing with the more serious business of life ahead.

"How tall they stand or how low they crouch are all important parts of how our pets communicate with one another," explains Benjamin Hart, D.V.M., Ph.D., professor of physiology and behavior at the University of California, Davis, School of Veterinary Medicine and author of *The Perfect Puppy: How to Choose Your Dog by Its Behavior*. "It can also be a big part of how we communicate with them. We definitely give them a different message when we're kneeling down to their level than we do when we're standing straight up 4 feet above them."

Leaning over your dog can be intimidating. That's because one way dogs assert their dominance is by putting their chin over another dog's shoulder, forming a T with their bodies, which can be very threatening.

THE NEED TO DOWNSIZE

It's not merely our height that can make us intimidating. Because our faces are so high up, dogs and cats have a hard time seeing our expressions. This can cause problems since our faces are the first place they look for important information, such as when their next meal is coming, when we're taking them for walks, or what our moods are like. When they can't see our faces, they aren't sure what to expect.

"Cats and dogs know that they need to interact with our faces when they want to know what we're thinking or they want our attention," explains Dr. Hart. "When we're walking around with our heads up high and not looking down at them, it's hard for them to read us. Even when we do look down, small dogs and cats can still have trouble seeing our expressions. That's one of the reasons some pets jump up on us. They want better face-to-face contact."

It isn't necessary to walk around on all fours or encourage your pets to jump up in order to have a better relationship. But there are times when you'll want to adjust your height and body language to make your presence a little less daunting and to help pets understand you better.

Make yourself smaller. One of the best ways to help pets feel like part of the family is to interact with them on their level, says Ira B. Perelle, Ph.D., a certified applied animal behaviorist and chairperson of the development committee for the Animal Behavior Society in Bloomington, Indiana. "Unless I need to assert my authority for some reason, I always crouch when I'm working with animals," he says. "By bringing my whole body down to their height, I'm telling them that I really want to interact with them in a friendly way."

A low body position is especially helpful when you want them to know you're ready to play, adds canine researcher Marc Bekoff, Ph.D., professor of environmental, population, and organismic biology at the University of Colorado in Boulder. "When I really want to play with my dog, I approach him like another dog would—on all fours, head-on." By imitating body language to initiate play, you're approaching pets as a mutual friend, he explains.

Some trainers advise people not to stoop to their dogs' level because it may weaken their position as the "dominant master" in the family. But as long as your dog is well-behaved and friendly, it really isn't a concern, says Dr. Wright. "Often, the best relationship we can have with our pets is when no one has to repeatedly assert their position of dominant or subordinate. We're all just having a ball as respectful, equal partners in the family."

Hug them to your legs. Dogs who are somewhat aggressive or

WHAT'S MY PET SAYING?

Behavior

Frequent Barking by a Small Dog

What It Means

"Don't Step on Me!"

People often speculate that small dogs like Chihuahuas and toy poodles must have a bit of a Napoleon complex—that they bark more than they should because they're trying to make up in sound what they lack in size.

It's true that small dogs are often big barkers, says John C. Wright, Ph.D., a certified applied animal behaviorist; professor of psychology at Mercer University in Macon, Georgia; and author of *The Dog Who Would Be King* and *Is Your Cat Crazy?* But it's not because they're insecure about their height. "They've learned from experience that when big dogs or people come too close, they get knocked around or stepped on. So they send out a warning," he says.

slow to do what you want may start feeling cocky if you bring yourself down to their level. In these cases, it's best to maintain your full height, says Liz Palika, a trainer in Oceanside, California. "That means standing up and looking dominant, especially when you're telling them what you want them to do," she says. "This doesn't mean you shouldn't show affection or praise your dog for doing the right thing. Instead of bending or crouching down to his level, stay upright and just hug him to your leg. You're showing affection while still maintaining a position of control."

Talk with your hands. Since dogs and cats spend much of the time craning their necks to see what they're supposed to do, it's helpful to teach them hand signals to go along with commands. Your hands are closer to the level of their faces, so even if they can't see your face, they can always look at your hands as a backup, says Cathy Jobe, founder of Waterloo Farms, a dog-training facility in Celina, Texas.

Raise them up. Unless you have a large dog, it's not always easy to get down to your pet's level when you want to talk or play. An alternative is to bring him up to yours—or to encourage him when he does it on his own. "Cats learn pretty quickly that they should jump up on your lap or on a piece of furniture when they want to get your attention or to be petted," says Dr. Hart.

If you don't allow your cat on the furniture but still want to give him the opportunity to jump up and say hello, you can build a small shelf for him, suggests Dr. Wright. "This will give him the chance to get closer to your face. Plus, cats enjoy high places where they can safely scope out their environment."

Sit down and say hello. When it comes to showing affection, dogs and cats are very "face-oriented." Many cats will show their affection by actually head-butting you. "Dogs also enjoy face-to-face greetings and will often rub muzzles with other dogs or rub the cheeks of people," says Dr. Bekoff. "That's one of the reasons dogs jump up on owners when they walk through the door. They want to get closer to your face."

You can cut down on your pet's jumping up and still get some face-to-face greeting time by sitting down to say hello. If your dog

A Cut Above

At 5-foot-2 and 105 pounds, Cathy Jobe of Celina, Texas, barely outweighs her German shepherd, Fratz Vom Teuchelweld. Yet she placed second overall and led her U.S. team to a first-place win at the rigorous Schutzhund World Championship competition, a vigorous contest that tests the character, courage, stamina, trainability, and resiliency of German shepherds in open terrain and stadium exercises.

Jobe trains 30 to 40 dogs a year for personal and home protection and has mastered a field that's traditionally been dominated by large men, many of whom feel that dogs respond best to deep voices, large physiques, and other "male" traits. But Jobe has proved that size doesn't always matter as much as an ability to communicate in ways that dogs can clearly understand.

"I don't use intimidation to train my dogs," she says. "People could save themselves a lot of pain and aggravation if they only realized that most dogs want to be good. It's up to you to show them the proper behavior, then praise them or give them a treat when they do the right thing—and only when they do the right thing. If you reinforce good behavior, your dog will respect and listen to you no matter how tall or short you are."

keeps jumping up, try ignoring him when you walk in the door. Then, when he's calmed down, sit down and greet him at his level. He'll learn that he'll get more face time when he acts a little less exuberant.

Teach children to act tall. Young children frequently have trouble getting respect from pets in the family because they're often about the same size. From a pet's point of view, children may resemble one of their littermates and not someone they need to respect, says Palika. To turn this around, teach children to make themselves "bigger"—by speaking in a lower voice, not squealing, and giving commands in a descending tone of voice. It usually doesn't take long for pets and children to learn to listen to and respect each other, regardless of how tall they are.

CHAPTER 18

The Etiquette of Eye Contact

When it comes to making eye contact, pets and people don't exactly see eye-to-eye.

People use eye contact primarily to express interest in each other. Parents admonish rebellious children to look at them when they're talking. Men try to make eye contact with the women of their liking. And lovers gaze at each other for hours on end. Even though no one likes being stared at, psychologists note that we consider it most polite when the people we're talking to establish eye contact, linger for a few seconds, glance away, then look back. We often lock eyes for about 60 percent of the time we're together.

Among dogs and cats, however, eye contact has less positive meanings. Dogs make eye contact in order to establish dominance or signal an attack. They become a little unnerved when we look at them too long, even when it's in the most loving of ways.

"Dogs, in particular, can become temperamental when it comes to eye contact," says John C. Wright, Ph.D., a certified applied animal behaviorist; professor of psychology at Mercer University in Macon, Georgia; and author of *The Dog Who Would Be King* and *Is Your Cat Crazy?* When dogs lived in packs, the alpha, or dominant member, would give others a stare that said, "I'm in charge." Less dominant dogs would acknowledge his superior status by looking away—unless they wanted to challenge his authority. Then they'd stare right back.

"There are some very dominant dogs who will interpret almost any direct eye contact as a threat," says Dr. Wright. "And there are some who are so subordinate that you can't force their muzzles up to make direct eye contact with you."

Cats are less likely than dogs to respond, either positively or negatively, to direct eye contact, although some do interpret it as

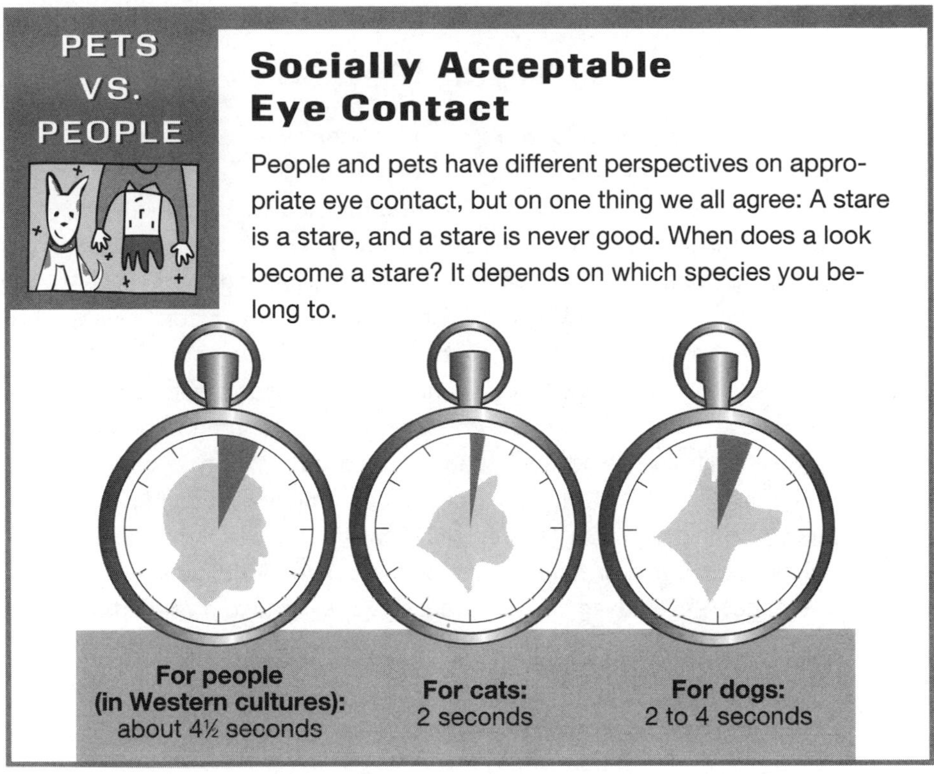

a threatening gesture, says Dr. Wright. "Cats aren't pack animals, so they're not quite as concerned with such behavior. But when a cat stares directly at another cat for longer than 2 seconds or so, that is still often considered a threat."

KEEPING AN EYE ON EACH OTHER

Despite these radically different feelings about eye contact, most households aren't filled with pets and people staring each other down or fleeing from each other's glances, says Stephen Zawistowski, Ph.D., a certified applied animal behaviorist and a senior vice president of animal sciences and science advisor for the American Society for the Prevention of Cruelty to Animals in New York City. "We learn to adapt to each other's ways fairly well," he says. "We look at our pets to help figure out what they need from us. And our pets learn to look to us for signals of what they can and can't do—when they can go out, for example, or when they'll get their next meal."

Watch Me

Like humans, dogs and cats won't respond to anything unless they're paying attention in the first place. So it's important to encourage your pets to make eye contact with you whenever you're trying to teach or tell them something.

You can teach dogs to look at you with a technique called "watch me," says Liz Palika, a trainer in Oceanside, California. Once they learn to look at you on command, you'll find it's much easier to communicate other messages—everything from obedience commands like "sit" to instructions like "get out of the kitchen."

Most dogs will learn the "watch me" command fairly quickly. It's a lot harder to teach cats to make eye contact. Many cats, in fact, will only look at you when they darned well feel like it. One way to get their attention is to combine a verbal command with a friendly gesture—for example, calling your cat's name while raising your hand, says Palika. The combination of motion and sound will get your cat's attention. At that point, you can proceed with whatever message you're trying to give—letting your cat know you want to play, for example, or that it's time to get his supper.

Hold a treat in one hand and stand a few feet in front of your dog. Tell him to sit, then say, "Watch me!" while pointing to your eye with the hand holding the treat. When he makes eye contact, give him the treat and a hearty "Good boy!"

You may find that your dog is making more eye contact with the treats than with you. If this happens, you may need to lift his head with your hand while giving the command. Only give him the treats when he looks right in your eyes.

When you understand how your pets understand and relate to eye contact, you can use it to teach obedience, praise them for good behavior, admonish them for wrongdoings, and generally form a better relationship. You can also use this understanding to know when (or whether) to make eye contact with animals other than your own, especially strays, to avoid unwanted conflicts.

Greet them indirectly. It's one thing to come home to your pets and greet them with a look in the eye and a happy grin. It's quite another to greet animals you don't know in the same way, says Emily Weiss, Ph.D., curator of behavior and research at the Sedgwick County Zoo in Wichita, Kansas. "Certainly, your own dog knows what you mean. But when you smile and make direct eye contact with a dog you don't know, you're essentially baring your teeth and giving the signal, especially to very aggressive dogs, that you're the boss and are looking to fight," she says. Cats don't react in quite the same way, although they, too, may interpret your friendly gesture as a menacing threat.

When greeting an unfamiliar dog, make brief eye contact and give a small smile instead of a big grin, Dr. Weiss advises. Then look away and go about your business. A friendly but slightly indifferent attitude will convey your positive intentions without putting him on the offensive, she says.

Teach your pet not to stare. Just as dogs and cats don't like it when you stare at them, you probably don't care for it when your pets stare at you, particularly when those stares are saying, "C'mon, just one bite of that sandwich!" or "Let's do something *now*."

"Dogs, especially, can get in the habit of staring at you in demanding ways," says Liz Palika, a trainer in Oceanside, California. One way to teach your dog that staring isn't polite is to give him a sharp, dominant stare and tell him in a low, descending voice to go lie down. Or you can interrupt stares by looking away yourself and maybe yawning. This lets your dog know that you need a break, she explains.

Looking away doesn't work with cats, Dr. Wright adds. You'll need to get tough by giving them a direct stare and saying no. "They'll learn that your staring precedes your startling them with a firm 'no', and they'll get the hint to stop what they're doing to avoid being reprimanded," he says.

Assert your authority. Most dogs understand that the humans in their lives are the ones in charge. It makes sense because people are taller and give the orders. But some dogs, particularly among the larger breeds, may challenge your authority if they aren't convinced that you're the true leader. "Looking right at them lets them know who's boss," Palika says. This technique also can work with dogs you don't know. "If a strange dog is approaching you and is simply standing tall and looking interested, you can outdominate him," she says. "Stand tall, stare at him, and say, 'Go home!' in your best growly voice."

This technique only works for dogs who haven't already made the decision to challenge you, she adds. Staring at a dog who's already growling or showing his teeth will probably just make him more determined. "If a strange dog approaches you with his hackles up and his ears up and forward, and he is snarling or growling, by all means don't make direct eye contact," she says. "Look away or look down. Slump your shoulders. And turn sideways. This will make you appear submissive to the dog, and he'll be much less likely to attack."

Some people are hesitant to look away from a threatening dog because they're afraid of looking weak, adds Dr. Wright. "Actually, the opposite is true. A dog can pick up your fear by looking at your eyes. If you look away, he'll understand that you're not showing fear or an aggressive interest in what he's doing."

Cats are a lot smaller than dogs, so people aren't threatened by aggressive felines in quite the same way. But an angry cat can do a lot of damage very quickly, so you don't want to give him an edge. "If you stare at a cat for more than a few seconds, he will often make a high-pitched chirp and hightail it out of there," says Dr. Wright.

Use your eyes for instruction. Though it's generally best to avoid prolonged eye contact with animals that you don't know, eye contact with your own pets can be very helpful, especially during training. "The only way your pet will know what you want him to do is if you have his undivided attention, which means he has to look at you," says Cathy Jobe, founder of Waterloo Farms, a dog-training facility in Celina, Texas. "He should learn to look to you to see what he should do, whether that's to sit, retrieve, or simply go entertain himself."

Break your gaze for a time-out. Training can be stressful for dogs because they're paying such close attention for long periods of time, trying to understand your every move. By watching your

WHAT'S MY PET SAYING?

Behavior

Staring

What It Means

"Get in Line"

Most dogs consider staring to be the ultimate in rude behavior, but Border collies don't see it that way. Bred to herd sheep, these intelligent, hardworking dogs are genetically programmed to stare . . . and stare. They don't give you the eye in order to launch a threat or to say they're boss. They're just trying to herd you—or to figure out if you want them to herd something else.

"Unlike most herding dogs, who use physical force like nipping and biting to herd farm animals, Border collies were bred to use intimidation through eye contact," says Nicholas B. Carter, Ph.D., executive director of Border Collie Rescue in Gainesville, Florida. "They circle around the flock, all the while fixing the sheep with an intense stare."

What works in the fields can be a problem in the living room, however. Border collies don't just herd sheep, Dr. Carter says. Given a chance, they'll herd people and other pets as well. This sometimes gets them into trouble. Sheep quickly get in line when confronted with a long stare, but people keep moving. This drives Border collies crazy, and they'll sometimes use their teeth to move the "herd" to the proper place.

You can't reduce a Border collie's urge to herd, says Dr. Carter. But you can make him a little less vigilant by holding still when you're getting eyed. "When you see him staring at you and circling around, just freeze," he says. "When you freeze, the herding instinct goes away." At least for a while.

dog closely, you'll know when he needs a break. "Dogs use what are called calming signals to say, 'Hey, I need a time-out,'" Palika says. "What they usually do is break eye contact with you, look away, and yawn or scratch their necks. By doing this, they're letting you know it's time to take five."

You can use the same maneuver when *you* need a break, Palika adds. "I have an Aussie who is a pretty committed working dog. When she's looking to me for something to do, she can be pretty intense. So, I'll give her a calming signal by looking away from her and yawning. It doesn't work 100 percent of the time, but sometimes she gets the idea and gives me a break."

Watch your emotions. Dogs and cats look to us for reassurance and affection. When we're upset, even if it's not at them, they recognize it and get upset themselves, says Dr. Wright. It's not uncommon, for example, for people to give their pets a "look" that was really intended for their boss or spouse. "Even dogs who don't respond adversely to eye contact will reel when you give them a stare while you're angry," he says.

Of course, if you're angry with your pet for something he's done wrong, it's okay to let him see that. But if you're really upset because of something else, remind yourself not to look directly at him until you calm down. This way, he won't be left on edge wondering what he did wrong.

Give the look of love. Even though people and pets perceive eye contact in very different ways, it's not always a complicated issue. Sometimes a stare means nothing more than "I love you." "It's pretty obvious when your pets are looking at you for no other reason than to express their affection," says Dr. Wright. It works the other way, too. Dogs and cats will often watch their owners' eyes for signs of affection. So don't feel as though you have to withhold eye contact. In fact, you may want to give your pets looks of love a little more often. "That's what you have them for," he says.

CHAPTER 19

Watch Your Tone of Voice

It's a complaint trainers hear all the time: The dog obeys the men in the family but ignores the women. And cats? If often seems as though they don't listen to any member of the household *any* of the time.

It's true that dogs and cats have selective hearing—they have a way of suddenly going deaf when you're telling them to do something that they don't want to do—but they do listen. "They simply don't respond to words the way people do," says Stephen Zawistowski, Ph.D., a certified applied animal behaviorist and a senior vice president of animal services and science advisor for the American Society for the Prevention of Cruelty to Animals in New York City. "They absorb the whole picture of how we speak, including pitch, timbre, tone, and modulation, in order to understand our meaning."

Whether you know it or not, you may be saying one thing with your words but something entirely different with your voice, leaving pets to decide for themselves what it all means.

Call of the Wild

To understand how pets hear us, it helps to understand how they speak to and hear each other. Dogs, for instance, rely on just a handful of sounds, like barks, growls, or whimpers, says John C. Wright, Ph.D., a certified applied animal behaviorist; professor of psychology at Mercer University in Macon, Georgia; and author of *The Dog Who Would Be King* and *Is Your Cat Crazy?* Barking, as you and your mail carrier know, is a way of sounding alerts. It can be good news, like "Hey! There's a deer!" or bad news, like "There's an intruder." Dogs bark when they're excited. Growling tells the receiver to hit the high road or else. And whimpering is a submissive sound that dogs use when they want attention.

Cats have developed a slightly more intricate language. They use soft chirps to call kittens, woeful meows to ask for dinner, demanding cries during mating season, deep growls to defend territory, and staccato clicks to show their excitement at finding prey. But they're similar to dogs in that they use a few general sounds to send a variety of messages.

Compare the half-dozen or so sounds that dogs and cats use to the roughly 100,000 words that people use, and you can begin to understand the language barrier. Compounding the problem is the fact that our pets don't even hear the same way we do.

SPEAKING THEIR LANGUAGE

People depend greatly on their sense of hearing and, thanks to the telephone, can hold entire conversations without seeing one another. But animals don't do this, says Dr. Wright. "They depend on visual cues from your body language, sound cues from the tone of your voice, and olfactory cues from the way you smell every bit as much as they depend on the words you're saying—and maybe more."

They can also hear things that we can't hear, says Patricia Simonet, Ph.D., a certified applied animal behaviorist and assistant professor in the science and humanities departments at Sierra Nevada College in Lake Tahoe, Nevada, where she teaches and conducts research in animal behavior, animal communication, and animal intelligence and cognition. Dogs and cats have exquisite senses of hearing. Dogs, for example, have hearing that's sensitive enough to distinguish between a B and B-flat played on a piano, and they can pinpoint the exact location of a noise in a fraction of a second. But pets tend to focus only on things that are relevant to their lives. This means your cat will become fixated on the rustling of a mouse in a wall several feet away but will tune out the sound of your voice. And if you aren't conveying a message that your dog understands, she'll ignore you no matter how much you yell.

"You need to modulate your voice to make it sound more like your pet's own language," says Dr. Zawistowski. "It's what some folks call a dog trainer's voice. It works on pets, and it even works on kids." Here's how it's done.

Listen, then speak. When you want your dog or cat to pay at-

WHAT'S MY PET SAYING?

Behavior
Talking Back

What It Means
"I Know What People Like"

Dogs usually respond with attentive silence when people speak to them. Cats, on the other hand, may talk back with a series of chirps and meows. Especially talkative are Siamese cats, who sometimes seem as though they're giving detailed accounts of their days every time you walk into a room.

What makes cats so chatty? Unlike dogs, who have a limited range of vocal sounds, cats have a rich vocabulary of chirps, meows, and clicking sounds. They rely on these sounds to communicate with other pets as well as with people. They've discovered that we aren't very observant when it comes to reading their body language, but that we do pay attention when they speak, says Myrna Milani, D.V.M., a veterinarian in Charlestown, New Hampshire, and author of *DogSmart* and *CatSmart*. "People have bred cats to be very vocal because that's what we respond to."

People who live with cats learn to distinguish many of their usual sounds. A short little meow, for instance, is generally no more than a hello, while longer or sharper meows usually mean they want something.

tention to what you're saying, modulate your voice so that it resembles the way they sound when they mean business, says Dr. Zawistowski.

"Listen to dogs or cats when they're telling each other to stop what they're doing or to stay away. They start at a normal tone and drop down through the registers into a low growl," says Dr. Zawistowski. "When you say, 'Sit' or 'Stay,' your voice should do the same thing. Start in your normal voice, or maybe just a notch lower, and use a descending tone. Your pet will pay attention to the change in your inflection."

You can use a similar technique when you want your pet to come to you. In this case, however, use the modulation they use when summoning each other. "If you listen to mother cats mewing for their kittens, pups whining for their littermates, or even wolves howling to summon the rest of the pack, you'll notice that their tone starts low-to-normal and then goes up," says Dr. Zawistowski. "When you call out, 'Come here, girl,' your voice should have a rising inflection to catch your pet's attention."

Animate your praise. Dogs and cats respond favorably to slow, low-pitched sounds, says Dr. Wright. "When your dog or cat does the right thing, let her know you appreciate it with a drawn-out, animated 'Go-o-od gi-i-irl,' using a low, almost cooing tone of voice."

Don't raise the volume. Though the temptation can be strong, try to resist yelling or shouting at your pet. To your pet's way of thinking, shouting indicates that you don't mean what you say. "Too many folks mistake changes in intonation for changes in volume and just get louder and louder. Like people who don't speak your language, your pet doesn't understand you any better when you're shouting," says Dr. Zawistowski.

Startle them away from bad behavior. Like people, cats and dogs will stop in their tracks when they hear a sudden sound. "When you catch your pets in the act of scratching the furniture or digging the carpet, deliver a loud, startling noise like 'Nah!' or 'Ah! Ah!'" says Dr. Wright. "It will grab their attention and stop the unwanted behavior. Then divert their attention to something you approve of, like one of their favorite toys. Then praise them with a soothing tone when they do the right thing."

Teach children to talk down. Children and pets aren't always the best mix because dogs and cats don't always know what to make of the high-pitched, excited sounds children make. "Young children need to watch their tone of voice around dogs," says Liz Palika, a trainer in Oceanside, California. "They have a tendency to scream or squeal in high-pitched tones, which to dogs sounds like one of two things: a puppy who wants to play or a rabbit that they should chase." Plus, kids tend to run around flailing their arms, which further excites dogs into action. "They should learn at a young age to say, 'No!' in a descending voice and not to run away from dogs," she says.

Cats also respond unfavorably to children's high-pitched voices. "Cats have very sensitive hearing, and a child's whining can be simply intolerable," says Dr. Simonet. "Fortunately, unlike dogs who may chase or pounce at noisy children, cats will just walk out of the room and get away from the sound."

Drop your voice. The reason men sometimes have better luck with training is that their voices naturally descend at the ends of sentences, giving a growl-like sound. Women, on the other hand, have higher-pitched voices, and they often raise their voices at the ends of words and sentences. To dogs, this makes them sound more like littermates than the leaders in charge, says Emily Weiss, Ph.D., curator of behavior and research at the Sedgwick County Zoo in Wichita, Kansas. "They sound like they want to play," she explains. "And the more impatient people get, the higher their voices tend to go—and the more excited their dogs become."

Drop into a growl when delivering commands, suggests Dr. Weiss. "You don't have to yell," she adds. "Just practice vocal control."

Rustle up something for kitty. Cats' ears are exquisitely designed to enable them to locate tiny prey lurking in high grass. In fact, their tympanic membrane—a structure in the ears that picks up frequencies—is most sensitive to rustling sounds, like those made by mice in a wall or rabbits in a field. You can take advantage of this when you want your cat to come to you. Gently rustle paper or a plastic bag while calling your cat, using an upward-inflected voice. You'll sound like prey, and she'll come from wherever she is to find you.

Take the edge off. People are often bewildered by the fact that their dogs and cats will happily come when they're called, except when it's time to take a bath or go to the vet. "Even though you may not hear it, you have just the slightest edge to your voice at times like this. Your pet can pick it up in a split second, and she'll hightail it the other way," says Dr. Wright.

It's hard to control what you do unconsciously, but you can often fool pets with a little mental trickery. "Before calling my pet to go to the veterinarian, I literally block the vet completely out of my mind and convince myself that we're going off to do something fun," says Dr. Wright. "It works every time."

Assuming your pets are leash-trained, you can make yourself sound even more convincing by stopping off at the park on your way to the vet. This way, you won't sound guilty—or feel quite as dishonest about fibbing.

Reward them for listening. Dogs and cats listen best when they know a reward is coming. "This is especially true for cats," says Dr. Simonet. "People think cats are untrainable, but that's not true. You can teach cats intricate tricks as well as very basic commands, so long as it's clear that there is something in it for them, like a treat, when they listen. And dogs basically live to please and be praised. So always give them lots of positive reinforcement when they listen."

CHAPTER 20

Make Your Hands Safe Instead of Scary

People communicate with their hands in many different ways. In the United States, an extended hand is an invitation to shake and be friends. In China, where people aren't as physically intimate, extending a hand is somewhat presumptuous—the response will likely be a polite but distant "no thanks." Do you want to say that everything is fine? Use the "okay" hand sign. Try the same thing in Brazil, and you'll have just said something unprintable.

If hands are this confusing to people—who, after all, have two of their own—imagine how confusing they are to dogs and cats, who have nothing like them. "We make sudden and seemingly threatening moves all the time without even knowing it," says Larry Lachman, Ph.D., an animal-behavior consultant based in Carmel, California, and author of *Dogs on the Couch* and *Cats on the Counter*.

Think about hands from a pet's point of view. Dogs and cats have a hard time relating to the ways we use them. All of the things we do with our hands, like greeting, reaching, and picking things up, they do with their mouths and noses, says Dr. Lachman. So there's automatically a little confusion. More important, the way we use our hands when we're feeling friendly may be perceived by dogs and cats as being somewhat aggressive. "When we reach toward their faces, as people always do with animals, it can trigger a strong defensive response because they haven't had a chance to get close to us in a way that is familiar and comfortable," he says.

Dogs and cats are adaptable, of course, and they learn to associate people's hands with good things like treats and affection. But they always remain leery of strangers' hands, and even sudden hand movements from their owners can make them uneasy.

Awkward Greetings

Dogs and cats have been domesticated for thousands of years, but many of their attitudes and perceptions are rooted in the ancient past, when they lived wild and apart from people. Greetings were important rituals in their lives because making a bad first impression invariably led to fights. Some things just weren't done—moving suddenly, for example, or putting a paw over a dog's head.

People, of course, have their own ways of doing things, and we assume that what's comfortable for us is also comfortable for dogs and cats. Reaching down and picking up a cat, for example, seems like the most natural thing in the world for us. But many cats dislike this form of physical familiarity, and they certainly don't like being forced into it. Reaching out to dogs is another greeting that seems right to us, but to dogs it doesn't make a lot of sense, and some actually dislike it, says Dr. Lachman.

There are many hand movements and gestures we use that pets perceive as unmannerly or threatening. Here are some examples.

Picking them up. Cats and small dogs often seem skittish around new people. It's not that they're naturally high-strung but rather that they've learned that people can't resist picking them up. "Sometimes all a cat sees is this giant creature bending over her and reaching out its arms to scoop her up," says Steve Aiken, an animal-behavior consultant in Wichita, Kansas. "That's fine if the cat is accustomed to and comfortable with being held, but there are many cats who never get used to it no matter how long they live with you."

Reaching over them. When one dog wants to show another dog who's boss, she'll walk up and put her chin or paw on the other dog's shoulders. Among dogs, this is a direct challenge, the equivalent of a person walking up and shoving her face close to yours. Dogs who are laid-back and submissive will accept this greeting from a more dominant dog, while those who are dominant themselves are likely to give their own challenge.

Even though you are not a dog, dogs read you as one. When the first thing you do is put your hand on top of a dog's head or shoulders, the dog thinks you're saying, "I'm in charge," even though the message you really want to give is "Hi." This rarely causes problems for dogs in the family, but strange dogs may perceive this greeting as presumptuous, at best, or even as a direct and hostile challenge, says D. Caroline Coile, Ph.D., a researcher specializing in canine senses, who raises and shows salukis near Tallahassee, Florida.

Putting your hand out. Most of us have been taught to greet strange dogs with an outstretched hand. The idea is that this gives them the opportunity to sniff us and recognize that we're friendly. Sometimes it works, but many dogs will view the outstretched hand as a threat. "Walking toward a strange animal with your hand out is pretty invasive," says Liz Palika, a trainer in Oceanside, California. "Some dogs will react defensively, and some might even launch a counterattack and nip your hand."

MAKING GOOD IMPRESSIONS

People who travel to other countries are advised to read up on customs and expectations in order to avoid making embarrassing faux pas when greeting their hosts. Things are less complicated when you're greeting dogs and cats. Their natural tendency is to like and accept people. Even if you do something they dislike, they're usually willing to try again. But rather than giving messages that you don't intend, it makes sense to use your hands in ways that make them feel safe and comfortable.

Let them approach your fist. Cats are tiny compared to people, and they understandably get nervous when people swoop down from above. A good way to greet them is to crouch down to their level and, rather than reaching out with both hands, make a fist and put it slightly in front of you. "When you hold out a fist at their level, it looks like another cat's head to them," says Aiken. "Generally, the cat will approach the fist and greet it by head-butting it and rubbing against it." Once this preliminary gesture is out of the way, cats will usually feel more comfortable about being picked up, petted, and handled.

Greet them with a pencil. Cats introduce themselves to other cats by approaching tentatively until they're just about nose-to-nose. Simulating this "nose greeting" will help ensure that you get a warm reception from an otherwise aloof cat, says John C. Wright, Ph.D., a certified applied animal behaviorist; professor

The Sign for "Sit"

Dogs who work a lot with people can recognize and respond to dozens of hand signals. Since pets are intensely aware of body language, hand signals are a great way to reinforce or even replace spoken commands, says Emily Weiss, Ph.D., curator of behavior and research at the Sedgwick County Zoo in Wichita, Kansas. "One of the easiest to teach is the hand signal for 'sit,' " she says.

First, hold a treat in front of your dog to get her attention. Then, with your palm up and the treat visible in your fingers, raise your hand until it's slightly over your dog's head (this is the hand signal for "sit").

As your dog lifts her head to watch the treat, her back end will automatically go down. As it does, say, "Sit!" When her bottom is all the way down, give her the treat and plenty of praise.

of psychology at Mercer University in Macon, Georgia; and author of *The Dog Who Would Be King* and *Is Your Cat Crazy?* "For most cats, all you need to do is stick out a single fingertip, pointing at the cat down at her level, and she'll give a nose greeting to your finger," he says. "Other cats, however, might not want to get that close to you right away. In that case, try holding out a pencil, eraser-end first, for them to greet. Most of the time, this will be enough to warm them up to you."

The nose greeting is considered very formal and polite, and it isn't necessary when you're dealing with cats in the family or cats you know, Dr. Wright adds. But it's a great way to break the ice when you have a new cat or are greeting cats you don't know.

Stay below nose level. Experts in animal behavior say that it's always wise to keep your hands to yourself when you're approaching an unfamiliar dog for the first time. But eventually you're going to want to bring your hands into the open. No one's quite sure about the best way to do this. Some behaviorists advise greeting dogs with your hands palms up, which is an open, unthreatening gesture. Others suggest keeping your palms down with the fingers slightly curled, which makes your hands look smaller and less threatening. Either approach is probably fine as long as you keep your hand below the level of the dog's nose, says Dr. Wright. "As long as you don't move your hand from below the head to above the head, the animal will perceive you as less threatening."

The same approach works for cats, says Aiken. "When you are meeting a cat for the first time, it's always a good idea to keep your hand as well as your forearm below the level of her head," he says. "This way, you're much less likely to come across as aggressive."

Let them approach you. People are more direct in their greetings than are dogs and cats, who prefer an oblique, deferential approach. To make them feel comfortable, Palika recommends not greeting them at all with your hands. "Let dogs approach you while you keep your hands in your pockets or by your sides," she says. "This allows them to sniff your pants leg and get a sense of you without worrying about what you're going to do with an outstretched hand."

Pet them low. Just as dogs and cats are suspicious of hands that come down from above, they also prefer being petted lower on their bodies, at least at first. Dr. Coile recommends petting dogs under the chin or on the chest. This conveys affection without giving the unintended message that you're trying to dominate them. "This is especially good when you're interacting for the first time with a dog you don't know well," she says.

In Love and Play

Even though dogs and cats don't have hands of their own and sometimes have trouble understanding what they're all about, they're very attuned to body movements of all kinds. You can use hand signals to communicate much more clearly than you can with language alone. Even simple gestures will help pets under-

WHAT'S MY PET SAYING?

Behavior
Attacking while Being Stroked

What It Means
"I Don't Like Stroking All That Much"

People say that you should never bite the hand that feeds you. Well, you shouldn't bite the hand that pets you either, but plenty of cats don't seem to know that rule. They'll purr and look perfectly content while being stroked, and then they'll suddenly turn and sink their claws or teeth into the nearest skin.

"Some people refer to them as three-stroke cats," says Benjamin Hart, D.V.M., Ph.D., professor of physiology and behavior at the University of California, Davis, School of Veterinary Medicine and author of *The Perfect Puppy: How to Choose Your Dog by Its Behavior*. "These are cats who will let you pet them three or four times, and then they'll lash out at you."

No one is entirely sure why cats do this. Unlike dogs, who crave physical contact, cats can take it or leave it—and they don't hesitate to let you know when they've had enough. In addition, stroking cats appears to rile them up somewhat. It's not that they're necessarily angry, but they do get aroused, and aroused cats may attack. Finally, it's possible that cats are just a little bit ticklish, and too much petting makes them uncomfortable—and annoyed.

stand what you're feeling and what you'd like them to do. More important, you can use your hands to show love and affection in ways that can't be expressed with words.

Make your hands exciting. It's been said that the way to a man's heart is through his stomach. That's certainly true for some men, and it's even more true for dogs and cats. "You don't have to give your dog or cat a treat every time you see her, but giving frequent, healthy food treats after playtime or when she's been particularly obedient reinforces the idea that your hands are associated with good things like food and fun," says Benjamin Hart, D.V.M., Ph.D., professor of physiology and behavior at the University of California, Davis, School of Veterinary Medicine and author of *The Perfect Puppy: How to Choose Your Dog by Its Be-*

havior. "Though our pets also respond to our hearty praises, they understand food more than anything else."

Pet early and often. As far as dogs and cats are concerned, petting is the best thing that your hands do. "Well-loved pets come to view your hands as the most rewarding part of your body," says Dr. Hart. "They're not only the appendages that feed them, but they're also what give them the most affection. If you make a habit of frequently petting your dog or cat, you'll likely find that they seek out your hands rather than avoid them."

Invite them to play. Dogs don't need a lot of encouragement to play, but they're not always sure if their people are in the mood. Among dogs, the clearest signal that it's time to play is what experts call a play bow, in which one dog lowers her front end and puts her rump high in the air. You can use your hands to signal the human equivalent of a play bow, says Palika. "If you want to say, 'Let's play!' try raising both hands way above your head, then drop them down to your knees," she says. "Your dog will almost certainly respond in a pouncy, excited way."

Confusion sometimes arises when people use this gesture in other situations, Palika adds. "Suppose a dog comes running up to someone who's a little nervous around animals, and the first thing that person does is raise her arms above her head. Big mistake," she says. "That only riles the dog up more."

Keep them steady. Young children and pets don't always get along as well as they should because children make a lot of sudden, erratic hand movements, says Katherine Houpt, V.M.D., Ph.D., a board-certified veterinary behaviorist, professor of physiology, and director of the behavior clinic at Cornell University College of Veterinary Medicine in Ithaca, New York. "Neither dogs nor cats respond well when people wave their hands around," she says. "In the best-case scenario, pets will just leave the room. In the worst case, they may bite or scratch someone."

It's helpful for children as well as adults to remember that dogs and cats interpret gestures in ways that make sense to them. In their worlds, rapid movements of any kind may be signs of danger, especially when the movements are coming right at them. Moving your hands slowly and keeping them low sends a clear signal that you're friendly and that you—and your hands—have only the best intentions.

CHAPTER 21

Talking with Scents

In the movie *Scent of a Woman*, the blind army colonel played by Al Pacino can tell a lot about women by their scent alone. "Chestnut hair, 22, and beautiful," he tells his companion, Charlie, as a young brunette takes a seat behind them. Charlie is completely blown away.

Obviously, Charlie never had a dog.

"People's sense of smell is *nothing* in comparison to dogs'," says Patricia Simonet, Ph.D., a certified applied animal behaviorist and assistant professor in the science and humanities departments at Sierra Nevada College in Lake Tahoe, Nevada, where she teaches and conducts research in animal behavior, animal communication, and animal intelligence and cognition. "People can detect big, obvious scents like a strong perfume or the smell of fish. But your dog can not only tell it's a fish, he might even be able to tell which stream it came from, what kind of chemicals were in the water, who handled the fish, and how long it's been there."

Cats also have an excellent sense of smell, though it's not quite as sensitive as dogs', says Dr. Simonet. "But they also rely on their olfactory senses to tell them who's been in their environment and to pick up countless details from the scent molecules in the air."

Why do dogs and cats have such exquisite senses of smell? The answer is simple: communication. Unlike humans, who depend mainly on speech, hearing, and vision to communicate, dogs and cats use smells to talk to each other, says Stephen Zawistowski, Ph.D., a certified applied animal behaviorist and a senior vice president of animal services and science advisor for the American Society for the Prevention of Cruelty to Animals in New York City. "They can get much of the information they need just by smelling one another as well as by smelling us," he says. "They can tell if we're friends or strangers, where we've been, and what kind of mood we're in. They can also leave scents for one another as we would leave written messages."

Humans will never completely comprehend all the information that passes through our pets' noses. But the better we understand how they use their most sensitive of senses, the better we'll be able to communicate.

Nose of the Dog

To put things in perspective, your dog's sense of smell is about 100,000 times better than yours. This means that he can distinguish and identify many times more scents than you can.

In addition, dogs "hang on to" scent much longer than we can. As we humans breathe in, scent molecules drift past the olfactory membranes and float out when we exhale. We get just a whiff of whatever the substance is. But dogs have a special chamber in their noses that traps pockets of air. This allows them to collect scent molecules until they have enough to identify the odor. And once a dog has pegged an odor, he never forgets it, says Dr. Zawistowski. Dogs have an astonishing ability to identify and remember different smells. "Just by sniffing a sidewalk telephone pole, your dog can tell not only which dogs have been there but also what they've had for dinner."

What's Your Smell?

Humans get to know each other by asking, "What's your name?" For dogs, the more important question is "What's your smell?" They use their super-sniffing ability to keep tabs on you. They can tell when you've been out getting food. They know when you've been near another dog or cat. They can even smell your mood, says Dr. Zawistowski.

This is why your dog insists on performing a sniff test when you come home at night, even though he obviously knows who you are. He wants to know what you've been up to. "People give off different scents when they're happy than they do when they're upset or displeased," says Dr. Zawistowski. "There's a saying that dogs can smell fear. Well, they can because they can smell a by-product of the cortical hormones we give off when we're scared. They can also smell when we're content and relaxed."

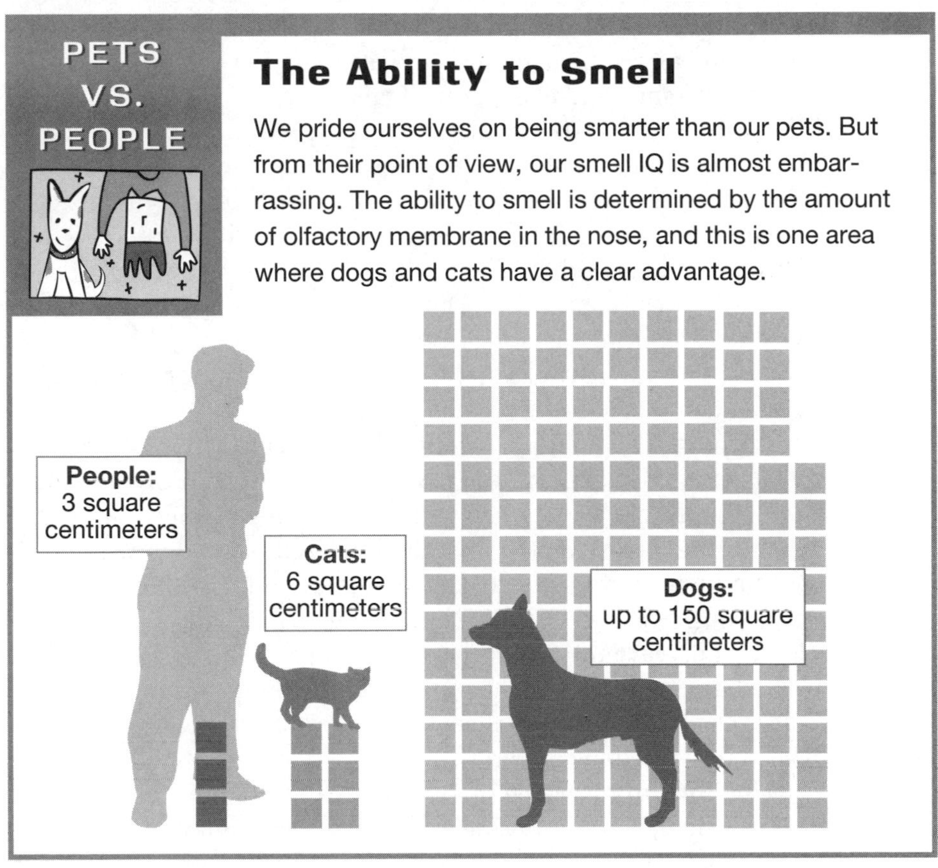

The Ability to Smell

We pride ourselves on being smarter than our pets. But from their point of view, our smell IQ is almost embarrassing. The ability to smell is determined by the amount of olfactory membrane in the nose, and this is one area where dogs and cats have a clear advantage.

This amazing sense of smell makes it very difficult to lie to dogs, adds Dr. Simonet. You might be saying, "It's okay, come here," and your body language might be saying, "I love you." But if you're really thinking, "Boy, you're in trouble when you get here!" he's going to catch that scent and stay away as long as he can because *that's* the sense he trusts most. This is why dogs often run and hide when you're getting ready to go to the vet or after they've chewed a pair of shoes. "They're not psychic," says Dr. Simonet. "They don't necessarily know they've done something wrong. But they may smell that you're upset."

Dogs will never master human speech, but you can take advantage of their exquisite "nosiness" to communicate a little more clearly—not only for training and solving behavior problems but also for performing everyday tasks, like finding your car keys. Here's how.

Say hello with a scent. Introducing your pet to someone new, especially a new member of the household, isn't as simple as exchanging names and making small talk. Your dog needs to "meet" the scent as well. "To make the smoothest introduction possible, try introducing the scent of the new person to your pet before they meet," suggests Dr. Zawistowski. "Bring home an article of clothing with the new person's scent on it and allow your dog to become familiar with it. Then, when the person shows up, your dog will already know his scent." This works particularly well when you're bringing home a new baby or a new pet, he adds.

Leave a little part of you behind. You can comfort your dog even when you're boarding him by leaving a little scent of yourself behind, says John C. Wright, Ph.D., a certified applied animal behaviorist; professor of psychology at Mercer University in Macon, Georgia; and author of *The Dog Who Would Be King* and *Is Your Cat Crazy?* Pick a toy that you think your dog will like (rub it between your palms to coat it with your scent) or a shirt that you've recently worn. Then, right before you're ready to leave him, leave the toy or the shirt behind. "This doesn't work for all dogs, and it won't work with cases of separation anxiety, but it can have a calming effect on a dog who gets a little agitated when he's left alone," he says.

Use low-proof scents. Even when our words are saying, "Come here, I want to hug you," our scents may be saying, "Avoid me like the plague." Some dogs dislike the smell of alcohol, which is a common ingredient in aftershaves and colognes. So if your dog is avoiding you or is acting agitated and you can't figure out why, it could be that there's something in the air. "There have been studies with aftershave in which dogs either completely avoid it or get aroused and actually roll in it. Neither is a reaction you want," says Dr. Wright. Even if you don't want to give up wearing scents, you should at least look for scents with low alcohol content, he advises.

Say no with a little Bitter Apple. Behavior problems can be hard to stop because dogs don't always understand what exactly the problem is. One way to help them get the idea is to involve as many of their senses as you can—especially the sense of smell. You can do this by using objectionable odors like that of Grannick's Bitter Apple spray, available in pet supply stores. "If your voice is saying no, and your body language is saying no, and the smell he's picking up is saying no, your dog is more likely to

NAME: Angus

OCCUPATION: Tracker

The day the suspect made a break for it, police helicopters and squad cars converged in McHenry County, Illinois. Fortunately, Angus was there, too.

As his handler, Corporal William Shreffler, can attest, Angus is proof of the saying, "You can run, but you can't hide." After picking up the suspect's scent, the rusty-brown, 90-pound bloodhound led William through the woods and across a creek, occasionally letting out a howl to signal to William that they were getting close. Angus led him to a fallen tree. As they approached the hunted man, he popped up and surrendered.

Angus and his fellow bloodhounds belong to the Du-Page County K-9 Unit, which is called out more than 100 times a year to track fugitives and missing people. "Bloodhounds are second to none for tracking," says William.

"They can pick up a human scent from almost any object that's been handled by a person and follow it through thousands of other scents," he says. "We had one case where a young mother abandoned a baby in a cardboard box. There must have been about 20 people at the scene, but Angus found the right scent and led us right to the mother's door."

Angus is William's companion as well as coworker. But even at home, when Angus is off-duty, sometimes a phone call will send him right back out on the trail. "When a kid in the neighborhood is missing or someone needs help finding a lost elderly or disabled relative, they know who to call," William says.

And Angus always knows what to do.

get the idea," says Dr. Wright. When your dog is chewing or digging, for example, spray Bitter Apple—or put some rubbing alcohol—on areas where you don't want him to go. "If one scent doesn't work, try another," he suggests.

Teach him to be your guide. Though you should always carry a compass and map when you're out hiking, you can also teach your dog to be an invaluable backup system. "Your dog's sense of smell is a wonderful homing device," says Dr. Simonet. "He can read your scented trail like a big neon sign. All you have to do is say, 'Take us home!'"

First, of course, you have to teach him what the words mean. The next time you're taking a short walk, go for a small distance, then turn around and say, "Take us home," and make your return trip, says Dr. Simonet. Next time, walk a little farther and do the same thing. "Your dog will learn to associate the words with finding and following the trail you came out on," she says. "Our dog actually saved our butts one time when we were out without a compass and became confused about which way was home."

You can also teach your dog to find items around the house, like your car keys, says Dr. Simonet. "Make it a game. First, identify the item you want your dog to find. Let him sniff it. Then hide it in an easily retrievable location and give a verbal command like 'find the keys.' The first couple of times, you can even let him watch you hide it. Always praise him profusely when he finds it. After several times, he'll be able to find the item on command."

Project good feelings. Since dogs can smell all sorts of chemicals that humans release when they're upset, they often get upset at the same time, says Dr. Zawistowski. "In packs, when one dog is stressed, they all get stressed. The same thing can happen at home. If you're wired up, your dog will be, too, no matter how hard you try to calm him down." When your dog is acting up, it's worth pausing to check your own emotions, he advises. Once you're relaxed, you'll be surprised how calm your pet is, too.

Cats: Just Sniffing Through

It's quite unlikely that your cat runs up to you when you walk in the door and tries to stick his nose in embarrassing places. This isn't because cats are more polite than dogs. It's because they don't depend quite as much on smell to collect the latest news.

"Cats are more likely to move from one sense to another, taking in the whole picture as they get closer to you," says Dr. Wright. "When you first walk in, they eye you up, taking in your body language and appearance. Then their ears kick in as they listen to the tone of your voice. As you get closer, they use their sense of smell to pick up additional information. They don't just rely on their noses as their first line of information."

Cats can still smell circles around people, however. They have roughly 67 million cells in their olfactory bulb—the place where they register scents—which is 15 million more than their human companions. Like dogs, they also have a special chamber in their noses, called a Jacobson's organ, which allows them to taste the air and pick up scents, mainly from other cats.

GARFIELD WAS HERE

Like dogs, cats use their keen sense of smell to keep tabs on where you've been and who you've been with. Unlike dogs, they customarily "mark" their owners, giving you a distinctive scent that identifies you as being part of their territory.

"Cats do a lot of time-sharing," explains Dr. Zawistowski. "Since they generally don't like to occupy the same area at the same time as other cats, one will go by and mark an area so the others know he's been there and how recently. Then the other cats will be able to share that space accordingly."

Cats have scent glands in their cheeks, which is why they rub their heads against objects in their territory, including you. This leaves their unique feline scent behind for others to find. When they're feeling defensive about their territory, they may spray their area with urine, giving a more pronounced signal of their presence.

"Marking is not a once-and-done thing," adds Dr. Wright. "The older a scent is, the less regard cats have for it. It's like they're saying, 'George was here, but it was a long time ago, and now I'm here.' If George wants to keep his presence known, he has to keep marking." This is one reason vets recommend having cats neutered, which reduces their territorial urges.

As with dogs, there are many ways you can use scents to communicate more clearly with cats. By applying certain odors like a mild bleach solution around the house, you can help stop common problems like scratching the furniture or urinating on the rug. You can also use smells to introduce them to new people.

Tell them another cat's coming. Since cats generally dislike sharing their immediate space, bringing a new cat home can trigger outbursts of hissing, scratching, and spraying. One way to reduce the tension is to let the cats communicate before they meet face-to-face, says Dr. Zawistowski. Keep the cats in separate rooms at first, he advises. While the "original" cat is in his room, let the new cat roam the house and leave his scent by rubbing against the walls and the furniture. "When he's done, put him back in his room and let the resident cat out so that he can roam and sniff and mark. Do this for a week, and by the time they meet, they'll be accustomed to sharing the space with each other."

Use scents to discourage scratching. Next to spraying, scratching is one of a cat's least desirable habits. It's also hard to stop because cats scratch for the same reason they spray. "Cats have sebaceous glands on their feet that leave an odor where they have scratched," explains Dr. Wright. "Plus, they leave behind a nice mark that shows where they've been, and the act of scratching sharpens their claws and gives them a good stretch."

Because they reap so many benefits from scratching, the idea is not to get them to stop entirely but to do it in appropriate places. When you catch your cat scratching where he shouldn't, you can rub the surface with rubbing alcohol or a chlorine-based bathroom cleaner, says Dr. Wright. These products have a smell that cats dislike, and they'll be more likely to turn their attentions somewhere else—preferably to a scratching post.

Clear the air. Some cats have the persistent and unpleasant habit of missing the litter box, or simply not using it at all. "This can be a perplexing problem, even for behaviorists, but sometimes the problem is right underneath your nose," says Dr. Wright. "There are two scent-related problems that are fairly common: one, the box smells too bad, so the cat avoids it; two, the box is so heavily perfumed that the cat finds it aversive."

Cleaning the box more often will take care of the first problem. For the second, the only solution is to go easy on room deodorizers and avoid scented cat litter. "I've been in houses where there are so many perfumed room deodorizers, potpourri bowls, and plugged-in air fresheners that the cat just goes anywhere because every place, including the litter box, smells the same," says Dr. Wright. "As long as you keep the box clean, you won't be able to smell it, but your cat will."

Avoid ammonia. When cats answer nature's call in the wrong places, like in the closet, the usual instinct is to bring out heavy-duty cleaning products to annihilate the smell. "It's a natural reaction, but it's not always the best idea," says Dr. Wright. Ammonia-based cleaners remind cats of the smell of their own urine, so they'll often return to the same spot. A better approach is to clean the area with an enzymatic cleaner or a product that contains ingredients with less attractive smells, like chlorine-based cleaners or a mixture of rubbing alcohol and vinegar, he says. These products have smells that cats dislike, and they'll be more likely to turn their attentions somewhere else, preferably to a litter box.

CHAPTER 22

When Affection Isn't a Favor

From a human point of view, physical affection is a very good thing. Holding and petting a warm, furry body is very comforting and can lower blood pressure and reduce anxiety and depression. And for dogs and cats, it's just as beneficial. Experts have found that stroking pets lowers their heart rates to healthful levels—not just at the time, but for up to 24 hours afterward.

"Pets and people are incredibly important to one another on many physical and emotional levels," says Alan Beck, Sc.D., director of the Center for the Human-Animal Bond at Purdue University in West Lafayette, Indiana. "They think of us as another member of their families. And we consider them a member of ours."

Unfortunately, that's precisely why people and their pets sometimes get into trouble. Even though we think of our pets as family, their lack of thumbs and our lack of fur is pretty convincing evidence that we're not related. "When we start treating our pets like people, and they start treating us like animals, we're bound to have miscommunication, especially when it comes to showing affection," says Myrna Milani, D.V.M., a veterinarian in Charlestown, New Hampshire, and author of *DogSmart* and *CatSmart*.

Differences of Opinion

Pets, especially dogs, are always so eager for attention that we assume that they like the same sorts of affection that people do. And to a certain extent, they do. Dogs and cats have been living with people for so long that they've come to understand what's expected of them—and what they can expect in turn. They know that rubbing against a knee is often followed by the rattle of the biscuit box, or that they invariably get a belly rub when the front door opens at the end of the day.

There's a difference, of course, between understanding why we do things and appreciating it when we do them. Some of our most common expressions of affection are actually the ones that dogs and cats like least—or are ones that tend to lead to behavior problems at some point.

Hugs. Among people, a tight hug is a wonderful sign of affection. Among dogs and cats, however, it can feel a little threatening. To survive in the wild, dogs and cats had to be able to use their bodies and move about freely. Being held down or restrained usually meant they were in big trouble. So even though people give hugs as signs of affection, you can't expect pets to always respond favorably, says Scott Line, D.V.M., Ph.D., a board-certified veterinary behaviorist in Winston-Salem, North Carolina.

"Cats and dogs show their affection by nuzzling muzzles or touching with their paws," adds Dr. Milani. People can take a lesson from this by stroking their ears or faces or simply getting close and letting them make physical contact. Even though many pets will tolerate hugs, it's rarely their first choice for affection, she says.

Cooing. People tend to talk to pets the same way they talk to babies—with high, cooing voices. Rather than interpreting this as love, however, pets see it as submission, says D. Caroline Coile, Ph.D., a researcher specializing in canine senses, who raises and shows salukis near Tallahassee, Florida. "High-pitched sounds make you sound too much like a littermate or, worse, a puppy. And not too many dogs respect puppies."

When you want to praise pets and still maintain their respect, it's helpful to drop your voice a little lower, says Dr. Coile. "Speaking in low tones gives your voice authority in your pet's eyes, even when you're saying how sweet and precious he is."

Spoiling. Pets are a lot like children. They love affection when it's special. Give them too much too often, and they start feeling as though they deserve it. This is especially true when the affection is "unearned"—when you give them treats every time they ask, for example, or speak warmly no matter what they're doing or what they've done, says Dr. Milani.

Acting rambunctiously. Pets encourage this type of affection, but in their world it means something different than it does in ours. Dogs and cats interact with each other in very physical ways. They jump on each other, put their paws on each other's shoulders, or play-fight until one gives up. They assume that people play the same way.

"A dog who jumps up on you may be saying hi, but he's also making a statement about his place in the household," says Dr. Milani. "He's putting himself on the same level, or above, you. If you greet that behavior with a pat and a kiss, you're giving the green light to other, less desirable behaviors, like begging for food, being snappish, or general disobedience."

Even if you don't mind when your pets take certain liberties, such as giving you a slobbery kiss or jumping on the kitchen table to say good morning, you wouldn't want them to act that way with others. Pets get mighty confused when their owners encourage an affectionate face licking, then scold them for doing it to someone else. "Pets don't do well with mixed messages," says Dr. Milani.

Good Loving

Affection is among the most powerful emotions that pets and people share. As with any strong emotion, however, it needs to be given judiciously—not only at the right times but also in ways dogs and cats can understand.

Praise them when they deserve it. People use affection for many reasons: to reassure pets when they're frightened, to reassure themselves when they're feeling guilty, and simply because it feels good to do it. There's nothing wrong with giving lots of affection, but pets respond best when the affection is related to something good that they've actually done, says Benjamin Hart, D.V.M., Ph.D., professor of physiology and behavior at the University of California, Davis, School of Veterinary Medicine and author of *The Perfect Puppy: How to Choose Your Dog by Its Behavior*.

"Affection is one of the most effective tools for behavior modification," he explains. When your dog behaves well, reward him with lots of affection. When he doesn't behave well, don't give him any affection—unless he starts doing something right. Then

WHAT'S MY PET SAYING?

Behavior
Licking Faces

What It Means
"Feed Me"

Every day when Dave Pryor comes home, his two dogs, Sonja and Annabelle, shower him with kisses. It's clearly a gesture that shows how much they love him, says Pryor, a computer Web designer in Emmaus, Pennsylvania.

The dogs, however, have a different opinion. Experts in animal behavior believe that while dogs do enjoy face-to-face contact, face licking is also a leftover behavior from their puppy days. It's a gesture that says, "Hey, give us some food!"

"Mother dogs carry food for their pups in their stomachs," explains Patricia Simonet, Ph.D., a certified applied animal behaviorist and assistant professor in the science and humanities departments at Sierra Nevada College in Lake Tahoe, Nevada, where she teaches and conducts research in animal behavior, animal communication, and animal intelligence and cognition. "When the pups want some, they lick around her mouth. She'll disgorge the food by vomiting in front of the pups. It's a very intimate, instinctual behavior."

There's obviously love involved, too, she adds. After all, if the only reason dogs licked faces was to get food, they would give it up after a few failed attempts. But they keep doing it, probably for physical reassurance. "They lick us and we pet them," says Dr. Simonet. "They feel loved, and we're both happy."

praise the heck out of him. "You may feel bad when he looks at you sullenly, but you're not doing him any favors by rewarding him when he's done something wrong," says Dr. Hart. "You're only confusing him, and confused dogs aren't very happy or well-behaved dogs."

Keep the treats separate. Even though biscuits and other tasty foods are very special rewards, they shouldn't be used as a substitute for actual affection, says Alex Brooks, director of Alex

Brooks School of Dog Training in Des Plaines, Illinois. "You don't want your praise and affection to be any less meaningful to your pet just because you don't have a biscuit in your pocket."

Consider the breed. "Our domestic pets have been bred to have vastly different personalities, and some breeds need and want more affection than others," says Dr. Hart. "Golden retrievers, Labradors, terriers, and small lap dogs crave physical affection, so petting is very important to them. More aloof dogs, such as Chows, couldn't care less—you'll actually annoy them with a lot of contact."

Cats have fewer distinct breeds than dogs, but they also vary in their desires for affection, says Ira B. Perelle, Ph.D., a certified applied animal behaviorist and chairperson of the development committee for the Animal Behavior Society in Bloomington, Indiana. "Siamese cats, for instance, tend to be very physically affectionate, while Persians are a little more standoffish."

Keep a polite distance. Dogs crave physical contact, but cats tend to be ambivalent about it. Even though some cats will happily rub against your leg or sit next to you, they get a little nervous when they feel their personal space is being violated, says Steve Aiken, an animal-behavior consultant in Wichita, Kansas. "In a cat's world, when other cats get too close, it's usually a sign of aggression. Even their mating is aggressive."

Cats don't hate physical contact, he adds, and even cats who aren't physically affectionate will make an effort to put up with it. "Generally, they'll warm up over time and get used to some petting here and there, but you can also find alternative ways to show your affection, like playing with them using some of their favorite toys," says Aiken.

Pet the chin, not the head. Unless it's done in fun, people aren't comfortable when other people pat the tops of their heads, because it feels condescending. Dogs feel pretty much the same way, says Wayne Hunthausen, D.V.M., an animal-behavior consultant in Westwood, Kansas, and coauthor of *Handbook of Behaviour Problems of the Dog and Cat*. "In dog body language, any time one dog puts his chin or a paw on another dog's shoulder or over his head, it's a dominant gesture," he says. It's his way of saying, "I'm in charge."

Most dogs don't object strenuously to being patted on the head, although it may cause negative reactions in those who are fearful or unusually aggressive. Nearly all dogs enjoy being touched under the chin or on the chest, however.

Shorten the goodbyes. Cats won't object to huge, sentimental farewells when you leave the house for the day, but it may cause problems for dogs, Brooks says. "A lot of people hug and kiss and fawn over their pets like they're never going to see them again. And guess what? The dogs worry that they're never going to see them again."

The best show of affection when you're leaving for the day is something short and sweet, he adds. Give your dog a quick pat, a quick goodbye, and head out the door. "That way, he'll recognize these comings and goings as a usual part of the day, not as something to become worked up about."

Putting It Together

CHAPTER 23

Choosing the Right Puppy

When you're up to your knees in fluffy, squiggling, sloppy puppies, saying yes to one is easier than saying no to all the rest. They all love you, they all need homes, and they're all adorable. But you have to choose, and what you decide is going to change your life for the next 10 to 15 years.

Breeders, trainers, and other animal experts have come up with long lists of things that you can tick off like so many items on a tax form before making your choice. Picking a puppy isn't like filing a 1040 form, however. Ultimately, your heart is going to trump your head.

That's fine most of the time, since nearly every puppy can grow up to be a great dog, says Bernadine Cruz, D.V.M., a veterinarian in Laguna Hills, California. But a great dog isn't necessarily the right dog.

Maria Stone, an advertising representative in Philadelphia, learned this the hard way when she brought her new dog home. She had wanted a dog who didn't need a lot of grooming and was big enough to make her feel safe in her inner-city neighborhood. She bought a Labrador, a breed that combines imposing size with an almost carefree coat. What Stone didn't know was that Labrador puppies almost vibrate with energy and that their hyperactive behavior can continue for years. They're a handful even for experienced owners. Max was her first dog.

"The first few years were miserable," she remembers. "Max never quit moving. Even when he was relaxed, his whole body would twitch as if it were on a spring. It was exhausting just being around him. Then there was the chewing—he ate everything he could reach. To be honest, a day didn't go by that I didn't think about taking him back. He turned out to be a great dog, but I'd never go through that again."

IT BEGINS WITH BREED

A lot of people tell similar stories, says Dr. Cruz. Just about every dog is going to be a nut until he's at least 18 months old. Like children, dogs go through growth spurts, awkward phases, and willful adolescence. The adults they eventually become, however, depends to a large extent on the breed.

Breeds of dogs differ significantly in various aspects of behavior, says Benjamin Hart, D.V.M., Ph.D., professor of physiology and behavior at the University of California, Davis, School of Veterinary Medicine and author of *The Perfect Puppy: How to Choose Your Dog by Its Behavior*. You need to ask yourself when choosing a puppy if the breed is going to be a good match with your family and lifestyle. If you work all day and go out every night, you probably don't want a high-energy dog like an Airedale, Labrador, or Border collie. You'll also want to choose a breed that house-trains well.

Some dogs bark more than others. Some are territorial. Some are aggressive toward people and other pets. Some demand lots of affection, and some would just as soon be alone. So before you break out the checkbook and buy a leash, collar, and cedar-filled bed, you need to think about the type of dog you want to live with. Here are some examples.

- A high-voltage dog. All puppies have tons of energy, but some breeds maintain that energy throughout their lives, says Dr. Cruz. Terriers, Border collies, Pomeranians, Chihuahuas, Jack Russells, Pekingese, and Lhasa apsos are very energetic and excitable. They also tend to bark a lot—not a great trait if you live in an apartment.
- A sleeper dog. Most of the hounds, especially bloodhounds and basset hounds, and Old English sheepdogs and mastiffs are very easygoing. They like exercise, but they're also happy to relax and sleep all day. For busy people without a lot of time, these can be perfect dogs.
- A leader dog. Akitas, malamutes, Chow Chows, and huskies are very independent and strong-minded. They're good choices for people who are strong-minded themselves and are willing to put

NAME: Sam

OCCUPATION: Nanny

At the Waltham research center in Leicestershire, England, where veterinarians do nutritional research, dozens of puppies spend their days taste-testing foods. The puppies are well cared for, and there's a long list of people waiting to adopt them.

The puppies spend several weeks at the center after they've been weaned from their mothers. Dorm life, as you might expect, has a way of making them unruly. That's where Sam, an elderly Labrador retriever, comes in. Sam is essentially a nanny, says Josephine Wills, D.V.M., former director of scientific affairs at the center. The puppies are all kept in kennels. Workers make a point of rotating Sam among the different groups. "He babysits the puppies and plays with them, and in the process he teaches them some manners," she says.

Between the ages of 2 and 4 months, puppies learn a lot about how they should and shouldn't behave—when not to play too rough, for example. Sam offers lessons in etiquette. When the puppies are overly rambunctious, a quick growl puts them back in line.

"He's a natural role model for them," says Dr. Wills. "He's also a wonderful asset for us because he helps the puppies learn to be polite and civilized."

WHAT'S MY PET SAYING?

Behavior
Chin Biting

What It Means
"Hello"

When you snuggle a 6-week-old puppy in your arms, you're likely to feel a little lick and bite on your chin. It's not because he's discovered a lunchtime leftover. He's just giving a typical puppy greeting.

Among puppies, a lick on the chin is considered a friendly salutation. It's also a sign of respect, which is why puppies often greet older dogs that way. Naturally, they do the same thing with people.

The bite that follows the lick, however, is something else. Puppies are born chewers. They'll bite anything that gets near their mouths—including Mom when they're nursing. Mom dogs quickly put a stop to it, but it takes time for puppies to learn that biting isn't welcome in other places either.

in the time to train them. Because of their assertive natures, they're generally not good choices for families with small children.

• An Einstein dog. Three of the smartest breeds are German shepherds, Border collies, and poodles. Their intelligence can be a mixed blessing. They can learn anything you care to teach them, but they require an enormous amount of mental stimulation and companionship to keep their minds busy.

• A watchdog. All of the assertive breeds, including Dobermans and Rottweilers, make excellent watchdogs, says Dr. Hart. So do the terriers, although they have a tendency to bark even when it's not required.

PREDICTING PERSONALITY

Even though dogs of the same breed tend to have certain traits in common, such as the need for exercise or the tendency to snap, you can't predict with certainty what kind of adult a puppy will grow up to be any more than you can predict what a child will be like. What you can do, however, is get a sense of a puppy's personality and disposition, says Dr. Cruz. Puppies who are good-hearted and affectionate usually grow up to be good-hearted and affectionate adults. Dogs who are nervous and suspicious when they're young will probably be that way when they're older.

The best clue you'll get is to meet the mother, says Karen L. Campbell, D.V.M., professor of dermatology and endocrinology at the University of Illinois College of Veterinary Medicine at Urbana–Champaign. By the time they are 6 weeks old, puppies have picked up an incredible amount of knowledge from their mothers about how to behave. The things they learn during this impressionable period tend to stick with them, she explains. And of course, some traits are inherited, and puppies get half their genes from their mothers.

"When you visit a breeder, you may be able to see the father, too," says Dr. Campbell. Look at how the parents respond to people. Do they make friendly eye contact, or do they stare? Do they enjoy being touched? Do they show friendly interest in you without launching into over-the-top excitement? All of this tells a lot about the puppies as well.

It's not always possible to meet the parents, but there are other ways to get a fix on a puppy's personality, says Dr. Campbell. As a general rule, small dogs, especially the terriers, tend to be a little more excitable than larger dogs. And males tend to be more aggressive than females. Here are a few additional things to look for.

Check enthusiasm with a cheeseburger. Puppies should be enthusiastic and eager to play with people. A good way to test this is to give them a rubber cheeseburger. "Most alert, playful puppies will look at a toy with interest when you pull it out and chase after it when you toss it," Dr. Campbell says. Rubber cheeseburgers are a good choice because they make squeaky sounds that puppies like. This test also gives a sense of whether the puppy is inclined to fetch, she adds.

Most puppies will be curious about the cheeseburger. Some, however, will be startled by the squeaky sounds. If they're too frightened to play with it after a minute or two, they may be too nervous to make good pets.

Roll them over. Dogs don't lie on their backs for just anyone—and they're certainly selective about doing it with other dogs. Rolling them over is a good test. "You want a puppy who doesn't

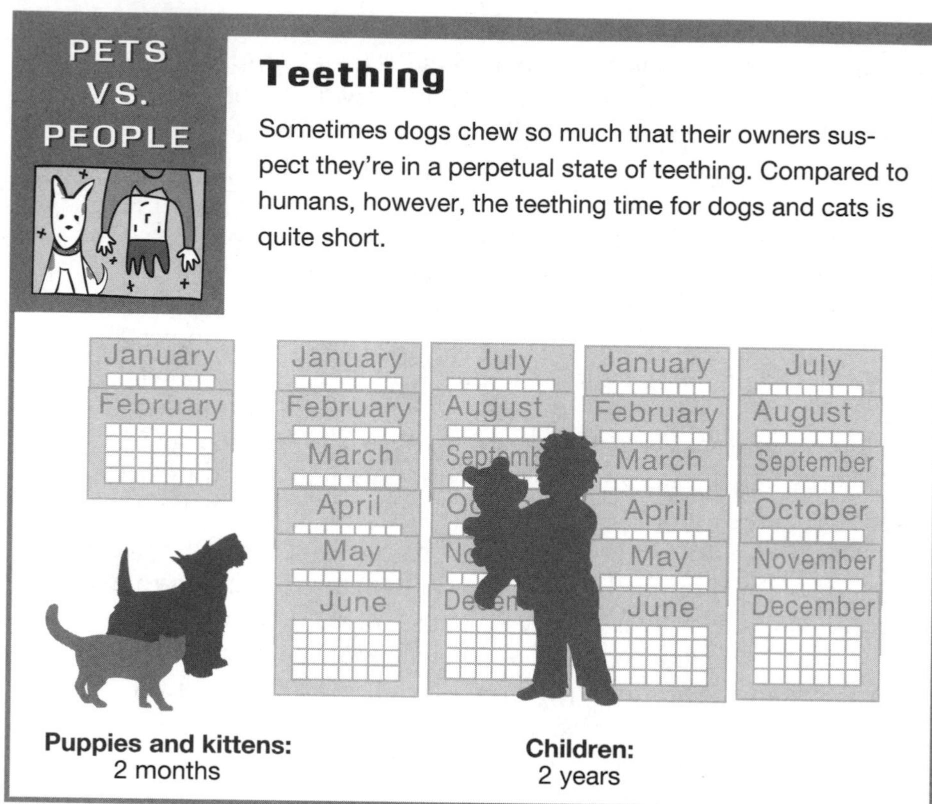

struggle much," says Dr. Campbell. Conversely, you don't want a dog who's so shy and timid that he urinates on the spot.

Tickle their toes. This is another test to determine how compliant a dog is going to be. "Pick up a foot and see how the puppy reacts to having you handle it," says Dr. Campbell. Dogs dislike having their feet touched. Most will struggle a bit, but they shouldn't struggle too much. This test has a practical purpose, too. Dogs' feet need regular attention. You may not want a dog who refuses to let anyone trim his nails or care for the pads.

Look him in the eye. The way a puppy looks at you says a lot about his personality. Puppies who stare with intensity are going to be dominant and could be hard to handle. Those who avoid all eye contact are very shy, and it may be hard to establish a good relationship. You want a dog who isn't nervous about meeting your eyes but who looks away when you keep staring.

Pay attention to mouth-play. Even though teething doesn't start until a puppy is about 12 weeks old, some are chewing fiends almost from the time they're born. A puppy who's constantly putting things in his mouth—like your fingers—may turn into an adult chewer, says Dr. Campbell.

Watch how he treats his littermates. "There are two puppies who should be your last choice in any litter," says Dr. Campbell: "The one who seems to be the leader, who is usually the most rambunctious of the bunch, and the shy one who hangs back from the group." The ideal puppy falls somewhere between these extremes, she explains.

Get the family history. A dog who got his start in a whelping box in a family's kitchen has a much better shot at the good life than one raised in a puppy mill—a breeding operation designed to churn out lots of puppies without giving them a lot of personal attention, says Dr. Cruz. When it's time to choose, look for puppies who have been handled often and given lots of love right from the time they were born.

CHAPTER 24

Choosing the Right Kitten

As director of the Humane Society of North Texas in Fort Worth, Tammy Hawley has plenty of experience choosing cats. Not that it's done her much good. Her most recent kitty acquisition chose her, as is so often the case. "Tweety came in through my dryer vent," Hawley says. "She started sneaking in at night to eat my cats' food. I would stay up to visit with her. By the time I finally caught her, she was ready to stay."

Even if Tweety had played harder to get, Hawley would have felt comfortable choosing her for a pet. She was curious, friendly, outgoing, and resourceful—in short, everything you could want in a cat. But relationships between people and cats don't always go that smoothly. There are kittens who daintily step into the litter box, only to abandon it later in favor of the houseplants. Or those who carefully sheathe their claws when playing, then turn into hand-scratching, couch-destroying tigers. Choosing a kitten is an inexact science at best, but there are ways to make good guesses about what kinds of cats kittens will grow up to be.

Easy to Please

People don't ask all that much from their cats. A purr here, a rub there, some quiet time on the lap—these are the qualities (along with proper litter-box deportment) that make for perfect pets.

When you're choosing a kitten, the main thing to look for is how she responds to handling, says Katherine Houpt, V.M.D., Ph.D., a board-certified veterinary behaviorist, professor of physiology, and director of the behavior clinic at Cornell University College of Veterinary Medicine in Ithaca, New York.

Look at Me!

In shelters crowded with hopefuls, kittens have pretty standard routines for drawing attention to themselves. They race to the front of their cages. They stick their paws through the grilles. Sometimes they climb up the doors, looking as cute as they know how to be.

But some kittens are born entertainers, and one in particular developed a PR stunt all his own. "When people came through the cat room looking for adoptable kittens, this little stinker would dip his paw in his drinking water, wait for just the right minute, and flick water at them," says Tammy Hawley, director of the Humane Society of North Texas in Fort Worth.

He didn't stop there. When people stopped to see where the water was coming from, he would open his eyes wide and stick his wet paw through the cage. "He was truly his own marketing agent," Hawley says.

With tactics like that, it's hardly surprising that he quickly found himself a home. And according to his owners, he never tried the water trick again. Apparently, he was smart enough to get attention, and smart enough to know when to quit.

Let her make the first move. When you're looking over a litter of kittens, be a little standoffish at first. Wait to see which of the kittens approach you, says Dr. Houpt. These will be the ones who are adventuresome and eager for human contact—qualities that will only magnify over time.

Look for wide-open eyes. Kittens who are born and raised without a lot of human contact sometimes grow up wild, or feral. Feral cats rarely make good pets, says Stephanie Frommer, shelter project coordinator at the Massachusetts Society for the Prevention of Cruelty to Animals in Boston. You can tell the difference just by looking at their eyes. Feral cats have a very distinctive look because they squint at visitors. "Kittens should look at you wide-eyed and with curiosity," she says.

Choose an adventurer. Kittens are born curious, and they spend a lot of time exploring their surroundings. Watch the kittens who pounce, play, and boldly go where no kitten has gone before—these are the ones who will be well-adjusted and fun to be with, Frommer says.

Do the Ping-Pong test. There are some things a happy kitten can't resist, and a Ping-Pong ball is one of them. Frommer recommends taking a ball with you to the shelter. Before choosing a kitten, roll the ball across her line of sight. If she goes for it—and most kittens will—you'll know she's eager and enthusiastic. A cat who ignores the ball or watches it suspiciously probably won't make the best pet later on.

Do the neck test. Kittens who get testy with Mom—or with motherly humans—are going to get testy with anyone. One way to test their temperament is to pick them up by the scruff of the neck, just like their mothers would. Most kittens will wiggle a bit, then calm down. "Kittens who really struggle often grow up to be aggressive," says Dr. Houpt.

Lift her legs off the ground. Try this temperament test for kittens, from Bernadine Cruz, D.V.M., a veterinarian in Laguna Hills, California: Slip a hand under the kitten's belly near the hips, then hold her in the air so her front half dangles. Keep her up for about 30 seconds. "A good kitty will kind of hang there for a minute and think about it," says Dr. Cruz. "A more temperamental kitty, well, she'll try to eat you, and that personality is not going to go away."

See how they play. Litters of kittens, like packs of children, have bullies, babies, and leaders. You can tell a lot about them by the ways they interact.

- Kittens who are perpetually stalking their siblings' tails and generally horsing around will be the most outgoing and playful.
- Kittens who are willing to play but don't initiate a lot of games on their own will generally grow up to be more laid-back.
- Kittens who totally ignore their littermates and don't show much enthusiasm may not be in the best of health. They're not the best choices.

Meet Mom. "The single best temperament test for any pet is the temperament of the mother," says Dr. Houpt. There is a genetic connection between a mother and her kittens, and the mother's behavior tells a lot about how kittens may behave as adults. "In the 7 or 8 weeks that most kittens live with their mothers, they learn a good portion of what they're going to learn over their entire lives," says Dr. Houpt. Mother cats who are fearful will raise fearful kittens—and the kittens will probably stay that way throughout their lives.

WHAT'S MY PET SAYING?

Behavior
Hiding in Shopping Bags

What It Means
"I'm Taking Cover"

There may be no better cat toy in the world than a paper bag. Drop one on the floor, upright or on its side, and it acts like a kitty magnet. Cats climb in, hunker down, turn around, and peer out as though their view of the world has entirely changed.

The reason cats love paper bags is that they provide great cover. As natural hunters, cats are always interested in finding the best vantage points from which to watch the world without being noticed themselves, says Tammy Hawley, director of the Humane Society of North Texas in Fort Worth. The paper bag is like a hunter's tree-stand. Cats can watch their "prey" going by and wait for the perfect moment to pounce.

What they don't seem to notice is that the rustling of the bag always gives them away. But they don't care. Bags make them feel as though they're invisible, and that's almost as good as the real thing.

BREEDS AND TEMPERAMENTS

You won't see a lot of purebred cats outside the showring, mainly because people don't concern themselves as much with cats' breeds as they do with dogs'. If you're looking for a purebred, however, you can use the breed line to get some idea of what a kitten will grow up to be like. For example:

Ragdolls. This breed got its name for an obvious reason. "They just go limp when you pick them up," Hawley says. "I've never met an aggressive ragdoll in my life. They're just happy to be alive."

Persians. These are very independent cats, and they like the finer things in life. "On television, you always see Persians eating from silver dishes and being carried around on satin pillows, and honestly, that does seem to be how they like to be treated," says Hawley. Persians are unlikely to come when you want or to show much interest in playing—unless it was their idea first.

American shorthairs. This very common breed tends to be smart, playful, and good with children, says Hawley. They enjoy learning and are one of the few breeds that will readily do tricks to please their owners.

Devon rex and Sphynx. These are two very unusual-looking breeds, but they're among the most agreeable cats out there. "They're very, very sweet, but they require a lot of care because they tend to inherit health problems," Hawley says. Both breeds, for example, have almost no hair. They get cold easily and are vulnerable to sunburn. They're strictly indoor cats.

Siamese. As with Persians, Siamese are independent cats who are either affectionate or not, depending on their moods. They're also very chatty, with a distinctive, yowling voice that puts some people off. They may also be standoffish at times.

CATS ARE NOT DOGS

People often make the mistake of using the same personality tests for kittens that they use for puppies. It never works because dogs and cats simply don't react the same ways, says Dr. Houpt.

People buying puppies, for example, will sometimes roll them on their backs to see if they're calm and submissive enough to be petted. Try this with cats, and you'll get a handful of claws. "A cat on her back is in an 'all-my-weapons-are-showing' position, with her claws open," says Dr. Houpt. "Nothing about this position is going to tell you what kind of kitty she's going to be."

Another puppy test is to drop a set of keys to see how jumpy they are. Most puppies will accept the noise, but cats have a very strong flight instinct. They'll probably react by scramming. "For them it's a healthy fear, not an overreaction," Hawley says.

CHAPTER 25

Picking a Good Older Pet

Captain couldn't cut it anymore on the racetrack. The veteran greyhound had lost a step on the competition and was unceremoniously "retired"—a code word in the racing industry for "scheduled for euthanasia."

Fortunately, Captain was spared this fate when he was adopted by the Andres family of Jamestown, North Carolina. Now, at 9 years of age, he's just hitting his stride as a family pet.

Captain is among the thousands of older dogs and cats across the country who have gotten second chances with new owners. In return, they give their new families all the love, affection, and companionship they can muster. "I wasn't sure that we were ready for another dog," says Chris Andres. "But the whole thing has worked out so well that we have *four* greyhounds now."

For many people, owning a pet from the kitten or puppy stage is an important part of the bonding process. And that's okay. Yet there are tens of thousands of mature pets in city pounds, foster homes, and rescue shelters who are looking for the same break that Captain and his crew got. If you're willing to handle a brief adjustment period, older cats and dogs can be every bit as wonderful as pets that you've raised from infancy.

In fact, adopting an older pet has major advantages over buying a puppy or kitten. For starters, there's cost. Purebred kittens and dogs from breeders can cost hundreds, even thousands, of dollars, while you can acquire an older pet for less money than you'd spend on a week's worth of groceries.

In addition, there's often less doubt about what you're getting into. An 8-week-old puppy may weigh less than 10 pounds—but could quickly grow into a boisterous, shoe-chewing, 80-pound bundle of joy who eats puppy chow by the pound. An older pet, on the other hand, is usually well past the chewing, housetraining, and general growing-up phase.

Age also makes a difference when you're looking for a pet who has the right temperament. "We like to tell people that what you see is what you get," says Janice Barnard, an animal behavioral counselor with the American Society for the Prevention of Cruelty to Animals (ASPCA) in New York City. "By the time a pet is a few years old, his outlook on life is pretty much set. You can look at a dog or cat and tell whether he's outgoing or quiet, friendly or a little reserved. It can be much tougher to tell that with a puppy or a kitten."

Finally, don't underestimate the warm feeling you'll get from knowing that you've saved a perfectly wonderful pet from life in a shelter—or worse. Nationwide, nearly two out of three pets that arrive in animal shelters are put down because they can't find proper homes. "Adopting an older pet is an act of pure love," says Siri Wine, director of the Siamese Cat Rescue Center and Siamese Rescue Alliance in western Virginia. "You're not only doing the pet a great service, but you're doing your bit to help with a major problem, too."

TAKE YOUR TIME

Picking the right older pet takes a little work. You'll have to assess your wants and needs and make sure that you're really ready to adopt a new family member. You'll also need to go through an adoption process that could take anywhere from a few hours to a few months, depending on what you're looking for. You'll want to make sure that you find a healthy pet, or at least are prepared for life with an animal who has special needs. And you'll have to steel yourself for the rush of emotions you may feel when you walk into a shelter and realize that saying yes to one pet means saying no to dozens of others.

"It's not always as simple as coming in, pointing to a cat, and taking him home," says Barnard. "You need to take your time because you're talking about a decision that can affect your family for years to come."

Before you pick a particular pet, of course, you'll need to pick a species. Both cats and dogs can be great companions, provided you give them what they need to prosper. Dogs require more maintenance than cats. They need to go outside for exercise and to relieve themselves several times a day. They thrive on contact with family members and other dogs. Cats, meanwhile, tend to be more solitary, although many crave attention and affection. Cats can do quite nicely in a family where no one is home during the day. Many are perfectly happy being left home for the weekend with food, fresh water, and daily visits from a friendly neighbor.

"It's a question of lifestyle," says Hedy Litke, director of animal placement for the ASPCA. "If you're someone who's on the go and is often out of the house, you'll probably want a cat more than a dog. But if you are home during the day and can take the pet outside and romp with him, maybe you're better off with a dog."

Once you've made the decision to get a cat or dog, it's time for a little more thinking and a lot more research. Do you want a big dog or a small dog? A frisky cat or one who's a little more mellow? One who needs a lot of grooming, like a long-haired cat or a Pekingese, or a "self-cleaning" version, like a short-haired cat or a Chihuahua?

This is where breed books can be very useful. Bookstores and libraries usually have many books on cat and dog breeds, listing temperaments, size, grooming requirements, friendliness around children and strangers, specific health concerns, life expectancy, and tons of interesting breed-specific quirks. Spend a few days or a few weeks thumbing through the books. You'll develop a feel for whether you're looking for a terrier or a hunting dog, a tabby or a Persian.

Of course, you may need to compromise a little when it comes to breed. Although shelters often have purebred pets available, most dogs and cats you'll find are of mixed stock. It's usually pretty easy to pick out the main breed or breed types in a pet. A 4-pound pooch with long, silky hair, for example, probably doesn't have much German shepherd in him. Even though the pets aren't of pure parentage, they'll probably exhibit many of the traits of their dominant breeds. A dog that's part Labrador probably has the same sweet disposition as his purebred cousins, Litke says.

Your First Visit

The next step in finding the right pet is visiting an animal shelter. Almost every county, city, or town in America has a place to adopt pets who have been given up by previous owners for some reason or other. Call ahead to make sure someone will be on hand to answer your questions. And when you go, take along all the people who will be living with the pet, from children to grandparents. "You're talking about adding a family member, so everyone has to be in agreement," Litke says.

Now comes the truly difficult part: picking one pet from the field of qualified candidates. So many cats and dogs—it's hard to make up your mind. Although it sounds a little cold, Barnard says, you have to approach this process as though you were buying a used car. "It's very important to stay focused on your wants and needs," she says. "A lot of people come in, see a pathetic-looking pet, and feel so sorry for him that they ignore their better judgment and adopt him. But it really doesn't do anybody any good to take an underdog when he's just not going to work out."

Shelters want you to select the right pet, not the one they figure will be the hardest to place. This keeps them from getting "rebound" pets—dogs and cats who are returned by the adopting family because they can't take proper care of them. "No reputable shelter is going to try to steer you toward the wrong animal," Litke says. "It just doesn't make sense in the long run."

A Few Simple Tests

When you spot a pet who looks like a winner, it's time to check him out a little more closely. With permission from the shelter personnel, mingle with the pet. Ask if you can use a quiet room to sit for a while. How does the cat or dog react to this new setting? Does he sit in the corner or try to hide? Is he too effusive for your tastes? A well-tempered pet will be friendly, but not overbearing, Barnard says. It's important that you feel comfortable with the animal. But remember that a shelter is a high-stress environment for many pets, especially cats. "Often, all you can catch is a glimpse of the true personality," she says. "But it should be enough to give you some guidance."

You should definitely avoid pets who react to you aggressively with snarls, scratches, or bared teeth. It's true that the pets are under stress and that this can make them cranky. But you don't want a pet who reacts this way at home when life happens to get a little hairy.

Shelters encourage people to ask a lot of questions. How did the animal get here? Was he abused? Is he housebroken or litter-box trained? Does the shelter have his health history? Do they

Breed Rescue

It certainly wasn't Malcolm's fault. He was as loyal as a Scottish terrier could be—and that's pretty loyal, even by dog standards.

His owners, however, weren't nearly as devoted. When they decided to have a baby, they showed Malcolm the door, even though he'd been a family member since he was 8 weeks old.

Unlike many such stories, this one has a happy ending. Malcolm found a new home, thanks to the Scottish Terrier Club of America's rescue program. Dozens of breed-specific rescue programs have sprung up in recent years, trying to find homes for dogs with hard-luck tales like Malcolm's. Rescues provide an alternative to regular shelters and pounds, especially for soft-hearted people who favor particular breeds.

"It's really the best of both worlds," says Siri Wine, director of the Siamese Cat Rescue Center and Siamese Rescue Alliance in western Virginia. "You can get a purebred animal and still get that great feeling from saving a cat or dog from a bad situation."

Being a rescuer isn't always as simple as filling out an application and toting home a pet. Many rescue groups require extensive reference checks and even home visits, says Daphne Branzell, a national rescue coordinator for the Scottish Terrier Club of America. Even after all the checks, she says, she won't allow an adoption unless she has the right gut feeling about the new owners.

The rescue movement got started when concerned animal lovers started saving "retired" racing greyhounds. Since then, the rescue movement has placed thousands of pets nationwide. You can find local rescue organizations for the breeds you're interested in from breeders, vets, or American Kennel Club chapters. Many rescue organizations also have Internet sites that feature pets currently trying to find homes.

know anything about his breed background? Contrary to what most people think, only a minority of pets at shelters are strays. Most come from families that simply couldn't keep them anymore. So shelter personnel are likely to have lots of information available.

It's very important to make sure that you're getting a healthy dog or cat. His eyes and nose should be clear, without redness or a discharge. His mouth should be clean, and his breath should smell relatively fresh. The ears should be clean, and the coat should be full, since patchy fur may be a sign of health problems. If you suspect there's a problem, ask about it. Most times, people at the shelter are aware of the pet's health troubles and can tell you what's already been done to correct it and what remains to be done. Many shelters have veterinarians on staff to answer questions. If they don't, ask if you can have the pet examined by a vet prior to adoption.

THE PAPERWORK

Pets aren't the only ones who have to pass inspection at the shelter. Before you can adopt a pet, you'll have to prove to the staff that you're able and willing to be a good owner. This shouldn't upset you, Litke says. It's in the best interest of the dog or cat as well as you.

People at the shelter will want to know if you have the proper facilities for the pet you've chosen. If you want a pet who needs room to romp, but you live in an apartment, you're probably asking for trouble. You'll be asked about your motivation, too. Are you adopting this pet for the right reasons, like companionship or friendship, rather than to give him to a college roommate as a prank? You'll also be asked about your ability to pay for food and health care. Most shelters will check a few references by telephone and make a decision on your application within a few hours. Others may want to do a more thorough search that could last a few days or more.

In the end, Litke says, many people realize they're just not ready for the commitment. Nearly two-thirds of the people who visit a shelter leave without adopting. While some will return later and choose a pet, a good number will realize that they're getting in too deep. "It's better that people know this up front," Litke says. "You may decide that you're better off without a pet at this point in your life."

BRINGING HIM HOME

Introducing a dog or cat to his new home can be a little stressful for everyone. So it's best to prepare a little beforehand, especially if you already have other pets. "You're talking about a major disruption in your current pet's life," Wine says. "Pets are creatures of routine and territory, and a new animal can disturb both of those things."

When you bring a new cat home, Wine says, it's best to confine him to one room at first so that he can get his bearings. Make sure that the room is well-lit, well-ventilated, and has water and a litter box in handy places. It's best to keep him in a room that has places to hide, such as under a bed or behind a sofa. "Cats will often disappear for a while when they arrive in a new place," Wine says. "This is perfectly normal. They just want to make sure that they're safe before they reach out."

After a few days, you can expand your cat's horizons by letting him have two rooms to explore. Don't be in a hurry—you don't want to overwhelm your new housemate. Within a few weeks or a month, he'll be ready to roam the whole place, and he won't spend so much time out of sight.

Introducing cats slowly to new environments is especially important when you already have a cat. Keeping them separate for a few weeks will allow them to smell, hear, and maybe even see each other, while preventing conflicts that can arise from face-to-face meetings, Wine says.

The same basic pattern works for dogs as well. Limit his explorations to one or two rooms for a few days, then gradually expand the available space. Unlike new cats, dogs are eager to socialize almost right away, so don't be stingy with the sweet talk. "Everyone in the house should spend time with the dog, petting him, walking him, and playing with him," Litke says. "It's vital that the dog understands he's part of the family."

If you already have a dog, it's probably best to arrange a neutral place for them to meet. Litke suggests taking both dogs to a park and allowing them to get to know each other for a couple of hours. That way, your resident dog won't feel so intimidated when the new guy shows up at the garage door. Expect a little growling or barking the first few days while the dogs work out the kinks at feeding time and other situations.

It's not only dogs and cats who go through an adjustment period. Your life will undergo some changes, too, ranging from 2:00 A.M. dog walks and find-the-kitty panics to unscheduled trips to the vet. Many first-time pet owners go through a brief period of what can only be described as buyer's remorse. "You start wondering what the heck you did," Barnard says. It can be tough for a while, but love usually wins out in the end.

CHAPTER 26

Choosing and Using Names

When Edward Cooper of Potomac, Maryland, needed a name for his new black Labrador, he immediately thought of his first loves: baseball and the Baltimore Orioles. His team's beloved downtown stadium gave Cooper the inspiration he was looking for. He named his dog Camden Yards.

The name may seem like a strange choice, but those who work with dogs and cats say that Cooper hit a home run. By naming Camden after something close to his heart, Cooper will convey affection and respect every time he uses Camden's name—and these are feelings that pets, with their highly tuned senses and piercing intuition, quickly recognize and identify with.

What's in a Name?

People are sometimes tempted to be clever when picking names for their pets—like the bartender who named his dog Swizzle Stick. There's nothing wrong with being whimsical, but your pet's name is the first and most important word he learns, says Laura Kleiman of Chadds Ford, Pennsylvania, a trainer and coordinator for Independence Dogs, an organization that trains dogs to be working companions for people with disabilities. It's the gateway to the lifelong relationship you're going to share, and you don't want to treat it too lightly. Names communicate caring, trust, and respect, and choosing the right name will strengthen the bonds between you.

Keep it simple. "You want to choose a positive name that's easy to say and isn't too long," Kleiman says. Choosing a name that's too long—like the unfortunate Airedale who was saddled with the moniker Arrobee Londonderry Airendale—means you won't use it often. Since you need to use your pet's name when-

MESSAGES AND MEANINGS

Nothing but "Trouble"

How many times can a dog run away before he gets hurt? One small Dalmatian named Trouble in Santa Fe, New Mexico, was near the point of finding out. Everyone in the neighborhood knew who Trouble was because he was *always* in trouble.

Trouble had a hard time staying put. He was constantly escaping from his yard. Once he got out, he went around the neighborhood and tipped over trash cans. The animal-control officers knew Trouble by name. But no matter what Trouble's owners tried, they couldn't get him to calm down and stay home.

Tired of constantly bailing Trouble out of trouble, they finally called Kate Solisti-Mattelon, a professional animal communicator in Littleton, Colorado. It didn't take her long to conclude that Trouble was a very nice dog with a very bad name. "Sometimes animals have a very clear sense of their names," says Solisti-Mattelon. "When you name a dog Trouble, that's what you're going to get."

The solution turned out to be easy. Trouble's owners renamed him Max. Once he was used to his new, dignified name, he started getting calmer. "It took a while because he really was full of bad habits, but changing the name made all the difference," says Solisti-Mattelon.

ever you want to get his attention, you want it to be short and sweet. It will be easier for you to say and easier for him to understand.

Make it unique. Dogs and cats can understand quite a few words, but they aren't able to make fine distinctions between different sounds, Kleiman says. You want to be sure that the name doesn't sound too much like other words you'll also be teaching him, especially commands. Names such as Joe or Noah can be a real problem because they sound an awful lot like "no"—and that's not a concept you want pets to associate with their names, says Steve Lindsay, a dog-behavior consultant in Philadelphia.

Keep it positive. There's a natural tendency to give names that reflect our own attitudes—or at least our own senses of humor. With the exception of a few notable rock stars, most people

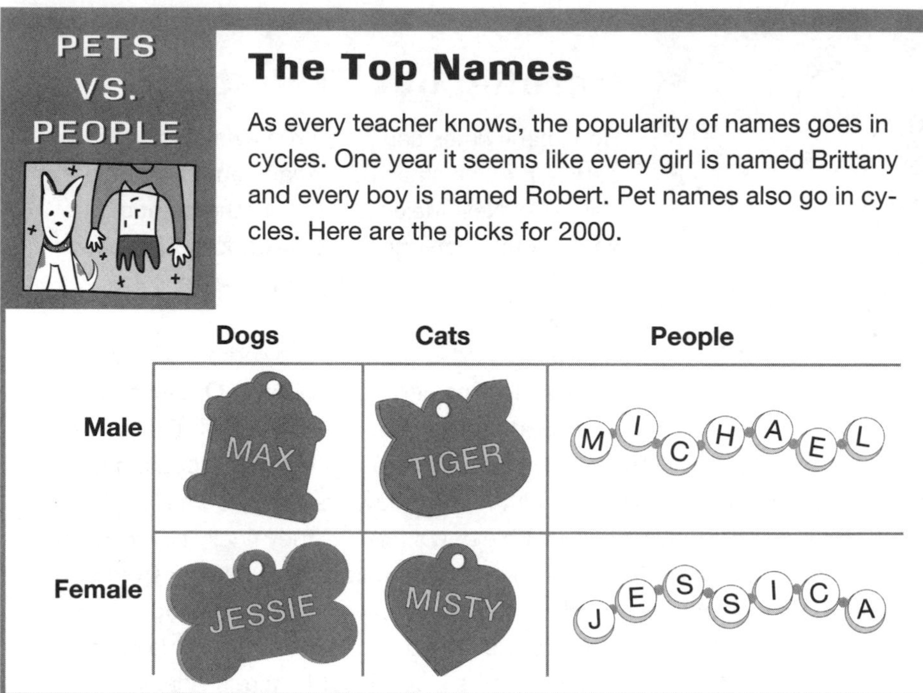

PETS VS. PEOPLE

The Top Names

As every teacher knows, the popularity of names goes in cycles. One year it seems like every girl is named Brittany and every boy is named Robert. Pet names also go in cycles. Here are the picks for 2000.

	Dogs	Cats	People
Male	MAX	TIGER	MICHAEL
Female	JESSIE	MISTY	JESSICA

manage to resist this tendency when naming their children. It's just as important to be respectful when naming dogs and cats. A name like French Fry will certainly make people smile, but your pet may find himself wondering why everyone seems to be laughing at him.

"A name like Killer can automatically communicate a negative image, and that may affect the way you or other people perceive your pet," adds Liz Palika, a trainer in Oceanside, California.

HELPING PETS LEARN THEIR NAMES

Dogs and cats don't have the same facility with language that we do. It's difficult for them to distinguish their names from the thousands of other words they hear every day. To help them learn their names more quickly—and, just as important, form positive associations with their names—here are a few things you'll want to do.

• "Name them as soon as they come into your home," Kleiman says. "Use the name a lot, and when you see them responding to their name, praise them."

• Always say the name in an upbeat, positive way, says Bob Sessions, a canine search specialist in Montgomery County, Maryland. "Over time they'll begin to say, 'Gee, this human always says this one word whenever he picks me up—he must be talking to me!' "

• While your pet is learning his name, go ahead and give him a reward whenever he responds to hearing it. You don't have to do this indefinitely, but during the first few months, it will help him understand that the sound of his name always predicts good things to come.

• Whether your pet is a youngster or a senior, don't use his name when you're angry or giving discipline, Sessions says. Pets who form negative associations with their names—when, for example, you say something like, "Rex, come and look what you did!"—will be much less likely to respond positively to other sorts of training, where using the name is essential to get their attention, he explains.

CHAPTER 27

Teaching Commands

We humans have a lot of resources to help us behave properly in polite society. Miss Manners tells us which fork to use. Ann Landers gives helpful tips on getting along with spouses and coworkers. And Peggy Post tells us how to plan the perfect wedding.

Dogs and cats can't turn to books or newspapers for advice. They can't ask us for guidance, either. They depend on us to take the initiative and let them know what types of behavior make us happy and which will land them in the doghouse. The only way we can communicate these lessons is with commands.

There's something about the word *command* that makes people a little uncomfortable. We don't like it when people give us commands. Why should dogs and cats like it any better?

This is one way in which pets and people are very different, says Rolan Tripp, D.V.M., affiliate professor of applied animal behavior at Colorado State University Veterinary School in Fort Collins and author of *Pet Perception Management*. People believe that once they reach adulthood, they're more or less free to do as they please. Dogs, however, don't believe in equality. Whenever two or more dogs come together, they quickly decide which dog has more status and which dog has less. Those with less status see it as their job to obey higher-ranking dogs. And they react to people in the same way, says Dr. Tripp. They assume that we're the "top dogs" in the family, and they expect us to tell them what to do, just as higher-ranking dogs tell them what to do.

Cats are a little different. Because they evolved as solitary animals, they didn't develop the same sense of social hierarchies as dogs did. But they still understand that people control something that's very important—the food supply. As anyone who lives with cats knows, the best way to get them to do anything is to offer them food.

HOW PETS LEARN

Dogs and cats understand far more than people give them credit for. Highly trained service dogs, for example, can learn dozens (in some cases, hundreds) of words and phrases, including such things as "turn on the light" and "find the car." Even pets without formal training can easily learn basic commands such as "sit" and "come" in a training session or two.

They don't learn automatically, however, any more than children do. It takes a little work to teach them things that you want them to know. But once you know their hot buttons—the things that get them excited and that they respond to—it happens very quickly.

Every pet has different likes and dislikes, but they all respond to rewards. That's true of people, too. If someone were to give you money every time you did a certain thing, you'd do that thing more often. In fact, this happens every day—we call it work. This type of learning, called positive reinforcement, works just as well for dogs as it does for us. We ask them to sit, they sit, and we give them the cookie. They learn to associate the command with the action, and the action with the reward. It's a very simple, effective way of teaching.

Cats respond to positive reinforcement, too, but not as automatically as dogs. When you give cats commands, they pause for a moment to sift through all the possible scenarios before deciding if they're going to obey. Suppose, for example, you want to teach your cat to come when you call. Praise or food by itself won't do it. You'll also have to link the command with a very specific situation. When your cat hears the command "come," he puts it all together: "It's six o'clock *and* I haven't eaten *and* my owner is home *and* she's walking toward the food bowl *and* she made the sound 'come'—in that case, I'm going to come running." If you give the command in any other context, such as when you aren't planning to fill his bowl, you'll be more likely to get a bored yawn than instant obedience, says Dr. Tripp.

TRICKS FOR GIVING TREATS

Nothing focuses a dog's mind better than food. Professional trainers know this, and usually they keep a few biscuits or dried liver bits in their pockets. At first, dogs don't know what commands mean. But they will know that pleasing their people earns

WHAT'S MY PET SAYING?

Behavior
Head Cocking

What It Means
"I'm Gathering Information"

When dogs are trying to figure out what people are saying—or what that rustling behind the wall is all about—they'll cock their heads, first one way, then the other. It looks as though they're deliberately trying to be adorable, but what they're really doing is gathering as much information as they can.

Every time a dog shifts his head, he's seeing something from an entirely different angle. This allows him to collect additional data to calculate such things as distance and rate of movement. In addition, cocking the head allows him to see faces from different perspectives, which makes it easier to recognize subtle facial expressions and gather social cues.

Head cocking helps dogs hear a little better, too. When they're puzzled by something they're hearing, moving the head and earflap helps direct more of the sound waves directly into the ear. We do a similar thing when we try to pull in a weak radio station by switching from stereo to mono. The quality may not be quite as good, but the monodirectional sound is a little louder and clearer.

them something to eat. Even when they begin to distinguish different sounds, it's still the food—along with other rewards, such as praise—that keeps them concentrating.

The problem with using food as a reward is that dogs come to expect it. There's going to be trouble when you ask your dog to do something, and you don't happen to have a biscuit in your hand. The only way to prevent this is to keep your dog guessing. Give him treats *sometimes* when he obeys commands. Other times, give him praise but no food. From his point of view, it's like playing the slot machines: He doesn't have to win every time. The mere possibility of winning is enough to keep him motivated. And because dogs have people-pleasing personalities, praise is a powerful reward in its own right.

Cats, on the other hand, have cat-pleasing personalities. They don't depend on people as much as dogs do, so praise isn't as important to them, says Rob Bloch, owner and head trainer of Critters of the Cinema in Lake Hughes, California. But food is. You can teach cats to do everything that dogs can as long as you coax them with food. "Baby food works well," he adds.

How to Give Commands

People who take their dogs to obedience classes usually learn how to give a few commands, such as "sit," "stay," and "down." For most dogs, these are enough. The basic commands are mostly geared toward keeping dogs under control when they're on a leash, getting groomed, or waiting to be fed. Dogs who learn these commands are generally more sure of themselves than those who haven't had any training at all. And, of course, they're easier to be around. So learning the basics is good for both people and their pets.

Cats can learn all of the same commands that dogs can. But since cats usually don't accompany their owners in the car or on walks around the neighborhood, most people don't bother teaching them. This is too bad, because it's a lot of fun when cats wave bye-bye when you ask them to or come running on command.

Regardless of the commands that you want your pets to know, the principles for teaching them are very similar. Here's what experts advise.

Always say the name first. "You have to get their attention, or they won't even hear the command," says Joanne Howl, D.V.M., a veterinarian in West River, Maryland, and former president of the Maryland Veterinary Medical Association. "When you say their names first, they know they need to listen—it's like telling them, 'Hey, you!'"

The best names, incidentally, are those with two syllables, and the best commands have one, she adds. This makes it easier for pets to tell the difference. "Think what happens when you say something like, "Ralph, come," Dr. Howl says. "To pets, they both sound alike at first. When a name has two syllables, pets know it's an 'attention' word, and they'll be ready to hear the command that comes next."

Speak deeply to dogs. Trainers have noticed that dogs respond best to commands when they're given in a low, slightly guttural

NAME: Tyler

OCCUPATION: Actor

People who insist that it's impossible to train cats have obviously never seen Tyler at work. A former shelter cat, Tyler went on to become a starring member of the touring Friskies Stage Show, which features felines at their creative, obedient best. He has also appeared in Friskies commercials and in the movie *Star Trek: Generations*.

Tyler is actually part of a team of feline actors who play the same cat. "You have to train them within their personalities," says Rob Bloch, owner of Critters of the Cinema in Los Angeles."A layabout cat is not going to run and jump. A food-driven cat is more active, and he's not going to lie around." That's why the cat who's running on the *Enterprise* may be the active Tyler, while the one lying on the deck is more likely to be a loafing look-alike named Brandy. The cats aren't exact doubles, though, so the camera never cuts straight from one to the other.

Tyler walks on a leash as obediently as any dog, and he walks on his hind legs almost as gracefully as he walks on four. He also responds to commands to push things with his feet, rub against people or objects, and bang happily away on a piano.

Unlike dogs, who work to please their masters, cats will only work for food. Tyler's trainer taught him to stand upright, for example, by holding food over his head while giving the command "high." When Tyler stood as tall as he could, he got his reward—and once he understood that, the rest, as they say, was history.

voice. "A low pitch means serious business because it's similar to the sound of a mother's growl," says Dr. Howl. You don't want to give high-pitched sounds. To a dog that's like yapping—it may be annoying, but it's not something to be taken seriously.

Make mouse sounds for cats. Unlike dogs, cats don't even notice low-pitched commands. They do notice commands that are given in a high voice, maybe with a little bit of a "sss" preceding them. The "s" sound gets their attention, and the high tone sounds similar to the pitches that rodents make—and no cat is going to ignore that.

Speak in a normal voice. Dogs and cats aren't recruits, and you're not a drill sergeant. You don't have to bark commands, but you don't want to speak softly either. Speaking in your normal voice or a little louder will get their attention right away and let them know that you're serious about what you're saying.

Coax them with your eyes. "Making eye contact is important when you're giving commands to dogs or cats," says Dr. Howl. "Some people think it works kind of like a 'mind meld' because of the connection you form with your pets. In addition, to dogs, looking them in the eye is both a challenge and a command—it lets them know you're higher in rank and need to be obeyed."

You don't want to stare at dogs you don't know or those who are acting aggressively, she adds. It won't make them want to obey; it will make them mad. But it's fine to make eye contact with cats at any time.

Give yourself big posture. Dogs are very conscious of size because in their world, bigger dogs tend to be the leaders. You can get them to view you the same way by standing up straight when giving commands, says Dr. Howl. "Dogs and cats read our entire way of speaking, not just the words," she says. "For dogs, you want to stand tall and act like you're an authority figure."

Shrink for cats. Bigger is better for dogs, but for cats, bending slightly at the knees and making yourself look smaller makes commands much more effective. "Cats are very small compared to us," Dr. Howl says. "You don't want to appear threatening, just sincere. If you stand up tall, they may get the message 'I'm in trouble,' and they may take off."

CHAPTER 28

10 Step-by-Step Training Lessons for Dogs

Imagine for a moment that you've just walked into an imposing office building for a job interview. Before you meet with the boss, you're given a form to fill out. On the line that says "Education," you write "3 weeks."

Five minutes later, you're back on the street—jobless, needless to say.

The truth is that human beings, with all their enormous brainpower, would have a very difficult time getting by if their educations added up to only 3 weeks. Yet that's about how much training dogs get. They may attend puppy school a few nights a week or spend a few hours practicing sits and stays in the backyard. Some even learn a few tricks. But most of the time, it doesn't go any further. And their owners can't seem to figure out why they run out the door without waiting for permission or tug on the leash as though it's a perpetual invitation to play tug-of-war. It's not that dogs don't want to please, they just don't know any better.

Quite a few people are convinced that dogs don't need education. But they do. Learning new things gives them stimulation, confidence, purpose, and satisfaction. They don't necessarily need months or years of training. But giving them the opportunity to learn a few basic skills is good for everyone, dogs and people alike, says Robin Kovary, director of the American Dog Trainers Network in New York City.

Skills give them freedom. Dogs who haven't learned basic etiquette tend to spend a lot of time alone because people, to put it bluntly, can't stand to have them around. Those who have gone through basic training, however, get the run of the house since they don't bark or jump on guests. They enjoy being allowed to hang around with their people. Their less educated friends, on the other hand, often get banished to a bedroom, says Kovary.

Skills broaden their horizons. Dogs who haven't been leash-trained won't hesitate to dislocate your shoulder should they see something exciting across the street—and walks aren't a lot of fun when you spend the whole time struggling to contain 40 pounds of unruly excitement. More than a few dogs spend their days looking longingly at the leash, hoping they'll get more than the usual "do your business" kind of walk. Those who heel nicely, or at least refrain from lunging, get more opportunities to explore because their owners enjoy taking them.

Skills make everyone happier. If there's one thing all dogs crave, it's time with their people. From their perspective, nothing beats leaning against your leg while you watch a movie or hopping in the car to go somewhere fun. Well-mannered dogs get a lot of opportunities to bond because they're very easy to be around. Their less mannerly friends, on the other hand, often feel lonely because people don't spend a lot of time with them.

Dogs don't have to be Lassie to learn the basics. They don't even have to go to obedience school, although they'll learn a little faster when they're getting professional attention. Most of the things dogs really need to know are easy to teach at home, Kovary says. It takes a little bit of time at first, and a box or two of treats. But once they've learned a few lessons, everything else comes much more quickly.

DEAD

Every dog should know how to play dead on occasion. For one thing, it's a great party trick. You can ask your dog, "Would you rather vote for Joe Blow or be dead?"—and everyone will laugh when she flops over. More pragmatically, it's easier to brush dogs when they obediently lie on their sides.

Dogs who already know how to lie down won't have any trouble learning this trick.

1. Let your dog see a treat in your hand, then tell her to lie down.
2. As soon as she's down, tell her, "Dead." At the same time, hold the treat near the ground and slide it a few inches beyond

her head. As she follows the treat with her eyes, she'll automatically roll onto her side and put her head on the ground. She'll raise her head when you praise her—and that's when she gets the treat.

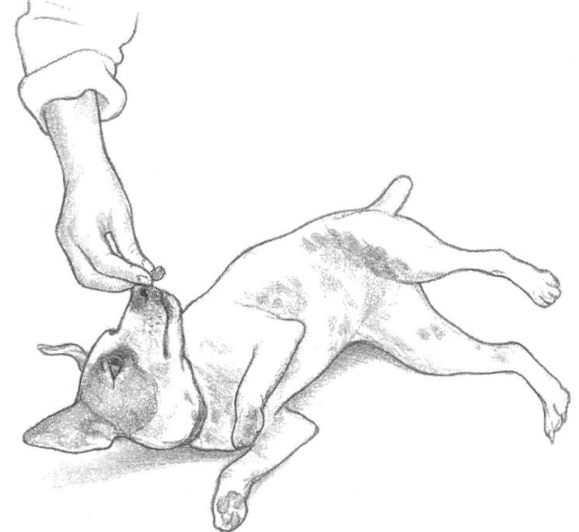

When dogs move their eyes to follow a treat, their bodies will naturally roll the same way.

SIT

This is probably the most important lesson that dogs learn. Dogs who are told to sit understand intuitively that it's time to be respectful and listen for instructions. Sitting gives them a chance to calm down when they're being hyper. And it's the easiest command to teach. Most dogs will learn to sit in just a few lessons.

1. Stand in front of your dog. Presumably, she'll be standing, too. Hold a treat a few inches in front of her face. At this point, you'll have her full attention.
2. Say, "Sit," and simultaneously move the treat upward over her head. She's not going to take her eyes off that treat. As her head goes up, her back end will automatically go down. As soon as it touches ground, tell her, "Good dog!" and give her the treat.

DOWN

The second pillar of good training is the "down" command. It's not as easy to teach as "sit," which is surprising in a way because dogs will lie down in a heartbeat. But folding up all their legs and quelling their energy long enough to lie down requires quite a bit of concentration. You might not see great results for a week or two, but it's worth teaching. For one thing, dogs are more comfortable lying down than sitting up, and you can use this command to give them a break during walks. It's also great for dealing with behavior problems such as barking, says Brian Kilcommons, a pet-behavior specialist in Gardiner, New York, and coauthor of *Good Owners, Great Dogs*. "Most dogs find it difficult to bark when they're lying down," he says.

1. While your dog is sitting and facing you, hold a treat a few inches in front of her face.

2. Tell her, "Down," and simultaneously lower the treat toward the ground, then outward a few inches, so it's not quite under her muzzle. Once again, her eyes are going to be locked on the treat. As she leans forward to get it, she'll automatically land in a "down" position.

When you lower a treat toward the ground, your dog's body will follow.

TAKE IT NICE

Dogs who are eager for a piece of food or a soggy tennis ball will sometimes forget that there are human fingers at the other end. To make sure that your fingers and your dog's teeth don't occupy the same space at the same time, you'll need to teach her to "take it nice."

1. While your dog is sitting and facing you, offer her a treat and say, "Nice" or "Take it nice." Your voice should be emphatic, not angry, but make it obvious that you mean business.

2. At first, most dogs will try to grab the treat. When that happens, pull your hand out of reach, then offer it again. After a few

lunges, your dog will learn that she isn't going to get anything unless she moves more carefully. When she gently reaches out to take the treat, hand it over and give her some praise.

STAY

This is among the hardest commands to teach because most dogs would rather run around than be still, especially when they're young. In addition, teaching "stay" requires that dogs be in one place and the humans some distance off—and dogs tend to get distracted and wander off to sniff some bushes. The trick to teaching "stay" is to remain as close to your dog as possible while she's learning. After a while, you'll be able to move farther and farther away.

1. It's best to teach the "stay" command when dogs are sitting on grass, dirt, or a carpet. "Don't try to teach it on a slippery floor," Kilcommons says, since dogs' feet can easily slide out from under them.
2. Whether your dog is sitting or lying down, put your palm a few inches in front of her face and say, "Stay." Trainers usually recommend saying the dog's name before giving a command. This doesn't work, however, when you're teaching "stay," Kilcommons says. Hearing their names gets them excited and makes it hard for them to hold still.
3. After giving the command, move backward a step, then quickly come close before your dog has time to move. Then give her a reward. Each day you practice, you'll be able to move farther apart, Kilcommons says.

OUT

This command is short for "out of your mouth." When you consider the types of things that dogs pick up, chew on, and swallow—some of which, like chocolate, are quite dangerous—it's obvious that this is a command they should know well, says Deborah Manheim, a trainer in Brooklyn, New York.

1. Give your dog a toy, something that she likes and will gladly put in her mouth.
2. Once she's got hold of it, show her a treat and hold it under her nose. Dogs like toys, but they like food better. Most will

NAME: Jessie

OCCUPATION: Cheetah Liaison

Most golden retrievers live with human families, but Jessie has a wilder calling. Ever since she was a puppy, the 7-year-old dog has worked at the world-famous San Diego Zoo as a chaperone for the zoo's best-known ambassador, a cheetah named Chobe.

Chobe often travels on business, visiting television stations and attending educational events and fund-raising parties. He gets rattled when he's around bright lights and strange noises—and those who spend time with a cat as big and as fast as a cheetah know that being rattled can be a real problem.

Jessie provides stress relief. She accompanies Chobe whenever he leaves the zoo, and her placid acceptance of lights, cameras, and action help him be calm, too.

"Chobe really needs Jessie," says Kathy Marmack, animal training supervisor at the zoo. "He chirps for her when she isn't around. And he's started to butt her with his head, which for cheetahs is a sign of affection. She slurps him back."

Jessie has shown so much talent and affection that trainers at the zoo have begun introducing her to other animals, among them leopards, tigers, a kinkajou, a badger, and a reindeer. "Jessie has an incredible way with all animals," Marmack says. "She's so incredibly gentle and good. I've never seen a dog like her."

gladly make the swap. As soon as she opens her mouth to drop the toy, say, "Out," and give her the treat. Practice several times a day until she'll drop the toy on command even when you don't have a treat.

Given a choice between food and something that happens to be in their mouths, dogs will happily take the food.

COME

As with the "stay" command, "come" is a tough one to teach. Dogs who are out of reach may pretend they don't hear anything. Even when they understand the command, they're often reluctant to quit what they're doing. You'll have to keep your dog under control and within reach when you first start teaching "come."

1. Have your dog sit and stay at one end of the room while you walk to the other. If your dog hasn't learned how to stay yet, you'll need to ask someone to hold her and keep her from running over.

2. Put a lot of enthusiasm in your voice and say your dog's name, followed by "Come!" As long as you sound happy and eager, your dog is going to come barreling over. It also helps to squat low and hold your arms open. Dogs understand that this is human body language for "c'mon over." Praise the heck out of her when she arrives.

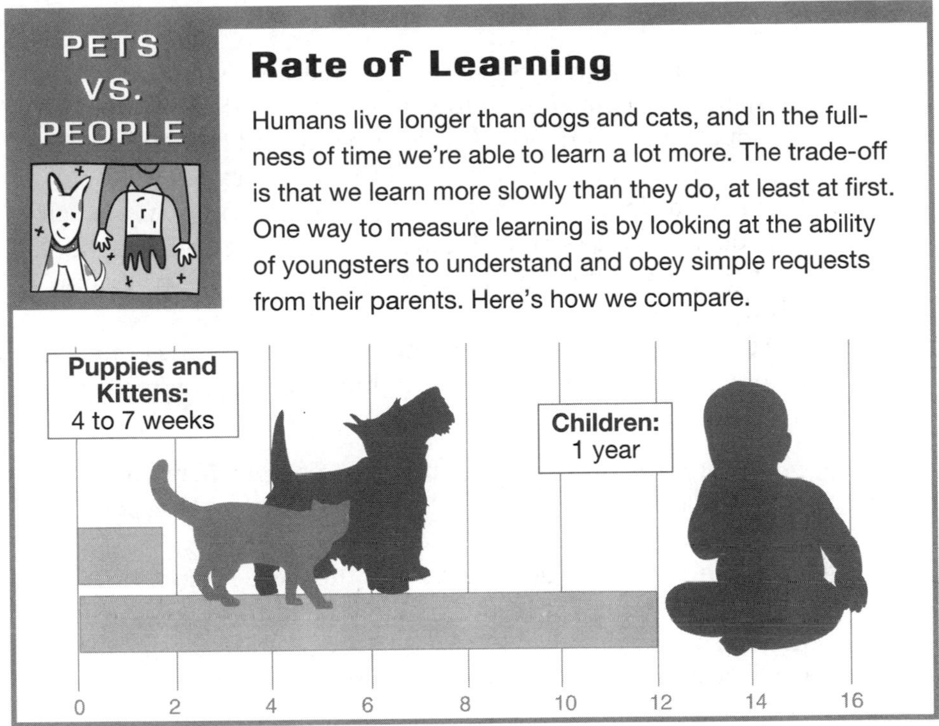

3. Once your dog has mastered this command in the living room, increase the challenge by doing it from across the yard. Once she's doing that reliably, take her to a park and practice there.

Since dogs love people and nearly always want to be with them, they'll usually come right away when they're called—unless they have a reason to think twice. People tend to yell "Come!" when their dogs have done something wrong. This is a mistake because dogs remember the situation and thereafter will always wonder what your motives are.

Here are two rules that trainers recommend: Call your dog to you only when you're happy, and go to her when you're giving discipline. Even when you're merely ending something fun—by snapping on the leash after a run, for example—it's best that you do the approaching. This way, she'll understand that "come" always means something good is about to happen, and she'll be eager to respond quickly.

GO TO YOUR PLACE

If you value your personal space, you'll want your dog to understand the command "go to your place." It's the equivalent of "get out from underfoot." The idea isn't to send her to her room to be alone. It's just to give yourself (or your guests) a little more room. Your dog may have a favorite place already, or you can pick one. Regardless of the location, it should be within sight of the family, so your dog will understand that she isn't being punished.

Your dog will have to know how to lie down on command before she can learn this trick, but otherwise it's easy to teach.

1. Use a dog biscuit to lure her to the place where you want her to go. Encourage her to lie down, point to the place, and say, "Down, place."
2. When she lies down, give her the treat. Combining the command ("place") with the gesture (pointing) reinforces the lesson, so most dogs will learn it quickly. Within a week or two, you'll be able to just say, "Go to your place" or "Place," and your dog will walk over and lie down.

QUIET

If your dog barks more than you'd like, well, welcome to the club. All dogs bark. Some do it a little, and some do it all the time. "For dogs, barking is like breathing," says Deborah Loven Gray of Washington, D.C., author of *Your Dog's Life*. You can't expect them to stay totally silent. On the other hand, you don't have to put up with a lot of woofing.

Gray recommends letting dogs bark once or twice to get it out of their system. After that, they need to be told, "Quiet."

1. Do whatever it takes to get your dog barking. Acting excited might do it. Or having someone ring the doorbell. Or jumping up and down a few times.
2. After she's barked a few times, give her a treat and say, "Quiet." Dogs who are eating aren't barking. It won't take her long to link the command with the anticipation of food, and the very thought of food will keep her quiet.

Get Your Toy

There are several reasons that dogs should know how to get their favorite toys on command. It lets them know when you're in the mood to play. It gives them a chance to run around while they figure out where the heck they left their toys. And it saves you from having to get down on all fours and scrounge under the couch.

1. Toss one of your dog's favorite toys a few feet in front of her. Tell her, "Get your toy," and act excited until she picks it up.
2. Once the toy's in her mouth, crouch down, open your arms wide, and say, "Get your toy!" Praise her well when she brings it over, and let her play with it for a while. Then do the whole thing again a few times.

CHAPTER 29

Four Step-by-Step Training Lessons for Cats

Every state has laws regulating the training of dogs. In Connecticut, for example, you may need both a hunting license and a training permit before teaching dogs to hunt. In none of the 50 states, however, will you find a law regulating the training of cats. This is probably because legislators, like most folks, don't consider cats trainable to begin with.

It's not the people's fault. Cats themselves foster the impression that training is a "dog thing" that has nothing to do with them. Their usual response to commands is to turn around and lick their tails or to slowly blink their eyes as though to signal their profound indifference to anything their people ask.

But this is largely an act. Like a tattooed biker dressed in chains and leather, a cat's indifferent or even hostile exterior is just a mask for a soft heart and sharp mind. Cats have a deep—if secret—desire to please. But they're also independent-minded creatures for whom dignity is more important than giving pleasure. So they'll never learn as readily, or at least as eagerly, as dogs. Still, most cats do enjoy making their people happy, and if sitting on command is what you want, they'll be willing to give it a try, says Karen Payne, a cat trainer in Miami.

One reason it's fun to teach cats simple tricks is the amazed attention you'll get from the people who watch you. Cats who actually obey commands are about as rare as bikers who do needlepoint. It happens, but it's rare enough to turn heads.

FLATTER FIRST, TEACH SECOND

Dogs crave people's attention. Cats like it but don't depend on it. So you can't expect cats to learn things just to please you. "Think of cats as self-fulfilled actresses," says Kay Cox, a pet counselor in Gilbert, Arizona. "They work to please themselves. So forget about commanding a cat. You must *request* that they work with you. When they respond, reward them with petting and treats."

The trick to training cats is to practice the three Rs—request, response, and reward. Here's how they work.

Request. You can bark orders at dogs, but you need to purr them to cats, says Cox. "Stroke her ego and ask nicely," she says. Use a happy voice and mingle in some praise. "You're so smart, Kitty, can you sit?" works better than "Sit!"

When giving cats commands, however, you need to say the command word—in this case, "sit,"—more crisply than the singsong praise words. The extra emphasis will help your cat connect her actions to the command.

Response. When your cat makes a move to honor your request, it is called a response. It may not be the complete trick, just a move in that direction. The first time you ask your cat to sit, for example, the response is any lowering of her rear toward the ground. Later, when she has a better idea of what you're after, the response will be a full folded-haunch sit that lasts for several seconds or longer.

Reward. Cats are sensitive creatures who demand praise. If you expect your cat to respond to you, you'll have to recognize her response right away. This is called the reward. Simple praise is a powerful reward for most cats. "They love to be told they are brilliant and beautiful, and that you are in awe of their intelligence," says Cox. Giving them food never hurts either.

SIT—TECHNIQUE #1

Most dogs learn to sit by the time they are 3 months old, but most cats never do learn this simplest of skills. That's unfortunate

NAME: Princess Kitty

OCCUPATION: Actor

When Karen Payne heard a thump outside the patio door of her Miami home, she had no idea that she was about to meet the smartest cat in the world—or that the Siamese mix, whom she named Princess Kitty, was about to launch her on a new career as a professional trainer.

As Karen soon discovered, Princess Kitty loved doing tricks. "Sit" and "stay" were merely warmups. She quickly learned to roll over, fetch, and play dead. She did card tricks and was sufficiently talented that the Magician's Local union invited her to be a member. And she played a passable version of "Three Blind Mice" on the piano.

With so many natural talents, it was inevitable that Princess Kitty would end up in show business. She appeared on television and in films and commercials. She got a few modeling assignments and made countless personal appearances. "She was a working cat," Karen says. "And she was the consummate professional."

When Princess Kitty was shooting a commercial for the Florida Lottery's Fish-Finder game, for example, she had to act as though she were scratching off a winning ticket. She cheerfully repeated the scene more than 90 times before the director was satisfied.

The highlight of her career was working with children. "We visited more than 20,000 kids in hospitals and schools," Karen says. Princess did her tricks, of course, but she also cuddled. She was so popular that Karen started a fan club, which attracted letters from children around the world.

because cats who sit on command never fail to impress the neighbors. Here's how to do it.

1. Put your cat on a stool, preferably one with a small seat. This gives her less room to roam and makes it more difficult for her to simply take off.

2. Give a series of gentle pushes on her rear end while saying, "Sit." If she doesn't fold her haunches quickly, move in a little closer. As she shifts her body to look up at you, her rear will automatically lower. The moment her tush touches the seat, tell her how awesome she is, Cox says.

Sit—Technique #2

Some cats get distracted when people touch them. It may be easier to teach them to sit by using treats.

1. Pick up a small morsel that you know your cat loves—cheese is always a good choice. Hold it between your thumb and forefinger and make sure your cat sees it.

2. Move the food slowly toward her nose, then pass it between her ears and let it hover behind her head. Tell your cat, "Sit." Her eyes will be fixed on the food, and when she tilts her head back, she'll drop her rear. That's when you give her the food.

Come to Mama

If you've ever opened a can of cat food only to discover that your cat has magically materialized at your ankles, you'll understand how easy it is to teach cats to come. All you have to do is take control of their natural instincts.

1. Get your cat's attention, then show her a treat you're holding in your hand, Cox says. While her eyes are fixed on the food, pat your chest with the same hand. The result is a silent command and a fast, energetic response.

2. When your cat comes running, capitalize on her success by stroking her ego. "Give your cat a big reward," Cox says.

Freeze!

This isn't a showy trick, but you'll find it's useful the next time your cat takes advantage of an open door and flies out—and you're able to stop her cold with one simple word.

1. Cats interpret certain sounds as meaning "danger," and their response is to stop in order to size things up. "If you hiss sharply, most cats will freeze immediately," says Payne. "For some a soft 'shh-shh' works better. Others respond to a whistle." Practice one or more of these sounds, varying the pitch each time, until you find the one that causes your cat to plant herself firmly and look straight at you.

2. Since a cat's natural instinct is to flee after freezing, you'll have to teach her that approach is better than retreat. As always, food is a very strong reward. When your cat freezes, quickly reward her with food as well as praise. She'll learn that "shh-shh" is her cue to stop and come forward—and eat.

WAVE BYE-BYE

Cats have a natural desire to grab moving objects. You can take advantage of this instinct and teach them to wave. "I use a peacock feather for this trick," says Cox. "It's pretty and fun, and cats can't resist slapping at it."

1. Waggle the feather in front of your cat to get her attention. Tease her into raising her paw by sweeping the feather slowly

Cats are crazy for anything that moves and will "wave" at a feather. If you say the word *wave* and give them food when they do it, they'll learn to wave on command.

up from the ground to above her head. Your cat will quite naturally follow the feather with her eyes, sit down as it passes over her head, then reach up to touch it as it dangles above her. Once she reaches out for the feather, pull it away and give her lots of praise.

2. When your cat is reliably reaching up, start moving the feather up and down an inch or two above her head, saying, "Bye-bye" at the same time. Your cat will follow the feather with her paw, making it look as though she's truly waving. "You can usually lose the feather after 3 or 4 days," says Cox. Use your hand to make the same gesture. With a little practice, you'll be able to wave from across the room, and your cat will wave right back.

CHAPTER 30

Fun and Games

Pets like to play. No, they *love* to play—and not only because chasing a stick or wrestling with string is the equivalent of a canine or kitty coffee break. Dogs and cats play when they want to blow off steam. They play to improve their balance and coordination and sharpen their hunting skills. And they play because it's fun.

Cats have always been frolicsome, largely because their skill as hunters depended on it. Birds, mice, and other prey have sharp hearing and quick reflexes. Catching them isn't easy. A cat in the wild who tried to hunt without taking a few practice runs was likely to go to bed without supper. Play got them ready. The stalking, pouncing, and paw patting that kittens and older cats indulge in is the equivalent of Michael Jordan practicing free throws. It gives them a chance to hone their eye-paw coordination and to discover which moves work and which don't.

Cats today aren't thinking about hunting when they tumble across the carpet. They rarely see a mouse, much less catch one. But the instinct to hunt is very much with them, and the games they like best, like stalking human toes that poke under the bed, look an awful lot like hunting.

Dogs in the wild didn't play very much once they'd outgrown their gamboling puppyhoods. Today, however, they play all the time—not just when they're puppies, but throughout their lives. The reason for this is that they've been bred for thousands of years to be compliant and dependent on people. Put another way, they've been bred to act puppyish, a process called neoteny, says Rolan Tripp, D.V.M., affiliate professor of applied animal behavior at Colorado State University Veterinary School in Fort Collins and author of *Pet Perception Management*.

Unlike cats, who lived solitary lives, dogs have always lived with other dogs or, more recently, with their human "packs." So they're not very good at amusing themselves when someone's not around to play with them. And although they hunted for food,

Toys Pets Love

We give children colored blocks and alphabet magnets. Pets deserve some special toys as well. Here are a few you may want to try.

For Dogs

Bite a Bone. This is a hard nylon bone with a ¼-inch channel on top. You can smear peanut butter or cheese into the groove. Dogs will happily lick, chew, and work it over for hours.

Soft Bite Floppy Disc or Nylabone Gumabone Frisbee. They fly like Frisbees, but the soft material won't hurt your dog's mouth or gums.

Kong. This is a bouncy, sturdy rubber chew toy with a small hole that can be packed with food. Dogs have to work to get the food out, which keeps them busy. And the rubber is durable, so it can withstand a lot of jaw work.

For Cats

Crazy Circle. A small ball rolls inside a plastic track. The ball can't fall out, but it moves easily, and cats love batting it around.

Cat Dancer. This consists of an enticing toy that dangles at the end of a springy length of wire. The bouncing action gets cats' attention, and they enjoy the thrill of the hunt.

they didn't depend on stealth or lightning reflexes as much as on sheer speed and endurance. Play for them isn't so much surrogate hunting as it is for cats. Mainly it's about showing affection and feeling close to their people. And it's a great way to burn off energy after a day spent sleeping on the couch.

THE POWER OF THREE

Pet toys are big business. Walk into any pet supply store, and you'll discover hundreds of toys: brightly colored toys, toys with squeakers, beef- and pork-flavored toys, even toys you fill with food. With so many choices for entertainment, dogs should be living in play heaven. But mostly they don't even notice. Given a choice between a $15 dog toy and your leather sandals, most dogs will reach for the sandals.

Dogs aren't very discriminating, explains Karen Wilson, a trainer in Christiana, Tennessee. When they're lavished with toys, they begin to think that everything must be fair game. "Dogs don't need any more than three toys," she says. "Otherwise, the whole world becomes their game."

Once dogs move beyond puppyhood and become adults, they begin to figure out which things belong to them and which don't. But when they have too many choices, it's harder for them to tell the difference—especially when their toys include things like little plastic shoes, which, as far as dogs are concerned, look very similar to a $100 pair of Guccis. That's why you should buy toys that don't have the slightest resemblance to your own possessions, says Marty Becker, D.V.M., a veterinarian in Bonners Ferry, Idaho, and coauthor of *Chicken Soup for the Pet Lover's Soul*.

Play Hard, Play Safe

As few as 15 years ago, most pets didn't have a lot of toys because the pet-supply business hadn't yet become a megadollar industry. Dogs and cats were hardly deprived, of course. Just as 6-year-olds can spend hours playing with "spaceships" that look a lot like empty cereal boxes, dogs are perfectly happy chasing tennis balls, chewing sticks, or wrestling with their people on the carpet. Cats are even easier to entertain. A piece of string or a bottle cap on the floor can keep them busy for hours. As long as games are physical and, in the case of dogs, give them a chance to interact with others, they'll keep at them until they collapse with a tired thump in the corner.

Cats play only for their own amusement and quit when they're ready. Dogs, however, are always following the leader. They're so intent on pleasing their people, they'll keep running, jumping, or wrestling even when they're exhausted. Intensely physical games are good as long as you don't let your dog play herself into pain.

To ensure that games are fun as well as safe for dogs and cats, here are a few tips that you may want to try.

Make sure they get traction. For dogs, playing on a hardwood or tile floor is like spinning around a parking lot after a snowstorm. They take off at full speed, then lock their brakes and go skidding the rest of the way. They think it's fun to slip and slide, says Dr. Tripp. Dogs rarely get hurt on slick surfaces, but it can happen, especially when they're older and their joints aren't limber enough to take the stress. Playing on carpet or outside on grass or dirt is a little safer and less risky—not only for dogs but for breakable possessions as well.

Throw low. Most dogs like to chase things. They also like to

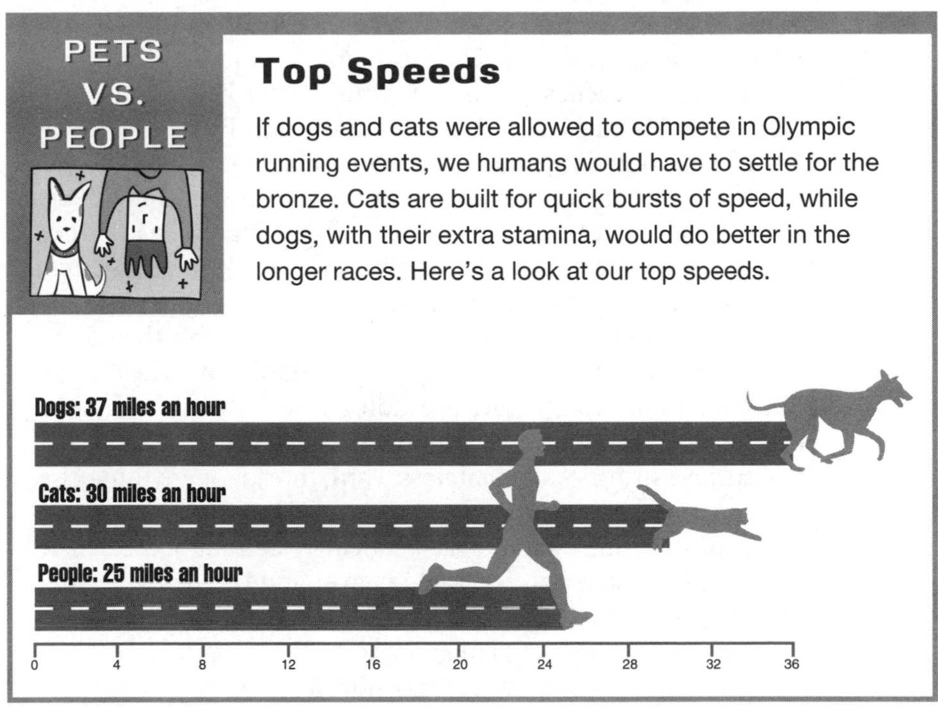

catch things. Without hands, they use their mouths, which is fine when they're catching a tennis ball. It's not so fine when a hardball descends after a long throw or when a stick comes down sharp end first. Throwing things low to the ground gives dogs the thrill of the chase without the risk of catching something they'll later wish they hadn't.

Buy for the breed. Just as dogs have different predilections and talents depending on their breed, they also have different tastes in toys. The retrievers, for example, have been bred to put things in their mouths. They love toys they can mouth and carry around. Terriers, on the other hand, were bred to hunt small game, which is why rodentlike squeaker toys tend to get them going. The people at pet supply stores can tell you which toys work best for different breeds.

Get them in shape for play. Dogs and cats are built for motion, and they can twist and run a heck of a lot better than we can. But pets do get out of shape when they haven't been active. Going airborne with a half-gainer to snag a sailing Frisbee is going to leave your dog with a limp or even a bad back if you don't work up to it first.

Apart from doing the obvious, like using walks to get your dog in shape before starting vigorous athletics, you'll generally want to avoid any game that requires jumping, says Linda Flaherty, a trainer who teaches at Lloyd Animal Medical Center in Stoughton, Massachusetts. If you're throwing a Frisbee, throw it low so your dog doesn't jump to get it. Throw balls so they roll straight, rather than careening off at an angle. Dogs aren't likely to hurt themselves when they're running straight ahead. Once their muscles are warmed up and they're back in shape, just about any game becomes fair game.

Pick up the string. Cats are generally more sensible than dogs. They play when they want and quit when they want. They're less likely than dogs to get hurt overdoing it. But there's one game that injures cats every year: playing with string.

Cats love string—or dental floss, yarn, thread, or anything else that resembles a long, whippy mouse tail. Their favorite game is pouncing on string that's dragged enticingly in front of them. The dangerous part is when the game is over and the string lies defenseless on the floor. Their thinking seems to be, "You've gotten away long enough—now I'm going to swallow you whole."

It's hard to imagine anything more innocuous than a few inches of string, but every year veterinarians treat cats with internal injuries caused by string wrapping around their insides. Playing with string is fine, Dr. Tripp says, as long as you pick it up when the game's done. In addition, remember to close sewing kits and keep balls of yarn out of sight and out of reach. Cats will play even when they're alone, and what they play with, they'll sometimes swallow.

ROUGH AND TUMBLE

Dogs are intensely physical. They lean into each other, put their paws on each other's shoulders, and generally make a lot of physical contact. And they do the same things with people. Their love of contact sports isn't a bad thing. It makes them feel close and connected to the people they love best. But there's also an edge of competitiveness, and sometimes a game turns into something more.

It's not something they consciously think about, but dogs define all of their relationships in terms in power. In multidog families, the various dogs quickly sort themselves into a social hierarchy, with "top dogs" having the most power and "bottom dogs" having the least. Ever since dogs started living with people, people have generally been the ones in charge, and dogs accept this. But some games are competitive. There's going to be a winner and a loser, and dogs like to win. But winning, in their mind, sometimes changes the way they think about their people. "There has to be a leader in dog-human relationships," Flaherty says. "If you don't take that position, the dog sees that job as vacant and will take it."

Tug-of-war, for example, is a great game. Dogs love pulling on things and pitting their strength against an opponent. But it's not a good choice of entertainment for every dog. A dog who's assertive in other ways is going to take tug-of-war very seriously. She's going to want to win. And whether she wins or loses, she's still going to see herself as competing with you—and no one wants to find themselves at one end of a rope with an assertive Rottweiler at the other end.

Actually, the size of the breed isn't important. Some big dogs are pussycats, and toy dogs can be little Caesars. The real issue is the temperament of the breed. Poodles have been bred to be compliant, so they're less likely to see tug-of-war as a serious conflict. Chihuahuas, on the other hand, can be quite assertive. You may find yourself holding one end of the rope as your pint-size competitor chews her way up the other.

Regardless of the games you play, dogs need to understand that you're playing for fun and not as serious competition. More important, they need to understand that games, no matter who "wins," aren't symbolic of relationships in the family.

Stay in the lead. Running games are a lot of fun, and most dogs enjoy chasing people. That's fine. Just don't change direction and start chasing your dog, Flaherty says. Once dogs get it into their heads that having people hot on their heels is a great game, they'll look for ways to make it happen. Like grabbing your shoes and taking off. As long as they think it's all in fun, they'll keep running, periodically looking over their shoulders to make sure that you're still close behind. "You'll look like a fool chasing your dog all over," Flaherty says.

Play on people-time. Dogs don't want to wait for their people to decide when it's time to play. So they give reminders—like bumping your hand with a slobbery ball or standing 6 inches away and staring until you notice. You want to be approachable, and it's fun when dogs tell us so plainly what they want. But playing with them every time they ask makes them assume that they have a certain amount of power, says Dr. Tripp. At the very least, your dog will get spoiled. Dogs with more assertive temperaments may get pushy.

Go ahead and play when your dog asks—but first, make her think that the whole thing was your idea, Flaherty recommends. When she approaches, have her sit and stay for a moment. Make it clear that she's doing some work for you. Wait a few seconds, then go ahead and throw the ball or pull the rope or run around. The game is now your brilliant idea, and your dog is reminded that you're the one in charge.

Insist on the "no-teeth" rule. Canine teeth and human skin occasionally occupy the same space at the same time. Dogs use their mouths as we use our hands. And when they play, those teeth can make contact—either accidentally or because they're playing with people the same way they play with dogs. It's one thing when dogs use their playful teeth on each other. It's not fine when they do it with people, Dr. Tripp says. Even when your dog nips by accident, he recommends acting very disgusted, ending the game, and walking away. Your dog wants more than anything to have your attention. Taking that away sends a strong signal that teeth aren't a part of the games you're willing to play.

Stand in the winner's circle. Parents often let their children win when they're playing games. Children—and adults—need to win occasionally to stay engaged and to keep their confidence up. But dogs put a lot of stock in who wins and who loses because it's one way they have of knowing who fits where in the social scheme. Winning games against their people may encourage them to rethink their place in the family—and this is when problems with aggression usually begin.

If your dog is trying to pull something away from you, for example, don't let her turn it into a strength game. Instead, simply get out the doggy treats and offer her one. As she drops whatever it was she was pulling, praise her and give her the treat, says Liz Palika, a trainer in Oceanside, California.

CHAPTER 31

You're in Charge

When everything is said and done, there's only one universal truth about cats and dogs:

They like you. They really, *really* like you.

Take a quick peek in the mirror. From your pet's point of view, you are the cat's meow. The dog's whiskers. The ever-loving bringer of food, toys, and treats.

It's enough to give a human a big head. Yet there's a flip side to all this unabashed affection. It's responsibility. Put simply, if you don't do something for your pet, it's not going to get done. From guiding behavior to filling food bowls, the burden is on you to make sure that your pet has a happy and healthy life.

"Pets look to you for many things," says Madeline Gabriel, owner of Enjoy Your Dog training school in San Diego. "They may want your company. They may want your leadership. They may just want your attention. Whatever it is, you have to figure out how to give it to them and keep the relationship going strong."

Pets are pretty forgiving creatures, which is good since there is much trial and error in the animal-human bonding business. But once you figure out how to set the tone and act like the leader that your pet wants you to be, you'll reap the benefits for years to come.

Cats and dogs both have four legs, two eyes, and fur that sticks to every surface known to man. But that's pretty much where the similarities between them end, especially when it comes to building a good relationship with people. Each craves your attention and affection, and each expects it to be delivered in very different ways.

What Dogs Want

There's an old saying about sled dogs in Alaska: "If you're not the lead dog, the scenery never changes." The implication is that followers have a pretty humble life. From a dog's perspective, however, there's no shame in being number six in line, looking at the tail of the dog in front of you day after day. "Dogs want order and stability more than anything else," says Gabriel. "They want to know where they fit into the world."

Dogs are pack animals, meaning that all of their instincts tell them that it's best to be part of a family—either a family of dogs or of people. In wild packs, where dogs live together, there's always a leader, called the alpha dog. This is the one who runs the show. No one questions his dominance. What he says goes.

In the civilized world, however, this leader goes by a different name: you. Dogs understand that the people in their lives run the show. People, on the other hand, aren't accustomed to being "alpha." There's a sense that leadership involves a lot of heavy-handed sternness. But it doesn't. It means being active and in control. It means setting reasonable rules and expectations and keeping to them so that dogs know what's expected. It means solving problems when they occur. It means praising good behavior and properly correcting bad behavior. It means meeting the needs of everyone in the pack so that balance and order—what dogs want most—is always maintained.

Trainers often say that there's no such thing as bad dogs because dogs always follow their leaders. Any behavior problems that may occur are ultimately caused by a breakdown of leadership, says Andy Bunn, a trainer in Charlotte, North Carolina. Somewhere along the line, the alpha leader has failed to meet a need—like giving a dog the opportunity to relieve himself outside or giving him the proper things to chew on or providing enough exercise so that he isn't tearing around the house with nervous energy.

WHAT CATS WANT

Unlike dogs, cats aren't the least bit interested in all this follow-the-leader stuff. They're solitary carnivores by nature and have a very different mindset than their pack-hunting peers. Alpha leadership works great for dogs. It can be a disaster when it's applied to cats.

"If you treat cats like dogs, you'll only frighten them," says Betsy Lipscomb, a cat-behavior consultant and president of the Wisconsin Cat Club in Milwaukee.

Different Dogs, Different Expectations

Cats are very similar in the ways in which they interact with people—and in the types of mischief they get into. Dogs, however, have tremendous variability because they've been bred to have different personalities. When you're deciding what types of rules to enforce and what to expect, you need to take your dog's breed into account.

- Tracking dogs such as beagles and Labrador retrievers have an incredible sense of smell, which means they're going to insist on putting their noses just about everywhere. It's hard for them to go for walks without stopping for sniff breaks.
- Hounds tend to be barkers because that was their way of calling their masters during hunts. Herding dogs such as Shetland sheepdogs are also pretty vocal. They barked to control their flocks, and from their point of view, the people in their lives are part of their flocks.
- Greyhounds and whippets are called sighthounds because they were bred to hunt by sight rather than scent. They're very alert to movement and have strong instincts to chase, which is why when you encounter cats, you'll want to tighten the leash.

Cats don't respond to authoritative leadership. Giving orders to cats and insisting that they follow them will only leave them feeling afraid, unaffectionate, and even hostile.

What cats do want is predictability. *They* want the freedom to come and go as they please, sleep where they want, or eat like a horse at one meal and pick at their food the next. They don't want humans to have the same freedom. They're most comfortable when everything happens on a predictable schedule and in the same ways. Moving the furniture around may be exciting for people, but cats hate it. When their routines are disrupted, they get nervous, which is about when they decide to retire to the back of a closet for 2 days.

SHOWING THE WAY

We've all encountered dogs or cats who are totally out of control. The signs are everywhere: scratched-up furniture, soiled carpets, mauled shoes, upside-down food dishes, and, somewhere off in the corner, a disgruntled human muttering something about "that darned cat" or "that &g$% dog."

"Most of the time, problems with behavior occur when owners just don't know how to take charge," Gabriel says. "Almost without exception, it's possible to have an active, happy pet who doesn't wreck the house or act like he owns the place."

Until dogs and cats learn how to sign leases and move into their own apartments, it's perfectly reasonable to expect them to conform to our wishes. Ultimately, that's what they want, too. But it's not going to happen without guidance, gentle prodding, and a little ingenuity.

Look at everything. Dogs and cats don't have the objectivity or human understanding to look at the big picture of their lives. Is everyone getting along? Am I acting in ways that people appreciate? Are my owners doing everything they should to make me happy? These are big issues, and only leaders—the people—have the ability to look at all the little details to make sure they add up to a harmonious whole.

The relationships between pets and people are complex, of course, just as they are between parents and children. You don't want to focus only on small things and neglect to look at the big picture, Gabriel says. Children, for example, can be thoroughly rotten one minute and absolute gems the rest of the day. Dogs and cats are the same way. It's up to their leaders to correct the small, negative things without losing sight of the fact that things are pretty good the rest of the time.

Take care of the energy first. Pets need serious playtime. They want to interact, romp, jump, and generally act silly. Give them every opportunity to do so, because a great deal of bad behavior is caused by nothing more than boredom, Gabriel says.

For dogs, the best approach is to take them for long, brisk walks once or twice a day. This allows them to burn off energy while expanding their horizons and keeping them mentally stimulated. After that, play in the house or the yard for a while. When they've calmed down a little, get all snuggly with them, Bunn says. This is serious bonding time.

You'll want to be a little less direct with cats. Playfully batting them with your hands or feet can get them more wound up as well as playfully aggressive—which, with their fast reflexes and sharp claws, you don't want to encourage, Lipscomb says. She recommends keeping them busy by playing with one of those fishing-pole toys that has a stuffed mouse or a ball on the end. Cats love these toys because the flying, bouncing tip reminds them of prey. It gives them a chance to run around and unleash their hunting instincts. She advises playing until they're so worn out that they can only flop on their sides and swipe at the toy with their paws.

Anticipate problems. Most behavior problems are entirely predictable. Cats need to scratch, and they aren't going to be selective about what they reach for. Puppies are going to chew no matter what. By anticipating your pet's natural needs and then taking care of them, you'll prevent nearly all of the common behavior problems that people have to deal with. Give your cat a good scratching post before he starts working over the wing chair. Give puppies an assortment of rawhide or nylon chews. Clean the litter box every day, and put out a few extra boxes for spares. Dogs and cats have certain basic needs that have to be expressed. Helping them be themselves in their human environments allows you to guide and control their behavior so that it doesn't break out in unexpected, and irritating, ways.

Don't take things personally. It would take the patience of a saint not to get angry when you come home after work and find a pile on the carpet or discover that the trash has been strewn around the house. But it's almost impossible to get angry when you realize that your pet truly didn't have any choice. Maybe he didn't have time to do his business in the morning, or you ran out of food and were planning to feed him later. Regardless of the issue at hand, dogs and cats *never* do things just to be bad, Lipscomb says. They had some need that their leaders weren't taking care of, and that's invariably when problems start to happen.

Teach in ways they understand. Since the people are responsible for making things run smoothly, it's ultimately their job to help dogs and cats understand what they should and shouldn't do. Dogs and cats learn things in different ways, however, so you'll have to customize your approach.

The easiest way to stop dogs from doing certain things is to reward them for things you do want. Suppose your dog has been mooching at the table. Don't waste time yelling or scolding. Lead him away from the table, have him sit or stay, then praise him well. You can reward him with a treat if you want, but it isn't necessary. The idea is to show him what types of behavior make you happy, rather than scolding him for those that don't. "When a dog figures out that you're happy with him for doing something, he'll do it all the time," Gabriel says. "That's one of the great things about dogs. They aim to please."

Cats are trickier to manage because they don't depend on human approval anywhere near as much as dogs do. Rather than rewarding them for good behavior, trainers recommend making their bad behavior seem less desirable. Take a cat who keeps jumping on counters. Yelling or swatting him off won't help. He'll get a little nervous around you, but the counters will be just as appealing as they were before. A better strategy is to make the counters less appealing—by setting out some empty cans in precarious positions, for example. The next time your cat jumps up, he'll encounter a clattering cacophony of noise. He's not going to like that at all and may decide that the counters aren't so much fun after all. The great thing about surreptitious teaching is that your cat will never suspect that you had anything to do with it, Lipscomb says. He won't be nervous when you come near, but he'll be *very* nervous about those horrible counters.

Be confident and consistent. People are always making exceptions for certain situations. We might eat chicken breasts with our hands when we're alone, but we'll use a fork in a restaurant. Dogs and cats, on the other hand, can't make these distinctions. "You can't get mad at a dog for jumping on the bed one night if it was okay to do it the night before," Gabriel says. "That sends a very confusing message."

Just as dogs and cats crave predictability, they also need reassurance. Alpha dogs, for example, are always sure of themselves. They exude confidence, and other dogs feel more comfortable because they know things are taken care of. It's the same in our families. Dogs and cats have very sharp intuition and will sense immediately when people are unsure of themselves. This makes *them* feel insecure, and that's when they tend to start acting up. So whatever rules you decide to establish, follow through consistently and with gusto and confidence. Your pets will follow your lead and be grateful that someone's keeping an eye on things.

When Communication Breaks Down

CHAPTER 32

Aggression toward People

One of Suzanne Clothier's more puzzling moments as a dog trainer came as she handled an allegedly aggressive dog under his owner's watchful eye. As she worked with the dog, the owner said, "I can't believe he hasn't bitten you yet."

Clothier, a trainer and co-owner of Flying Dog Press in St. Johnsville, New York, wasn't sure if the dog's owner was surprised or merely disappointed. "I wasn't bitten because I watched the dog for even the smallest sign that he was beginning to feel threatened by me," she says.

As Clothier and other trainers can attest, dogs and cats are masters of nonverbal communication. They watch our body language and give off plenty of their own. They invariably provide clues when they're feeling scared, possessive, or dominant. The problem is that people aren't always paying attention. When we fail to understand their subtler signals, dogs and cats are forced to use loud, dramatic ones, like growling or biting. They learn very quickly if dramatic signals are going to get our attention. They essentially say to themselves, "Ah, this she understands. I'll do it again if I have to."

There's no mistaking the signals when dogs and cats get aggressive. A long stare, accompanied by a growl, a hiss, or a tail swishing back and forth, means you're facing a serious threat, says Victoria L. Voith, D.V.M., Ph.D., a board-certified veterinary behaviorist in Dayton, Ohio. What's not so obvious is why the animals we love and trust sometimes act this way.

Natural Behavior

Aggression is a lot more natural than we think—in pets as well as people. The behavior of a hard-driving executive pushing to close a deal is not so very different from the behavior of a dog trying to maintain dominance. Humans don't bite or growl, but they're driven by some of the same motivations, like competing for resources or finding a mate. "People don't like to consider that aggression is part of a pet's natural repertoire," Clothier says.

Due to the influence of testosterone, males are more likely than females to show signs of aggression, which usually begin in a pet's early years. But aggressive tendencies are highly individual. Some dogs have dominant personalities, while others are timid or retiring. Even though some breeds, like German shepherds, have reputations for being aggressive, any dog, given the right (or wrong) circumstances, can show a flash of temper, teeth, or claws.

Dogs and cats have been domesticated for thousands of years. They depend on us for just about everything. We're bigger than they are. We control the food supply, and we determine where they sleep. It's natural for pets to look up to us and, most of the time, respect us.

In some families, however, the balance of power shifts away from people and toward the pets. This doesn't happen overnight, and it's not deliberate. But people sometimes give their pets—especially their dogs—a little too much deference. They step aside when their dogs brush against them. They give them food when they demand it and gingerly step away from the food bowl when they're eating. Or they'll let their dog sleep on the couch because he grumbles when they try to push him off. After a few months or years of accepting privileges, dogs naturally get the idea that they, and not their owners, are in charge.

This type of conflict occurs because people and pets see things differently. From a human point of view, giving dogs nice things is a way of saying, "I love you," Clothier explains. From a dog's point of view, receiving too many privileges is interpreted as "I'm setting the rules." And once a dog feels that he's in charge, he'll sometimes act aggressively to protect his privileged status.

Aggression is less of a problem in cats, if only because they're smaller and less likely to inflict serious damage. But cats do act aggressively at times, especially when they've recently had a fright. A cat who's been in a fight, for example, will sometimes get so worked up that he won't calm down for hours. If you get in his way or reach out to pet him, you might bear the brunt of

Mean on the Street

Owners are often amazed when their mild-mannered dogs, who act like ladies and gentlemen around the house, turn into macho bullies whenever they go for a walk. Rather than politely greeting passing dogs, they act as though every social encounter is a matter of national defense.

While some dogs dislike (or distrust) other dogs, the problem is probably originating at your end of the leash, says Suzanne Clothier, a trainer and co-owner of Flying Dog Press in St. Johnsville, New York. If you get tense when you see another dog approaching, your dog will detect your anxiety. "Once he spots that, he may begin acting aggressively," she says.

The problem may be compounded when you tighten up on the leash, which slightly raises your dog's head. Among dogs, a high head position is often perceived as a challenge. This means a passing dog may get the wrong idea, which in turn can put your dog on the offensive.

To keep canines calm, here's what Clothier recommends.

- Keep the leash loose when another dog approaches. The idea is to maintain enough tension to control your dog, but not so much that it pulls his head upward.
- Since dogs can readily detect human emotions, it's important to stay calm yourself when the two of you are around other dogs. Clothier admits it sounds silly, but she sometimes advises people to sing to themselves or recite a fairy tale, like *Goldilocks and the Three Bears*. "How uptight can you be when you're talking about a blonde and three bears in the woods?"
- Keep him moving. It's difficult for your dog to act aggressively toward other dogs when the two of you are walking briskly, Clothier says. When you're approaching another dog, don't give them time to mount a challenge. Walk quickly past or abruptly change course. This will keep your dog's attention focused on you instead of the other dog.

his stress—a type of behavior called redirected aggression. "Your cat may be crouching down, his pupils will be dilated, and his ears will be flattened back," says Pam Johnson-Bennett, a feline-behavior consultant in Nashville and author of *Twisted Whiskers* and *Psycho Kitty?* "If you stick a hand out in an effort to calm him, you may be scratched or bitten."

KNOWING THE SIGNS

Dogs and cats don't rely only on our verbal communication. They're very good at reading nonverbal cues and are highly aware of our posture, muscular tension, and facial expressions. They can even detect changes in mood by the way we smell.

Humans, however, aren't quite so discerning. We often miss the signs that indicate our pets are gearing up for an aggressive display. A dog that is staring and raising the fur on the back of his neck looks plenty aggressive. But if he's leaning away from you at the same time, he's probably just bluffing. Staring is another sign of aggression, at least some of the time. But it's entirely possible for pets to stare at their owners merely because they want to play and are trying to get their attention. "The greatest act of love is to pay such close attention to your pets that you can read all the subtleties," Clothier says. "That's all they're asking for."

Dogs who are at the point of aggression will usually point their ears forward and raise the hair on the back of their necks, says Wayne Hunthausen, D.V.M., an animal-behavior consultant in Westwood, Kansas, and coauthor of *Handbook of Behaviour Problems of the Dog and Cat*. They'll often give a long, hard stare, and their tails will be high and may be stiffly wagging back and forth. They'll also lean toward you, putting their weight on their front feet. Dogs who display one or more of these signs are feeling extremely short-tempered, and some type of aggression may be imminent.

Cats are less predictable than dogs in signaling aggression. They'll often start out by lashing their tails—a sign that their patience is wearing thin, says Johnson-Bennett. You'll want to watch the paws, too. When your cat smacks you with his paw, leaving the claws sheathed, consider it a warning. If you keep doing whatever it is that's making him irritated, the next step is likely to be a bite or scratch. Other signs that cats aren't feeling friendly include flattened ears, raised hair, and tense muscles.

TURNING IT AROUND

A dog or cat who truly wants to hurt you can do so with lightning speed. That's why it's important never to ignore or excuse aggressive behavior in your pet. It won't go away by itself,

Clothier says. But there are ways that you can relate to dogs and cats that will make aggression less likely to occur. Here's what experts advise.

Be the boss. Dogs evolved as pack animals, living in societies in which every dog knew his place, and the leaders were rarely challenged. Dogs are naturally inclined to accept people as their leaders, and it's up to us to assume that role. This means making it very clear, from the time your dog is a puppy, that your word is law. If you tell him to get off the couch, he should hop off quickly. He should step out of your way when you walk across the room. And he certainly shouldn't get cheeky when you tell him to do something that he doesn't want to do.

Puppy and obedience classes are a great way to help your dog understand that he needs to look to you for direction, Clothier says. Even if you're not interested in intensive training, setting clear guidelines and enforcing them regularly will help prevent aggressive impulses from rising to the surface.

Give them room to move. Dogs and cats are much more likely to act aggressively when they feel that they don't have any other option—because they're "trapped" in a corner, for example, or you're clutching them when they're trying to get away. When your pet's body language is saying, "I'm getting nervous, and I'd like to be left alone," it's probably time to back off, says Dr. Hunthausen.

Neuter the boys. Since aggression is often caused—or at least influenced—by the male hormone testosterone, neutering pets is often the best way to stop aggression from becoming a problem, says Dr. Voith.

Play calmly. Dogs enjoy physical play. They crave human contact, and the more you rub and pet them, the happier they'll be. Cats, on the other hand, aren't wild about being touched, at least not all the time. When you rub a cat's belly, for example, a momentary purr of pleasure can quickly change to a paw-slap or even a bite, says Johnson-Bennett. The only solution, when it comes to physical contact, is to pay close attention to your cat's body language. He'll let you know when he wants to play and when it's time to give it a break.

Get some help. Even though it's normal for dogs and cats to occasionally feel aggressive, they should never take these feelings out on you, says Dr. Hunthausen. Pets who are regularly growling, hissing, or biting have a problem. It could be a physical problem that's making them cranky. They could have stress in their lives that you're not aware of. Or they could be feeling a bit uppity, as though they have the right to push you around.

Regardless of the cause, it's important to stop aggression before it becomes a habit—and before you get hurt, says Dr. Hunthausen. Start by scheduling a checkup with your veterinarian.

If your pet gets a clean bill of health, the next step is to see a professional trainer or behaviorist. Most problems with aggression aren't that hard to treat as long as you catch them early, Clothier says.

CHAPTER 33

Attacking Feet or Hands

From pets' point of view, hands and feet are nearly perfect prey toys. Fingers flutter like wings, and toes, usually spotted from under a bed or chair, wiggle like little animals. Plus, there are those lovely screams of surprise that let them know they've hit the mark.

Except in cases of aggression, dogs usually don't attack appendages, although puppies sometimes find our "paws" a little too tempting to resist. Cats, on the other hand, react strongly to movement, and that's what makes our hands and feet such attractive targets.

No one enjoys being ambushed with needle-sharp claws or teeth first thing in the morning, but you shouldn't take it personally. Cats don't launch attacks because they like causing pain, says Pam Johnson-Bennett, a feline-behavior consultant in Nashville and author of *Twisted Whiskers* and *Psycho Kitty?* They do it because it's fun.

Preparing for the Future

Puppies and kittens spend a lot of time playing, either with littermates or with other pets or their human owners. They do it because they have a lot of energy and enjoy tumbling around. But there's also a deeper purpose. The things they do in play, like stalking, clawing, wrestling, and biting, give them practice for things they'll do in life.

When a kitten stalks and pounces on a toy or a length of string, she's simulating a real hunt. "Play predation" helps cats sharpen their reflexes and hone their skills so they'll be more successful when the real thing comes along. Dogs do similar things, especially herding dogs like Border collies and Shetland sheepdogs. Bred to keep sheep and livestock in line, they occasionally have a tendency to nip at people's heels. "Herding dogs look for things to herd," says Suzanne B. Johnson, Ph.D., a certified applied animal behaviorist in Beaverdam, Virginia.

The urge to use your hands or feet for target practice isn't motivated only by instinct, of course. Dogs and cats have a lot of energy, especially when they're young, and chasing things that move is a great way to blow off steam and have some fun at the same time. Pets who don't get much exercise or who spend a lot of time alone will often launch ankle attacks because they don't have other opportunities to play, says Sharon L. Crowell-Davis, D.V.M., Ph.D., a board-certified veterinary behaviorist and professor of anatomy and radiology at the University of Georgia College of Veterinary Medicine in Athens.

"From a cat's perspective, playing with people works really well," she adds. "We jump up and down, yell, and squeal. Your cat doesn't know that 'kill the ankle' is a bad game. She just knows she wants to play."

Pets also use their claws or teeth when they want some attention, says Kate Gamble, a feline-behavior consultant in Auburn, California. "Cats often reach out with their paws as you are walking by," she says. "It isn't so much play as 'Hey, remember me?'"

Dogs are active and energetic, and they enjoy interacting with people. They instinctively respond to quick movements, so when people are running around, they want to participate, and they sometimes use their teeth to do it. "Children are more often targets of this kind of behavior because they move fast and like to run," says Dr. Johnson.

Soft Mouths, Velvet Paws

Older pets play less than puppies and kittens, but they never outgrow the pleasure of using their teeth and claws. Unlike the youngsters, however, they've learned to "inhibit" their bites and scratches, Dr. Crowell-Davis says. This is why a dog can gently mouth your hand without applying painful pressure and why a cat can bat at your hands or toes without causing a painful scratch.

Pets learn fairly early that their teeth and claws can be dangerous when not properly used. The way they learn is by playing

Nice to Meet You

People shake hands or hug when they meet, and we take it for granted that dogs enjoy up-close-and-personal greetings, too. But hugging or touching paws isn't part of their vocabulary. In fact, dogs think that the typical human greeting is downright rude.

"A common complaint is 'I was just reaching down to pet her, and she turned around and bit my hand,'" says Sharon L. Crowell-Davis, D.V.M., Ph.D., a board-certified veterinary behaviorist and professor of anatomy and radiology at the University of Georgia College of Veterinary Medicine in Athens.

Dogs are more circumspect than people and rarely approach strangers directly. Instead, they often sidle up to people or other pets. It's their way of showing respect and proving that they're not a threat, says Suzanne B. Johnson, Ph.D., a certified applied animal behaviorist in Beaverdam, Virginia.

Dogs are never going to understand human rituals, so it's up to us to greet them in ways they feel comfortable with.

- When meeting a strange dog, it's best to let her approach you instead of putting out your hand, says Dr. Johnson. "People think they should offer the dog the back of their hand, but the dog doesn't know the back from the front."
- Dogs are a lot shorter than we are, so we naturally bend over to rub the tops of their heads. Among dogs, however, this type of body language is viewed as a threat, and you could get a negative response. "It's better to allow the dog to sniff, then stroke her on the chest once she's given an indication it's okay to do so," says John C. Wright, Ph.D., a certified applied animal behaviorist; professor of psychology at Mercer University in Macon, Georgia; and author of *The Dog Who Would Be King* and *Is Your Cat Crazy?*
- The best way to introduce yourself is to kneel or sit on the ground. Dogs feel more comfortable when strangers aren't higher than they are, he says.
- Dogs don't mind a little eye contact, but locking eyes for more than a few seconds is considered very rude and can make some dogs feel threatened, says Dr. Wright.

roughly with their littermates. A puppy who bites too hard is going to get bitten back. A cat who uses her claws too roughly is going to get a response—and it won't be a positive one. It doesn't take long for dogs and cats to learn how rough they can be without causing pain or getting a forceful reaction in return. "If your cat were really trying to hurt you, those scratches and nicks would be a lot deeper than they are," Dr. Crowell-Davis explains.

Dogs and cats try to treat people with the same courtesy, but there's one thing they forget. Unlike their littermates, people don't have fur, which makes us more sensitive to teeth and claws. So even though those morning attacks are meant to be playful, they're often painful.

PERSONAL PROTECTION

It's natural to get a little riled when your cat launches a successful attack or your dog bites too hard. Yelling doesn't help very much because pets may not understand what the problem is. The only useful approach is to help your pet understand that this type of play isn't appreciated. There are lots of ways to do this. Here's what experts advise.

Tucker them out. The more you play with dogs and cats, the less likely they are to be filled with pent-up energy—lying in wait for convenient feet or hands to come within reach, says Dr. Crowell-Davis. For dogs, all you have to do is snap on a leash and walk or run for 30 to 40 minutes a day. Cats love toys that move, like balls or a string dragged across the floor. Don't bother with stationary toys, even those containing catnip. Your cat will assume the toy is dead and probably won't show a lot of interest.

Make attacks less fun. Pets who attack hands and feet are trying to have a good time. One way to make this pastime a little less fun is to arm yourself beforehand with a squirt gun or an air horn. As soon as you see an attack coming, spritz them with water or blast them with the horn. Not only will this startle them and stop the attack, but they'll learn that this type of play has uncomfortable consequences. "When I'm working with a family, we'll typically have squirt guns positioned all around the house," says Dr. Crowell-Davis.

Distract them with toys. No matter how tempting your hands and feet are, dogs and cats are just as willing to go after something else. You can often forestall attacks by tossing a Ping-Pong ball or rolling a tennis ball across the floor, says Dr. Crowell-Davis.

You can also use toys to help dogs learn that your hands aren't made for chewing. No matter how gentle your dog is, never let her mouth your hands or nip at your heels. If she starts, quickly slip her a toy to chew on. If you start this when they're young, most dogs will learn to keep their teeth to themselves later on.

Don't make the mistake of putting toys away while your cat is still wide-eyed and excited, Johnson-Bennett adds. If you do, you can be sure that the next foot or hand your cat sees is going to be fair game. Wind the game down slowly, as though the "prey" is on its last legs. At this point, your cat will naturally calm down, she says. In fact, she'll probably wander to the food bowl because cats like to eat when they're done with the hunt.

Speak their language. Cats don't always understand the word *no*, but they're very clear about hisses—they're a threat they understand. "If I catch my cats doing something wrong, I hiss at them," Dr. Crowell-Davis says. "They look at me just like they would another cat—with sort of a 'Wow, I'm in trouble' look."

Cats who are getting ready to launch an attack will stare intensely at your ankles and twitch the ends of their tails.

Border collies and other herding dogs will always crouch down before heading for your heels.

CHAPTER 34

Attacking Paper

Among the hundreds of behavior problems that trainers deal with, attacking paper is pretty low on the list. It isn't dangerous. Pets don't get sick from doing it. And while it may be annoying, it's not going to put a household into turmoil. Yet, it's surprisingly common. Nearly all dogs and cats do it sometimes, and it's not a pretty sight.

No one enjoys coming home and discovering that the mystery novel they were reading was shredded into bits or that the toilet paper was pulled from the roll and scattered over the carpet. It's difficult to read a newspaper when your cat keeps batting it with her paws. And just try wrapping a present when the paper acts like a magnet for furry feet. As long as it crinkles and tears, some pets, cats especially, can't resist getting involved.

Adults in Training

"It's common for puppies and kittens to destroy almost everything around them," says Steve Aiken, an animal-behavior consultant in Wichita, Kansas. Part of this is pure play, but there's also a deeper reason. The games young pets play prepare them for the serious business of life. For cats, stalking and pouncing on the newspaper is a warmup for the hunting they'll do as adults. For dogs, shredding a novel is a way of understanding their world. Children get experience by looking at things and touching them. Dogs get the same experience by holding things in their mouths and chewing them.

Paper seems to have a special appeal. The way pets attack and shred paper is similar to the way their ancestors would shake and shred prey. The fact that paper tears easily is probably an added incentive for cats. Just as they scratch tree bark to mark their territory, scratching at paper leaves a visual reminder that they were there. Paper may be even better because the claw marks show up easily, says Michele Arnoto, programs manager of Tree House Animal Foundation in Chicago.

JUST HAVING FUN

Lacking our cognitive abilities, dogs and cats react to things on a very physical level. The things that give them pleasure are those that trigger one or more of their senses. Tearing at paper probably feels as good to them as a foot massage does to us. And the sounds of tearing are very satisfying. So when you come home one day and discover bits of toilet paper throughout the house, it's probably not because your pet is angry or upset. She's probably just having fun, says Linda Colflesh, a trainer in Boiling Springs, Pennsylvania.

Pets do destroy things when they're anxious or frightened, she adds. Dogs who panic when they're left alone, for example, will often chew and rip up everything they can find, including paper. You can tell a lot about their motivation by watching their body language. If they seem like they're having fun, and if they're just as likely to attack paper when you're home as when you're gone, you can be pretty sure that there isn't a deep, underlying reason you need to worry about.

Cats are more likely than dogs to attack paper, because their ears can detect higher frequencies. The sound of crumpling paper gets their attention almost instantly. In fact, pet supply stores sell cat toys that are nothing more than little sacks. When cats play with them and run across them, they make crinkling sounds just like paper.

THE NEED FOR ACTION

Pets are much more likely to go to town on paper when there isn't a lot happening in their lives, Aiken says. They need just as much mental and physical stimulation as people do. When they're not getting a lot of exercise or a chance to interact with their people, they get bored. That's when they look for ways to entertain themselves. Pouncing on paper probably isn't their first choice of entertainment, but in a pinch, it's better than nothing.

It's not that they necessarily want to play with the paper itself, Aiken adds. What they may be doing is trying to get your attention. The time you spend wrapping a package or reading a newspaper is time you're not spending with them. So they give a few reminders, like pushing between the newspaper and your hands or walking across paper that's spread out on a table. Sooner or later, you're going to react. It may not be the most positive kind

MESSAGES AND MEANINGS

Paper from the Past

Had the CIA's evidence disposal unit known about Ch'a, it would have hired her on the spot. At one time, Ch'a, an American Eskimo dog, had a natural gift for reducing paper to its smallest possible parts. Everything was fair game: receipts, monthly bills, even postage stamps. If Ch'a could reach it, she'd shred it.

Ch'a's owner, September B. Morn of Bellingham, Washington, realized that she had to do something. She had gotten Ch'a from a rescue organization, and she figured something in the dog's past was causing her to be so destructive. As it turned out, Ch'a had been spanked regularly with a rolled-up newspaper. "No wonder she was determined to shred every paper she found," September says.

Once dogs are grown, it can be difficult to teach them new ways of doing things, especially when their behavior is related to something negative in their pasts. But September, a trainer and author of *Dogs Love to Please . . . We Teach Them How!* had an idea.

"I taught Ch'a to fetch me things that I threw for her, including bits of paper," she says. Each time Ch'a brought paper back, September gave her something good to eat. Ch'a was resourceful. She realized that she didn't have to wait for September to throw things. She began looking for opportunities. If she found a scrap of paper on the floor, rather than destroying it, she would take it to September, then eagerly wait for her reward.

The paper shredding stopped, and Ch'a never took it up again. Looking back, September realizes that punishing Ch'a for her behavior couldn't have worked. Ch'a shredded paper as a way of dealing with stress, and punishment would have added to that. By giving Ch'a an incentive to preserve paper, not tear it, she was able to convert a negative behavior into a positive one. "This gave Ch'a an outlet for her energy," she says.

of attention, but as any child would attest, negative attention is better than no attention at all.

Apart from giving pets more personal time and attention, there isn't a lot that you can do to discourage them from going after paper. What you can do, however, is make this practice a little less destructive by trying some of the following tips.

• Some trainers recommend ripping paper into pieces before you throw it in the trash. Pets get their pleasure out of ripping and tearing. Paper that's already in bits won't hold a lot of interest.

• Toilet paper and paper towels are common targets—not so much because they have irresistible textures, but because it's fun to grab one end and run, unrolling the whole thing. Some people have found that using upright holders rather than the horizontal kind is a good solution. It won't unroll as easily, so pets get less satisfaction out of playing with it.

• Rather than discouraging cats from playing with all paper, you can make paper toys just for them. If you make it clear that you're very happy when they play with these particular toys, that's where they're going to focus their attention. Cats can't resist paper that's been crumpled into little balls.

CHAPTER 35

Barking and Meowing

Larry Lachman, Ph.D., had learned to head for cover whenever Fagan went on a barking binge. Dr. Lachman, an animal-behavior consultant based in Carmel, California, and author of *Dogs on the Couch* and *Cats on the Counter* discovered that Fagan, his golden retriever mix, would sometimes bark (as well as whimper and hide in the bathroom) when an earthquake was pending.

Unlike Fagan, most dogs don't need an excuse to bark, and it doesn't take an emergency to set them off. Voices in the yard next door will get them started. So will the arrival of the mail carrier or the sound of sprinklers. Or they'll bark just to pass the time.

Cats are less likely than dogs to indulge in aimless noise-making, but they can be very persistent when they want something. And some breeds, such as Siamese, are much more "talkative" than others.

No one objects to occasional barks and meows, but some dogs and cats do it so much and so loudly that the people in their lives can't get any rest, Dr. Lachman says. It's frustrating for owners because they know their pets are trying to tell them something, but they can't figure out what that something is—and what they need to do to stop the noise.

Ancient Silence, Modern Noise

In the days when dogs lived by their wits and supper was a fast chase away, they didn't bark much because the noise would scare their prey. Puppies who hadn't learned the rules barked all the time, only to be shushed by the wiser adults.

The rules for survival changed when dogs started living with people. Far from being a liability, barking became an asset because people wanted their newfound friends to act as canine

MESSAGES AND MEANINGS

Reach Out and Pet Someone

Tammy Bryson was having a terrible time staying in touch with her friends and relatives, all because of Precious.

Precious, then a 2-year-old gray-and-silver tabby cat, had developed the annoying habit of meowing, loudly and persistently, whenever Tammy picked up the telephone. Tammy, a schoolteacher in Fayetteville, North Carolina, found herself interrupting phone calls in order to pay attention to Precious.

"She didn't meow that much at other times, only when I got on the phone," Tammy says. "It got to the point that I would lock myself in my bedroom just so I could have a conversation in peace. And the whole time, I would hear her crying outside the door."

For a long time, Tammy couldn't figure out what it was about phone conversations that put Precious's mouth into motion. Then she realized something. When she was talking on the phone, she would often absentmindedly pet Precious. "I realized that Precious came to associate my talking on the phone with being petted. When I wasn't petting her, she would meow to tell me."

Once Tammy made the connection, the rest was easy. She makes a point at the beginning of every phone conversation to put Precious in her lap and pet and cuddle her for a few minutes. "That's usually enough to satisfy her so that she'll go about her business while I finish my conversation," she says.

alarm systems. They bred and encouraged dogs to bark. And because dogs were no longer independent and responsible for catching their own food—and, in fact, they were bred to be docile—they became more and more puppyish in their behavior. They started barking more.

To human ears, barking is a lot of meaningless noise, but dogs send different messages by varying the pitch, sound, and timing of their barks. For example:

"I'm afraid." This is the least problematic type of barking from a human perspective because it only occurs when dogs are startled. You'll usually hear a quick series of yips or yelps when they respond to whatever made them nervous.

"You're in my territory, get out." A deep-throated bark is used as a warning to potential intruders. Even small dogs are capable of emitting surprisingly deep barks when they want to make themselves seem bigger and tougher than they are. This type of territorial barking can go on all day because some dogs view everyone from the mail carrier to a passing dog as an intruder.

"Give me some attention." All dogs crave attention, and some crave it more than others. Dogs who get nervous when they're apart from their owners—and, for some dogs, being in another room is like being on another continent—will often whine or bark to signal their need for reassurance.

"I'm bored out of my skull." Dogs who get bored when they're alone will sometimes entertain themselves by barking for hours at a stretch. This type of barking even sounds bored—rhythmic and monotonous. It's also the type of barking that results in your neighbors' calling animal control.

Unlike dogs, cats are entirely comfortable spending time by themselves. Before they were domesticated, they lived fairly solitary lives and didn't have a lot of companions to talk to. But modern cats understand that people depend on spoken language, and they're more than willing to accommodate them with persistent meowing. The usual messages are "Feed me," "Let me out," or "Pet me," says Kimberly Barry, Ph.D., a certified applied animal behaviorist in Austin, Texas.

What's the Message?

You can't stop pets from barking and meowing any more than you can stop people from speaking. Vocalizations are an essential part of their communications package. Pets who are always making noise, however, are trying to tell you something, and they aren't going to quit until you resolve whatever it is that's bothering them, says John C. Wright, Ph.D., a certified applied animal behaviorist; professor of psychology at Mercer University in Macon, Georgia; and author of *The Dog Who Would Be King* and *Is Your Cat Crazy?* "You need to understand their emotions and motivations in order to correct the noise-making."

Most noisy pets are looking for extra attention, he explains. And they aren't shy about demanding it. They'll keep barking or meowing until you stop whatever it is you're doing in order to attend to them. Food won't keep them quiet, at least not for long.

And they don't really want to go outside. They want to be catered to, and they'll keep asking for attention until they feel satisfied—and satisfaction doesn't come easily.

It's never easy to know for sure what's causing dogs to bark or cats to meow, adds Liz Palika, a trainer in Oceanside, California. She recommends keeping a journal for a few weeks in which you write down everything that's happening when your pet starts making noise. By putting together various clues—the time of day, who was home and who was gone, whether there were noises outside, and what sorts of activities were going on—you'll eventually see a pattern that will help you determine what's triggering the outbursts.

Once you know what's causing barking or meowing, you can move on to the next step, making it stop.

Ignore the noise. Yelling "Quiet!" rarely stops pets from barking or meowing. For one thing, they don't know what the word means. More important, they interpret your yelling as participation, and that can really get the call-and-response going.

"Whenever you look at, speak to, pet, or otherwise reward dogs and cats, you're reinforcing what they're doing at the moment," says Dr. Lachman. "It's important not to engage in these or other types of rewarding behaviors while your pet is vocalizing."

You can take the cold-shoulder treatment one step further by leaving the room whenever your pet starts making noise. Since barking and meowing are usually bids for attention, turning your back and walking away give a powerful signal. Dogs and cats are observant and resourceful, and when they realize that making noise isn't getting their message across, they'll do it less often.

Keep them occupied. Dogs and cats tend to make the most noise when they're bored and full of energy, says Dr. Barry. "Giving them something else to do can really help," she says. Take them for a walk or play in the yard. Drag a string across the floor for a few minutes or toss them a ball. Busy pets are usually quiet pets, and once they blow off steam, they'll be less likely to bark or meow later on.

Block stimulating sounds. Dogs' hearing is vastly superior to

It doesn't help to punish dogs for barking, but trainers sometimes recommend looking them in the eye, holding their mouths closed for a second or two, and telling them no. The combination of eye contact and a stern command puts them on notice that you're in charge and that they need to pay attention. And because dogs dislike having their mouths held closed, they'll begin to associate barking with this unpleasant sensation and will look for other ways to get your attention.

NAME: Thor

OCCUPATION: Police Dog

It was the worst situation imaginable. Two prisoners had escaped into thick woods, and Officer Jim Watson of the Mentor, Ohio, police department was crawling on his belly through thick underbrush in pursuit. With him was Thor, a 3-year-old German shepherd who had worked with Jim for more than a year.

"I couldn't see anything through the undergrowth," says Jim, now a master trainer for the North American Police Work Dog Association. "I was completely dependent on Thor to lead me through the woods."

But Thor, who had been trained in tracking, knew exactly where he was going. Jim's breathing quickened when he saw that Thor had stopped and was listening intently. Suddenly, Thor let out a low, deep growl—the signal he had been trained to use when suspects were nearby. Jim looked where Thor was looking and caught a glimpse of a red shirt. They were nearly on top of the suspects, and without Thor's warning, they would have crawled right into sight.

By taking the men by surprise, Jim had no trouble arresting them. As he learned later, however, he was lucky. The men confessed that they had been planning to stab Jim if he caught up with them. Jim and Thor returned to the area the next day and discovered two knives the men had buried.

Jim says he'll be forever indebted to Thor for saving his life. As for Thor, it was just another day on the job.

ours. This means they can hear—and respond to—things that we're not even aware of, from rustling in the bushes to the sound of a mouse in the ceiling. Increasing the level of background noise by turning on the radio, TV, or a fan will help mask many of the noises that cause dogs to bark, says Dr. Wright.

Reduce their anxiety. It doesn't happen very often with cats, but some dogs get so lonely and anxious when they're alone that they'll bark frantically. Their anxiety doesn't start when you shut the door, Dr. Wright adds. They usually start getting nervous when you're doing all the little things that indicate you're about to leave, like picking up your keys or putting on your coat.

You can reduce their overall anxiety by making these predeparture signals a little less meaningful. The way to do that is with sheer repetition, says Dr. Wright. On a day you're going to be home, for example, pick up your keys and rattle them as though you're going to leave—then sit back down. A minute later, rattle them again. Do this periodically all day long. Put on your coat and take it off. Open and close the garage door. Walk out the door and quickly walk back in. The idea is to strip away the concept of "leaving" from all these little gestures. After a while, your dog will understand that the rattle of keys doesn't mean very much, so his anxiety won't reach such a fever pitch when you're ready to go out the door.

CHAPTER 36

Begging

Your pet's ancestors knew better than to mooch from their companions. Regardless of what they wanted—food, affection, or a warm place to sleep—they knew that making demands wasn't the way to go. Pushy pets were either ignored or smacked for their presumption. When they wanted something, they either had to be tough enough to take it or quick enough to grab it without getting caught. Begging was out of the question.

Things changed when dogs and cats moved from the wilderness into the living room. They became completely dependent on their owners, not only for food and shelter but also for the affection they used to get from their companions. When they want something, they have to ask for it. "Pets don't beg from each other when they want something," says Kimberly Barry, Ph.D., a certified applied animal behaviorist in Austin, Texas. "They beg from humans because humans control their resources."

Now that dogs and cats have been domesticated for thousands of years, begging has nearly become their national pastime. Some begging isn't a problem, Dr. Barry adds. Cats who meow when their food is being poured, or dogs who stare hungrily when they're waiting for supper, aren't being unusually pushy. But some pets never take no for an answer. They stare at your fork as it travels from your plate to your mouth. They get underfoot in the kitchen and cry persistently between meals. Or, when they're in the mood for affection, they will nudge your hand, push against your legs, or climb in and out of your lap until you give them the rub they're looking for.

"Begging depends on your perception," Dr. Barry says. "Requests" that one person finds endearing may be a nuisance to someone else. But everyone has their limits, and unless you teach your pets that begging isn't appreciated, they'll continue to cross the line.

Underlying Motives

Regardless of what they want at the moment, dogs and cats beg in order to get humans to pay attention to them—and we, from the softness of our hearts as well as our desire to get a little peace, invariably give in. And because the rewards for begging, such as food, are the same rewards we give as a show of love, dogs and cats invariably get the wrong idea, says Elmo Shropshire, D.V.M., a veterinarian in San Francisco. "They beg because we have given them the message that we want them to do it."

Food is a good example. Dogs and cats love food, and we love feeding them. So we give them treats whenever we're in a good mood or they do things we like. It doesn't take them long to figure out that people like feeding them and there's no reason to be shy about asking for more. Their thinking probably goes something like this: "I like food, and you like feeding me. So hey, where's my biscuit?"

"Our habit of reinforcing positive behavior with food makes pets think that we want them to eat all the time," says Dr. Shropshire. "And when a pet begs and is rewarded with food, he feels like he's done something right."

There's similar confusion when pets beg for attention. We give them the most attention when we're happy with them. Even though we're not so happy when they follow us from room to room or pester us when we're trying to do something else, we're rarely so grudging that we won't relent and give them what they're asking for. Dogs and cats can't make the distinction between affection that's given willingly and affection that's coerced. Any affection, in their minds, means that they've done something good and we're happy with them. So they beg some more.

No More Handouts

Anyone who lives with an attention hog or a food mooch soon discovers that giving in "just this once" never stops begging. Whatever their original intentions, once pets learn that they can get the goods by demanding them, they're not about to be patient. They're going to either get what they want or drive you crazy until you deliver.

Begging will never be an issue if you never give in to your pet's demands, Dr. Barry says. But once dogs and cats start the habit,

MESSAGES AND MEANINGS

Duck Calls

As a client service representative for a busy medical laboratory in Lowellville, Ohio, Kathleen Snyder deals with demands all day long. The last thing she needs is more demands at home, which is why J. D.'s behavior was driving her crazy.

Schnauzers are known for their big appetites, but J. D.'s mooching was over the top. When Kathleen and her family sat down to eat, J. D. would sit at her feet, whine, and stare at her with eyes that broke her heart. To ensure that he got his point across, J. D. would sometimes jump up and put his paws on the table.

"We knew we shouldn't give in and feed him, but it was hard not to give in to those puppy-dog eyes," Kathleen says.

The one thing that puzzled her was that J. D. wasn't consistent in his mooching. Some days he never approached the table at all, while on others he wouldn't leave. Kathleen finally made the connection. On days when she was working at home, J. D. seemed perfectly content to snooze in the other room while the family ate. On days when Kathleen was out visiting clients, J. D. invariably came sniffing around as soon as the family sat down. Those were the same days, she realized, that he always brought her the duck.

J. D.'s favorite toy was a rubber duck. He often ignored the duck on days when Kathleen stayed home. But when Kathleen was gone all day, he met her at the door with the duck in his mouth. It was his way of saying that he wanted to play and get some attention.

Once Kathleen figured out the puzzle, the rest was easy. She and the rest of the family instituted a strict no-feeding rule at the supper table. They started feeding J. D. in the evening before they ate. And they started giving him extra attention, especially when they first got home. By the time they sat down to supper, J. D. was well-fed and had received his fill of attention.

"It took a few weeks, but eventually he realized that we would give him the things he craved before dinner but never while we were eating," she says. "He's been much more well-behaved lately, and mealtimes have been much more pleasant."

you'll need to be more creative in finding ways to make them stop.

Satisfy them with service. It may seem as though pets have insatiable appetites—for food or whatever else they desire—but they do have a satisfaction "ceiling," a point at which they've essentially had enough. You can help pets reach this ceiling by giving them what they want on a regular, predictable schedule, says Dr. Barry. Give them their food at the same times every day. Take a few extra minutes to play with them or take them for walks. Go out of your way to give them attention rather than wait for them to come to you. Once they understand that all things come to those who wait, they'll naturally get a little less demanding, she explains.

Be strong and ignore them. It's not the easiest solution, but the most effective way to stop begging is to make it unprofitable by never giving in. The drawback to this approach is that you'll have to live with a lot of meowing, nudging, or whining in the meantime. Pets who are used to getting what they want can be extremely demanding and persistent, and bad habits don't go away in a day or two, says Dr. Barry. You may have to put up with the begging for a few weeks or even months. It's worth gritting your teeth and going through with it, she advises.

Cure them with kindness. It's nearly impossible to share a kitchen or dining room with a mooching dog without scolding him, and even St. Francis would have yelled "Quiet!" after 20 minutes of feed-me-now meows. But venting your natural feelings will intensify their efforts because pets who are begging are looking for attention, and scolding and yelling are just other forms of attention, Dr. Barry says.

Rather than scolding pets when they beg, praise them when they don't, she advises. Suppose you're working in the kitchen and your dog happens to be staying out and minding his own business. Go over and pet him. Dogs and cats crave our approval, and experts have found that praising good behavior usually works better than punishing rudeness.

Be consistent. Dogs and cats are a lot like children. Even when they understand what they should and shouldn't do, they're always willing to push their advantage. No matter how strict you are most of the time, giving in teaches them that begging does pay off as long as they do it long enough. "If you're not consistent, you're almost like a slot machine," says Robin Kovary, director of the American Dog Trainers Network in New York City. "They know that if they keep pulling the lever, eventually they'll hit the jackpot."

CHAPTER 37

Biting

Tom Esau, a mail carrier in Portland, Oregon, has become proficient at reading dogs' body language. After getting three painful bites in 13 years, he's learned to pay attention to the ways that dogs are standing or looking at him when he approaches houses on his beat. Failing to do so, he's discovered, can result in less than a first-class reception.

People are always a little shocked when dogs and cats bite, but we shouldn't be. Just as we use our hands almost from the time we're born, dogs and cats use their teeth. Biting is a natural part of their behavior, whether they're playing with their littermates, hunting field mice, or defending their territory, says Wayne Hunthausen, D.V.M., an animal-behavior consultant in Westwood, Kansas, and coauthor of *Handbook of Behaviour Problems of the Dog and Cat*.

Pets learn the basics of biting at an early age. As they tumble about the nest, they learn to react quickly, a skill they will use in later life. They also learn to control their bites. At first, they bite with all the strength they can muster. Their moms and littermates don't appreciate this and bite them back. This is how they learn to "inhibit" their bites. By the time dogs and cats are grown, they have learned to control the strength of their bites, depending on the situation. They also learn when it is and isn't appropriate to bite.

While they're still young, however, puppies and kittens want to show off their newfound skills to their human owners. Unlike their littermates, however, we don't bite back when they get too rough. This means that they don't learn right away that biting humans isn't appropriate or appreciated, says Pam Johnson-Bennett, a feline-behavior consultant in Nashville and author of *Twisted Whiskers* and *Psycho Kitty?*

Biting isn't limited to play, of course. Some dogs and cats are naturally aggressive and temperamental and will bite at a moment's notice. More often, they bite when they're feeling frightened or threatened or merely because they want to be left alone. Cats, for example, enjoy being petted—unless you try to rub their bellies the way you would a dog's. Many cats dislike having their stomachs rubbed and will scratch or bite to let you know they've had enough.

Reading the Signs

Unlike mail carriers, who encounter strange dogs all the time, most of us don't get a lot of practice "reading" different animals. But it's worth learning their basic signals because any pet, if he's feeling uncomfortable or cranky enough, may bite on occasion, says Dr. Hunthausen.

Cats usually signal an impending bite by lashing their tails back and forth. Dogs are a little more expressive. When the tail is held straight up and rigid, it means a dog is at high-alert, says John C. Wright, Ph.D., a certified applied animal behaviorist; professor of psychology at Mercer University in Macon, Georgia; and author of *The Dog Who Would Be King* and *Is Your Cat Crazy?* They'll also be staring, their weight will be distributed toward the front feet, and their ears will rotate forward. "When these aggressive dominant signals are displayed at the same time, you need to be careful," he says.

Don't be fooled by a wagging tail, Dr. Wright adds. While dogs often wag their tails when they're happy and excited, they also swish them around when they're feeling aggressive. The only way to tell the difference is to look at other body signals, such as staring or an upright, tense posture.

Esau has developed his own method for determining whether or not a dog is unhappy about the mail service. "A dog with his tongue out won't bite," he says.

Behaviorists have discovered the same thing. "It wouldn't be prudent for an aggressive dog to leave his tongue hanging out, because he might bite himself," says Dr. Hunthausen.

Setting the Limits

Even though bites from strange dogs—and, less often, from strange cats—get most of the media attention, the majority of bites occur at home, says Dr. Wright. It's not that every friendly family pet is harboring an evil twin inside. It's just that dogs and cats, like people, go through periods when they're not feeling well and are crankier than usual. Or they occasionally get resentful because their food isn't being respected or someone is crowding their personal space. Humans argue when their nerves get stretched. Pets, unfortunately, sometimes bite.

Even though it's helpful to understand why pets bite, don't waste time trying to rationalize your dog or cat's behavior, says Suzanne Clothier, a trainer and co-owner of Flying Dog Press in St. Johnsville, New York. It doesn't matter if your pet is frightened or upset or is protecting his food. Pets should never bite people, and it's up to you to make sure that they get this message loud and clear.

Play peacefully. Since dogs and cats are naturally inclined to use their teeth in play as well as in defense, you need to help them understand that people aren't appropriate targets. Many owners give their pets mixed signals. They encourage biting play from puppies or kittens, but are surprised and angry when the same pets give them a painful bite. You should never let your pets mouth your hands, unless all they're doing is licking, says Dr. Hunthausen. Giving them appropriate chew toys will provide an outlet for their biting urges. The idea is to help pets understand that hands are good for many things, like pouring food in a bowl, but they're not to be confused with play toys.

Give a stern lesson. Even playful bites can cause damage, so a zero-tolerance policy is essential. The next time your pet bites, look him straight in the eye and tell him "No!" says Dr. Hunthausen. Then ignore him for a while. Dogs—and, to a lesser extent, cats—crave our company, and a stern reprimand followed by a temporary cold spell will drive home the point that biting brings regrettable consequences.

Dogs and cats are sensitive to our moods, and, in most cases, showing displeasure will get the message across. Don't try to reinforce the message by smacking dogs or cats, Dr. Hunthausen adds. It won't help them learn any better, and it could make them afraid of your hands.

Complain in his language. One way to teach dogs not to bite is to let out a yelp as soon as their teeth touch your skin. Yelping is the sound their littermates made when they were bitten too hard, and dogs remember these early lessons. "Your dog will say to himself, 'Boy, these people are really sensitive. I have to be careful with them. Because if I bite too hard, they get up and stop the game,'" Clothier explains.

Yelping works with grown dogs, but it's more effective if you start doing it with puppies, Clothier adds. As soon as puppies hear a yelp, they'll usually pull back and say they're sorry by flapping their ears back and offering apologetic kisses.

Don't pull away. The hardest thing in the world is to hold your hand still when your cat chomps down, but it's the best way to make him stop, says Johnson-Bennett. Cats are attracted to moving objects, and yanking your hand away almost guarantees a second bite. She recommends keeping your hand still while letting loose with a high-pitched "ouch." Then give your cat the cold shoulder. This will help him understand that the good times end when he bites.

Respect his food. If there's one hot-button issue for dogs, it's a threat to their food. Even though most dogs respect their owners enough to let them walk near their food or pick up the bowl before they're done, some get extremely worked up and will growl or bite to protect what they perceive as theirs. This type of aggressive response is always a problem and should be treated by a professional, says Dr. Hunthausen. In the meantime, it's a good idea to give your dog plenty of space while he's eating.

Give cats time to relax. Like a 2-year-old who won't give up his tantrum, cats are slow to calm down. Cats who have been in fights, for example, may stay wound up for hours, even though they seem calm to you. It's not a good idea to try to calm frightened cats right away, Johnson-Bennett says. They won't appreciate your efforts to give comfort and may lash out with a sudden bite, a type of behavior called redirected aggression. Give them a few hours to calm down on their own, she advises. They'll let you know when they're ready for company again.

CHAPTER 38

Chasing Cats

Sunny, a 3-year-old yellow Labrador mix, wakes up each morning and searches for his feline housemates, Emily and Edison. As soon as he spots them, he turns on the turbo. What ensues is a high-speed chase. Sunny knocks into tables and chairs and topples lamps as he chases first one cat and then the other.

"Sunny is obsessed," says Claire Stephens of Williamsburg, Virginia. "He zeros in on the cats. And once he's going after them, he doesn't listen to me."

Sunny is just doing what comes naturally. The impulse to chase small animals—especially those who dart, swerve, and twist—is essentially hardwired into the canine brain. Most dogs don't mean any harm when they chase cats. They don't think about why they're doing it, and they wouldn't know what to do with a cat even if they caught one. They're just heeding an ancient imperative: "If it runs, it might be food, so you'd better grab it."

Ancient instincts aren't the only reason dogs chase cats. Humans have something to do with it, too. They've bred dogs to chase rabbits, foxes, and many other types of small game. To a dog, cats don't look all that different from rabbits. Cats know this, which is why they often take off even before a dog shows much interest. Once they're in motion, dogs start getting very interested.

Fortunately, dogs rarely chase the cats they live with. For one thing, they know they're not supposed to. More important, they probably view these cats to some degree as canine surrogates. They eat, sleep, and play in the same general area. So they may think of them as being little dogs—not very much fun to play with, but not to be chased either. Also, feline housemates are likely to stand their ground, and most dogs would just as soon avoid the risk of getting scratched.

All in Fun

From a dog's point of view, chasing cats is a lot of fun. Some cats think it's fun, too. As long as you don't mind the turmoil, and your cat doesn't mind the thrill, there's nothing wrong with letting them play, says Micky Niego, an animal-behavior consultant in Airmont, New York. "My cat, Olive, loves to play with my dogs," Niego says. "My bull mastiffs may gently pin her, and she'll playfully box them without using her claws. She'll escape, then come back for more."

Since chases may begin in fun and turn serious later, you have to be sure that your cat really is a willing participant. Here's how to tell.

- Cats who are feeling frisky will often initiate chase games by thumping dogs on the head. It's their way of saying, "Tag, you're it," Niego says.
- Dogs with good intentions may respond to a cat's initial thump by lowering their front legs and sticking their rumps in the air. Behaviorists call this a play bow, and it means that dogs are happy and ready to play. Dogs who stand stiffly or stare at the cat, however, are taking the whole thing much too seriously.
- Once a happy chase is under way, cats will run silently, without hissing or growling. "The minute I hear a hiss or a low growl, I know the dog has crossed the line, and I stop the play," Niego says.
- Dogs who are playing are anything but silent. They'll bark like crazy, usually with high-pitched yelps. These are the sounds that happy dogs make. Deeper, growly sounds mean dogs are feeling irritated or aggressive. "Even if you're not sure, you can never make a mistake by interrupting them," Niego adds. "If they truly want to continue playing, the cat will go back to the dog."

Interrupting a fight is the safest thing to do for the well-being of your pets. But keep in mind that pets who are fighting may not discriminate between your hand and the other pet, and you may get bitten or scratched.

Tigers and Teddy Bears

The desire to chase cats varies among different breeds. There are always exceptions, but dogs bred to stalk and kill speedy prey, such as beagles, greyhounds, and terriers, tend to show the most interest in cats, says Roger Valentine, D.V.M., a veterinarian in Santa Monica, California. Irish setters and Labrador retrievers, on the other hand, have been bred to retrieve prey, not kill it. And because their traditional prey has already been downed by human hunters, they don't usually respond to motion as much as other dogs. On the occasions when they do chase and catch cats, they're unlikely to hurt them because they're "soft-mouthed" predators. They've been bred not to bite hard or leave teeth marks.

Herding breeds such as Border collies and shelties are a curious mix of these two extremes. They're bred to chase livestock and move it in certain directions. They do chase cats—often not to catch them, but to herd them.

Mixed Signals

The vast majority of dogs today are far removed from their traditional jobs. They aren't vicious. They aren't looking for prey. They don't herd sheep or chase foxes, and neither did their parents or grandparents. Yet they still chase cats. Old instincts certainly linger, but there's also a benign reason for this behavior: They want to play.

Dogs are exceptionally playful. They romp around with people and other dogs, and they're certainly willing to play with cats. Cats, while they're certainly amenable to fun and games, don't indulge in play as much as dogs do. And they don't always understand that most dogs have good intentions. So the canine message of "Let's play" is probably misinterpreted by cats as "You're prey." Naturally, they take off. Dogs sense their fear, and this, in turn, trips their ancient prey drive. So what begins as a friendly game can turn into something more serious.

Slowing Them Down

Cats are very fast, and most dogs are relatively slow. They don't catch cats very often, but the chase itself can be a problem. Apart from the risk of household damage, cats who are always getting chased start feeling nervous and insecure. They may indulge in nervous behavior, like spraying. They also tend to get sick more than calm cats because their bodies are perpetually flooded with powerful fight-or-flight hormones, which may weaken immunity.

Once dogs discover the joys of chasing cats, it takes some work to make them stop. Dozens of generations may have passed

MESSAGES AND MEANINGS

The Reformation of Roxy

Pit bull terriers have a reputation for being fighters, but Roxy was pure love—or at least it seemed that way. For over a year, she lived happily with two cats, Frick and Frack, in a New York City apartment. They even took naps together.

Everything changed when Roxy turned 18 months old. She was as friendly as ever with her owners, but her formerly friendly interest in the cats became something more sinister. She didn't play with them. She stalked them, and it was clear what might happen if she caught them. Her owners were shocked and scared, not only because Roxy's personality had undergone such a radical change but also because they knew what pit bulls are capable of. So they called Bob DeFranco, a trainer and executive director of the Animal Behavior Center of New York.

To their relief, DeFranco knew exactly what was going on. Dogs have an adolescent phase just as people do, and they can get equally rebellious and belligerent. Dogs reach adolescence at different times. Roxy, DeFranco told them, was in the thick of it.

The only way Roxy was going to get along with the cats was if her owners enforced a few strict rules, DeFranco said. He advised them to keep Roxy in a crate for a few hours each day. The idea wasn't to punish her, but to allow the cats to roam the house without being afraid. This would help Roxy understand that they had just as many rights in the house as she did. He also recommended that they put the cats' food bowls up on a counter and elevate the litter box. This would make the cats feel more secure. And when they felt calmer, Roxy would be calmer, too.

He taught them how to read Roxy's body language. It was fine if Roxy showed interest in the cats. It wasn't fine if Roxy started staring, leaning forward, or putting her tail out stiffly—all signs that she was getting aggressive.

At the first sign of any of these signals, he explained, they needed to order Roxy to lie down. As soon as she did what they said, they were to encourage her to chase one of her favorite toys—then praise her when she did. It took about 2 months, but the effects of the new rules were dramatic. "Roxy learned that playing with a toy was far more rewarding than chasing a cat," says DeFranco.

since your dog's ancestors chased anything besides a dog biscuit, but underneath their sweet natures and careful breeding, dogs will always be predators at heart, says Micky Niego, an animal-behavior consultant in Airmont, New York.

You can't force dogs to ignore their basic instincts. Instead, give them something that's even more compelling—the urge to listen to you. Here's a four-part plan that trainers recommend.

1. Clap your hands. Once a chase is under way, all the commands in the world won't stop it because your dog won't even hear what you're saying, says Kimberly Barry, Ph.D., a certified applied animal behaviorist in Austin, Texas. She recommends clapping loudly as soon as your dog shows the slightest interest. This will focus her attention on you and away from the cat.

2. Keep your voice low. As soon as your dog is looking at you, tell her, "Leave it." Your voice should be stern but low. Yelling is counterproductive. "To dogs, that's like saying, 'Gentlemen, start your engines,' " says Niego. "It will only escalate her desire to chase."

Running after a dog who's chasing a cat also adds fuel to the fire. Ancient dogs always hunted in groups. Your dog may interpret your sudden motion as a sign that you're taking part in the hunt. It's better to stand still while giving the "leave it" command, says Dr. Valentine.

3. Give them something better to do. Dogs who are told to stop doing something that they really want to do have to make a choice: They're either going to listen to you or they're going to give in to the emotions of the moment. You can make the choice easier by immediately redirecting their attention to something else that they like. It might be a toy that's on the floor. Or it could be you, assuming you run a few steps in the opposite direction. The idea is to give your dog a way to release some of that excitement in a more socially acceptable way.

4. Remove the temptation. Dogs are much more likely to chase cats they don't know than those they see every day. This tends to be a problem when people who already have cats bring a dog home for the first time. Even though the dog is unlikely to catch the cats, you don't want her to get in the habit. One solution is to move all of the cats' belongings—the litter box and food and water bowls—to high places, says Dr. Valentine. This gives cats a safe place to retreat to and ensures that the opportunities to chase are kept to a minimum.

CHAPTER 39

Chewing

Stormy is a good dog with a very bad habit. He chews everything he can find, and he doesn't seem to know how to stop. His passion is evident in the mounting pile of debris in the yard outside Laura Whittaker's home in Franklin, New York. There are splintered boards that used to be part of the deck. Two pairs of mutilated shoes. Some ragged horseback riding tack and the remnants of a welcome mat. The pile is likely to grow because Stormy, a 2-year-old Labrador, shows no sign of outgrowing his habit, Whittaker says.

At least he's in good company. All dogs like to chew, and the retriever breeds are especially fond of it, says Marty Becker, D.V.M., a veterinarian in Bonners Ferry, Idaho, and coauthor of *Chicken Soup for the Pet Lover's Soul*. "If you distill a Lab down to his essence, you'll find two neurons connected to a set of teeth," says Dr. Becker, whose own Labrador, Sirloin, culminated his chewing career by gnawing the Christmas decorations—bulbs, extension cords, and all—from the outside of the Beckers' house.

Though retrievers are among the worst offenders, they hardly have the chewing market cornered. Just as humans use their hands to express their feelings, dogs use their teeth. They chew when they're happy or sad. They chew when they're bored. And sometimes they chew just because it feels good to do it.

Cats have their own forms of vandalism, but they're rarely chewers, adds Robin Downing, D.V.M., a veterinarian in Windsor, Colorado. "Cats tend to be destructive with their claws," she says. "They're rippers and tearers. It's dogs who are the gnawers."

A Natural Urge

Dogs explore the world with their mouths. When they're young, they will mouth and chew anything they can get their mouths around, just as human babies do. By chewing and tasting their way through their environments, puppies soon learn what tastes good and what doesn't, which textures they prefer and which they'd rather avoid. They also learn what will pass for food in a pinch—and for puppies, food is rarely far from their minds. A puppy's urge to chew peaks between 14 and 24 weeks. That's when they are teething, and chewing helps ease their aching gums, explains Dr. Downing.

Most dogs outgrow the urge to chew and turn to other entertaining habits, like digging up the yard. But some dogs continue to be oral throughout their lives. In part, this is because they may have been bred for generations to work with their mouths—by retrieving ducks, for example. Anyone who owns retrievers will attest that they don't have to be taught to retrieve. Whatever you throw, a retriever will pick it up and carry it in his mouth. And if you don't take it back, he'll gladly settle down to chew it.

"Chewing is one of the most basic dog behaviors," says Dr. Downing. "They don't think too hard about doing it. It comes naturally."

An Emotional Release

Once dogs outgrow the teething stage, they begin to be more discriminating in the things they chew, and they don't have the same compulsion to do it. It takes some trial and error, but they eventually understand which things in the house they're allowed to chew (their toys) and which they're supposed to leave alone (couches, shoes, handbags). Some dogs, however, never learn this basic lesson. If they can reach it, they'll chew it. In fact, they seem almost driven to chew, and it's not a good sign, says Dr. Downing. It usually means that something's out of balance in their lives, and they're coping with their uncomfortable feelings by chewing. Some of the reasons include the following:

Boredom. Grown dogs who do a lot of chewing are usually bored, says Inger Martens, a trainer and behavior consultant in Los Angeles. Chewing is one way dogs burn off energy that they're not releasing in other ways, she explains.

Anxiety. Just as people bite their nails or smoke more when they're nervous or anxious, dogs chew. It's a way of releasing negative feelings and consoling themselves, says Dr. Becker. Some dogs will chew anything when they're upset. Others are more selective and will only chew things that, in their minds, represent the problem. Dogs who are afraid to be alone, for example, will sometimes chew doors or window frames. And they often chew objects that they associate with their owners, like gloves or shoes. It's not their way of saying they're ticked off, he says. They do it because the objects smell like their owners, and that's the canine equivalent of comfort food.

Habit. Dogs may chew on sofas or socks simply because no one ever taught them not to. Dogs need this type of guidance, especially when they're young. A mother dog always corrects her pups when they chew on things that she considers inappropriate, such as her ears. Humans, on the other hand, don't understand the canine rules and sometimes let puppies chew whatever they want. After a while, chewing becomes a habit. Once dogs develop a taste for solid oak or fine upholstery, it's not easy to make them stop.

DIRECTED CHEWING

Since dogs chew as naturally as they breathe, it would be impossible—and cruel—to make them stop. Yet you don't want to sacrifice your personal belongings to your dog's voracious pleasures. The solution is to compromise: Encourage dogs to chew, but make sure they understand what constitutes an appropriate chew toy. As long as you're consistent and vigilant for a few weeks, most dogs learn pretty quickly to distinguish a soggy tennis ball from your favorite shoes. Here's a plan that trainers recommend.

- Before teaching dogs what they can't chew, give them something they can. Pet supply stores are packed with chew toys, ranging from rubber balls and nylon bones to pig ears. Dogs have preferences just as people do, and you may have to try a few different chews until you find the one your dog likes best, Dr. Downing says. Bright colors are essentially meaningless to dogs, so don't spend extra money to get a bright red or electric green chew. Shop for texture and consistency; most dogs like toys that provide a little *al dente* resistance. One of their favorite toys happens to be the cheapest: Nearly every dog adores used tennis balls, and you can usually find a few in the grass or bushes surrounding neighborhood courts.
- Since dogs are intensely attracted to odors, new toys don't always generate a lot of excitement. People understandably get

NAME: Heide

OCCUPATION: Product Development Director

When it's time to choose the year's most valuable employee, Miles Handy knows who he'll honor: his director of research and development, Heide.

A 13-year-old beagle, Heide has unfailing instincts for what the dogs of America want. Her job is to test every variety of treat and rawhide chew produced by Oink-Oink in Detroit. Heide has absolute veto power, Miles says. If she doesn't like it, he won't sell it, because there's a good chance other dogs will turn up their noses, too.

So far, Heide's judgment has been impeccable. In just 4 years, Miles's company has expanded from a one-man operation to a national operation that produces nearly 100 different products, with a state-of-the-art processing plant, high-tech smokehouses, and an automated packaging line.

Heide's sophisticated tastebuds were what launched the company in the first place. Miles bought a pig ear chew at a trade show and brought it home. Heide loved it. "I knew that if Heide liked them, they'd sell," he says. He quickly went into mass production, producing pig ears in flavors ranging from pizza and Cheddar cheese to cool mint.

In 1997, Miles decided it was time to share the wealth by appointing a canine board of directors. Today, six other dogs have joined Heide in the R&D department. Each dog (with a little human help) completes a "Paws Up, Paws Down" form for every product.

discouraged when they buy a fancy chew toy for $10, only to watch their dog sniff it for a moment before returning to the tatty sneakers he was working over. Dogs chew your possessions largely because they have your scent, so it's a good idea to "mark" new toys by rubbing them between your palms for a while, says Dr. Downing.

• As soon as your dog starts chewing an authorized toy, show some excitement, suggests Dr. Downing. Praise and play with him. Throw the toy so he can grab it and bring it back. He'll discover that this particular toy has lots of potential, and he'll keep returning to it to repeat the fun. At this point the toy is truly his, and you're ready for the next step: Teaching him what he can't chew.

• Whether you have a puppy or an older dog, the first weeks of a stop-chewing program are the toughest because you're trying to break old habits—or prevent new habits from taking hold. Once dogs get the opportunity to chew something they shouldn't, the pleasurable experience is something they'll remember. So you essentially have to act like a doggy cop, keeping your dog in sight all the time.

When you catch him putting something in his mouth, quickly take it away and replace it with his toy, praising him when he takes it, says Dr. Downing. When you're not around to supervise, keep him in an area where he doesn't have access to temptation. If you can deny him the opportunity for unsupervised chewing for a few weeks, you'll be able to reinforce the idea that his toys are acceptable for chewing, while yours are not.

• It's not uncommon for dogs to get fixated on particular objects, like shoes or chair legs. Since it's nearly impossible to supervise dogs all the time, you may want to apply a pet repellent to the target areas. Repellents such as Grannick's Bitter Apple spray or cream have a terrible taste, and most dogs will stay away from objects that have been treated. You don't have to use a repellent forever, Dr. Downing adds. Dogs learn from experience, and after thinking "Bleghh!" a few times, they'll be more likely to view their toys in a more appreciative light.

Bitter Apple and other repellents aren't always effective, she adds. "My dog will eat anything with Bitter Apple on it," she explains. Be prepared to experiment a bit. Hot-pepper sauce can be a very effective deterrent, although you'll want to test it first to make sure it doesn't stain.

PETS VS. PEOPLE

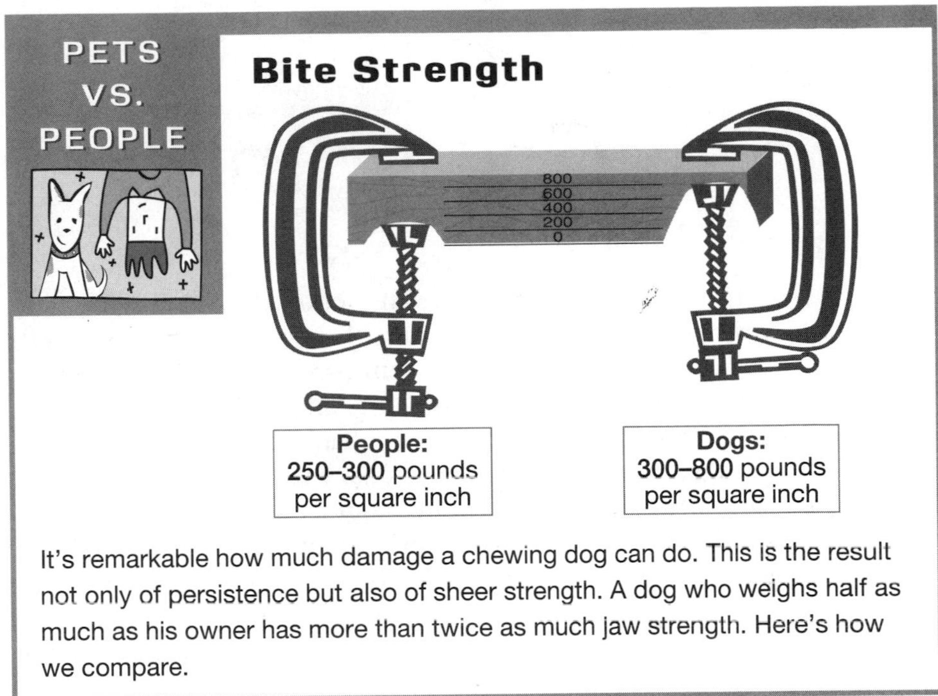

It's remarkable how much damage a chewing dog can do. This is the result not only of persistence but also of sheer strength. A dog who weighs half as much as his owner has more than twice as much jaw strength. Here's how we compare.

• Since dogs who don't get a lot of exercise and don't have a lot to do are the ones most likely to chew, it's essential to help them burn off excess energy, Dr. Downing says. Chasing a ball or going for regular walks allows dogs to blow off steam. Active dogs get to be tired dogs, she adds. This means they'll be more likely to spend their time napping rather than chewing.

CHAPTER 40

Crowding

Every species has a different notion of personal space, that invisible circle of privacy that separates what's private from what's public. For humans, personal space averages about 2 feet. We start feeling uncomfortable when people we don't know come any closer than that.

Dogs and cats also have personal spaces. Their zones of privacy, however, are different from ours. Cats demand a lot of personal space, and they take it for granted that everyone else does, too. For some dogs, however, personal space is measured by the hair-width—they just can't get close enough. This is fine when they're with other dogs, but it can make people feel a little claustrophobic.

"Dogs find great comfort in having physical contact with humans," says R. M. Alev, D.V.M., a veterinarian in Skokie, Illinois. This can be very pleasant when you're in the mood for some furry company, but some dogs won't quit crowding. They sit on your feet when you're working. They try to follow you when you walk into the bathroom. They do everything possible, in other words, not to let you get more than 3 inches away.

Ever Closer

When you watch dogs playing together, it's easy to see how they can crowd the people in their lives. They're in constant physical contact—sniffing, pawing, nuzzling, and wrestling. "Dogs are programmed to be social animals," says D. B. Cameron, D.V.M., a veterinarian in Nevada City, California. They can't talk verbally from a distance the way people can. They depend on physical contact to express themselves. So what people call crowding, dogs would call communicating.

Cats are much less likely to crowd their owners. All cats, from lions in the wild to Persians in city apartments, have a natural tendency to be solitary and apart. Cats never lived in groups the way dogs did, Dr. Cameron explains. So when your cat is all over you—rubbing against your legs, climbing on your lap, and kneading your stomach with those sharp little claws—she probably isn't trying to communicate anything special. She's just enjoying the physical contact.

"Cats set the ground rules for physical contact," says Dave Frederick, D.V.M., a veterinarian in Woodstock, Illinois. "They'll come to you when they are ready, and they'll plop themselves on your lap or across your chest, whether it's a good time for you or not."

LOOKING FOR COMFORT

Even though most dogs enjoy physical contact, they differ tremendously in the degree to which they try to get close to people. Those who were removed from their litters before they were ready tend to keep a greater distance later on, says Carol Lawson, a trainer in Garfield Heights, Ohio. Those who spent more time with their littermates and who interacted a lot with people when they were young tend to crave physical contact as they get older, she explains.

"Dogs sometimes have days when they're feeling uncommonly needy, just as humans do," Dr. Cameron adds. A dog who can't bear to be alone even for a few minutes may have woken up feeling insecure. Dr. Cameron thinks that clingy behavior may occur more often during long, dark days, suggesting that some dogs may have the equivalent of seasonal affective disorder.

Dogs who have been frightened—by the crash of thunder, for example—are the ones most likely to pad around after their owners, adds Carlos Davila, a trainer in Parma, Ohio. This type of crowding usually diminishes after the original scare is over, but some dogs keep doing it—either because their confidence was badly shaken or because crowding has become a habit, he says.

Dogs don't necessarily crowd their people because they're insecure. In some cases, they may be responding to our insecurities. "Have you ever noticed that your dog crowds on days when you are under extreme stress or you don't feel well?" says Dr. Cameron. "Some dogs have an uncanny ability to be nurturing and supportive."

CROWDING FOR CONTROL

You would think that dogs who perpetually follow their owners around the house are the most timid and insecure. But sometimes the opposite is true. Dogs who are unusually assertive will sometimes use physical contact as a way of signaling their independence and leadership. Watch two dogs when they're playing. One of the dogs will invariably be much more physical than the other. She'll deliberately use her body to dominate the other one by leaning, pushing, and shoving. Dogs do similar things with people when they're attempting to increase their leadership within the family.

"They might do something as subtle as brushing up against you when you pass in a narrow hallway," says Terry Miller, a trainer in Cleveland Heights, Ohio. Dogs who do this aren't insecure. Rather, they're trying to make *you* insecure in order to bolster their own social power.

LOSING THE SHADOW

It may be natural for dogs to nose into your personal space, but it's not something you have to live with. In fact, you shouldn't. Regardless of the message they're sending—"Reassure me" or "I want you to move first"—it's a sign that they aren't coping very well on their own. The longer that dogs are allowed to crowd their people, the more they start to believe that this is the way things are meant to be. "The only way to deal with dogs who are annoyingly underfoot all the time is to be lovingly firm," says Dr. Cameron.

Walk away—in a straight line. Dogs who crave attention have a neat trick for making sure people notice: They refuse to budge. Don't make a detour, Dr. Cameron says. Walk right through them, even if that means pushing them out of the way with your knee or foot. This conveys two messages: one, that your needs come before theirs; and two, that their job is to pay attention to you, not the other way around. Dogs who get accustomed to accommodating people tend to be less clingy than those whose owners accommodate them.

Send your message silently. Scolding dogs for getting too close is counterproductive. For one thing, scolding makes dogs nervous, and nervous dogs get more insecure. It also gives them attention, and that's what they want above all else. "Walk away from them without saying a word," says Dr. Cameron. "Sometimes dogs are happy to get even negative attention, and scolding them could encourage them to continue the behavior."

Give extra attention, but only at certain times. Some dogs are so needy for attention and reassurance that it seems downright cruel to ignore them. You aren't doing them any favors by giving in when they crowd you, says Dr. Cameron. Dogs view the world very simply. When they're insecure and get loads of attention, they figure it's because you're nervous about something, too. On the other hand, giving them attention when they're *not* acting clingy lets them know they're loved without giving the message that you approve of the way they're acting, Dr. Cameron explains.

CHAPTER 41

Digging

When Brendan and Matilda Murphy moved to their new home in Olive Branch, Mississippi, they looked forward to playing on the thick, soft lawn—a nice change from the weed-choked yard at their previous house. Francine, their 18-month-old yellow Labrador, noticed the lawn, too. But after a 9-hour drive, 2 days of being shut in the garage while the carpet was replaced, and a harrowing 8 hours watching from her crate while men from a moving company hauled everything inside, her plans were a little less innocent: She was going to tear it up.

Within 3 hours, Francine had virtually destroyed the turf, leaving mammoth holes that made the pretty yard look more like something from *Caddyshack* than the grassy retreat her family had paid for.

Francine went into the earth-moving business in order to release pent-up energy and anxiety. But that's just one motivation for digging, says Rolan Tripp, D.V.M., affiliate professor of applied animal behavior at Colorado State University Veterinary School in Fort Collins and author of *Pet Perception Management*. Some dogs, like Francine, do it to relieve stress. Others dig in order to create a comfortable place to lie down. And still others do it because the dirt is there and, hey, it's fun.

The reason dogs turn to digging as opposed to, say, destroying furniture is that the urge is wired into their personalities. Dogs have been digging for thousands of years. At one time, it contributed to their survival because it allowed them to store food or stay warm in the winter. Dogs today don't have to worry as much about staying warm, but the instinct remains.

For some breeds, digging is more than just a natural inclination—it's the mission they're born to. Terriers, beagles, and dachshunds, among others, have been bred for generations to run down small prey and dig for it when it dives underground. The urge to dig is part of who they are.

Cats scratch the ground a little bit to cover urine and droppings, but they don't dig digging the way dogs do, says Dr. Tripp. Even if they did, they're smaller than dogs and don't engage in prolonged periods of physical activity. They couldn't do much damage to a yard even if they tried.

SAME HOLE, DIFFERENT REASONS

Back when dogs spent most of their time on farms or ranches, no one thought of digging as being much of a problem. But the advent of sprawling yards and precious, well-tended gardens transformed a perfectly normal behavior into a real problem.

Digging becomes an issue when owners and their dogs disagree on where, when, and how it should be done. Owners who dream of golf course–quality turf and backyard botanical gardens have a hard time reconciling their desires with the urges of their dogs, who probably doze off while thinking of wider, deeper, more plentiful holes. You can't extinguish a dog's inherent desires to dig, says Dr. Tripp. But once you understand what's bringing these desires to the surface, you can usually discover ways to reduce or eliminate the damage.

Some dogs dig just for fun, he adds, and this type of digging can be very difficult to stop. Others, however, are trying to solve a problem, and digging is their solution. Dogs who are digging for answers fall into a few main categories.

The Climate Controller. The most practical of all diggers are those who do it to stay cool in summer and warm in winter. Northern breeds such as huskies and malamutes do a lot of digging in the summer because their coats are really too heavy for temperate climates, says Wayne Hunthausen, D.V.M., an animal-behavior consultant in Westwood, Kansas, and coauthor of *Handbook of Behaviour Problems of the Dog and Cat*.

Even though the ground is a great insulator, it isn't perfect. It doesn't take long for holes to warm up or cool down, depending on the air temperature. Dogs sensibly respond by digging even deeper—or, when that fails, by digging a new hole.

The Escape Artist. Dogs who dig at fences or gates—or in some cases at the floors in front of outside doors—are saying, "Let me out of here," Dr. Hunthausen explains. It's not that they're necessarily unhappy where they are. They're just inter-

NAME: Jed
OCCUPATION: Earth Mover

A dog who knew what was good for him wouldn't dig in Emma Sweeney's garden. The coauthor of *The Complete Idiot's Guide to Gardening* and *Perennials: A Growing Guide for Easy, Colorful Gardens*, Emma takes her precious patch of earth very seriously. But Jed, Emma's 6-year-old Labrador retriever, had always been a little bit impulsive. Besides, he loved the feel of soft, tilled earth against his paws. "The garden was getting to be a real mess," says Emma, of Clinton, New York.

Emma couldn't decide whether to ban Jed from the yard or to let him slowly drive her out of her mind with fury. But one day, as Emma was thinking about how excited Jed got about the prospect of "helping" her garden, she remembered a friend's advice. "She said that if your dog doesn't have a job to do, he can get depressed," Emma says.

So she decided to give Jed the job he was asking for: She made him her digger.

Instead of turning Jed away when she picked up the shovel, she started urging him on—not that Jed ever needed much encouragement. Emma discovered that Jed could easily do the digging that she was laboring over all by himself. "In the spring or the fall when I'm planting, I start to dig with my shovel, and then I say, 'Jed, dig,' and he comes and digs up that spot. His favorite thing is to find roots that have to be torn out because then he gets in a wrestling match, too."

ested in something on the other side. It could be an intriguing scent or sound, or they could be trying to find a playmate.

The Lonely Heart. Dogs are social animals. Most get used to spending time alone, but some go crazy when their owners go away. This condition, called separation anxiety, is most common in dogs who have been abandoned at some point or who have had several owners, says Dr. Tripp. Dogs with separation anxiety usually do their digging at doors, under windows, or near other barriers that they feel separate them from their owners. These dogs don't really have a specific goal in mind. They're just so filled with stress and anxiety that they have to do something, anything, to make the feelings go away. Digging is a common way of coping, although some dogs get more destructive and will chew on door frames, furniture, or anything else until they're feeling better.

The Workout Fanatic. Some dogs dig for the same reason people run: They need and like the exercise. "People sometimes think that when they put their dog out in that big backyard in the morning that the dog will run laps and wear herself out before they get home," says Inger Martens, a trainer and behavior consultant in Los Angeles. "In fact, those dogs spend most of their days lying by the door waiting for someone to come home—at least, the parts of the day they don't spend digging holes to China."

The Mutt in a Rut. "Lots of dogs dig out of boredom," Martens says. This is most common in high-energy breeds such as Labradors, terriers, and hunting dogs. They have a lot of energy, and digging provides an outlet. And it doesn't take much to get them started: A leaf falling on the ground will draw their attention, and they'll start turning dirt to see what's down there. "What begins with curiosity can become a habit," she says.

LIBERATING THE LAWN

Since dogs can't tell you why they're digging, getting them to stop can be a challenge. About all you can do is make some educated guesses about what digging category your dog belongs in and find some ways to satisfy her instincts to excavate. Sometimes this is easy. A dog who's digging burrows in order to stay cool may give it up when she's given a cooler place to rest. Dogs who have been bred to dig or who dig for the love of it present a tougher challenge because they don't *need* anything except the digging itself. Your path to a smooth backyard may have a few holes while you look for workable solutions. Veterinarians usually recommend trying a variety of tactics. Sooner or later, you'll find the one that works best for you.

Keep her busy. Taking your dog for a walk, preferably before you let her loose in the yard, can mean the difference between intact turf at the end of the day and a yard reminiscent of a minefield. One or two walks a day is enough for some dogs, but others need a lot more exercise. Dr. Tripp recommends coming home at lunch and giving your dog an extra walk. If your schedule doesn't permit this, you may want to hire a dog walker or trade favors with a neighbor. Dogs who get a lot of exercise are a lot less likely to dig, he explains.

Provide a comfort zone. If you suspect that your dog is digging to regulate her body temperature or to give herself a comfy den, you can take a load off her mind by providing it for her. In winter, an insulated doghouse furnished with a few old blankets will make cold, dreary holes seem downright uncomfortable. In summer, try filling a child's wading pool with a few inches of cool water, suggests Dr. Tripp.

Regardless of the temperature, dogs sometimes dig in order to create a small, enclosed space that makes them feel comfortable and secure. You can improve on nature by making a better den. Put a wooden box in a quiet, sheltered part of the yard and fill it with old blankets or a load of straw. Put a few of your dog's toys in the box, then stand back while she makes her explorations. Any sensible dog will prefer a straw-lined box to a cold, cramped hole, and your yard's appearance should start improving fairly quickly.

Garden privately. Dogs look to their owners for leadership, and when they see people digging in the yard, they want to join in—then look surprised when their owners are not as thrilled with their handiwork as they are, Dr. Hunthausen says. Even though it's a lot of fun to spend time in the yard with your dog, you'll have to make some compromises when there's a digger in the family. If your dog can't see you digging, she'll be less likely to do it on her own, he explains.

Keep them busy. Dogs who dig invariably have too much extra time on their paws, says Dr. Hunthausen. Whether they're digging to while away the hours or to console themselves during

WHAT'S MY PET SAYING?

Behavior
Burying Bones

What It Means
"I'm Protecting My Leftovers"

Dogs may not really know why they bury bones, but the habit is an old one, says Benjamin Hart, D.V.M., Ph.D., professor of physiology and behavior at the University of California, Davis, School of Veterinary Medicine and author of *The Perfect Puppy: How to Choose Your Dog by Its Behavior*. It began in the days when dogs lived in packs and hunted for large prey, such as antelope, deer, and moose. Even for a pack of dogs, a moose is a pretty hefty meal. Without an icebox in sight, dogs wisely buried their leftovers. This kept the food fresh and helped ensure that other dogs didn't come along and swipe it.

Dogs don't have to worry anymore about preserving food from one meal to the next, but their ancient urges have them excavating backyard treasure troves anyway, says Dr. Hart. Whether they're burying a hefty bone or a favorite toy, they hate to see anything go to waste—and they certainly don't want anyone else to get it.

the long, lonely hours that you're gone, they need jobs to keep them busy. Try some of the following strategies.

- Get a hollow rawhide bone or rubber chew toy and fill the inside with a sticky treat such as canned dog food, melted (and cooled) cheese, or peanut butter. Dogs will spend hours trying to get to the goods inside.
- Put out a Buster Cube. Available in pet supply stores, the Buster Cube is a nifty hollow toy that you fill with dry food. As your dog pushes the cube around, it periodically drops a piece of food. It's designed to release enough food to keep dogs motivated, but not so much that they finish the game in a hurry.
- Organize a dog-visiting co-op. If you live in a neighborhood with a lot of dogs, you may be able to interest other owners in swapping dog-sitting (and dog-walking) services. Some people are always home during the early evening, while others are free

at lunchtimes. If you get enough people interested, your dog will have the excitement of meeting her friends every day, and the exercise and mental stimulation will take her mind off the lawn, Dr. Hunthausen says.

Make old holes undesirable. No matter how much you discourage dogs from digging, they're invariably attracted to the scene of their original crimes. It's worth taking a few minutes to make old holes less "diggable," says Dr. Tripp, by filling them with rocks, for example, or by covering them with chicken wire or a tarp.

Spay or neuter your pet. The urge to meet and greet the opposite sex respects few boundaries, certainly not boundaries that dogs can dig under. More than a few yards are peppered with holes near the fence, made by dogs who started mining to find love. Once pets are neutered, the instinct to escape recedes in a few weeks or months, says Dr. Tripp.

Give in and watch the fun. Some dogs, either because of breeding, temperament, or simply the love of the sport, will never quit digging. You can't fight fate forever, but you can direct it a little bit by giving your dog one place where she's allowed to dig. Choose an out-of-the-way spot, lead your dog to it, and encourage her to dig, Dr. Tripp recommends. The best way to get her started is to get on your knees and do a little digging yourself. When she takes your cue and puts her feet in motion, praise and encourage her. It won't take more than that to keep her happy.

CHAPTER 42

Drinking from the Toilet

Imagine a stale puddle of water that's been sitting in 80° heat all day, maybe with a few hairs floating on top. Now imagine a bubbling stream of cool, refreshing water. It's pretty obvious which one you'd choose—and which one dogs and cats prefer. It explains why they'll sometimes make a detour around their water dishes and pad down the hall to the bathroom for a quick thirst-quencher.

From a human point of view, the idea of drinking from the toilet isn't very appealing. But dogs and cats don't have our inhibitions about bathroom business. All they see when they look at a toilet is a big, porcelain water fountain, a king-size source of cold refreshment that's renewed like a magic spring many times a day. The water's always fresh. It's always available. And there may be a bit of an aftertaste, which, to them, makes it taste even better.

"Most pet owners leave out water for their pets in a plastic bowl, and it often sits there for several hours or even days," says Nicholas Dodman, B.V.M.S. (a British equivalent of D.V.M.), professor of behavioral pharmacology and director of the behavior clinic at Tufts University School of Veterinary Medicine in North Grafton, Massachusetts, and author of *Dogs Behaving Badly* and *The Cat Who Cried for Help*. "As the water warms up to room temperature, you can see bubbles form around the sides of the bowl as the dissolved air comes out. I'm sure that by that time it doesn't taste very fresh."

There's another reason pets sometimes ignore their water bowls in favor of the toilet. In hot weather especially, people sometimes forget to keep the bowls full. Dogs and cats, finding their usual springs dried up, go off in search of other supplies.

They find the toilet, quench their thirsts—and remember. Even if you never let the bowl run dry again, your pet may decide to keep returning to the place he had success.

MORE THAN GOOD TASTE

The toilet isn't the only source of water in the house. For cats, a dripping faucet or the moisture left in a bathtub provides more than enough water to keep them going. Yet they often seem to prefer the toilet anyway. Part of this is probably due to their curiosity. Both dogs and cats are attracted to novelty. Toilets make gurgling and whooshing sounds that pets may find intriguing, says Wayne Hunthausen, D.V.M., an animal-behavior consultant in Westwood, Kansas, and coauthor of *Handbook of Behaviour Problems of the Dog and Cat*.

Cats have an additional reason to drink from the toilet. They originated in the African savannah, where water was scarce. A bubbling spring was more than just intriguing; it kept them alive. On some level, cats have probably retained an interest in all things flowing. They hate getting wet, yet it's not uncommon for them to put their paws into the toilet or under faucets to feel the moving water, Dr. Hunthausen explains.

A toilet may not be as clean as a bowl of water, but this is hardly a deterrent for pets, Dr. Dodman adds. They think nothing of eating and drinking things that humans wouldn't touch. In fact, for some, the smellier and dirtier things are, the more pets seem to like them. This usually isn't a problem. Even though toilets may harbor bacteria, pets rarely get sick from drinking the water—unless someone in the family happens to be infected with organisms such as *E. coli* or salmonella, in which case pets drinking toilet water may get sick, too. "Fortunately, cats and dogs have very strong gastric acid that helps protect them," he explains.

BRING THEM BACK TO THEIR BOWLS

Even though drinking from the toilet is generally harmless, no one really wants to listen to pets slurping it up. Then there are the wet splashes on the seat and floor, and the wet-mouthed kisses that make everyone a little squeamish. "Having your dog take a drink, then come up and kiss you on the lips would be

Hard Drinkers

It's common for dogs to empty their water bowls once or twice a day. Some breeds, however, seem to be perpetually thirsty, regardless of their size. Tracking dogs are notorious for their water consumption, says Amy Ammen, a trainer in Milwaukee and author of *Training in No Time*. It's not because of their size or activity levels. It's because they use their noses all the time. In the process of sniffing, a lot of moisture escapes from the olfactory system.

"Tracking dogs and search-and-rescue dogs drink incredible amounts of water," she says.

about the same thing as sticking your hand in the toilet and rubbing the side of your face," says Dr. Hunthausen.

Keeping pets out of the toilet is probably a good idea. Closing the lid will deter cats and most dogs. But no one's going to remember to close the lid all the time, and some dogs have been known to nose it open. So you may want to make a few other changes as well.

Give them moist food. Dogs and cats are creatures of convenience, and they're generally disposed to drink from their bowls rather than make a long trip down the hall to the toilet. When they're unusually thirsty, however, they may find themselves visiting both their water bowl and the toilet. One way to reduce their thirst is to feed them wet food now and then, says Dr. Dodman. "Wet food is about 75 percent water, so in the process of eating a meal, they're also having a drink."

Upgrade the water bowl. Most food and water bowls these days are made from plastic. Plastic is inexpensive and durable, but it also picks up odors. Pets who routinely bypass their bowls and head for the toilet may simply dislike the taste of the water they're getting. Bowls made from stainless steel or ceramic are tough and easy to clean, and they're less likely than plastic to have off tastes.

Give them ice water. This doesn't work for cats, but you can encourage dogs to come back to their water bowls by putting in a few ice cubes. Dogs love ice. The cold feels good going down, and they enjoy crunching it, says Amy Ammen, a trainer in Milwaukee and author of *Training in No Time*. The more they look forward to an icy treat, the less likely they'll be to wander to the fountain down the hall.

You don't have to put ice in the bowl every day, she adds. Dogs respond very well to what trainers call intermittent reinforcement. Giving them ice sometimes but not always will encourage them to keep coming back, ever hopeful that they'll hit the jackpot.

Ask your veterinarian about toilet additives. Some people add chemicals to toilet tanks to give them a perfumed scent. This can be a great way to keep pets away at the same time, says Dr. Dodman. "To us it smells clean, but most animals really dislike these odors," he says.

You'll have to be careful what you buy, however, since some toilet-cleaning products may be toxic for pets. Your veterinarian can tell you which products will keep pets away and which are too toxic to use.

CHAPTER 43

Dung Eating

Sydney, Australia, has a big-time problem with dog poop. Every day, canines there generate more than 100 tons of the stuff, much of which piles up on public sidewalks and park paths. To solve this unpleasant situation, politicians voted to import 25,000 exotic dung beetles from Africa and the Mediterranean. The inch-long insects have been given *carte blanche* to roam city streets and devour the droppings, making Sydney safe for sandals again.

Now, it's unlikely that your backyard will ever be that much of a minefield. But it's quite possible that your dog may decide to show you his best African dung beetle imitation by eating dung, either his own or another pet's. Called coprophagia, dung eating is almost exclusively a problem with dogs. (Cats who eat dung probably have a medical problem, and you'll need to call your vet.) It's also a not-so-subtle form of communication. Your pet could be telling you anything from "I'm hungry" or "I'm bored" to "Mom used to do it, so I just don't know any better."

Experts believe that most dogs will sample dung at least a few times in their lives. Fortunately, there's usually very little risk to your pet's health. About the only thing your dog may pick up—besides a world-class case of bad breath—is an intestinal parasite such as tapeworms. While it's always a good idea to have your dog's stool checked for parasites at least once a year, it's especially important for dung eaters.

Why Dogs Do It

Before deciding how to keep your dog from eating dung, it's important to understand why he's so attracted to the stuff in the first place. Veterinarians suspect that the problem starts in early puppyhood. When a dog has a litter, she often keeps her nest clean by eating the stools of her pups. This serves two purposes, says Michele Zajac, D.V.M., a veterinarian in Scranton, Pennsylvania. Removing the stools helps keep the den free of diseases and intestinal parasites. It also keeps the smell down—an important factor in the wild, where strong odors can attract predators to the helpless pups.

Coprophagia is mainly an issue with young dogs, Dr. Zajac adds. Because puppies explore with their mouths, some discover that dung tastes good enough to eat. Eating dung is not as much of a problem with kittens. Mother cats sometimes eat the stools of their young, but kittens rarely mimic the behavior.

Some puppies continue to eat dung once they're out of the nest and exploring the world. Dogs perceive their environment much more with their noses than with their eyes. Scents in the air provide a world of information about their surroundings, and nothing screams "Here I am!" louder than animal stools.

The scent is not only powerful, it can also provide clues about who's eating what and what other animals have been in the area. Since a dog's sense of taste is closely linked to his sense of smell, eating stool may help him gather some additional intelligence.

Dogs usually outgrow the urge to eat dung by the time they reach their first birthday. "They just seem to lose the desire for it," Dr. Zajac says. "If your dog hasn't shown this behavior by the time he's full-grown, it's not too likely that he ever will."

Some dogs, however, get the taste for dung and never give it up. And a small percentage will pick up the habit in their later years. Experts aren't really sure why older dogs eat stools, but they have a few theories.

- Hunger. If a dog doesn't get enough to eat at mealtimes, he may try to quell his rumbling belly by eating stools.
- Confinement. A dog may eat dung in order to keep his cage clean.
- Boredom. Dogs, like children, tend to exhibit their worst behavior when they don't have anything fun to do.
- Observation. Watching another dog nibble on dung could rekindle your dog's old habit or get him started for the first time.
- Attention. Dogs enjoy getting attention from their owners, and eating dung invariably does the trick, says C. A. Tony Buffington, D.V.M., Ph.D., professor of veterinary clinical sciences at the Ohio State University in Columbus.

Even though dogs appear to have a natural need or desire for dung, there are ways to stop the habit. Here's what veterinarians recommend.

Eliminate the temptation. Your dog won't feast on stools unless he first finds stools to feast on. If you clean the yard every time your dog—or any other pet who happens to visit—leaves a deposit, you'll deny him the opportunity. "Just use your pooper-scooper, and you'll save a lot of trouble," says Dr. Zajac. "This is by far the simplest solution."

While you're picking up temptation, you may want to think about where you put the litter box as well. Many dogs will eat cat stools, and they see a litter box as a standing invitation. Veterinarians recommend putting the litter box in a place that's easy for your cat to reach but not so easy for your dog, such as in a closet with the door partly shut or on a high shelf that your dog can't reach.

Correct him quickly. Dogs learn pretty quickly, and what they need most is communication from you. It's always a good idea to walk your dog on a leash, and it's especially important when you're trying to stop him from eating dung. When he's starting to root around with his nose, firmly pull him away with the leash and walk in the other direction, says Dr. Zajac. You don't need to reprimand him, she adds. You don't want him to associate the dung with anger, pleasure, or attention. You just want him to keep walking. If you can keep him away from dung for a few weeks, he may gradually lose his taste for it.

Incidentally, don't try to chase your dog when he's already done the deed or actually has stools in his mouth, Dr. Zajac adds. He'll probably just interpret this as play, which means you'll have

Dogs are persistent foragers, and it's not always easy to keep them out of the litter box. One solution is to install a special catch that allows doors to open wide enough to admit a cat, but not enough for a bigger dog.

rewarded the dung eating by giving him a good game of chase. A better strategy is to distract him. Call his name or clap your hands. Then lead him away from temptation.

Keep him occupied. A busy dog is a happy dog. And a happy dog may keep his nose clean. If your dog has enough to keep him interested—balls to chase, rawhide to chew, companionship with other pets, and proper exercise—he'll be less likely to eat stools, Dr. Zajac says.

Feed him early and often. Since dogs sometimes eat stool just because they're hungry, you may want to change his feeding schedule. Try feeding him in the morning and again in the evening, Dr. Zajac suggests. Giving dogs two meals a day can help take the edge off their hunger and discourage unauthorized dining.

Consider adding fiber. Adding more fiber to your dog's diet can also help, says Kathalyn Johnson, D.V.M., clinical associate in companion animal behavior at Texas A&M University in College Station. "We're not sure why some dogs respond to this," she says. It may be that fiber changes the consistency of the stool, making it less palatable to dogs. Dr. Johnson recommends adding a teaspoon or two of Metamucil, which is very high in fiber, to your pet's food every day until he stops eating stool.

Try digestive enzymes. No matter how efficient your dog's digestive system is, some nutrients will slip through unused. It's possible that dogs can smell these unused nutrients in stools and decide to give them a second pass. Veterinarians have found that giving dogs digestive enzymes, which help them absorb more of the nutrients in their food, will sometimes stop them from eating dung.

There are several types of digestive enzymes that you can sprinkle on your dog's food. Adolph's Meat Tenderizer is a good choice, says Dr. Zajac. Use about ⅛ teaspoon for every 6 pounds of weight. Or you can use an enzyme called Prozyme, which is made exclusively for pets. The amount you use depends on the size of your pet. Follow the instructions on the label.

Give it a bad taste. Even though dogs probably don't love the taste of dung, they don't mind it, either. You can change things by sprinkling a product called For-Bid on your dog's food. Available in pet supply stores, For-Bid makes the smell and taste of stool even less desirable, says Dr. Zajac. Follow the directions given on the package. It usually works after one or two applications.

CHAPTER 44

Early-Morning Awakening

People who live with cats discover pretty quickly that they don't need fancy alarm clocks to get up in the morning. Many cats are early risers, and they firmly believe that people should get up at the same time they do, if only to fill the food bowl. And they can be quite determined about making their point: When a purr and cheek-nuzzle don't get results, they'll resort to more aggressive tactics, like batting your toes.

It's normal for cats to be awake at hours when people are sound asleep, often between 3:00 and 6:00 A.M., says Kate Gamble, a feline-behavior consultant in Auburn, California. Experts aren't sure why cats wake up so early. Tigers and other feral cats look for food before dawn, so it's likely that ancient hunting instincts propel modern cats out of their beds in the early hours, she says.

Dogs occasionally start their mornings early, but for the most part, they adjust their schedules to match their owners'. "When you're active, they're active," says Pam Johnson-Bennett, a feline-behavior consultant in Nashville and author of *Twisted Whiskers* and *Psycho Kitty?* "When you're tired, your dog is usually ready to jump on the bed and go to sleep, too."

Scheduling Changes

Even though it's normal for cats to be early risers, changes in their lifestyles or environments can cause them to wake up earlier than usual. "Cats hear things at night, especially between late February and early October, which is mating season," Gamble says. When they hear cats fighting or talking back and forth, they get excited and are less likely to sleep in, she explains.

In addition, people in the family may influence how much (or how little) cats sleep. If you're gone most of the day and don't give your cat a lot of attention in the evening, he'll have oodles of energy and will be more likely to stay up late or wake up early, Gamble says. It's essentially the feline equivalent of boredom: When nothing is happening, cats try to stir things up. Waking you up isn't as thrilling as chasing a bird, but it's better than doing nothing.

Cats don't get depressed as readily as people, but changes in their lives, such as a move to a new house or the loss of another pet, can put them in a funk, Gamble adds. "Often, they'll pick the early-morning hours to feel overwhelmed and let out a mournful-sounding meow." Older cats are particularly adept at waking their owners with continuous, piercing meows. "They don't know how loud they are meowing because they may have suffered hearing loss," she says.

RESTORING REST

In the distant future, when cats and people have spent another few thousand years together, it's likely that our sleep schedules will more closely coincide. Until then, cats will continue to wake up early—and encourage you to do the same—by running across the headboard, rattling the blinds, or knocking a glass of water off the dresser.

Nature's urges are a lot stronger than your desire to snooze for another hour, so there's no easy way to teach cats that mornings are for sleeping. Once you understand your cat's underlying motivations and desires, however, you can encourage him to sleep a little later, or at least to leave you alone while keeping himself entertained.

Satisfy their urges. Even though cats have been domesticated for thousands of years, their hunting instincts remain strong. On a typical "wild" night, cats would hunt, eat, and sleep—a routine that's hard to maintain in a modern apartment or townhouse. You can help cats sleep more soundly by simulating these ancient scenes—by playing with them for 20 minutes in the evening and feeding them afterward, says Johnson-Bennett. This gives them the sense that they've caught their prey and done a good day's work.

Gentle play is fine, Gamble adds. In fact, playing too energetically will rev your cat up and make it harder for him to sleep.

"People think that playing with their cats has to be high-energy, but cats don't kill prey that way," she explains.

Ignore the fuss. One of the most annoying tricks cats use to get their owners out of bed is also, unfortunately, one of the most effective. "They will get just out of range and meow or howl," Gamble says. "They know you have to get up to deal with them." And once they succeed in getting you out of bed, you can be sure that they'll remember this neat trick the next time. "The minute they get you up, they've won."

Since cats figure out what doesn't work just as quickly as they learn what does, it's worth gritting your teeth, covering your head with the pillow, and pretending to be asleep as long as they continue crying. Ignoring your cat may not help him sleep later, but he will learn that he's wasting his time trying to get you up. "You need to set clear boundaries so that your cat will understand what the rules are," Gamble says.

Go on the offensive. Like children who won't take "no" for an answer, cats don't always interpret a lack of interest as meaning "go away." You may need to respond more assertively to their morning incursions—by misting them with a spray bottle, for example, or bleating a tricycle horn. They'll figure out that it's better to let you sleep, Gamble says.

Help them adjust. Cats who have only recently started pestering you in the morning may be bothered by something that's happened in their lives. It could be something as simple as another cat visiting the yard. Moving to a new house can also be a problem. Giving your cat extra attention during the day and evening can help reduce stress and help him sleep more soundly. If you've recently moved, you may want to keep your cat in a small area at first, like the bedroom or a laundry room, Gamble says. When cats are tense, they don't like having too much territory. Keeping them in a smaller area, with their food and a litter box handy, will help them feel a little calmer.

Try an electric "waiter." Until your cat learns to operate the can opener, he's going to depend on you to fill his bowl—and he won't be shy about telling you when his tummy's rumbling. You can take yourself out of the picture by getting an automatic feeder, Gamble says. Available at pet supply stores, these ingenious gadgets can be programmed to open at whatever time you like. This means that you can feed your cat in the morning and save your sleep at the same time.

CHAPTER 45

Eating Grass and Plants

Americans spend billions of dollars a year on pet foods, including gourmet brands that dogs and cats probably dream about all night. So what do pets do after emptying their bowls of their exquisite contents? Some cats spend hours chomping the ends of carefully tended spider plants. Dogs may turn backyard gardens into all-you-can-eat salad bars, helping themselves to mouthfuls of grass or weeds. Then, as soon as they swallow their greens, they throw them back up.

It's not entirely strange that dogs occasionally make themselves a backyard salad, says Mary Beth Dearing, D.V.M., a veterinarian in Alexandria, Virginia. Dogs are omnivorous, which basically means that they'll eat anything that's put in front of them—insects, leaves, paper, you name it. Their bodies aren't really designed to digest grass and plants, but compared to other things they eat, greenery probably seems pretty appetizing.

Cats present more of a puzzle because they're mainly carnivorous. Even though they'll happily empty their bowls, they're predisposed to eat things they've chased, captured, and killed. They should have no need or desire for leafy stuff—and yet, most people with cats find that their houseplants look a little tatty because the leaves are getting chewed. Dr. Dearing suspects that cats aren't attracted to the taste of plants, but to the sight: It's possible that plant leaves and vines resemble mice tails, bird feathers, and other things that make cats pounce. And once they pounce, they're tempted to eat.

Greens Do the Body Good

Nature doesn't do things by accident very often. Since so many pets nibble on grass and plants, many veterinarians believe that

WHAT'S MY PET SAYING?

Behavior
Rolling in Catnip

What It Means
"I'm Bombed Out of My Head"

Scientists call it *Nepeta cataria*, but cats call it heaven. No one knows exactly why catnip gets cats in such a lather, but they suspect that most cats respond to nepetalactone, an oil found in the leaves. Some cats don't respond at all to catnip, while others get the rush of their lives, says Mary Beth Dearing, D.V.M., a veterinarian in Alexandria, Virginia. Veterinarians have noticed that some dogs like catnip, too.

After licking and chewing catnip, cats will roll around, rub their faces, shake their heads and twitch—behaviors that aren't seen at any other time. The catnip high only lasts a few hours, and it's entirely safe. The one exception is when cats truly overindulge in catnip or are unusually sensitive. Then they may hallucinate or, in some cases, scratch themselves compulsively.

Many people keep catnip in their gardens, which provides a nice "watering hole" for the neighborhood cats. Cats tend to prefer fresh catnip, although they certainly enjoy cloth toys that are stuffed with dried leaves. It's best to buy catnip products that are made in the United States; the catnip from other countries may have been treated with high levels of pesticides.

there's something in the greens that dogs and cats need nutritionally—either because they aren't getting it in their regular food or because they need a little more of it than pet foods provide. Dietary fiber is a likely candidate. Even though commercial pet foods contain quite a bit of fiber, dogs and cats might naturally seek out new sources as a way of keeping their digestion regular, says Dr. Dearing.

Puppies are much more likely than adults to eat grass, leaves, and even flowers. Veterinarians chalk up this behavior to simple curiosity, but there's some evidence that young animals eat greens in an attempt to purge worms or other parasites from the digestive tract. Plant foods are high in dietary fiber, and fiber stimulates the digestive tract to work more efficiently. So it's possible that puppies view grass and leaves almost as laxatives and eat them as a way of purging unpleasant things from their bodies.

Older pets are less likely than puppies to have worms, but they do get stomachaches, and they appear to nosh grass and weeds as a kind of homegrown medicine. "If their intestinal tracts are upset, sometimes they might feel better if they put something in their mouths," says Dr. Dearing.

Every medicine has side effects, however, and grass is no exception. Dogs and cats who eat a lot of grass frequently throw up afterward. Experts aren't sure if pets eat grass because they feel bad or if they feel bad because they eat grass. Either way, it makes sense. "If they do have an upset stomach and eat grass and vomit, it empties out whatever is irritating the stomach," says Steven R. Hansen, D.V.M., senior vice president of the American Society for the Prevention of Cruelty to Animals' National Animal Poison Control Center in Urbana, Illinois.

If dogs and cats only ate grass when they were looking mopey and under the weather, we could conclude that grass eating is their way of telling us that they're sick and that grass is a healthful tonic. But many pets look downright exuberant when they're munching like sheep in the yard or demolishing the plants on the windowsill. This has led many veterinarians to conclude that while dogs and cats may treat grass as a medicine, they also perceive it as a heck of a lot of fun—just another way of amusing themselves, says Robert Poppenga, D.V.M., Ph.D., associate professor of veterinary toxicology at the University of Pennsylvania School of Veterinary Medicine in Philadelphia.

This is certainly true of cats. Cats love string toys, so they'll attack anything that looks like one, even if it's a plant vine. They like to shred plant leaves and flowers, and while they're playing, they frequently swallow little bits.

Risky Business

Veterinarians may eventually discover why dogs and cats are attracted to plants, but for now, about all they can say for sure is that some pets have a powerful liking for them. This isn't necessarily a bad thing. Most dogs can easily pass a little bit of grass through their systems, and cats can nibble some houseplants without getting sick. Still, dogs and cats can't handle large amounts of greenery. At the very least, they're likely to throw up,

Fast First-Aid

If there's one thing dogs and cats are good at, it's throwing up. They do it much more often than people do, probably because nature anticipated that they'd be stuffing all sorts of nasty things into their stomachs.

Throwing up may not be pleasant, but it's often better than not throwing up. Pets rarely eat enough of a plant to do themselves serious harm, but sometimes they do. Those who have eaten plants such as amaryllis, crown of thorns, dumbcane, English ivy, and jonquil really do need to throw up, and if they don't do it on their own, you'll have to help.

"Giving 3 percent hydrogen peroxide is the best way to induce vomiting when an animal has eaten a poisonous plant within the hour and is not showing any abnormal symptoms," says Steven R. Hansen, D.V.M., senior vice president of the American Society for the Prevention of Cruelty to Animals' National Animal Poison Control Center in Urbana, Illinois. "It's very safe, very accessible, and very reliable."

To use this remedy, first give your pet a moist meal, like canned food, says Dr. Hansen. Then measure out 1 tablespoon of 3 percent hydrogen peroxide for every 15 pounds of pet. Don't mix it with water. Draw the solution into a needleless syringe (a turkey baster works just as well), put the tip toward the back of your pet's mouth between the teeth and cheek and gently squirt it in. Don't squirt it over the tongue, which may cause choking, he warns. Most pets will vomit within 15 minutes. If they don't, it's fine to give it one more time, he says.

Inducing vomiting isn't always necessary, Dr. Hansen adds, so you'll want to call your vet first.

and no one wants to deal with that. More important, pets who munch on grass or houseplants sometimes eat too much. For dogs, this can lead to an intestinal blockage or even bloat, a dangerous condition in which the stomach suddenly fills with air, says Dr. Hansen. And since many house and yard plants are toxic, poisoning is a real possibility.

Buy some strong shelves. Most houseplants aren't toxic, but some are—and these are often the ones that dogs and cats like to eat. You may be able to train dogs or even cats not to eat plants, but it won't be easy. It's a lot easier to put the plants up and out of reach.

• For cats, the most dangerous plant is probably Easter lily, which contains a compound that can cause kidney failure.
• For dogs, cycads (a type of tropical palm) and philodendrons may cause problems, says Dr. Hansen.
• Poinsettias can irritate dogs' and cats' stomachs.
• Dogs like peach and apricot pits because of the sweet pulp that clings to the surface. Dogs who eat the pits can get into trouble—not only because the pits are large and rough and difficult to pass in the stools but also because they contain enough cyanide to make dogs sick.
• Spring daffodils, tulips, and dieffenbachia contain oxalic acid crystals. When viewed under a microscope, the crystals appear as wicked little spikes. Pets who chew the leaves of these plants may have an allergic reaction to the chemical crystals. "They can cause pets to swell up and not be able to breathe," says Dr. Hansen.
• Holly and mistletoe leaves and berries account for many holiday poisonings. "Even the water in the Christmas tree stand is very irritating," says Dr. Dearing.

Use safer lawn chemicals. Grass that's harmless in small amounts can become quite toxic when it's treated with fertilizers and pesticides. In fact, many veterinarians wonder if it's not the grass itself that makes pets vomit but the chemicals that have been applied to it. Apart from keeping your pets off the lawn entirely—or supervising them all the time so they can't eat it—you may want to switch to products that are safer for pets.

There's a lot of disagreement about which products are safe and which aren't, so you'll want to ask your veterinarian for advice. In the meantime, keep your pets off the lawn for at least a few hours—or a few days—after chemicals have been applied. Fertilizers and pesticides start to break down once they're exposed to air and water, so lawns gradually get a little safer.

Even when you know your lawn is safe, other lawns in the neighborhood may not be. "You don't know what people are putting on their yards," says Dr. Dearing. "You just have to assume that it's something toxic and avoid it."

Give them a plot of their own. Some pets never get a hankering for grass and plants, and others seem to crave them. Rather than supervising all the time, you may find it's easier to provide what every salad-loving pet craves—a garden of her own.

You can buy small patches of organic grass at pet supply stores. The patches are easy to maintain, the grass grows quickly, and it has a nice, wholesome taste. "You put one of those out there for them, and they'll mow it right down," says Dr. Poppenga.

Give them more fiber. Even though veterinarians aren't convinced that pets eat grass in order to get more dietary fiber, you can hardly go wrong by adding more fiber to their diets. Foods that are high in dietary fiber such as lightly steamed green beans, canned pumpkin, and, for pets who will eat it, cooked oat bran or oatmeal will help the digestive tract work more quickly and efficiently. In addition, fiber slows the absorption of sugars in the intestine, which is good for pets with diabetes. Fiber may even help prevent hairballs in cats. Pets who get more fiber in their food bowls may be less likely to seek it out elsewhere, says Dr. Dearing.

CHAPTER 46

Eating Objects

Very little surprises Harold Striegel, D.V.M., a retired veterinarian who treated dogs and cats for nearly 30 years. But even he was startled when a client came into his office with a black Labrador retriever and claimed that the dog, named Wrigley, had eaten a padlock.

Wrigley appeared to be in perfect health, but Dr. Striegel decided to x-ray his digestive tract anyway. A few minutes after the procedure, he had the x-rays in hand. "Your dog didn't swallow a padlock," Dr. Striegel told his client. "He swallowed five of them."

Oral Knowledge

Wrigley's appetite for iron was sufficiently unusual that his story made headlines around the world. But veterinarians are accustomed to finding strange objects in dogs' insides. "Any veterinarian can tell stories about pets swallowing fish hooks, stones, GI Joe dolls, underwear, and just about anything else," says Saundra L. Kayne, D.V.M., a veterinarian in Carbondale, Illinois.

Dogs are distinctly oral. They put things in their mouths to check out the taste and texture, and, like toddlers who suck their thumbs, they find it comforting. Unlike toddlers, however, dogs never really outgrow the oral stage of learning.

"Through the taste, texture, and smell of objects, dogs gain an incredible amount of information about their environments," says Patricia McConnell, Ph.D., a certified applied animal behaviorist and assistant adjunct professor in the department of zoology at the University of Wisconsin at Madison. Puppies are particularly likely to mouth and swallow things. It helps them learn what's good to eat, what's fun to play with, and what they should stay away from.

Cats are less likely than dogs to swallow strange things. Partly, this is because cats are natural hunters who traditionally ate what they caught—they didn't scavenge the way dogs did. And because they're agile, they're more likely to explore things with their paws than with their mouths. When they do swallow something—string is a particular favorite—it's usually because they were playing and swallowed it by mistake. Their tongues have backward-facing projections, which means it's sometimes difficult for them to get rid of objects, especially clingy things like string, once they're in their mouths. It's usually easier just to swallow them.

BETTER THAN LYING AROUND

We generally assume that nature does things for a reason—that if dogs put things in their mouths, there must be good reasons for them to do so. But this isn't always the case. There's some evidence that dogs do most of their mouthing when they're bored, presumably because chewing and swallowing things is more entertaining than sleeping on the couch all day.

"Dogs need mental, social, and physical stimulation like they used to get in the wild," says Roger Abrantes, Ph.D., an ethologist, evolutionary biologist, and author of *Dog Language: An Encyclopedia of Canine Behaviour* and *The Evolution of Canine Social Behaviour*. Without opportunities to burn off energy and amuse themselves, dogs engage in what experts call stereotypy—small, repetitive actions that don't have a real function.

Humans do this, too, Dr. McConnell adds. "A girl may twirl her hair around her finger, and an executive may pace," she says.

Mindless mouthing probably makes dogs feel better because the activity stimulates the production of endorphins, chemicals in the body that make them feel good. "Chewing and swallowing is a great way for dogs to calm themselves," says Dr. McConnell.

A LEADS TO B

It makes sense that dogs put things in their mouths when they're bored. What's tougher to fathom is why they swallow them. Here are some of the theories.

Now or never. Dogs descended from wolves, and wolves often had to make do with pretty slim pickings. When food was available, they ate as much as they could hold. And if it turned out that what they ate wasn't nutritious or even food, well, it was better to be safe than sorry. "There was a great deal of famine out there, and dogs became very opportunistic and flexible in what they ate," says Dr. McConnell.

Who cares about taste? Human tongues have roughly 10,000 tastebuds, but dogs only have about 1,700. They're not very discerning about flavors. People can't imagine eating a golf ball or a strip of bark, but to dogs, they probably taste about as good as anything else.

Easy come, easy go. Since dogs aren't very choosy about food, and because they have capacious stomachs and the instincts to fill them, they get sick to their stomachs much more often than people do. So it may be that they'll swallow anything because they know they can chuck it back up if they need to, says Karen Overall, V.M.D., Ph.D., a board-certified veterinary behaviorist and director of the behavior clinic at the University of Pennsylvania School of Veterinary Medicine in Philadelphia.

Whoops. Dogs have much fewer facial and lip muscles than humans do. This means that they have relatively little mouth control, says Dr. Overall. They may find it's easier simply to swallow objects than to dump them once they've picked them up.

Mind over Mouth

Since dogs are naturally inclined to swallow things, and because the objects rarely cause physical problems, veterinarians don't get very excited when frantic owners call because their dogs swallowed the wrapping off a baseball or the latest Tom Clancy novel. Still, it's not a great habit to encourage. Some dogs do get intestinal obstructions. At the very least, no one looks forward to shampooing the carpet just because their dog got bored one afternoon, polished off a houseplant, and tossed it up later. Apart from the obvious solution of keeping mouth-size objects out of reach, veterinarians recommend keeping dogs busy enough so they don't need the oral entertainment.

Put them to work. Dogs enjoy creative challenges. Encouraging them to use their brains more often makes them less likely to depend on their mouths for entertainment. Sandy Myers, an animal-behavior consultant in Naperville, Illinois, has trained her golden retrievers to tote dirty clothes from the bedrooms to the laundry room. But it doesn't have to be anything that fancy. "Teach them to bring the newspaper, play hide-and-seek, or catch a Frisbee," she suggests. "When dogs are using up energy by stimulating their minds, they're probably not going to eat your new shoes."

Give them something to find. For untold numbers of generations, dogs have survived by searching mainly for food, but also for things such as shelter and mates. Satisfying their desire to search is a great way to take their minds off mindless mouthing, says Dr. Abrantes. Actually, you can satisfy two of their keenest desires—to eat and to search—by scattering the food across the floor rather than pouring it neatly in a bowl. "This simulates the foraging they used to do in the wild," he says.

Give them a problem to solve. Another way to combine food and mental stimulation is with a Kong toy. These sturdy rubber toys have a hole at one end where you can pour in a little kibble. "Dogs will push it and throw it around—they're using their brains to get all the food," says Dr. Abrantes.

CHAPTER 47

Fear of Being Alone

Imagine coming home from work and finding that the inside of your house is a remnant of the place you left. The carpet by the door is ripped, the bottom rungs of the banister are chewed to splinters, and your slippers are shredded in the hall. As you stare at the mess, your dog runs from the kitchen—and pees at your feet.

It's hard to believe that all this destruction is your dog's way of saying, "I missed you." And he didn't miss you just a little bit. He missed you so much that he was terrified you'd never come back. He panicked and took out his anxiety on the closest targets—all of which, unfortunately, belonged to you.

Dogs are deeply dependent on their ties to others for their sense of security and well-being, and they never learn to relish time alone. Most dogs get accustomed to spending time by themselves, but some truly suffer, and destructive behavior is their way of letting you know.

Dogs who have been abandoned, left at a shelter, or passed from owner to owner are the ones most likely to suffer from separation anxiety, says Wayne Hunthausen, D.V.M., an animal-behavior consultant in Westwood, Kansas, and coauthor of *Handbook of Behaviour Problems of the Dog and Cat*. Even dogs who are usually calm tend to get nervous when they're left alone more than usual.

Unlike dogs, who once lived in packs, wild felines hunted and lived alone. So even though modern cats enjoy having people around, they probably don't miss them nearly as much when they're gone, says Dr. Hunthausen.

The Faces of Anxiety

Dogs get destructive for many reasons, so a ruined pair of shoes doesn't always mean that they missed you. Since even the calmest dogs can go berserk for a lettle while when their owners leave the house, separation anxiety isn't always easy to recognize, says Rolan Tripp, D.V.M., affiliate professor of applied animal behavior at Colorado State University Veterinary School in Fort Collins and author of *Pet Perception Management*. But there are some common clues that you can look for. For example:

Vocalization. "Some dogs will bark for 8 hours running when they're left home alone," says Dr. Tripp.

Mouthing. Just as people clench their jaws, chew gum, or nibble on pens when they're nervous, dogs will often chew on furniture, shoes, socks, or anything else they can get their mouths around.

Hyperactivity. Some dogs cope with stress by frantically digging or running around.

House soiling. Messes in the house can be very clear signals that dogs are experiencing stress, says Dr. Tripp. Dogs think of the home as being their castle, and they have a deep reluctance to make messes where they live. Unless you have a puppy or an older dog who's losing control, house soiling usually means that they're out of control, he explains.

You're Safe Now

In his book *The Dog Who Loved Too Much*, Nicholas Dodman, B.V.M.S. (a British equivalent of D.V.M.), professor of behavioral pharmacology and director of the behavior clinic at Tufts University School of Veterinary Medicine in North Grafton, Massachusetts, tells about a dog who was so fearful and destructive when he was alone that his owner worried that he might have no choice but to put the dog to sleep. Feeling distraught over his decision, the man withdrew and completely ignored his dog for several days—at which point the problems abruptly stopped.

It seems paradoxical, but dogs who are fearful or anxious about being alone generally get worse when their owners are always lavishing them with attention before they leave and when they come home. That's why one of the best remedies for separation anxiety is to be matter-of-fact about leaving and coming home, says Benjamin Hart, D.V.M., Ph.D., professor of physiology and behavior at the University of California, Davis, School of Veterinary Medicine and author of *The Perfect Puppy: How to Choose Your Dog by Its Behavior*. The idea is to help dogs understand that people—their leaders—attach no more importance to leaving the house than they do to reading the newspaper or sweeping the floor. When they realize that their leaders are calm, dogs are calmer, too.

It's no easier for dogs to get over their fears than it is for people, but behaviorists have developed a system that can help dogs understand that leaving doesn't mean leaving for good. Here are seven steps they recommend.

1. Keep departures and arrivals calm. Don't give your dog a big goodbye when you leave. When you come home, ignore him for 15 to 20 minutes, Dr. Tripp advises. Later, when your dog is calm and you're settled in, give him a little extra attention.

2. Push the panic buttons. Dogs with separation anxiety don't get frantic only when their owners are gone. They work up to it gradually as they watch the "leaving rituals"—grabbing your coat, checking your keys, and walking to the door. Each of these cues raises their anxiety a notch or two. By the time you actually shut the door behind you, they may be in full panic. That's when chewing, digging, or barking usually starts.

"If grabbing the keys or picking up the lunch box is what puts your dog on edge, do it 50 times a day," suggests Dr. Hunthausen. The first dozen or so times, your dog will probably react with his usual look of anxiety. But if you keep doing it throughout the day, he'll realize that the sounds or gestures don't mean much of anything. He'll still get nervous when you leave, but he won't get quite as worked up beforehand, and that will help make him calmer.

3. Practice leaving. Once your dog is less frantic before you leave, it's time to get him used to the idea of actual departures. Again, the idea is to desensitize him—by going out the door and then immediately coming back in, 20 to 30 times a day, says Dr. Tripp. Vary the times and change the routines. If the garage door makes a big clatter, open and close it a few times. Start the car, then stop it and go back inside. Your dog will certainly be confused by all the commotion, but after a few weeks (or, for some dogs, months), he'll begin to attach less importance to each of these activities and will be less likely to work himself into a terror, he explains.

4. Teach the "stay" command. Dogs with separation anxiety like to keep their owners in sight all the time and will often follow them around like little four-pawed shadows. Teaching

Home Again

Ryan was trouble on four feet. The Pacific branch of the Irish Setter Club of America, which "rescues" dogs put up for adoption in that area, tried to place Ryan with every family it could find. But it never worked out. He would dote on his adoptive families when they were home, then tear up their things—the ones he wasn't urinating on—when they weren't home.

The club's rescue coordinator, Marilee Larson, said Ryan was always returned within a few days, with owners citing the worst case of separation anxiety they'd ever imagined. Rescue leagues are legendary for their determination to get dogs adopted, but Larson was afraid that Ryan was running out of options. On a long shot, she called a couple who had been looking for an Irish setter puppy and asked them if they'd be willing to consider a troubled adult dog.

It turned out to be an easy sell. The couple, John and Vicky Pierson of Clear Lake, California, had a soft spot for setters. They'd been forced to give up one of their dogs some years before when they moved into a smaller, rented home. Now they were ready for another. So they welcomed Ryan into their family.

Given his history, Ryan's first night was nearly miraculous. He wandered calmly through the house, peeked at the children in their beds, and got along great with the family's cat and their elderly setter. He fit in so well that the Piersons felt as if they already knew him.

Larson nervously called a few days later to hear how Ryan was doing. She was amazed to hear that Ryan hadn't shown the slightest sign of fear. He seemed so much at home, in fact, that he reminded the Piersons of Randy, the dog they had previously given up, and they were sure they were going to keep him.

Ryan *did* seem a lot like Randy, the way he related to the kids and how he sat with his bottom on the couch and his front feet on the floor, and the Piersons started to wonder. They took Ryan to their veterinarian, who reminded them of the scar Randy had on his foot from a surgery years before. It took him only a few seconds to trim the fur from the paw—and there was the scar.

Randy, it seems, had come home—and in recovering his family, he'd given up his fears.

dogs the "stay" command can be extremely helpful because it forces them to get used to your absences, says Dr. Hunthausen. A dog who learns to stay put for 10 seconds can learn to stay for longer periods of time. Each time you practice the command, go farther and farther away from your dog—just a few feet at first, but eventually into the next room. Even though you'll never put your dog in a stay position when you're leaving the house for the day, the daily practice will give him confidence and make him feel more secure when he's on his own. (For more information on teaching the "stay" command, see page 210.)

5. Giving dogs regular exercise is a great way to reduce their fears, says Dr. Hunthausen. Exercise makes dogs tired, and tired dogs don't have as much energy to devote to their anguish.

6. Dogs have an instinct called denning, which means they're most secure in small, enclosed spaces. Veterinarians often recommend crate-training dogs when they're young because the crate gives them a place where they feel safe, says Dr. Hunthausen. It's not always easy to crate-train older dogs, however. An alternative is to put your dog's bed and toys in a small, cozy space, like the laundry room. Once he has a place where he feels safe, you can leave him there when you leave the house.

7. No one feels very calm when they walk in the door and discover that the living room has been demolished, but it's worth taking a deep breath or two, says Dr. Tripp. Dogs have hazy memories under the best of circumstances, and they won't have the faintest idea why you're mad. And anger has a way of backfiring. If you unload on your dog, he's going to remember. The next time you leave, in addition to missing you so much that it hurts, he'll be scared that you're going to come home angry again. The extra anxiety may spur him to take on the kitchen—after he's done destroying the living room.

RAISING A CALM DOG

Experts estimate that more than 45 percent of puppies and older dogs experience some separation anxiety during their first few days with a new family. Some don't get over their fears. It's so common, in fact, that behaviorists recommend teaching dogs when they're young that being alone isn't scary. The way to do this is to apply positive boundaries within your home by providing a space where they'll feel secure, says Inger Martens, a trainer and behavior consultant in Los Angeles.

The day you bring a new dog home, create an area in a small section of the house, like the kitchen or a hallway, by sectioning it off with a baby gate. Put your dog's water bowl and toys in the area and generally make it comfortable. He'll come to think of this area as being his special place, and this will help reduce separation anxiety when you're gone.

In addition, dogs appreciate routines. You want your dog to understand right away that there are proper ways to do things. Be as consistent as you can. Feed him and let him out at the same times every day. Set aside some "quiet time" when he's expected to be by himself without bothering you. When he's quiet and behaving, praise him from across the room. If he starts acting up or getting excited, ignore him until he's calm again, Martens says.

"You wouldn't say to a child, 'There are the keys to the front door. I'll be back in 4 hours,'" she says. "You'd say, 'Okay, it's noon. We're having lunch, then you're going to do your homework, then you're going to go outside and play, and then we're going to go to sleep.'" What works for children works equally well for dogs. Once they understand that spending time alone is part of their usual schedule, they'll get used to it and expect it later on.

CHAPTER 48

Fear of Noises

She may be small, but P. D. won a big victory for dogs everywhere. Her owner, Abbi Taylor Guest of Decatur, Georgia, took the local animal-control department to court for fining her $150 after P. D. frantically broke out of her house during a thunderstorm and got scooped up by the animal-control patrol.

It came out in court that there were mitigating circumstances: P. D. had been hit by a car 2 years before her breakout. She suffered from separation anxiety. And thunderstorms scared the bejeezus out of the little mixed breed. Testifying on her behalf was a forensic doctor who stated that memories of the accident, combined with the rumbling of thunder, were so overwhelming that P. D. "was unable to distinguish between right and wrong" and should not be held accountable for her actions. The case was dismissed.

Though P. D.'s case is a bit unusual, more than a few experts would go to bat for dogs who are terrified of thunder. They believe that dogs have a nearly instinctive fear of loud noises, fears that have only gotten worse due to the increasing noise levels in modern life, says Katherine Houpt, V.M.D., Ph.D., a board-certified veterinary behaviorist, professor of physiology, and director of the behavior clinic at Cornell University College of Veterinary Medicine in Ithaca, New York.

"To top it off, they usually have something bad happen during a thunderstorm, like getting stuck under the bed or knocking over furniture while trying to hide," says Dr. Houpt. "The whole experience can be quite devastating." Their frantic behavior during storms, she explains, is really just a cry for help.

Do You Hear What I Hear?

Cats don't love loud noises and are sometimes skittish about gunshots or sudden claps of thunder, but it's mainly dogs who suffer—and who show their fears by shaking, shivering, or trying to hide, says Dr. Houpt. "Dogs' ears are more sensitive to those low, deep frequencies than cats' ears are. And though small dog breeds certainly can be afraid during storms, it's more common in larger dogs because they often hear those frequencies best."

It's difficult to imagine life as dogs hear it. Their hearing is about four times better than ours. What sounds like the faint rumbling of a distant storm to people more closely resembles the sound of God bowling a 300 on the rooftop to dogs. The problem is compounded because they hear very well at high and low sound frequencies. The sounds of thunder, fireworks, and gunshots, which come in at the low end of the sound spectrum, can be singularly terrifying. Sounds that are higher pitched, like electronic beeps and buzzes, are nearly unbearable for some dogs. The discomfort is most pronounced in collies and other herding dogs because they were bred to have extraordinarily sharp hearing in order to hear the faint call of a shepherd from several fields away. What's loud to us can be truly deafening for them.

BRAVING THE STORM

The fear of loud noises is among the more stubborn behavior problems that veterinarians treat. With a little work and patience, however, nearly every dog can learn to tolerate, if not appreciate, loud noises.

Create a safety zone. In their evolutionary pasts, dogs were den-dwelling animals, and they're still attracted to small, enclosed spaces, especially when they're frightened. "They like having confined quarters where they can feel sheltered from the elements," says D. Caroline Coile, Ph.D., a researcher specializing in canine senses, who raises and shows salukis near Tallahassee, Florida. "They can become particularly stressed when they feel exposed and vulnerable."

Dogs who are afraid of loud noises will invariably gravitate toward the smallest, coziest hiding place they can find—under beds, in the backs of closets, or in some cases even in bathtubs. You can help them feel more secure by creating special hiding places that they can consider their own, Dr. Coile advises. "Try putting a dog bed in some nook or cranny of the house, like beneath the stairs or behind a chair, where the dog can feel protected. That may be all she needs."

Take away the fear. Dogs don't process their memories and experiences as well as people do, which means their ninth thunderstorm or Fourth of July is just as scary and unexpected as the first. Since they won't learn from experience, it's up to their people to change their thinking so that loud noises don't frighten them anymore. Behaviorists deal with noise anxiety by using a technique called systematic desensitization. Put more simply, it means getting them used to noise, says Dr. Houpt.

The principles of desensitization therapy are complex, and there are many ways to go about it. The basic technique, however, is simple. Here's how it works.

- Gradually and gently expose your dog to very low levels of whatever it is she fears. For example, buy a recording of a thunderstorm and play it for about 15 minutes at a very low volume, says Dr. Houpt. At first the volume should be so low that your dog doesn't show any sign of fear. Every 5 minutes or so, give her a treat or praise as a way of rewarding her for being calm. This will help her understand that the sound she's hearing is a predictor of something good rather than something scary.
- On the second or third day, increase the volume just slightly until your dog starts looking a little bit uneasy. As long as she stays calm, give her praise and treats. You may want to do some basic obedience drills as well. This will help distract her from the noise and help her understand that good behavior is always rewarded, whether there's noise in the background or not.
- With daily practice, most dogs will start getting less fearful. They'll be able to tolerate louder volumes without getting frightened, and they'll be able to listen to the recordings for longer periods of time. What they'll discover is that loud noises—thunderstorms, fireworks, or anything else—really aren't such a big deal.

When you are doing desensitization therapy, you don't want to crank up the volume too high or too fast, says Dr. Houpt. Rather than helping your dog accept the noise, this will scare her half to death, she explains. Going slowly—for some dogs, it takes months to overcome their fears—is the best way to ensure success.

Reward calm behavior, not the fears. Whether or not you're practicing a desensitization program, you always want to act as though there's nothing to be afraid of. It's natural to want to re-

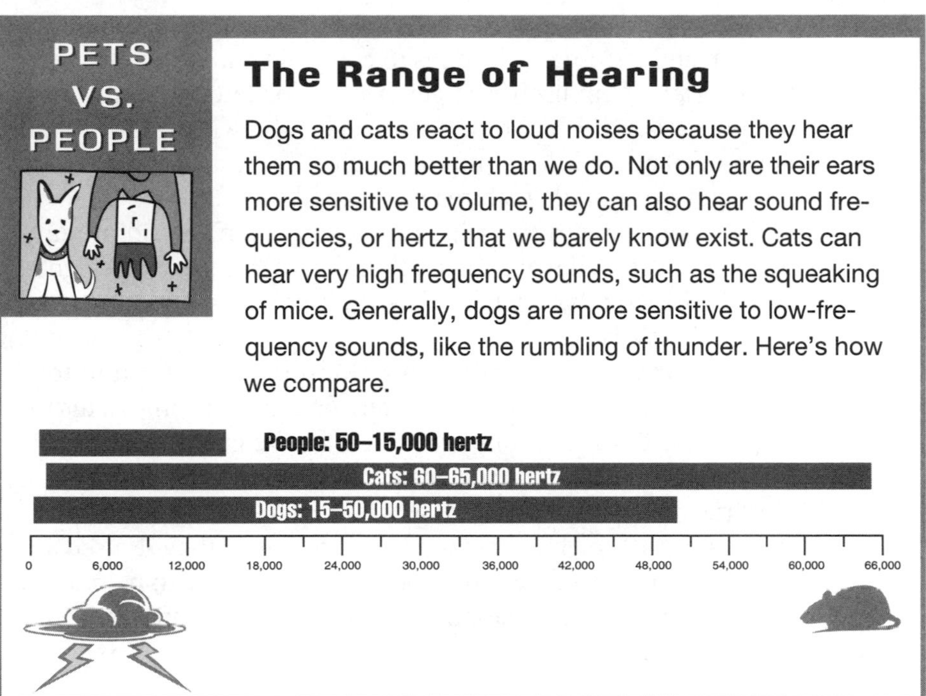

The Range of Hearing

Dogs and cats react to loud noises because they hear them so much better than we do. Not only are their ears more sensitive to volume, they can also hear sound frequencies, or hertz, that we barely know exist. Cats can hear very high frequency sounds, such as the squeaking of mice. Generally, dogs are more sensitive to low-frequency sounds, like the rumbling of thunder. Here's how we compare.

assure a dog who's trying to crawl behind a bookcase, but this tends to make the fear worse, says Alex Brooks, director of Alex Brooks School of Dog Training in Des Plaines, Illinois. "Though you don't want to treat a scared pet harshly, you don't want to coddle her too much either," he explains. "If you do, she'll learn not only that it's okay to be scared but also that being scared has its rewards."

Dogs always take their cues from their owners, he adds. When you act calm and relaxed, as though nothing out of the ordinary is happening, dogs will naturally be a little less frightened. At the same time, you need to help them understand that only good behavior gets rewards, never fearful behavior. So when your dog starts getting nervous, tell her to sit and stay, Brooks suggests. "Then praise her and reward her for being so good and sitting still. Repeat this every time there's a storm or other noises, and your dog will learn that she'll be rewarded if she sits and stays by your side."

Play in the rain. The fear of thunderstorms is probably the most common fear that behaviorists deal with. Dogs will never like loud noises, but you can teach them that thunderstorms can be fun in other ways. "I act as though it is just like any other afternoon and encourage the dogs to come out and play with me," Brooks says. "I praise them generously for fetching balls and romping around. Every time a storm starts brewing, I take them out and play for a few minutes again. Eventually, they learn through repetition that storms mean good times."

The problem with this is that most dogs aren't afraid of rain, but of thunder, and when there's thunder, there's sure to be lightning. Make sure that there's safe shelter before going out in the elements, he advises.

Ask your vet about medications. Most dogs can learn to tolerate loud noises, but some are so terrified that nothing seems to help. These dogs often improve when they're given sedatives or anti-anxiety medications such as fluoxetine (Prozac). Sometimes the drugs are used to help dogs get through difficult periods, such as Fourth of July weekends. More often, they're used in combination with a desensitization program. "They can help dogs get through drastic situations until the behavior-modification training takes hold," says Dr. Coile.

CHAPTER 49

Fear of Strangers

Dogs and cats are the world's best icebreakers. They're not at all shy about rubbing against visitors or putting their noses in "friendly" places. For the most part, they think that meeting new people is a lot of ear-rubbing, belly-scratching fun.

There's a good reason for their exuberant good nature. Dogs and cats have been domesticated for a long time. They're predisposed to like people, especially people that you like. But they don't always give their affection right away. They have an inherent tendency to be slightly wary of strangers until they're sure of their intentions. That's why dogs who happily greet people that you invite to the house will bark uproariously when they hear strange footsteps on the walk. Cats are more subtle and less vocal, but they're equally careful and will evaluate new people before they approach. It's not that dogs and cats are suspicious, exactly. It's just that thousands of years of evolution have taught them to keep an eye on things. Once they feel safe, their good nature is immediately apparent.

It's not very common, but some dogs and cats are completely terrified of people they don't know. They shy away from strangers—or hide behind furniture when people come to visit—and watch them nervously out of the corners of their eyes. Or they'll pull a vanishing act, disappearing under beds or in the backs of closets until the people go away.

Any pet can develop unreasonable fears, but it usually occurs in dogs who had relatively little contact with people during the first month or two of life, says Gary Shiebler, author of *A Search for the Perfect Dog*. "An undersocialized dog may respond badly to any new experience."

Reliving the Past

Dogs and cats remember a lot more than we give them credit for. While some pets are naturally shy, those who are deeply afraid of people may have had a bad experience with people in the past, and the memory of that makes it difficult for them to be trusting afterward.

While abuse can make pets afraid for the rest of their lives, it's often little things that happened when they were young that make them nervous later. A dog who received a painful vaccination, for example, may be afraid of veterinarians. A cat who once was startled by a loud voice and tumbled off a ledge may be afraid of loud people. One way to tell if fears are caused by general shyness or by a specific event in the past is to see how your pet responds in different situations, Shiebler says. If your cat is calm around women, for example, but becomes extremely nervous around men, you can be pretty sure that she associates men with something that's painful or frightening.

And from a pet's perspective, things we take for granted can be a little scary. For example, some dogs and cats get nervous when they see people who look a little odd—not because they have big noses or hair that's parted in a strange place, but because they don't resemble people at all. They could be wearing a big hat or have a backpack slung over a shoulder, which gives them an unfamiliar shape, says Patricia McConnell, Ph.D., a certified applied animal behaviorist and assistant adjunct professor in the department of zoology at the University of Wisconsin at Madison. Pets may suspect that what they're seeing is some strange lifeform, and they aren't sure what to make of it.

Similarly, some pets get nervous around children or people who make fast movements. In the distant past, things that were noisy or moved quickly were often dangerous. Dogs and cats haven't forgotten these evolutionary lessons, says Dr. McConnell. In addition, pets often get nervous around people who make *us* nervous. Our body language, facial expressions, and even scent tells pets when we're feeling edgy, and they may get edgy, too.

Breaking the Ice

Most people want their pets to be relaxed and comfortable not only when friends come to visit but also when "normal" visitors,

MESSAGES AND MEANINGS

Man's Best Friend

Samantha Norof was mystified. Whenever a man came to her apartment in Bronx, New York, Belle would hide or, in some cases, hiss and attack. Women, on the other hand, were greeted by a purring, friendly feline who didn't seem to have a care in the world.

Belle had a perfectly normal upbringing, and no one had ever yelled at or abused her. "I couldn't figure it out at first," says Samantha. "But after thinking about it, I realized that the one man she saw consistently was my building superintendent, who came over frequently for one noisy maintenance job or another."

Samantha suspected that Belle had been badly frightened by the noise and disruptions caused by the repairs and had apparently decided that all men, even those without tool belts, were not to be trusted.

Samantha decided to turn things around. To prevent additional frights, she started taking Belle to visit a neighbor whenever repairs were scheduled in her apartment. In addition, she encouraged her boyfriend to make a concerted effort to win Belle's heart. So the next time he came over, he brought a cat toy.

"It was basically a high-tech version of a feather on a string, Belle's favorite toy," Samantha says. "He played with her for a few hours, and now she loves it when he comes over."

Belle is still a little standoffish around men she doesn't know, but in most cases, she warms up pretty quickly—"as long as they spend a few minutes playing with her," Samantha says.

like the mail carrier, come by. A little "woof" provides a helpful alert, but a cacophony of barking every day quickly gets annoying, for owners as well as their neighbors. Dogs and cats with severe fears may need help from a veterinarian or behaviorist, but most pets can learn to be more comfortable around people. Experts use two techniques, called desensitization and counterconditioning, that help pets overcome their fears. The theories behind these techniques are complex, but the basic idea is pretty simple: to help pets understand that the presence of people is a sign of good things to come. Here's how it works, says Dr. McConnell.

Note: If there is any possibility that your pet could hurt someone, do not do this without a trained professional.

• Begin by identifying what it is that your pet fears. If your pet is afraid of nearly everyone, this part will be easy. But in many cases, dogs and cats are afraid only of certain individuals or types of people. Does your pet get frightened when she meets people outside or in the house? Do men trigger more anxiety in your pet than women do? Are there some situations in which your pet gets unusually nervous? Once you understand the types of people that trigger the fears, you'll know where to direct your energy later.

• Make a list of the things that your pet is most passionate about, says Dr. McConnell. For many dogs and cats, food is a clear winner. Or it could be the sight of the leash, a massage around the ears, or even happy words like "Play!" or "Come here!"

• Plan a time when the two of you can confront whomever your pet is afraid of, for example, by having a friend who is familiar with your pet ring the doorbell. What you want to do is expose her to a very low level of the frightening experience while giving her a very high level of her favorite treat. A minute or two before your friend arrives, give your pet several treats. This will put her in a happy frame of mind, says Dr. McConnell. Then open the door and let your friend come in—and give your pet several more treats. If you do this regularly, after a few weeks (or in some cases, months) your pet will begin to anticipate something good happening whenever the doorbell rings, she says.

• Once your pet is reacting calmly to a mild "threat," it's time to bump up the intensity level. Rather than having a friend ring the bell, for example, ask someone over whom your pet hasn't met before. As you did before, give her treats before the bell rings and after your friend is inside. (Better yet, have your friend throw or hand over the treat.) Your pet will realize that nothing awful is going to happen.

• Vary the routine by having different people come to the door at different times. You don't want your pet to get too comfortable in one routine, because she'll still be nervous in other situations. It's good to throw variety into the mix. For example, rather than giving her a treat yourself, have the visitor make the offering. Get several of your friends and coworkers involved: men as well as women, bare-headed people and people in hats, people who are quiet and people who are loud. The one thing you'll want to keep

WHAT'S MY PET SAYING?

Behavior
Barking at the Mail Carrier

What It Means
"I'm a Good Protector!"

Even dogs who are normally quiet and shy will often let loose with full-throated monologues at the bang of the mailbox door or the sound of footsteps on the walk.

From a human point of view, this daily display seems a little silly because dogs surely recognize the sound of the mail carrier. But dogs have a different perspective. It's not that they don't know who's approaching. They bark because it works, says Patricia McConnell, Ph.D., a certified applied animal behaviorist and assistant adjunct professor in the department of zoology at the University of Wisconsin at Madison.

Here's what happens: The mail carrier arrives, dogs bark, and the carrier goes away. The next day, the same thing happens. It doesn't take dogs long to realize they've stumbled on a neat trick: "Well, I sure scared him! He'd better not come back if he knows what's good for him!"

Of course, the mail carrier does come back, and dogs joyfully repeat their warnings—and then congratulate themselves for being such good protectors.

consistent at first is the treats—always give them before and after you introduce the "trigger," says Dr. McConnell.

• Once your pet has firmly made some positive associations—"Boy, I sure like it when the doorbell rings"—you can make things simpler by giving treats only after the doorbell rings. By this time, she'll probably be looking forward to company, and giving her a treat after the fact will reinforce the idea that people bring good things.

CHAPTER 50

Fighting with Other Pets

The classic barroom fight usually goes something like this:

"You come any closer, and I'm gonna pop you one!"

"Oh, yeah?"

"Yeah!"

And so it goes. Bluffing and blustering usually take the place of brawling, which is a good thing because getting socked in the nose hurts, and even the winner will walk away a little worse for wear.

Dogs understand this. They do a lot of squabbling of their own, both in the wild and in the domesticated comforts of home. With their hard teeth, strong jaws, and tough claws, they can do a lot of damage in a hurry. Which is why most fights don't progress beyond the huffing-and-puffing stage. The initial confrontation looks and sounds scary, but most of the time, the combatants stop short of actual combat and no one gets hurt.

"I ask people two questions: How many fights has their dog been involved in and in how many instances did they have to take him to the vet to have him sewn up," says Ian Dunbar, Ph.D., M.R.C.V.S. (a British equivalent of D.V.M.), a veterinarian and animal behaviorist in Berkeley, California, and founder of the Association of Pet Dog Trainers. Most people estimate about 20 times for the first question, and zero for the second, he explains. That's a fight-to-bite ratio of 20 to 0. "If these dogs are really trying to kill each other, they apparently aren't very good at it," he says.

Cat fights are a little different because by the time cats decide they're angry enough to attack, they go ahead and do it, which is why their fights often result in trips to the veterinarian's office. But they don't fight anywhere near as often as dogs, and when they do, it's usually over a mate.

Freeze!

If you've ever been outside at midnight and heard a sudden rustling in the trees, you probably responded by standing totally still—both because you wanted to hear better and because the fright caused your body to lock into place. Dogs often respond the same way when another, more assertive dog approaches and gives the who-are-you sniff.

There are two reasons for this sudden immobility. For smaller dogs, holding still helps ensure that they won't be mistaken for prey. In addition, standing still is known among behaviorists as a calming signal. It helps dogs stay calm in the face of impending threats, and it has a calming effect on other dogs as well.

Flashes of Temper

Most dogs—indeed, most animals—are friendly by nature. Even when they don't want to play or snuggle up with each other, they do want to get along in peaceful harmony. But they have tempers just as people do, and this means they can get ornery and disagreeable. "It's unrealistic to expect dogs to get along without having differences," Dr. Dunbar says. "We have debating schools; dogs have rough-and-tumble schools."

Dogs fight about all sorts of things, but their underlying motivations can usually be boiled down to the following three things.

Jealousy. This is probably the most common cause of disagreements in the family. Dogs crave their owners' attention and attach a lot of value to getting it. A dog who feels that he isn't getting as much attention as another pet will make his displeasure known, either with a warning growl or grumble or by actually getting physical.

Social status. Dogs who live together usually understand who's in charge and who's not. When they meet other dogs in the neighborhood, however, the social rules aren't established, and they'll sometimes fight to establish their place in the hierarchy.

Possessions. There's a simple rule among dogs: The dog with the bone—or the toy or the bowl of food—feels he owns it. The dog without the bone, the toy, or the food knows he wants it. It's part of dogs' nature to covet what they don't have and to defend what they do. Conflicts over possessions as well as conflicts over territory are usually resolved peacefully, if only because both dogs know the rules and are willing to abide by them—if not at first, then after a warning shot is fired.

The Rules of Engagement

Dogs are very physical in their interactions, both with people and with other dogs. When you consider how strong and fast dogs are, it's surprising that they don't hurt each other more often. But there's a reason for this. Puppies are always biting and tumbling over each other, and when they get too aggressive, their playmates either give a loud yelp or bite them back. Either way, they learn to control the strength of their bites, says Dr. Dunbar.

Even before this, their mothers teach them how much pressure they're allowed to put into a bite. When a puppy uses his teeth too much or too hard when taking milk, his mother will simply stand up and walk away. Along with her goes everything the puppy wants, such as comfort, softness, warmth, and milk. He soon learns how much bite is acceptable and how much is too much.

In a true fight, of course, all the rules change, although most fights aren't meant to inflict real damage but to make a point. When two dogs meet in a park, for example, there may be a few moments during which they'll jockey to establish their respective positions—and this may include growling, snarling, and biting. Unless they're truly serious about going to war, however, the bites will be "inhibited." The confrontation looks scary, but it's unlikely to result in real injuries.

Fights can escalate, however, and what begins as a bluff can turn into the real thing very quickly. You can never be sure that dogs aren't going to fight, which is why it's a good idea to lead your dog another way as soon as you see signs of tension. Dogs invariably signal their intentions, however, and you can make a pretty good guess based on their body language and behavior. Here are some examples.

A visible tongue. Dogs whose tongues are either lolling out of their mouths or zipping between their incisors—a movement that Dr. Dunbar calls lizard tongue—aren't anticipating a fight. Dogs who want to fight protect their tongues by drawing them back into their throats.

Guys and Gals

In the animal world, males are the fiercest competitors. A male dog who takes another male dog's bone had better be prepared for the consequences—or be fast enough to make a clean getaway. Possession may give him an edge, but he'll still have to defend his prize.

The rules change when a female takes the bone, says Ian Dunbar, Ph.D., M.R.C.V.S. (a British equivalent of D.V.M.), a veterinarian and animal behaviorist in Berkeley, California, and founder of the Association of Pet Dog Trainers. Once she has the bone, it doesn't matter very much what the male thinks. He can huff and puff, raise his hair, and growl ferociously. She's just going to keep gnawing. She's a female, and the bone's between her paws—and that means that canine law is on her side.

Bent elbows. One of the most dominant displays that a dog can make is to stand stiffly on his back legs while putting his front paws on another dog's back. This looks very threatening, and in some cases it is. Look carefully to see if one or both of the front elbows are bent. Bent elbows almost always mean that a dog wants to play.

Bowing. This is the giveaway signal. A dog who puts his front end close to the ground and raises his butt in the air is making what behaviorists call a play bow. No matter how loud the bark or ferocious the growl, the play bow always means that a dog has good intentions.

Making Peace

Some dogs have extremely aggressive personalities, either because they've been trained that way or because they're simply more assertive and temperamental than others. Dogs who always seem to be looking for a fight need to be avoided—unless they're yours, in which case you'll need the help of a professional trainer. Most dogs, however, can learn to be more accommodating of other pets, says Dr. Dunbar. Here are a few tips you may want to try.

Bring puppies together. It's certainly possible to teach old dogs new tricks, but it's a lot easier to start when they're young—and when you let other dogs do the teaching. Dogs who spend their formative months in the company of other dogs tend to be more easygoing and accepting than those who were raised only around people. More important, puppies teach each other bite control and other valuable lessons.

If there are other puppies or young dogs in your neighborhood, you may want to try to organize some puppy playtimes at a park or in someone's yard. Taking dogs to school for puppy training can also help a lot, says Dr. Dunbar.

Let them work it out. As long as your dog has never been hurt in a fight or shown a serious tendency to hurt other pets, you can safely ignore most altercations—assuming the other dog has similar inclinations, says Dr. Dunbar. Dogs need to work out for themselves such issues as social status and their place in the family hierarchy. So let them do it, he advises. The aggressive posturings and growls will usually start to diminish once dogs are sure of their place in the family.

Have them step outside. "My dogs can have a squabble if they want to, but it has to be less than 3 seconds long," Dr. Dunbar says. When they exceed the 3-second rule, he tells them, "Dogs outside!" This lets them know that they won't be allowed to finish their argument in the house and that they have to take it somewhere else. "What happens, of course, is that the dogs go outside and immediately turn around, face the door, and ask to come back in," he says.

Don't reward the growls. Growling can be an invitation to play, or it can be a threat. Either way, you don't want to reward it. People inadvertently do this when they try to calm their dogs by saying, "It's okay" or by petting them. Dogs don't need reassurance when they growl, says Dr. Dunbar. Giving any positive feedback at all will encourage them to get more assertive.

Ask your vet about neutering. In males especially, few things reduce the urge to fight more than having them neutered. Dogs who are neutered don't have to fight for mates, and they're less likely to be worrying about their place in the social hierarchy. Having them neutered will eliminate the urge to fight in 30 percent of dogs and will noticeably reduce the urge in another 20 percent.

CHAPTER 51

Finicky Eating

Dogs are known for being chow-hounds, and owners are always a little surprised when their voracious canines suddenly develop delicate tastes. Cats, on the other hand, have a reputation for being fussy about their food. In either case, the reality is more complex. Although some dogs and cats are particular about their food, no pet is born picky.

"Any creature that will enthusiastically munch raw mice and live grasshoppers is not by nature a finicky eater," says Myrna Milani, D.V.M., a veterinarian in Charlestown, New Hampshire, and author of *CatSmart* and *DogSmart*.

Dogs and cats establish their tastes for food in the first months of life. Up until they are 6 months old, they will eat almost anything. But after this first burst of exploration, they tend to dislike novel tastes, and some adults will flatly refuse to eat unusual food. Old cats, in particular, may refuse anything but the usual, preferring to go hungry rather than try something new.

In most families, people and pets quickly arrive at mutually agreeable menus, and everyone's happy. Problems occur when pets, for no apparent reason, stop eating their dinners and start begging for something different. Most of the time, the message they're sending you is "I'm spoiled, and I want you to fuss over me." But they also might be telling you "This food is bad" or "I'm sick today."

Different Styles

Before labeling pets as finicky, it's important to understand their normal eating habits. Dogs and cats approach mealtimes differently, and their unique eating styles have led many people to assume that cats are naturally finicky and dogs are naturally voracious.

Dogs inherited their eating style from their ancestors, the wolves. A 100-pound wolf can stuff 20 pounds of food into his stomach at one sitting, then go without eating for a few days. Some dogs prefer this style of eating—packing in a big meal every few days, with just a few nibbles in between. It's not the healthiest approach because dogs tend to get sick when they eat more than a pound of food at one time. But the feast-and-nibble cycle is a common pattern.

Cats have a different approach. "Wild cats eat lots of tiny meals," says Rebecca Remillard, D.V.M., Ph.D., a veterinary nutritionist at Angell Memorial Animal Hospital in Boston. "They'll kill a mouse and eat half of it, then come back in an hour and finish the rest."

A cat's digestive system is different from a dog's, she explains. Cats need small, high-protein meals as often as 10 to 12 times a day. While dogs are built to gorge and fast, cats are built to nibble and snack. What looks like finicky eating is really just efficient eating.

Pick and Choose

Once you understand how dogs and cats normally eat, it's easy to tell if your pet is following her ancestors' example or if she has merely decided to hold out for something better—and is willing to drive you crazy until she gets it. Pets who quit eating until you fork over some canned tuna or a tasty biscuit are taking advantage of your good nature. And as soon as you give in, they discover that picky eating has certain rewards.

Why do pets who used to eat everything suddenly turn up their whiskers at all but the choicest tidbits? Here are a few reasons.

"I'm tired of the same food." Even caviar can lose its appeal, and some dogs and cats want a change after eating the same food for a long time, says Lisa Smith, a pet-behavior consultant and veterinary hospital manager in Severn, Maryland.

"I'm bored." In the wild, the thrill of the hunt always preceded mealtimes. It got the digestive juices flowing in a way that a slow waddle to the food bowl doesn't. Finicky eating may be your pet's way of saying that she'd like more excitement in her life, especially around mealtimes, says Grant Nisson, D.V.M., a veterinarian in West River, Maryland.

"I'm lonely." Like people, some dogs and cats think that food is

MESSAGES AND MEANINGS

Saved with a Steak and a Saucer

Professional pet-sitters quickly discover that there's more to caring for cats and dogs than slapping some kibble in a bowl, especially when they're caring for the pampered whims of the whiskered set.

"One of my first jobs was to take care of this huge house while the owner was gone," says Rické Morgan, owner of Morgan's Menagerie in Shady Side, Maryland. Her charge was a little Maltese named Fatima. Fatima was happy to have company, and she wagged her tail and rolled on the floor in play. Everything seemed just peachy—until dinnertime.

"All she would eat was fresh filet mignon sautéed with canned peas and rice," says Rické. "It couldn't be turkey or chicken—just filet. And not just any peas—Fatima ate only LeSueur brand. Nothing else would do."

On the first two nights, Fatima consented to take a few tiny nibbles of food. Then she stopped eating entirely. "Every time I put the food down, she would sniff at it, sigh, and then throw herself down next to the dish," says Rické.

Fatima was obviously in mourning for her owner, who was going to be away for a lot longer than Fatima could go without eating. Rické, who was getting worried, tried everything she could think of to encourage the little dog to eat. She pleaded with Fatima, offered morsels by hand, and even acted as though she were going to eat the food herself. Nothing helped.

Rické decided that a cup of tea was just the thing she needed to quiet her nerves. She opened a cabinet and took out an earthenware teacup. Fatima raised her head and looked at her intently. Then Rické took out the matching saucer, at which point Fatima began jumping and barking wildly.

Always alert to canine communication, Rické played along. "I took the saucepan out of the drawer, banged it around as if I were cooking, and slipped the rejected filet out of her bowl and onto the saucer. I popped it into the microwave for a few seconds to get it warm, then I set it down on the floor with a flourish." Fatima ate every bite.

The saucer turned out to be the solution. Even though Fatima customarily ate out of a bowl, Rické says, the saucer reminded her of her owner and made her feel less lonely—and more hungry.

best enjoyed in the company of family and friends, Smith says. What they often get, however, is a bowl set down in a hurry as their owners leave the house in the morning.

"My food is spoiled." Warm temperatures can cause moist foods to go bad within an hour or two, and even dry food loses its savor fairly quickly. In addition, the grains used in dry foods occasionally get contaminated with molds, which gives them an off taste, says Dr. Nisson.

"I'm spoiled." Pets who are accustomed to getting handouts sometimes give their food a disgusted look, as though to say, "I'll die unless you give me something better." They're lying, of course. What they're really saying is that they have you wrapped around their paws, Smith says. Pets who insist on eating chicken breast or who only get an appetite after you've opened the fifth can of food are amusing themselves at your expense.

"I'm not finicky, I'm efficient." It's natural for cats and even some dogs to snack throughout the day. As long as they're healthy and their weight looks right, this is perfectly acceptable, and foisting food on them will only cause them to reject it, says Dr. Remillard.

"This food sure is filling." Pets who switch from a grocery store–brand food to a super-premium food such as Science Diet or Eukanuba will often eat less than half as much as they did before because the food is better for them nutritionally, says Dr. Nisson.

"I'm addicted." Just as people can develop strong cravings for chocolate or caffeine, pets can become addicted to certain foods. Once a cat tastes tuna, for example, she'll often refuse to eat anything else.

"I've never seen such weird stuff in my life." There's no accounting for tastes, and some dogs and cats will refuse anything that's different from what they're accustomed to.

"I don't feel well." Dogs who turn away from their usual food and reject choice offerings as well may be sick. You'll want to call your vet if they don't start eating within a day or two and if they are lethargic or have a fever, says Dr. Nisson. It's dangerous for cats to go very long without food, however. Call your vet if your cat doesn't start eating within 24 hours.

BRING BACK THE GUSTO

Dogs and cats are creatures of habit. Once they get accustomed to begging for—and receiving—special treats, it's extremely hard to get them eating normally again. And in the meantime, you'll have to put up with meows, moans, and perpetual mooching. It's not difficult to convince your pets to be less fussy, but it may take some time. Here's what experts advise.

Give them only pet food. Given a chance, dogs and cats will happily eat human food. Once they get a taste for it, they'll often skip their usual dinner in order to get the goodies. "If you knew you could have candy and cookies, would you eat your peas and potatoes?" says Ben Kersen, a trainer in Victoria, British Columbia, Canada. The only way to make their food more appealing is to stop giving them yours, he advises. Once pets understand that what they see is what they get, they'll be more likely to eat their dinners without complaining.

Hang tough. Pets can't open expensive little sardine cans by themselves, so what goes in their mouths is entirely up to you. It's aggravating to listen to plaintive cries or to be confronted with pleading eyes, but if you hold tough, nix the fancy snacks, and give them only pet food for a few days, there's a good chance their fussy habits will disappear, says David McMillan, a trainer and owner of Worldwide Movie Animals in Canyon Country, California.

Make mealtime more social. The sounds and smells of cooking and the companionship that's a ritual of mealtimes can have a powerful effect on dogs and cats. Pets tend to be less finicky about their food when they're allowed to eat in the kitchen or dining room along with the rest of the family, says Diana Philips, a trainer and owner of Spirit of the Moon Animal Talent in Gibsonton, Florida.

Count to 15. Many pets, especially cats, are accustomed to free-choice feeding, in which food is available all the time. This approach is usually fine, but for some pets, food loses its appeal when they've been looking at it all day, Smith says. A better approach is to put the food down for 15 minutes. If your pet hasn't eaten, pick up the food and put it away. By making food "scarce," your pet will probably value it more, she says.

Acknowledge her "tuna jones." Addictions die hard, and cats who crave a single food—usually tuna—may refuse to eat anything else. While a pure tuna diet isn't very good for cats, expecting them to go "cold tuna" is unrealistic because some cats will literally starve before eating something else, says Dr. Nisson. You'll have to ease your cat into a new eating style—by adding a little bit of tuna to the food you want her to eat. Each day, add a little less tuna. Within a month or two, most cats will be eating normally again, he says.

Feed them late. The appetite is partly controlled by the body's natural rhythms, and some dogs and cats simply aren't ready to eat until 9:00 or 10:00 P.M. "I find that many dogs have too much on their minds to feel like eating earlier in the day, so a late feeding really helps," says Kersen. Late-night feedings are especially helpful in summer, when high temperatures can make dogs and cats reluctant to eat.

Stimulate the appetite with exercise. Pets who do a lot of running around are much less likely to be bored than those who sleep on the couch all day, Kersen says. This is important because pets who are excited by life tend to eat more heartily than those who are lackadaisical. Exercise also burns calories, of course, which results in a heartier appetite. Veterinarians agree that healthy dogs and cats can easily use 20 minutes of vigorous play a day—all at once or, for older, less vigorous pets, in 5-minute increments.

Play hide-and-seek. For creatures who evolved as hunters, few things are more boring than a bowl of lifeless kibble. To stimulate your pet's senses along with her appetite, put the thrill back into eating by hiding small servings of food around the house, for example, and letting her sniff them out, says Joanne Howl, D.V.M., a veterinarian in West River, Maryland, and former president of the Maryland Veterinary Medical Association. It's not as exciting as catching a mouse, but it's as close to hunting as modern pets are likely to get.

Warm their food. Pets sometimes demand people food because it's smellier than their own—and smell, especially for cats, is just as important as taste for working up an appetite. Food that's heated in the microwave or doused with a little warm water releases more aromas than cold foods, Smith says. Don't make it too hot, however, because some pets will gulp food even when it's scalding hot.

Nip it in the nest. Dogs and cats establish many of their habits, including their willingness to try new foods, when they're young. One of the best ways to keep them from getting picky later on is to expose them to a wide variety of foods. Switch brands now and then. Give them chicken flavor instead of beef flavor. You may even want to give them small tastes of fruit, vegetables, and cheese, Dr. Nisson says. The idea isn't to get them accustomed to human food but to help them understand that new foods are also good foods.

Keep in mind, too, that fruits and vegetables are high in fiber and low in calories. If your puppy develops a fondness for crunchy carrots, apple slices, grapes, and sugar snap peas as treats, you could avoid a weight problem later on.

CHAPTER 52

Food Stealing

In the holiday film *A Christmas Story*, a horde of hounds breaks into a house and devours Christmas dinner just minutes before the feast is to be served. While few families have actually had to eat Chinese take-out on Christmas because of their pets' insatiable appetites and thieving ways, nearly everyone has lost something—part of a sandwich, a piece of cake, or a fresh piece of fish—to counter-surfing dogs and cats.

"Pets are natural-born scavengers," says Ben Kersen, a trainer in Victoria, British Columbia, Canada. Their ancestors routinely got their nourishment by sniffing around for extras, and dogs and cats continue to view food lying around as an open invitation to supper. Pilfering food is their way of saying, "This smells great, and I'm taking it."

Instincts may give pets the idea, but actually jumping up and taking food usually occurs when there's some sort of miscommunication in the family. "When dogs and cats grab a free snack, and you don't tell them not to, they think it's perfectly acceptable behavior," says John Fioramonti, D.V.M., a veterinarian in Towson, Maryland.

Things are a bit more complicated when pets steal food that you're getting ready to eat, either by grabbing it off a table or out of your hands, Kersen says. In dogs, at least, this type of utter disregard for manners usually means that they have so little respect for the people in their lives that they feel they have the right to take whatever they want, when they want it.

I Think That's Mine

Even though pets and people have similar views about what constitutes socially acceptable conduct, people understand that there are exceptions to every rule, while dogs and cats can't make the fine distinctions. People at a dinner party, for example, wouldn't dream of grabbing the serving platter out of their host's

MESSAGES AND MEANINGS

The Case of the Lost Loaf

Feeding a family of six is quite a chore, especially when food keeps disappearing. Karen Malcor-Chapman of Alhambra, California, couldn't figure it out. After every shopping trip, a single loaf of plastic-wrapped, soft, white bread would vanish. "It happened every time," Karen says. "It would just disappear from under our noses."

Whole-house searches usually found the bread tucked neatly under a bed. It was never damaged except for the wrapper, which was always punctured with hundreds of little pinholes. The tiny holes in the wrapper, and the fact that the loaf wasn't devoured, seemed to implicate Oliver, Karen's 20-pound white cat. But he was never in sight when the groceries came home, which eliminated him as a suspect—or so Karen thought.

After weeks of search-and-rescues, the family devised a plan to expose the loaf-lifting scam. After the next shopping trip, while various family members unloaded bags, Karen hid out and watched. While everyone was out at the car grabbing bags, Oliver sauntered into the kitchen. "He found the bread, grabbed it gently in his teeth, and tugged until it hit the floor," she says.

Still in hiding, she watched in amazement as the burly cat straddled the bag, grabbed the plastic wrapping in his mouth, stood up nearly on his tiptoes, and dragged it away. Karen crept slowly after him and peered under the bed, where he'd pulled his prize. There she discovered her normally dignified cat rolling like a foolish kitten on the floor, tossing and poking the loaf like it was a catnip toy. That's when Karen started laughing—and Oliver, mortified and caught in the act, dropped the loaf and ran.

Karen never scolded Oliver for his bread-stealing ways, but then, she didn't have to. "Oliver never stole it again," she says. She suspects that his embarrassment at getting caught was a lot more powerful than his love of the loaf.

hands and snatching the juiciest steak. At home, however, they'll often take food from a family member's plate. People understand that some kinds of "stealing" say more about familiarity than about disrespect.

This is where pets differ. Dogs, for example, have very strict rules about who eats what and when it gets eaten. Top dogs always eat first, and it's their right to choose their portions. This works fine when dogs are among dogs, because we expect to see a certain amount of grabbing and gobbling. But it doesn't work so well among people. When a dog decides that the sandwich in your hand is hers, she's telling you quite a bit about how she feels about your relationship.

"They aren't just being rude, they are telling you that you don't count," says Dr. Fioramonti. "They consider themselves to be boss." Since this type of food stealing signals a lack of respect, it's usually followed (or accompanied) by other types of disrespectful behavior, such as growling or ignoring commands.

Cats are just as likely to take food as dogs, but they have a different reason for doing it. Cats normally share their food, and they don't object when a companion nudges in, says Diana Philips, a trainer and owner of Spirit of the Moon Animal Talent in Gibsonton, Florida. Similarly, they feel perfectly free to raid your plate. It's their way of saying that they consider you to be an equal.

Hold On to Your Plate

Regardless of their reasons for doing it, pets who steal food aren't appreciated in the human clan. "You don't have to accept this behavior," says Philips. "Although it's normal for pets to want free food, they can learn to live without it."

Feed them only from their bowls. We often think of dogs and cats as being governed by instinct, but much of their knowledge is acquired in the same way people learn—by watching. "If you are constantly taking treats off the counter and popping them to your pet, she's going to learn that food comes from the counter, and she'll eventually try to get it herself," says Kersen. Dogs and cats who get food only out of their bowls soon learn to keep their eyes on the floor and their appetites out of trouble, he explains.

Don't let them score. With a combination of patience, persistence, and tenacity, dogs and cats invariably will find food that they shouldn't—and once it's in reach, they're very unlikely to walk away. You can't let them win because once they've been rewarded with success, they're going to keep trying, Philips says. "Always take the prize away," she says. "Even if it's ruined, don't ever give it back."

NAME: Bynoe
OCCUPATION: Customs Inspector

Most dogs in customs work are trained to search out explosives or carefully concealed stashes of marijuana. Bynoe's job is a little different. A 10-year-old yellow Labrador retriever who works for the Maryland Department of Agriculture, Bynoe sniffs hives of honeybees for signs of disease. By ensuring that the honeybee population stays healthy, Bynoe is directly responsible for protecting the state's beekeeping industry.

Sniffing bees is the easy part. As with every customs dog, Bynoe faces one formidable obstacle that is the biggest threat to his law-enforcement career: food. Dogs who work for a living have been known to nab an unguarded nibble from time to time, especially when they're relaxing at home. But Bynoe is cut of sterner stuff, which is a good thing because dogs who get distracted by tasty tidbits coming through customs invariably get fired, says Jerry Fischer, Bynoe's partner and the apiary (bee) inspector for the state of Maryland.

"When he's working, it's just impossible to distract this dog," Jerry says. "You can leave a steak on the table next to him, and he'll just ignore it."

Be sneaky in punishments. Since food stealing is such a common problem, experts have devised many creative ways for stopping it—like spritzing pets with water. Tossing keys on the floor nearby. Giving a blast on a whistle. What these techniques have in common, apart from the fact that they startle pets silly, is that they can be done from behind, out of sight.

"When pets know the corrections are coming from you, all you are doing is teaching them to sneak," Kersen explains. Giving them "invisible" reprimands, on the other hand, makes them suspect that the whole world is in on it. They'll be a little hesitant to steal when they suspect Big Brother is watching.

Create an ambush. Most pets have personal favorites, foods that they're always hankering for. You can take advantage of this by giving them a temptation that's too delicious to resist—and throwing in a little extra. "I take the juice that jalapeños are packed in, paint it on some food, and then set it out on a counter or tabletop," says Kersen. The spicy juice won't hurt them, but their mouths will temporarily catch fire—and they may decide that if this is the stuff humans eat, they don't want any part of it. Hot-sauce booby traps mainly work for dogs, he adds. Cats take the time to sniff and examine their food and aren't likely to be fooled.

Give an attitude adjustment. Since dogs who consistently steal food are suggesting that they're higher in the pecking order than their people, it's usually necessary to work on the underlying attitudes, says Dr. Fioramonti. "It's essential that they learn to respect you."

The best way to teach overbearing dogs some manners is to help them understand that nothing in life is free, that everything they value and cherish—food, walks, even trips to the yard—is controlled entirely by you. "Your dog gets nothing from you without working for it," Dr. Fioramonti explains. "In order to get her dinner, she has to sit when you ask. To get a scratch on her head, she has to lie down. Every time she wants something, make her earn it." The idea is to help them understand that you hold a lot of power. Once they understand that you're the "top dog," they'll be less likely to do things that violate basic good manners.

Keep them distracted. "Make sure that your pet always has something to do other than stare at the trout on the tabletop," says Philips. She suggests keeping a little food in the bowl to quell your pet's hunger pangs, while at the same time putting out toys or other fun things that will keep her attention off the counters or tabletops.

A NUTRITIONAL SIGNAL

Pets usually make a move for the chicken wings because one, they like the taste; two, they figure you won't mind; and three, they think they can get away with it. But there's also a fourth possibility: They aren't getting enough to eat.

Pets who eat with normal appetites but who always seem famished probably aren't getting all the nutrients they need, says Dr. Fioramonti. Most commercial pet foods supply all the nutrients they need, but some may contain overly large amounts of indigestible ingredients, such as fiber, and not enough protein. In addition, each pet absorbs nutrients differently, and some may not be able to absorb all the essentials from their usual food.

Even the best-quality food will leave pets hungry if they aren't

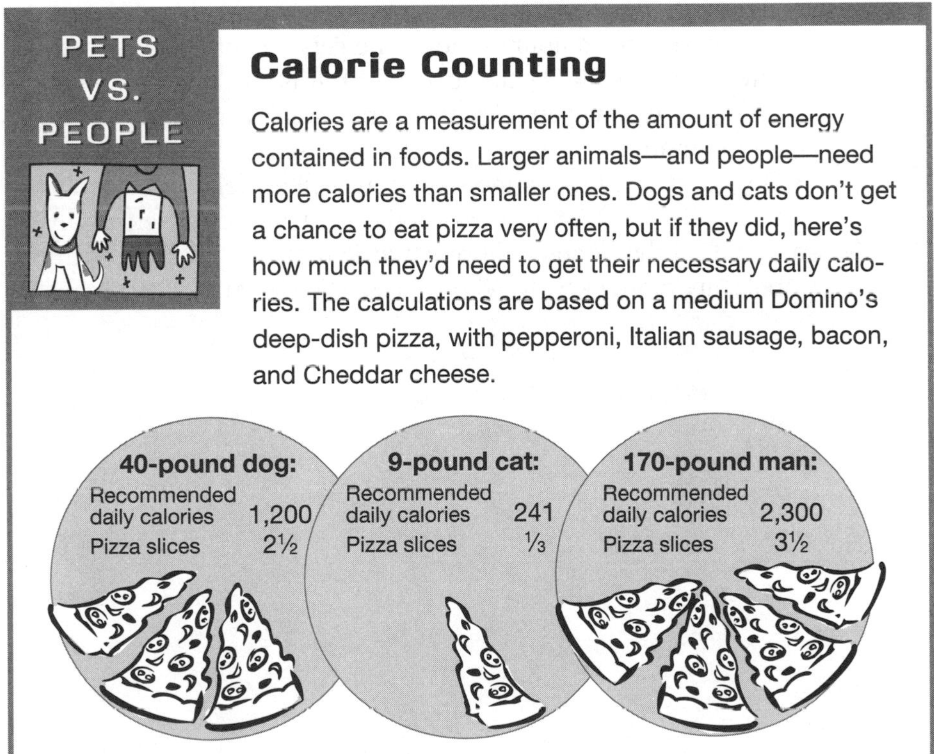

Calorie Counting

Calories are a measurement of the amount of energy contained in foods. Larger animals—and people—need more calories than smaller ones. Dogs and cats don't get a chance to eat pizza very often, but if they did, here's how much they'd need to get their necessary daily calories. The calculations are based on a medium Domino's deep-dish pizza, with pepperoni, Italian sausage, bacon, and Cheddar cheese.

	Recommended daily calories	Pizza slices
40-pound dog:	1,200	2½
9-pound cat:	241	⅓
170-pound man:	2,300	3½

eating enough of it. The average 10-pound cat needs to eat about 260 calories a day to feel full. For a 40-pound dog, it takes about 1,200 calories a day. "Growing kittens and puppies, athletic dogs, or pets who are pregnant or nursing might need twice that amount," explains Dr. Fioramonti.

Pets who aren't eating enough or who seem to be hungry no matter how much they eat need to be checked out by a veterinarian because medical problems such as parasites or hormone imbalances can cause out-of-control hunger and food stealing. But as long as your pet is generally healthy, it's usually not hard to increase the amount of calories she's taking in.

- Veterinarians sometimes recommend giving dogs and cats super-premium foods. Available from vets and pet supply stores, foods such as Nutro and Science Diet contain high-quality ingredients that are easily digested and absorbed.
- To make sure your pet is getting enough food, measure how much goes in the bowl and compare that to the recommendations on the food label, says Dr. Fioramonti. If you're not feeding her enough, you'll want to increase the amount a bit. As a test, try increasing the amount of food she gets by about 10 percent. If after a month, she's gaining weight but is still raiding food at every opportunity, you'll know calories aren't the problem, says Dr. Fioramonti.
- Dogs and cats love canned foods as well as delicacies such as pureed baby food. While these foods are nutritious, veterinarians have found that foods requiring a little tooth-work, such as dry kibble, are more likely to send "I'm satisfied" signals to the brain.

CHAPTER 53

Hiding

After parking his Plymouth sedan in a shopping-mall parking lot, Jeff Nichol, D.V.M., thought he heard a cat crying. He looked around and didn't see anything, but he still heard the cries. So he started searching for this poor, plaintive cat who obviously had gotten lost and was pleading for help. As he searched, the meowing brought him closer and closer—to his own car.

"Under the fender, near the front wheel, was my own cat," says Dr. Nichol, a veterinarian in Albuquerque, New Mexico. "I tried to grab him, but he backed away like a turtle backing into its shell. I finally just left him there and drove home. Two hours later, he came out and had dinner."

Dr. Nichol's story is a bit unusual, but his cat's ability to hide and then reappear is not. Cats have lean, light bodies and incredibly flexible spines. They can shimmy into the tiniest of spaces. And sometimes their habit of spelunking gets them into more trouble than they bargained for.

Hidden Comfort

Dogs and cats are attracted to small, dark places because they have a denning instinct. It goes back to their ancestors, who discovered that small enclosures not only were warm and cozy but also would protect them from predators. Some pets have retained these ancestral urges. They sometimes feel uneasy when they're in a wide-open space, like the middle of the living room. Their natural tendency, especially when they're scared or insecure, is to seek out small, hidden places, such as in a dark closet, under the bed, inside dresser drawers, or in the bathtub, says Scott Line, D.V.M., Ph.D., a board-certified veterinary behaviorist in Winston-Salem, North Carolina.

"It's a very natural and normal thing for pets to do," adds Ju-

PETS VS. PEOPLE

The Smallest Space They Can Fit Into

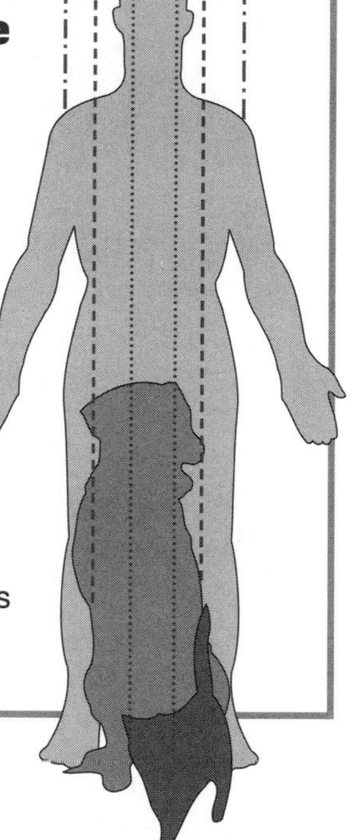

Cats have about the same number of bones as humans, but they're shaped in such a way that they have tremendous flexibility and can squeeze into spaces as small as the width of their heads. Dogs aren't as limber as cats, but, compared to humans, they're as flexible as Silly Putty, wedging themselves into any space as wide as their sides. People are limited by their shoulder width—you can't fit into a space that's narrower than your shoulders are wide.

dith Kaufman, a trainer in Norwalk, Connecticut. "We might consider it hiding, but they consider it nice and cozy."

Most dogs are a lot bigger than cats, so they aren't as adept at disappearing from view. But they have their own ways of making themselves inconspicuous. They'll lie with their backs against a sofa or a wall or curl up in a tight ball in a corner. This gives them the illusion of being in a den, and it allows them to see what's going on around them, says Kaufman. Like cats, they're more likely to hide when they're nervous, such as during thunderstorms, or simply to escape a bath.

Normal and Natural

Hiding really isn't a behavior problem because, apart from unauthorized car trips, it doesn't cause problems for owners. Nor does it mean that something terrible is happening in pets' lives, although a loud clap of thunder or a roomful of rambunctious children will send many pets scurrying for cover. Unless your pet is visibly frightened and hides all the time, it isn't anything to worry about, says Dr. Nichol.

The one exception is when your cat is getting into trouble. Because cats can squeeze into the smallest of places, they can essentially disappear and stay hidden for hours or sometimes days at a time. It's not unheard of for desperate owners to launch all-out neighborhood searches, putting up posters and posting "Lost pet!" ads in the classifieds, only to discover that their cat had been home all along, comfortably snoozing on the top shelf in the linen closet.

Cats don't always choose the safest hiding places, either. They crave warmth and can get very creative at finding it—under the hoods of cars, for example, or in clothes dryers if the doors are left open, says Dr. Nichol. As long as you're aware of this, you can make sure that your cat doesn't accidentally tumble-dry by keeping appliance doors closed, and it's a good idea to bang on the hood before starting your car in the morning.

CHAPTER 54

Hogging the Bed

Any couple with a California King mattress should expect to have enough room to lounge in comfort. Usually, they do—if they don't have pets. As soon as a furry bedmate climbs on board, that big mattress suddenly seems a whole lot smaller.

Dogs and cats are very good at lounging, and they like a lot of room to do it right. They'll sprawl on their sides with their legs stuck out in a W shape. Or they'll stretch lengthwise from the foot of the bed to the pillow. Or they'll flip over, lie on their backs with their legs in the air, and snore. Even small pets seem to occupy a disproportionate amount of space on the bed.

"There's no doubt that they get a lot of satisfaction from sleeping in the bed," adds Vint Virga, D.V.M., a veterinarian at the behavior clinic at Cornell University College of Veterinary Medicine in Ithaca, New York. Bedtime for them is a chance to get close to the people they love. And if they happen to take up a lot of room, well, it's no concern of theirs. They'll sleep just fine, even as their human bedmates toss and turn and desperately try to find a spot that isn't already taken.

Grab It When You Can

Dogs and cats are creatures of comfort. They spend a lot of their time sleeping, and it makes sense for them to get as comfortable as they can. While pets with thick coats or Northern heritages generally prefer tile floors to downy comforters, most dogs and cats think the bed is just about perfect. This is especially true of bony dogs like greyhounds. Unlike meatier dogs, they have to cushion that spine somehow, and it's hard to beat a good mattress, says Marsha Reich, D.V.M., a veterinarian in the depart-

PETS VS. PEOPLE

The Anatomy of Comfort

People often sleep on their stomachs, and pets hardly ever do. The reason for the difference is the spine: It curves differently in humans, dogs, and cats. What's comfortable for us isn't comfortable for them. Here's a back-to-back look at people and pets.

People: The lower part of the spine has two curves, which naturally support each other when we lie on our stomachs.

Cats: Cats have C-shaped spines with an added bend where the neck meets the chest. When they lie on their stomachs, they have to arch that bend backward. They're much more comfortable sleeping on their sides or curled up in a ball.

Dogs: Their spines are similar to cats', only straighter. This means that they can sleep on their stomachs for short periods. This position does require them to arch their backs slightly, so they generally turn over fairly quickly in order to sleep on their sides.

ment of behavioral medicine at the University of Pennsylvania School of Veterinary Medicine in Philadelphia.

"Dogs can be real opportunists, and many will simply take over their owners' beds," adds Robin Kovary, director of the American Dog Trainers Network in New York City. It's not that they're trying to be inconsiderate. They just want to get as much of a good thing as they can.

Status is part of all this, too. Humans who have risen in the world may wear Rolex watches. Dogs who aspire to leadership try to get taller. They associate height with power, and getting up on the bed makes them feel bigger and more powerful.

Cats are just as likely to gravitate to beds as dogs are. Comfort is part of it, but mainly it's because they're instinctively attracted to high places, says Dr. Virga. They feel safe when they're up high. Plus, the view from the bed is better than it is from the floor, and cats enjoy seeing what's going on around them. A big cat can take up just as much space as a small dog, but people are less likely to complain about it because cats are lighter and easier to move aside.

The exception is when cats develop a liking for a particular human hollow, such as the crook of the knees or between the neck and the shoulders. Cats who get this close to people at night may be taking advantage of their relative immobility to mark them with their scent, says Susan Ackermann, D.V.M., a veterinarian in Hellertown, Pennsylvania, who specializes in cat care. Or, like dogs, they might do it just because it feels good.

Reclaiming Your Space

Even people who love having pets in the bed tend to get tired of battling for space. In winter especially, no one wants to wrestle with 40 or 50 pounds of canine immobility just to find a warm spot. "The problem usually isn't hogging the bed as much as it is the response of dogs to being pushed over," says Dr. Reich. Some pets will gladly oblige, but others won't budge. Some even growl when their slumber is disturbed.

"Growling means that your dog is getting dominant or aggressive, and that's a problem," Kovary says. You paid for the bed. You wash the sheets. So it only makes sense that you should have first rights of occupancy. Now you have to convince your dog.

Puppies will learn quickly to get off—or stay off—the bed, but older dogs who have been sleeping there for years aren't going to give it up easily, Kovary says. You'll have to teach your dog that getting on the bed is a privilege and not a right.

- For starters, give your dog his own bed, Kovary advises. Put a dog bed on the floor, or just put down a pile of blankets. Make it comfortable and inviting.
- Once your dog understands that the new bed is his bed to use as he pleases, it's time to kick him off yours. Don't make a big deal of it. Just shove him off, lead him to his bed, and praise him or give him a biscuit when he settles down, even if it's only for a moment. Then go to bed yourself—and get ready to stay awake for the rest of the night. Your dog may understand that you don't want him there, but he's going to sneak up anyway. You'll prob-

ably have to sleep with one eye open for a few weeks. After a while, though, your dog will decide that *he's* not getting enough sleep, and he'll curl up where he won't be disturbed.

Cats are harder to train than dogs. If you truly want your cat out of the bed, about all you can do is close the bedroom door at night—and brace yourself for the mewing and scratching sounds that will follow. Cats are creatures of habit just as much as dogs. It may take awhile before they'll give up. Once they do, however, it shouldn't be an issue anymore, even when you leave the door open. The same force of habit that made the bed so attractive works the other way, too. Once your cat is accustomed to sleeping somewhere else, he'll be less likely to come back and burrow in again.

CHAPTER 55

House Soiling

Except for puppies (and sometimes kittens) who haven't yet learned to control their bodily functions, house soiling is rarely an accident. Pets who suddenly start making messes are trying to tell you something with their actions that they can't say in words. The message could be as simple as "I'm lonely" or "I'm not feeling very well." Or it could be "Hey, the litter box is a mess, and I'm not using it until it's clean."

It's hard to stay calm when you step on something you wish you hadn't or when the house is starting to smell like a cat box. But it's worth taking a deep breath and pausing for a moment to try to figure out what's going on. "Yelling isn't going to help," says Gwen Bohnenkamp, owner of Perfect Paws, a dog and cat training center in the San Francisco Bay area, and author of *From the Cat's Point of View*. "In fact, in many cases, it's only going to make things worse. You're not communicating anything to your pet except the fact that you're really mad. And she probably won't have the slightest clue why."

House soiling is one of the most frustrating and destructive of all behavior problems. Over time, it can lead to permanent odors or damage. Worse, it can cause a growing distrust between pets and their people.

Different Perspectives

Cats and dogs are pretty flexible creatures. They've adjusted to their lives with humans by applying old instincts to new surroundings. In other words, they do what comes naturally—no matter how "unnatural" the situation. This is why they quickly learn where they should and shouldn't make their pit stops.

Dogs and cats approach this issue differently. Dogs view the house as their den. It's the place where they eat, sleep, and play. Dogs in the wild don't want to eliminate in their dens, and domesticated dogs don't want to make messes in the house. Many house cats, on the other hand, have never stepped foot outside, and they take a slightly different view of their surroundings. Because the house is their whole world, they learn to associate different rooms with different activities. The kitchen is the place to eat. The sofa is the place to sleep. And the bathroom is the place to go to the bathroom, unless you put the litter box somewhere else.

Both of these approaches serve pets and their owners well. Once dogs learn to do their business outside, they will almost always continue to do so. Once cats accept a litter box as a suitable substitute for soft ground, you won't have too many surprises. At least, that's the way it's supposed to be. But sometimes, even after years of perfect behavior, dogs and cats will start going where they shouldn't. You know they're trying to tell you something, but it's not at all clear what that something is. Since your pet can't come right out and explain herself, you'll have to do what Sherlock Holmes always did: Start with the obvious explanations and solutions and work toward the more complicated ones.

• Check the litter box. While some cats will happily use the litter box even when it's been a few days since you changed the litter or cleaned out the clumps, others aren't so accommodating. "We flush a toilet every time we use it. Why should we expect a cat to accept a dirty toilet?" says Gregory Bogard, D.V.M., a veterinarian in Tomball, Texas.

Litter boxes don't have to be pristine, but it's a good idea to clean the box at least once a day. Then add a thin layer of new litter, Dr. Bogard suggests.

• Check your schedule. For dogs, the most common cause of house soiling is a full bladder. Even though some dogs can last all day without a break, you really can't expect a dog to go for long stretches without occasionally having an accident. And once she's had an accident, she's much more likely to have another one because she'll come to associate the smell of the "spot"—or the entire room—with doing her business.

The only solution is to let your dog out or walk her more frequently, says Dr. Bogard. People who work all day often try to slip home at lunch. Or they hire a professional pet-sitter to drop by once or twice a day. Vets often recommend training dogs to stay in a crate because dogs are extremely reluctant to eliminate in "their" space.

Litter Box Basics

Litter boxes are pretty simple things. But humans often manage to mess them up anyway. "There's no such thing as an accident for cats," says Gregory Bogard, D.V.M., a veterinarian in Tomball, Texas. "They always put it where they want it. If they don't like the way the litter box is set up, they'll let you know."

When your cat falls out of her routine, it's time for you to return to basics.

Supply enough boxes. The general rule is one box per cat, plus one. That means two boxes for one cat, three boxes for two cats, and so on, says Gwen Bohnenkamp, owner of Perfect Paws, a dog and cat training center in the San Francisco Bay area, and author of *From the Cat's Point of View* and *Manners for the Modern Dog*. This is especially important if your home has more than one floor or if you have a cat who tends to guard a box against use by another cat.

Forget the gizmos. Box lids, doors, and all those other fancy add-ons can distract or confuse your cat. "That stuff is for humans more than anything else," says Bohnenkamp. "All your cat wants is a quiet, open box to do her business."

Keep it clean. Veterinarians recommend cleaning the box every time your cat uses it and adding about ½ inch of fresh litter over the top. This disguises lingering odors and makes the box more appealing. It's fine to use scented litter as long as your cat doesn't mind, but the scents are really for human noses, Dr. Bogard says. "Cats are pretty tolerant, and most will use whatever litter you put down for them. But the cat's not fooled by the pretty scent. If the box is dirty, you might be tricked, but your cat is not."

Make it accessible. A cat can't use a litter box if the bathroom or closet door is closed. Try to find a place for the box that your cat can reach without crawling around, under, or through anything difficult. If you have to move the box, do so a little bit at a time—no more than a foot a day. Moving a box too quickly can confuse and distract cats, and unanticipated messes may be the result, says Dr. Bogard.

• Check her health. It's not uncommon for dogs and cats to get bladder infections, kidney stones, or other conditions that can make it hard for them to control their bladders or bowels. When they start having accidents after years of good bathroom habits and you can't figure out why it's happening, you should consider the messes a valuable warning sign and call your vet right away.

FEAR AND ANXIETY

Dogs and cats are creatures of habit. They're happiest when everything occurs on a regular schedule and in a predictable fashion. Any change in their routines, from moving to a new house to sharing their space with out-of-town guests, can be very upsetting. And they'll sometimes respond to stress with some unpredictable behavior of their own.

"It can take awhile, from a few days to a few weeks or even more, for pets to get used to change," Dr. Bogard says. In the meantime, about all you can do is give them extra attention at every opportunity. The more time you're able to spend with your pet—with extra walks, for example, or additional strokes at bedtime—the less likely she'll be to express her insecurity in inappropriate places.

Almost all pets are more prone to house soiling when they move to a new house, not only because the change is upsetting but also because they'll have to learn what rules apply to their new space. The best way to reduce the trauma of moving is to introduce your pet to one or two rooms at a time, especially if the new house is bigger than your old one. Keep her in the bedroom for a few days, Bohnenkamp suggests. When she seems comfortable there, let her explore the upstairs for a while. Then give her the run of the downstairs. Moving slowly like this helps prevent pets from being overwhelmed with the change, she explains.

"Cats don't always like excessive freedom," Bohnenkamp adds. "Keeping them in one fairly large room with the litter box can help them explore slowly and ease their anxiety." If your cat has an accident after exploring the house, move her back into the first room and wait a few more days, he suggests.

The same approach works just as well for dogs. Just to be safe, however, it's a good idea to keep them in a room with a floor that can withstand a few accidents, says Bohnenkamp.

It's not only anxiety that causes pets to lose control, adds Andy Bunn, a trainer in Charlotte, North Carolina. Any intense emotion, like the excitement they feel when you come home from work, may cause some dogs to urinate on the spot. This condition, called submissive urination, doesn't occur in cats, he adds.

WHAT'S MY PET SAYING?

Behavior

Urinating outside the Box

What It Means

"This Is *My* House"

When a male cat starts urinating in the house, you can be pretty sure the writing's on the wall—and he wants you to get the message: "This is my turf, and don't you dare mess with it."

It's common for unneutered cats to urinate on walls or furniture as a way of defining their territory. (Accidents on the floor, on the other hand, are usually caused by other factors.) Females occasionally spray, but it's much more common in males.

The easiest way to stop this type of house soiling is to have your pet neutered, says Gregory Bogard, D.V.M., a veterinarian in Tomball, Texas. This causes a drop in male hormones, making them much less likely to spray. It's important, however, to stop the problem early. Some pets who get into the habit of spraying will keep it up even when they've been neutered, he adds.

You can usually stop submissive urination by keeping your comings and goings low-key, Bunn says. When you walk in the door, don't look at, pet, or talk to your dog, he suggests. Just go about your business for a couple of minutes. Then ask your pet to sit, and greet her quietly. By that time, she'll be calm enough that she'll be less likely to lose control.

The same low-key approach works when you have guests in the house. As soon as they walk in the door, distract your dog by having her sit or lie down or by playing with her for a few seconds. "Just give her something to think about other than the new people," Bunn says.

Incidentally, it's a good idea not to stand over your dog when giving her attention or to move your hands too quickly, Bunn adds. For a dog who is naturally nervous, your looming body position will be perceived as a show of dominance, and she may urinate in order to show she's subordinate to your authority.

STAYING CALM

It's easy to get angry when your pet makes a puddle on the Persian carpet. But anger—or worse, punishment—doesn't stop house soiling. In fact, it can be counterproductive and will probably make your pet even more upset. "Rubbing a pet's nose in the mess doesn't deliver the message you think it does," Dr. Bogard says. "Your pet may feel bad, but she won't understand why you're yelling. If anything, scolding will teach her to be even more secretive about where she goes the next time."

Myths to the contrary, dogs and cats don't have accidents just to spite you. They're only trying to tell you that something is out of kilter, and they're confused and upset. So the best thing you can do is remain calm, says Dr. Bogard. Clean up the mess and use an odor remover to eliminate the scent. Then take a little time to figure out what's going wrong.

In the meantime, the best thing that can happen is that you'll actually catch your pet in the act. If you can distract her before she makes a mess by clapping your hands, for example, she'll probably stop what she's doing. That gives you the opportunity to gently take her where you want her to go—the litter box for cats and outside for dogs. When she resumes her business in the proper place, praise her in a low-key way and let her know what a good girl she is. You'll find that a little positive communication may be all it takes to get her back into the groove.

CHAPTER 56

Howling and Yowling

If you've ever spent time in Yellowstone National Park, you may have heard a haunting, melodic series of howls—the sounds of wolves communicating with other members of their packs. It's a sound you can't mistake for any other, and when you're sitting by a fire in the middle of the wilderness, it's a sound you'll never forget.

What sounds like poetry in the great outdoors, however, can be downright annoying when it's coming from next door—or from your own living room in the middle of the night. Like wolves, dogs and cats sometimes let loose with long, mournful howls or yowls. It's one of their ways of networking, either with other pets or with you, says Barbara S. Simpson, D.V.M., Ph.D., a board-certified veterinary behaviorist and a certified applied animal behaviorist in Southern Pines, North Carolina.

Household howling can put your nerves on edge, but it's worth paying attention to because your pet is clearly trying to tell you something—anything from "Here I am . . . where are you?" to "I'm so unhappy I can hardly stand it." Of course, some pets howl simply because it's fun, Dr. Simpson adds.

Sounding Off

Dogs don't have anywhere near the vocal range of humans. Most of their communication, in fact, involves scent and body position rather than barking or howling. Some dogs go their entire lives without a single howl, but others do it all the time. Arctic breeds like Alaskan malamutes and Siberian huskies are vigorous howlers who will sound off at a moment's notice. Hounds howl when they pick up an intoxicating scent. And even dogs who rarely howl, like poodles, will sometimes surprise their owners with a sudden *Arrooo* when they hear a siren or another howl-like sound. Of course, when one dog starts howling, others in the neighborhood often join in, just as their ancestors in the wild answered howls with howls, Dr. Simpson explains.

Howling is usually nothing more than the equivalent of dog chat, but it can also be a wail of distress. You'll rarely hear this kind of howling because it's most likely to occur when you're gone. Dogs are intensely social animals who don't like being alone. Some pets get so lonely and forlorn when their owners leave the house that they'll vent their grief by howling, sometimes for hours at a time. "Howling may be a vocal way for dogs to communicate loneliness and to seek contact with others," Dr. Simpson says. Your neighbors, on the other hand, are more likely to communicate *their* displeasure by taping an angry note to your door.

Unlike dogs, cats don't howl at sirens or to vent sad feelings. "From the cat's point of view, something big has happened, and yowling is one way they handle change," says Kate Gamble, a feline-behavior consultant in Auburn, California. Some likely reasons for feline yowling include the following:

- Age. Older cats who don't hear or see as well as they used to will sometimes yowl when they're feeling disoriented or isolated.
- Hormones. Unspayed female cats in heat will yowl to attract a mate—and the competing toms do plenty of yowling of their own.
- Boredom. Cats without a lot to do will sometimes yowl, either to express dissatisfaction or simply to pass the time.
- Changes in routine. Cats crave consistency, and change in their routine—or their owner's routine—will sometimes cause them to let loose with discontented yowls. It's their way of saying, "I can't handle any more excitement."
- Breed. Some breeds are more vocal than others. Siamese are much more likely to yowl than other breeds.

Other common causes of yowling include changes in diet, problems with the litter box, or, worst of all, rides in the car.

How to Stop Cats from Yowling

Since yowling is not a regular occurrence in cats, it's worth calling your vet if your cat starts making noise without an apparent reason. It doesn't happen often, but cats may develop nervous-system disorders that cause them to make yowl-like noises.

Even when your cat gets a clean bill of health—and in most cases he will—you'll still have to deal with the problem.

Turn on a light. Even though cats are superbly adapted to darkness, they don't always feel comfortable being left alone in a dark room. "Cats, especially older cats, don't see as well in the dark as we think they do, and they may become confused and frightened," says Annie Bruce, a cat-owner consultant in Boulder, Colorado, and author of *Cat Be Good*. When the yowling occurs mainly at night, you may want to put a night-light near where your cat sleeps and see if that helps, she suggests.

Provide a distraction. Cats will often yowl as a way of getting attention—or, more often, as a way of getting what they want. This is why some cats develop the habit of yowling when they approach a door, whether they want to go out or not. One way to break the habit is to toss them a toy as soon as the noise starts. This breaks their concentration and gives them something more exciting to do. "I keep a basket of Ping-Pong balls within easy reach," Gamble says.

Make rides more enjoyable. Taking your cat to the vet is always an adventure. If your cat's nerves aren't shot by the time you get there, yours will be from all the yowling. Putting your cat in a crate, cat carrier, or cardboard box will help keep him calm and less vocal. Position the carrier so that your cat can see what's going on around him, but not so that he can see out the window, Gamble adds. The sight of scenery whizzing by is more than some cats can handle.

Don't give him extra attention. When you respond with sympathy when your cat yowls, he'll quickly learn that this is a great way to get attention, Bruce says. No matter how much the sound is driving you nuts, ignore it, she advises. The less attention you give your cat when he's yowling, the less likely he'll be to keep it up.

Ask your vet about neutering. Both male and female cats are much less likely to yowl when they've been spayed or neutered, Bruce says. But the operation won't change their vocal habits for a month or more—the time it takes for reduced hormone levels to affect the brain. Once they do, you'll be rewarded with peaceful silence.

HOW TO STOP DOGS FROM HOWLING

Some dogs love nothing more than a good howl, so it can be a real challenge to make them stop. In fact, some dogs, like bloodhounds, are genetically programmed to howl, and about all you can hope to accomplish is to find other ways for them to amuse themselves. But it's usually possible to reduce the outbursts, Dr. Simpson adds, even when you can't stop them entirely.

Teach the "quiet" command. As long as your dog does his howling when you're home, you may be able to hush him by making it clear that you don't appreciate this form of dog talk. The minute your dog starts to howl, Dr. Simpson advises, tell him "Hush" or "Quiet," and give him a treat. Dogs can't howl and eat at the same time, so this will keep him quiet for a few seconds. Repeat the command when he resumes his howling, and follow it with another treat. After a while, he'll get the idea that being quiet brings tasty rewards.

"Of course, this probably won't work if you're often not home and your dog has the opportunity to go freestyle," Dr. Simpson adds. "A dog who is free to do what he wants may still howl."

Give him a job. Since some dogs howl when they're lonely and bored, you may be able to stop the habit by creating a more interesting environment. One of the easiest solutions is to give your dog a toy that keeps him busy. A good choice is Kong toys, which have hollow cavities that you fill with something tasty, like peanut butter or Cheez Whiz, Dr. Simpson suggests. He may spend so much time trying to get to the food that he'll forget to feel lonely.

"A client of mine fills hollow bones with peanut butter and calls them bye-bye bones," Dr. Simpson says.

Get him used to being alone. Some dogs crave companionship so much that they'll launch into plaintive howls as soon as you walk out the door. The only way to stop this kind of howling is to help your dog get more comfortable with the idea of being alone, says Dr. Simpson. She recommends using a technique called graduated departures. It works like this.

- Walk to the door and give your dog a command, like "sit" or "stay." Then walk out the door.

• Come back in after a few seconds, before your dog fully realizes that you left. Reward him with an exuberant "Good boy!"
• Go out the door again, for a little longer this time. Then come back in and reward him for being quiet.

"Do this many, many times when you're not actually leaving. Your dog will probably tend to get fairly ho-hum about the whole thing," Dr. Simpson says.

Get him a companion. Even dogs who aren't very social will feel more comfortable when there's another dog in the house. Making your dog feel like he's part of a pack will often reduce his need to howl, says Dr. Simpson.

CHAPTER 57

Humping

In 1956, Elvis Presley appeared on *The Milton Berle Show* and performed "Hound Dog" for a national audience. His hip gyrations and thrusting pelvis delighted millions of teenagers and horrified their mothers and fathers, thereby proving two things: that humping is a normal behavior of the young and energetic and that not everyone appreciates having to watch it.

Popular entertainers aside, people know enough to keep their hips under control, at least in public. But dogs are less discreet. Once they discover humping, some dogs will do it every chance they get—on pillows, other dogs, people's legs, or merely in the air. (Cats rarely hump unless they're mating.) It's embarrassing for owners to watch, but for dogs, it's rich in meaning. Humping conveys messages, such as "I'm the top dog around here" or "I'm bored, and this helps pass the time." And for dogs who are slaves to their hormones, humping doesn't mean much of anything, except perhaps "I'm senseless with desire."

Who's on Top?

The instinct to hump runs deep and occurs more frequently in males than females. After all, it's how puppies and kittens are made, and it plays a role in the species' survival. So it's not surprising that it crops up even in nonmating circumstances, like play. "Puppies often start humping from the first minute their little legs get strong enough to stand up to it," says Kay Cox, Ph.D., a pet counselor in Gilbert, Arizona.

What starts out as an innocent exploration, however, soon turns into a social statement. "The earlier a pup can manage to hump, the sooner he proves to the others that he's strong and bold, and he quickly becomes the leader of the puppy pack," says Dr. Cox. As puppies get older, humping becomes a deliberate type of one-upsmanship—the equivalent of power handshakes among businessmen—and some will continue to do it for the rest of their lives.

In dogs who are sexually intact, the urge to hump is largely driven by hormones, in females as well as males. "My girls go crazy when they come in season," says Danielle Buchheister, a Samoyed breeder in Mayo, Maryland. "They'll hump each other or my neutered males, and they couldn't care less what anyone thinks." Females go into season no more than twice a year, however, while male hormones are relatively constant.

The same hormones that drive dogs together may also spark an interest in the arms and legs of people. "The chemicals that interest dogs seem to smell pretty similar, whether they come from humans, dogs, or a laboratory," says Anthony Jenkins, D.V.M., a veterinarian in Powell, Tennessee. This is why dogs may sometimes be "attracted" to women during certain phases of their menstrual cycles or to women taking birth control pills. Humping can also be a result of mistaken identity—when, for example, a person has recently been around a dog in heat and has carried some of the scent away on his clothing.

Humping isn't always about power or sex. When dogs get wildly excited—from stimulating play, an exhilarating run, or just the joy of being alive—all the surplus energy has to go somewhere, and moving their hips seems to provide a satisfying outlet.

"When a pet suddenly takes up humping, he might be telling you that he's sick," Dr. Jenkins adds. Dogs and cats will sometimes hump pillows or other objects when there is an infection in the urinary tract or a problem with the anal glands. Illnesses can even trigger humping in *other* pets because of changes in the body's chemistry. A pet who's sick may find himself on the receiving end of a dog or cat who's attracted by the new smell.

RISKY BUSINESS

Humping is a natural behavior, and there's no way to stop it entirely. As long as it's confined to other pets, you're better off just ignoring it. "Humping pets are trying to negotiate who's the boss," explains Buchheister. "If you keep pulling them apart, nothing is going to get resolved."

Take your pet for a checkup, however, if he's only recently started humping. And you should definitely take action if he's humping people's legs or arms. "He may be telling you that he's

NAME: Dakotah

OCCUPATION: Actor

The burly yellow Labrador retriever had a captivating screen presence and a great résumé. His appearances in movies such as *Far from Home* and *Independence Day* with head trainer Frank Disesso marked him as a serious actor, but it was his quirky role in the television sitcom *Third Rock from the Sun* that brought Dakotah's smiling face—and humping hips—into America's homes.

In the show, Dick Solomon (played by John Lithgow) gives a dog to his girlfriend, Dr. Mary Albright (played by Jane Curtin), as a token of his romantic feelings. The script called for Dakotah to display some romantic feelings of his own, which he did by greeting Mary with a humping frenzy.

"Training him to hump was easy," says Sue Disesso, assistant animal trainer at Moe Disesso Trained Animals in Newhall, California. "We started by rubbing good smells of hot dogs all over the body of an actress. The sniffing naturally led to rudeness. Once Dakotah believed we were giving him permission to do it, he loved humping roles."

Acting and humping on demand require teamwork. Dakotah and Curtin spent a lot of time together off-camera learning each other's language. On the set, Dakotah would look for a slight change in Curtin's posture. A dip of her shoulders was his cue to start humping.

Canine humping is never dignified, but for Dakotah, it reaped more than a few Milk-Bones. His wages, food, housing, and trainer's fees came to about $1,000 a day.

in control and has no respect for you," says Dr. Cox. Humping often progresses to other, more serious forms of bad behavior, such as growling or snapping.

Check the hormones at the door. When hormones run high, some pets become nearly mindless humping machines and will latch on to anything they can reach. "It's almost cruel to make a nonbreeding animal go through this," says Dr. Cox. A trip to the vet for spaying or neutering will often put an end to sex-driven humping, and it only takes a few hours for the gonadal hormones to drop to less troublesome levels, although it may take weeks or months for the behavior to change.

Stop the preliminaries. Dogs rarely just leap on people's legs. They usually work up to it by getting increasingly physical—by persistently licking your hands or neck, for example. Once they get enough body contact, they think they can get away with anything, and that's when their hips start moving. "It should never go this far," says Steve Feldman, D.V.M., a veterinarian and behavior consultant in Clinton, Maryland. "When a dog starts getting pushy, tell him, 'No,' 'Off,' or 'Down,' and make him take a time-out until he's calm again."

Bump him away. "It may sound harsh, but when he comes up on you, push him away with your knee and give him a very firm 'Off,'" advises David McMillan, a trainer and owner of Worldwide Movie Animals in Canyon Country, California. The idea isn't to give him a painful slam but to let him know that your leg isn't available for this type of behavior. "With two or three firm corrections, it may be all over with," he says.

Learn the language of leadership. Dogs usually mount people's legs for the same reason they mount other dogs—to show how tough and dominant they are. You can turn this around by showing them that you, not they, are in charge. "Dogs need rules," says Dr. Feldman. "We're not helping our pets at all if we don't take the lead and give them the rules they need to live by."

He recommends playing the "nothing is free" game. In other words, make your dog work for everything. Make him sit before you put food in his bowl. Don't give him a snack unless he lies down first. Don't let him out the door unless he sits and waits for your command. Consistently doing this teaches dogs that their owners set the rules, and once they understand that, they're less likely to take liberties with their owners' legs.

Deal with the personal issues. Dogs and cats sometimes hump pillows because they're handy and can't resist a rude advance. But some pets are merely responding to the scent of certain people. "If your dog is after a particular pillow, you need to figure out who's been sitting there and deal with issues between him and that person," explains Dr. Cox.

Learn their limits. Many dogs, and even the occasional cat, are sensitive to stimulation, and a lot of grooming, petting, or playing may get their hips moving. Pets are pretty consistent in their responses, so it won't take long to figure out how much play or physical contact they can stand before they start getting physical, says Dr. Cox.

CHAPTER 58

Jealousy

There's a fundamental difference in what dogs and people expect from each other. People first. We're busy with friends, spouses, and children. We read magazines and browse the Internet. We go to work in the morning and out to dinner at night. Our dogs are important parts of our lives, but they're not the only parts.

Now, dogs. Apart from food and going for walks, there's only one thing they really care about: us. No matter how friendly they are with strangers or other pets in the family, we're the ones they look to for attention, affection, and love.

It sounds like a relationship that's destined to fail. But dogs are resilient. They come to understand that they'll never get all the attention that they'd like, and, generally, they adjust well enough. But sometimes they don't, and that's when jealousy becomes an issue.

Some dogs show their displeasure by pushing between their people and whoever happens to be sitting too closely. Or they'll get between you and your newspaper. Or, less often, they'll get snappy toward people or pets whom they see as rivals.

It's almost impossible to overestimate the intensity with which dogs view their owners, says Benjamin Hart, D.V.M., Ph.D., professor of physiology and behavior at the University of California, Davis, School of Veterinary Medicine and author of *The Perfect Puppy: How to Choose Your Dog by Its Behavior*. Your companionship is probably the most valuable resource you can offer your dog. When that resource is threatened because you're busy with something or someone else, nearly every dog will feel pangs of anxiety, and some will act out their emotions in the worst possible ways.

A Lifetime of Friendships

Dogs have always lived in families. Long before people started pouring their food in bowls, they lived with close-knit families of dogs. Some of these families were as small as three or four dogs. Some were much larger, with a dozen or more dogs hunting, playing, and sleeping together. Because of this social heritage, dogs crave companionship every bit as much as people do.

Jealousy may arise when dogs feel that they're at risk of losing some of their special status within the family. Suppose you have a new boyfriend. No matter how friendly he is, your dog is going to view him as competition. A similar thing happens in families who get a new pet. A puppy or kitten may look harmless, but to the dog who's lived there all along, this interloper will be getting attention that he feels is his—and he's not going to like that.

Cats are much less likely than dogs to act possessively toward people. This is probably because they didn't evolve within close-knit families the way dogs did. Even today, they don't require very much human attention—certainly not as much as dogs, says Susan Ackermann, D.V.M., a veterinarian in Hellertown, Pennsylvania, who specializes in cat care.

This doesn't mean that cats are always happy when new people or pets come into their lives, she adds. In some cases, in fact, they can get downright disagreeable. This has less to do with jealousy than with their need to occupy their own space. Cats are very protective of their yards, their homes, and their litter boxes. "The dominant cat needs only to look at another cat to let him know where he stands," says Dr. Ackermann.

MAKING PEACE

Dogs who get jealous in one situation invariably get jealous in others, and the behavior tends to escalate. A little cute nose-nudging can easily become not-so-cute destructiveness or aggression. So you'll want to help your dog understand that there's nothing to be jealous about and that you aren't going to put up with it.

Love him at 6:15. Actually, the time doesn't matter, but dogs need regularity in their lives, and this is true of loving no less than of walking or eating. Having specific times when you give your dog all the attention he wants gives him something to look forward to. More important, it helps him get the message that he can't have it all the time. When the appointed time (or times) comes around, play with your dog. Feed him. Tell him how smart he is. Then ignore him. This way, he'll get two messages: that he's still tops in your eyes and that there are limits to what you're willing to do.

Ignore the pleas. Dogs who are looking for attention can be incredibly persistent. The nudging, barking, or whining can go on for hours—or days. When your dog is acting up this way, it's usually best to ignore him, says Dr. Hart. He has to learn that attention comes when you want to give it, not when he demands it. Give in even once, and you'll set the training back weeks, he adds. So wear some earplugs. Give the neighbors earplugs. Do whatever it takes to be firm and hold your ground. Sooner or later your dog is going to relent—unless you give in first.

Turn rivals into friends. A good way to help dogs accept newcomers in their lives is to load them with attention *only* when their rival is around, suggests Trish King, an animal-behavior consultant in Novato, California. It's hard for dogs to stay resentful when the presence of this person or pet brings such promising rewards.

Let dogs be dogs. It's extremely common for dogs to be jealous of other dogs who join the family. And when dogs get jealous, fights may break out. Unless they're actually drawing blood, stay out of it, says Joan Guertin, a dog trainer in Branson, Missouri. Dogs have to work out their respective roles in the family, and that includes their status. Any interference from you is going to be interpreted by one of them as favoring the other, and that will make the competition more intense.

Respect the outcome. Once the dust has settled and dogs have taken on their respective roles, humans have to respect those roles, says Robin Kovary, director of the American Dog Trainers Network in New York City. Don't feel sorry for the "loser." Rather, support the winner. Feed him first. Give him attention first. Let him go outside before the other dog does. The dogs are perfectly happy in their respective roles, and there won't be resentment—unless you start interfering by pampering the subordinate dog, in which case they'll have to settle everything all over again.

Occasionally, two dogs will be relentless in their attempts to outrank each other, Kovary adds. Most dogfights aren't serious, but some are. If the problems continue, you'll probably need to see a trainer or a behaviorist to get some help.

Bring dogs together away from home. Since jealousy is often inevitable when a new dog comes into the family, you might as well do what you can to reduce the intensity. One of the best ways to help prevent a serious confrontation is to introduce the dogs for the first time away from home. After they've spent some time together, bring them home at the same time. That way, the resident dog won't feel as though he has to defend his territory against the newcomer. Once they've spent time together, even if they didn't get to be friends, they're less likely to be enemies when the new dog takes up residence, Kovary says.

CHAPTER 59

Jumping On Counters

Every high surface in your home has probably been occupied by a cat from time to time. Kitchen tables, bedroom dressers, and windowsills are just a few of the favorite hangouts for cats who can't keep their feet on the ground.

Cats have muscle and bone structures that are designed for jumping. This means that they can reach counters and other high places about as easily as people can step over a curb. They explore high, out-of-the way places partly to satisfy their curiosity and to get a clearer view of what's happening at ground level, says John C. Wright, Ph.D., a certified applied animal behaviorist; professor of psychology at Mercer University in Macon, Georgia; and author of *The Dog Who Would Be King* and *Is Your Cat Crazy?* Plus, jumping up on tables and counters allows them to say hello to people at face level.

"They feel safer when they're high off the ground and away from potential harm from dogs and other animals," adds Dr. Wright. "High places give them great vantage points to scope out the ground below for mice and other prey. And when cats live in close proximity with other cats, they often seek higher places than the others to establish themselves as 'top cat.'"

Protecting Your Space

No one would complain if cats limited their vertical excursions to bookshelves or windowsills. But they're just as likely to land in the middle of the supper table during meals or on the counter near the defrosting fish. And despite their reputation for grace and balance, more than a few cats have miscalculated their jumps and sent expensive crystal goblets crashing to the floor.

Yelling at cats doesn't teach them much of anything—at least, nothing you want them to learn, says Dr. Wright. Although a high-volume "No!" will send them flying off a counter, they don't associate the message with the behavior that caused it. "What you'll end up with is a cat who learns to be afraid of the person who is yelling," he explains. "Not only will he start to avoid you—behavior you obviously don't want from your pet—but also he'll just start waiting until you're out of sight to jump on the counters."

This doesn't mean that you have to tolerate paw prints on your favorite china. It does mean giving up scolding in favor of more persuasive—if somewhat sneaky—techniques. You can often persuade cats to think that they don't *want* to get up on tables or counters, without making yourself look like the bad guy.

Give them a ledge of their own. You can't train cats not to jump, because their urge to go high is so deeply ingrained. But you can give them socially acceptable alternatives to the kitchen table. Dr. Wright recommends putting up a comfortable window seat where they can perch. Or you can buy a cat tree and put it in front of a window. "That way, they'll have a high place that's not off-limits," he says.

Set a trap. Cats rarely act in predictable ways, and it's discouraging to go to the trouble of putting up a cat tree or window ledge only to discover that your cat still prefers the dining room table. "You can help cats learn about forbidden zones by setting harmless booby traps that are designed to startle them, but not hurt them," says Katherine Houpt, V.M.D., Ph.D., a board-certi-

Cats don't like noise or sudden movements, and Snappy Trainers provide both. Used as training aids to keep cats off counters and tables, Snappy Trainers make a loud noise and fly up in the air when they're triggered by inquisitive feline feet.

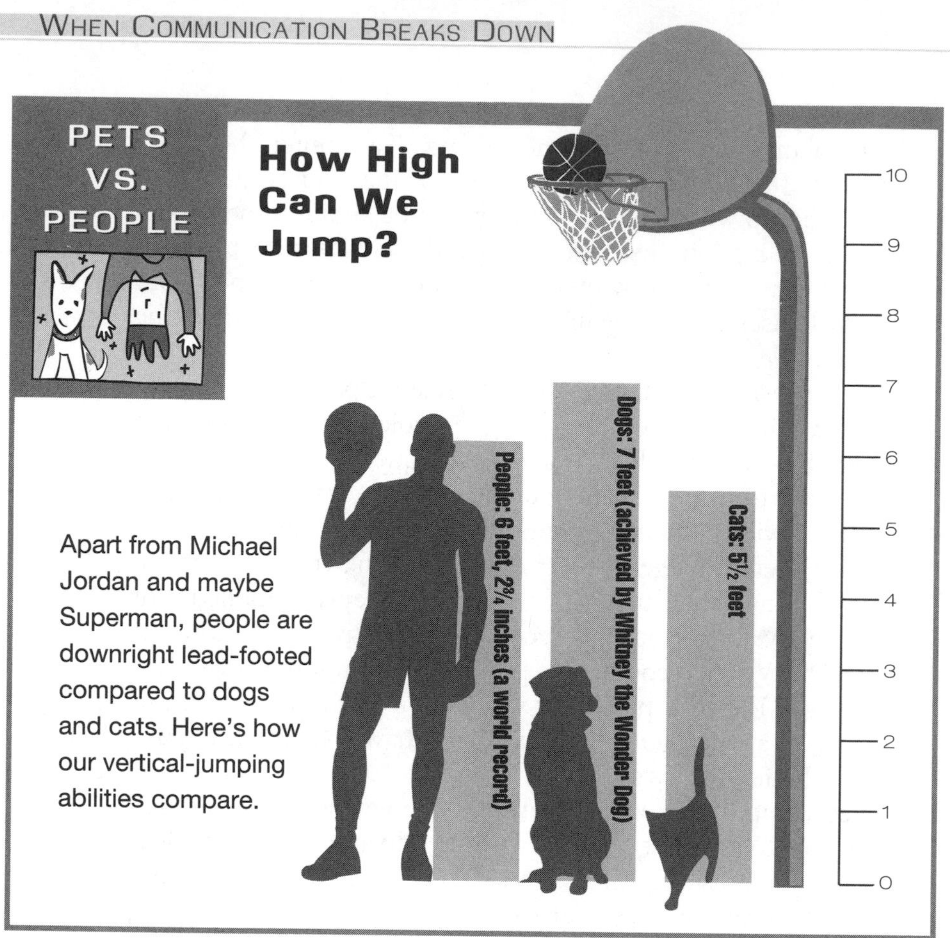

fied veterinary behaviorist, professor of physiology, and director of the behavior clinic at Cornell University College of Veterinary Medicine in Ithaca, New York.

She recommends using "mousetrap" trainers, available in pet supply stores and catalogs. Called Snappy Trainers, they have large plastic paddles attached to springs. "When the cat jumps up, he triggers the trap, which flies up and makes a loud sound and a lot of commotion," Dr. Houpt says. "It doesn't slap him, but it does scare him." Cats learn quickly, and after a few scares, they'll usually decide to limit their explorations to other, less tumultuous places.

Water down their enthusiasm. A quick way to discourage jumping is to give cats a quick spritz of water, preferably from behind when they don't know you're there. A spray of water that appears to come from nowhere will startle the heck out of them, and they won't blame you for the sudden fright. "If you don't want to worry about wiping up the water, you can use a can of compressed air, like the kind used to clean computer keyboards," says Dr. Houpt. "Cats dislike blown air as much as they do water."

Make their feet uncomfortable. If there's one thing cats hate almost as much as getting wet, it's getting their paws all sticky, says Steve Aiken, an animal-behavior consultant in Wichita, Kansas. "Cats meticulously groom their paws because back in the days when they were hunting for their next meal, they couldn't afford to have their claws and paws in less than prime hunting condition," he explains. That's why double-sided tape is a superb deterrent for keeping them off counters and other surfaces.

"In places where you don't want your cat to jump, lay down some strips of cardboard covered with double-sided tape," says Aiken. "Your cat will dislike the feeling of the tape residue on his paws and will decide on his own to stay away from those areas. It usually takes only once or twice to change even a well-established jumping behavior." Another trick is to cover surfaces with plastic carpet runners, turned upside down. The bottom sides have pointy plastic nubs that are very uncomfortable for little cat feet. You don't have to leave the runners out indefinitely—just until your cat begins to think that all of his favorite places have those horrible surfaces.

Give a double message. Traps by themselves are effective training tools, but experts in animal behavior usually recommend combining them with a visual cue of some kind—sort of the feline equivalent of a warning sign. "Drape the counters with pieces of waxed paper that hang slightly over the edge," says Dr. Wright. Cats who have been scared by the traps will quickly make an association between the paper and the commotion. At that point, you can get rid of the traps, but leave the paper in place for a week or two as a visual reminder. Most cats will continue to be distrustful of the general area.

You don't have to leave the paper up forever, he adds. After it's been on the counter for a week or two, take it away for a day, then put it back the next. Then take it away for 2 days and replace it again. Keep doing this for a few weeks. Your cat will never be sure when that awful paper is coming back, and he'll probably decide to stay away for good, says Dr. Wright.

CHAPTER 60

Jumping Up

The average Rottweiler weighs about 100 pounds, while the average American woman weighs about 135. Those 35 extra pounds don't help much when all 100 pounds of dog take a flying leap to welcome you home.

One of the most common complaints among owners is that their dogs leap up whenever they or other people walk in the door, leaving paw prints on jackets and skirts or even knocking people over. It was once thought that dogs jumped up as a way of asserting dominance, much as dominant dogs in packs put their paws on the shoulders of more submissive pack members. Most animal behaviorists now believe that dogs jump up simply because they're excited to have company. It's their exuberant way of saying, "Hi! Hi! I'm so happy to see you!" Cats do their share of jumping, too—onto bookshelves, kitchen tables, and windowsills—but they rarely jump up on people.

"Dogs have learned to be very face-oriented," explains Benjamin Hart, D.V.M., Ph.D., professor of physiology and behavior at the University of California, Davis, School of Veterinary Medicine and author of *The Perfect Puppy: How to Choose Your Dog by Its Behavior*. "They know that if they want to be noticed, get petted, or find out information that affects them—like when they'll get their next meal—they need to have us look at them. They jump up to get our attention."

This doesn't mean that you have to put up with dogs in your lap or paw prints on your pants. It just means that you have to teach them better ways to get noticed.

What Goes Up Must Come Down

Since dogs have a natural tendency to go airborne, it's not always easy to teach them that jumping isn't the best way to get your attention. What you can do is to show them appropriate alternatives, praise them when they get it right, and consistently follow up bad behavior with consequences. "Our pets genuinely want to have a good relationship with us," says John C. Wright, Ph.D., a certified applied animal behaviorist; professor of psychology at Mercer University in Macon, Georgia; and author of *The Dog Who Would Be King* and *Is Your Cat Crazy?* "It's up to us to communicate in such a way that they understand what we want them to do or not to do." Here are a few tips you may want to try.

Turn a cold shoulder. Since dogs jump up because they want to be noticed, the best thing that you can do is to ignore them when their paws leave the ground, says Katherine Houpt, V.M.D., Ph.D., a board-certified veterinary behaviorist, professor of physiology, and director of the behavior clinic at Cornell University College of Veterinary Medicine in Ithaca, New York. "Your dog wants attention. If you start pushing him down or waving your hands around, that's exactly what he's getting," she explains.

Rather than pushing him away, turn away from him and fold your arms across your chest, she advises. "At first he may keep trying to jump up on you. But if you keep ignoring him, eventually he will learn that his jumping up isn't working, and he'll sit down. When he does, you can say hello and pet and praise him."

Tell them straight. Dogs look to us to tell them what is and isn't appropriate, and giving clear commands will help them understand what's expected, says canine researcher Marc Bekoff, Ph.D., professor of environmental, population, and organismic biology at the University of Colorado in Boulder. When your dog jumps up, hold out your hand in a "stop" gesture and forcefully tell him "Off," he suggests. Good behavior only comes from clear communication, he explains. When your dog knows that you're displeased with one type of behavior, he'll naturally try other things that please you more.

Trainers used to recommend raising a knee to discourage persistent jumpers. The idea was to bump their chests, reducing the momentum and giving them an uncomfortable jolt. The problem with this technique is that a knee raised too forcefully can hurt a dog. Most experts now believe that it's better to use the force of your authority—and your voice—than to get physical.

Give praise and more praise. "People sometimes make the mistake of always punishing, punishing, punishing. But dogs don't really know what to do until you show them by praising them when they behave in a way that you like," says Cathy Jobe,

Obedient Jumping

Dogs who jump on people usually need refresher courses in good manners. But some go airborne because they're very well trained. It's their way of communicating with people who can't "hear" them any other way.

Just as Seeing Eye dogs provide guidance to the blind, hearing dogs are invaluable to those who have lost some or all of their hearing. These specially trained dogs are taught to make physical contact with their owners in response to a variety of daily sounds. "When the phone rings, someone knocks on the door, or an alarm sounds, the dog finds the owner, jumps up, and starts pawing her legs to get her attention," says Michael Sapp, chief operating officer of PAWS with a Cause in Wayland, Michigan. "Then the dog either takes the owner to the source of the sound or, in the case of a fire alarm, leads her out of the house."

Most service dogs are large breeds such as shepherds or retrievers, but hearing dogs tend to be small breeds, Sapp says. "If you're standing at the sink washing dishes and the phone rings, you don't want a 90-pound Rottweiler jumping up on you to let you know."

founder of Waterloo Farms, a dog-training facility in Celina, Texas. You don't want to give your dog attention or affection while he's jumping up. You do want to shower him with praise when he greets you calmly or sits when you tell him to. "Dogs want to be good," she explains. "But the only way they know when they are being good is when you praise them."

Come down to his level. Your dog craves face-to-face interaction, which is pretty tough when your face is 5 to 6 feet off the ground, and his is 2 to 3 feet lower. Dogs try to close the gap in the only way they can—by jumping up. "Dogs also can find our height a bit intimidating, especially if we're towering over them," says Ira B. Perelle, Ph.D., a certified applied animal behaviorist and chairperson of the development committee for the Animal Behavior Society in Bloomington, Indiana. "It's a real pleasure for our pets when we sit down and interact closely with them," he says. "I try to crouch or sit as much as possible when I'm among four-legged animals."

Show by example. It's annoying when dogs jump up, but it's not entirely their fault. We practically invite them to do it when we make a huge production about coming home. "Dogs pick up on the excitement levels of those around them," says Stephen Zawistowski, Ph.D., a certified applied animal behaviorist and a senior vice president of animal services and science advisor for the American Society for the Prevention of Cruelty to Animals in New York City. "If you come in the door making a commotion, waving your arms, and being very loud, it's understandable that your dog will respond by jumping up."

You can help your dog stay calm by being calm yourself. When you come home, give your dog a warm but sedate hello. Then go about your business for a while. Only when you've settled in and the usual homecoming energy is lower should you give your dog your full attention.

CHAPTER 61

Killing Mice

Cats have reputations for being great hunters, but any Las Vegas bookie would put his money on the mouse. Despite their great reflexes and predatory instincts, cats only succeed, on average, about once in every three attempts.

This is good news for the mice. It's not so good for the people who live with the cats and have to deal with the carnage when their pets do hit the jackpot. It wouldn't be so bad if cats actually ate the mice—but often they don't. Like big-game hunters who mount trophies in the study, cats apparently like to display their successes, usually in the form of mousy bits on the carpet or on the front steps.

Dogs certainly aren't averse to hunting—in the wild, they do it all the time—but they generally don't bother with mice. Mice are quick, and dogs are relative slowpokes. While cats succeed a third of the time, dogs wouldn't even come close to that. In addition, dogs traditionally lived with other dogs and ate communally. A dog who proudly brought home a mouse to share with six to eight hungry companions wouldn't get much of a welcome.

Natural-Born Killers

Cats are true carnivores, meaning that they depend on meat to survive. Today, they get most of their meat protein in commercial cat food, so there's no reason for them to hunt mice. They do it anyway, though, probably as a sort of predatory hand-me-down, says Myrna Milani, D.V.M., a veterinarian in Charlestown, New Hampshire, and author of *DogSmart* and *CatSmart*.

The instinct to hunt runs deep, Dr. Milani adds, and it's triggered by several things, hunger least of all. Mice move quickly, and cats are attracted to movement, she explains. Mice make high-pitched squeaky sounds that cats, with their remarkable sensitivity to high frequencies, hear as clearly as we hear a taxi horn. The squeaks get their attention and appear to stimulate

WHAT'S MY PET SAYING?

Behavior
Lining Up Mice

What It Means
"I'm Keeping Things Neat"

Cats are known for their finicky natures, so perhaps it's not surprising that after they've killed a few mice, they'll sometimes line up the bodies next to each other in perfect alignment, right down to the curls in their tails.

"I once talked to someone who said that she found 20 mice lined up that way," says Annie Bruce, a cat-owner consultant in Boulder, Colorado, and author of *Cat Be Good*. "Their heads all faced the same way in perfect rows."

No one's sure what cats are thinking when they neatly display their kills. It may be nothing more complicated than a way of getting people's attention. Then again, it may be one more manifestation of their desires to keep everything neat and orderly. "Some cats may just be neatniks," says Tim Howell, D.V.M., a veterinarian in Indianapolis.

their appetites. Finally, cats learn how to behave by watching other cats. A cat who has rarely encountered mice and doesn't show much interest when she does would suddenly get excited if she saw another cat making a play for it.

Instinct goes only so far, however. Domestic cats have been living with humans for thousands of years, and ever since they began finding food in their bowls, hunting mice has become more of a hobby than an occupation. Some cats hunt all the time, but quite a few never get into the habit, presumably because they have lost some of their instinctive behaviors in the years they've spent with us.

BAD FOR A MOUSE, GOOD FOR MOUSEKIND

There's a tendency for humans to view the relationship between cat and mouse as one between villain and victim. This is certainly true when you're talking about one cat and one mouse. But from nature's point of view, both cats and mice, as species, benefit from their cat-and-mouse games, says Dr. Milani.

When spring rolls around, for example, mice are a little sluggish. There are plenty of inexperienced youngsters and older, less agile adults. Thanks to cats, only the hardiest mice survive to see the winter. This helps ensure that future generations of mice will be fit and healthy. And cats, through no intention of their own, have guaranteed themselves a food supply for the coming years.

The cats, for their parts, aren't born expert hunters. They have to learn speed and technique before they can reliably eighty-six a mouse. So they fail a few times, learn from their mistakes, and refine their hunting techniques. A fast, agile mouse who gets away teaches the cat to be smarter next time. And the mouse, of course, is grateful to get another chance.

A Little Bit for Me, a Little Bit for You

It's not so bad that cats hunt mice—after all, it's what they've always done—but they seem to do it more for thrill than for food. They aren't satisfied until they've proven their prowess to their people—which is why you may wake up in the morning and find mouse innards on the kitchen floor.

"I've had cats who brought their mice to the outside door, then sat down and ate them, but not until I noticed them," says Ellen Perry Berkeley of Shaftsbury, Vermont, author of *Maverick Cats: Encounters with Feral Cats*.

It's not that they're showing off, says Dr. Milani. They are probably acting as though we're their family members. Mother cats usually teach their kittens in two stages, she explains. First, they bring home dead mice. This gives the kittens a chance to smell mice and start thinking of them as food.

As the kittens get older, Mom starts bringing home live prey so they can practice. "A cat who does this is not bringing home a gift," says Annie Bruce, a cat-owner consultant in Boulder, Colorado, and author of *Cat Be Good*. "She's trying to show humans how to hunt and eat, and it may be a chance for her to show us that she's the one in charge as well."

Things get a little complicated because cats don't bring home only whole mice, dead or alive. They often select a body part or two, like a liver or tail. It's possible that cats don't like these parts and so are willing to give them up. More likely, they do it because organ meats are very high in nutrients, and if they think of us as their kittens, it's the proper thing to do, says Dr. Milani.

NO CRIME, NO PUNISHMENT

Since hunting comes naturally to cats, you can't expect them to give it up just because you dislike finding the remains. And eating mice is perfectly healthy, as long as the mouse hasn't eaten some type of poison first, says Tim Howell, D.V.M., a veterinarian in Indianapolis.

Still, accepting cats' instincts doesn't mean that you have to indulge them. Here are a few ways to keep the mousy madness at manageable levels.

Stay very still. Should you come across your cat in the act of stalking, ignore your natural instinct to interfere, says Dr. Milani. The odds are on the mouse's side in any event. If you do try to drive your cat away, your movement may have the opposite effect and stimulate her "kill phase." If you stay still and don't provide the movements that stimulate cats' hunting instincts, she may lose interest and walk away.

Bring your cat in at twilight. Mice and cats are most active between dusk and dawn. That's when outdoor cats do most of their hunting. Cats who come inside when the sun goes down won't get a lot of opportunities to hunt, Bruce says.

Give your cat a surrogate. Since cats' cravings for mice are driven more by instinct than by actual desire, you can often satisfy them with fake mice. This doesn't mean tossing a stuffed mouse on the carpet and leaving it there. Cats hunt moving prey, and things that just lie there are about as exciting as a beanbag chair. Dr. Milani recommends hanging a mobile from the ceiling and attaching a catnip mouse. It should be low enough so that your cat can bat it, but not so low that she can capture it easily. "As soon as she jumps up and hits it, the whole thing moves, so your cat can get quite a workout," she adds.

Don't bother with bells. Kind-hearted people often fit their cats' collars with little bells in order to warn potential prey—songbirds as well as mice—that they're approaching. This probably doesn't work very well for preventing mouse kills, says Dr. Milani, because most cats will simply develop new hunting strategies to compensate for their "disability." Feeding cats won't keep them away from mice either, she adds. You can prove this for yourself by giving your cat a big meal, then showing her a mouse, a butterfly, or a bug. She's still going to go after it.

CHAPTER 62

Kneading and Nursing

You can tell a cat is truly ecstatic when her eyes turn dreamy, her sides vibrate with rumbling purrs, and her paws stretch and relax as though she were kneading dough. It sounds idyllic—unless she happens to be lying on your lap, and those kneading claws are going through denim and into skin.

It's flattering that cats love us so much that they'll knead and nurse as though we're mom cats giving them a meal. And in a way, that's exactly what they're doing. Within minutes of birth, kittens climb onto Mom's belly, latch onto a breast, and begin kneading her tummy. The combined action of pumping paws and sucking lips stimulates the flow of milk, ensuring that the hungry kitten gets a bellyful of the ultimate comfort food.

As cats get older, they retain the memory of these intimate and comforting moments. Most adults lose the urge to nurse, but the kneading impulse hangs on. "It's how they express a sense of safety and satisfaction," says Joanne Hibbs, D.V.M., a veterinarian in Knoxville, Tennessee.

Alone Too Soon

Cats view their owners as the source of all good things: food, petting, protection, and love. That's how they viewed their mothers, too. Most cats don't have any trouble distinguishing people from parents. But some cats, especially those who were weaned before they were 8 weeks old, may harbor a feline fantasy that people really are their moms. These are the cats who tend to nurse as well as knead, says Dr. Hibbs.

Most kittens outgrow the nursing stage by the time they are 6 months old. Of the small group that keeps doing it, it's usually saved for special occasions—a little nibble at night, for example,

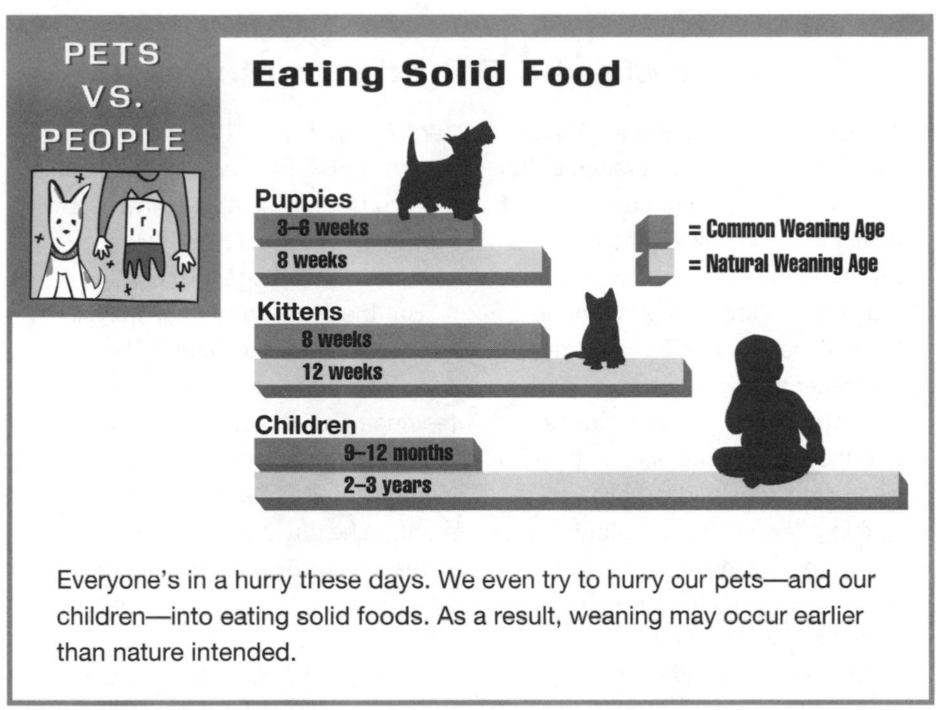

Everyone's in a hurry these days. We even try to hurry our pets—and our children—into eating solid foods. As a result, weaning may occur earlier than nature intended.

or a kiss hello when you come home from work. "It's not that it's necessarily bad for a grown cat to suck on her owner, but it is juvenile behavior," says Dr. Hibbs. Like Peter Pan, your cat may be telling you that she doesn't want to grow up. She'd rather be your little kitten forever.

LOVING BUT PAINFUL

No one complains about a little kneading and the occasional kitty kiss. But some cats knead and nurse so aggressively that it gets uncomfortable to have them around. In rare cases, this may be caused by an imbalance of chemicals in the brain—a condition that often can be corrected with fluoxetine (Prozac) or other medications, says Dr. Hibbs. More often, cats are simply reliving comforting moments from their kittenhoods. They aren't thinking about what they're doing. It's all unconscious—and difficult to stop.

Keep the claws short. Kneading is an instinctive behavior, just as lapping up milk or purring is instinctive, says Dr. Hibbs. Cats who have tendencies to nurse and knead won't give up these behaviors easily. "I tell people to clip their cats' claws once every 3

How Mishka Found Her Mom

It was a cool fall day when Pamela M. Rose, a medical librarian in Buffalo, New York, caught a glimpse of a wild kitten in a field. The tiny brown tabby was scrawny and matted, and too young to fend for herself. Her mother, Pamela knew, had recently been killed by a car.

Watching the kitten disappear into the weeds, Pamela and her husband, Joel, decided to save her. Within a few weeks, the kitten, whom they named Mishka, had been caught in a humane trap, lured by the smell of sardines.

Mishka was terrified at first. Pamela grabbed her firmly by the scruff of the neck, much like a mother cat would hold a kitten. "I started brushing her, and I sang to her," Pamela says. The brush strokes imitated a cat's tongue, and singing is as close as a human can come to purring. Within a few minutes, the kitten began to relax.

But the struggle to tame Mishka had just begun. For weeks, Pamela sat in Mishka's room, singing and feeding her. Slowly, the kitten crept closer. Within a few weeks, she allowed herself to be touched. In a month, she shyly crawled into Pamela's lap. Then one day, she timidly began to knead Pamela's belly. A purr, deep and throaty, came rumbling out of the tiny cat. "When she started kneading me, I almost cried," Pamela remembers. "It was like this poor orphan had adopted me as her mother."

weeks, more often if the claws get sharp sooner," she says. This won't stop your cat from kneading, of course, but it will be a lot less uncomfortable for you.

Pad the paws. Trimming a cat's claws is about as easy as giving them pills. An easier way to reduce the discomfort of kneading is to apply a product called Soft Paws—little caps that fit over the toenails and cover the sharp points with smooth latex. You'll still have to trim the nails periodically and reapply the caps, but you'll be a lot more comfortable in the meantime, says Lisa Smith, a pet-behavior consultant and veterinary hospital manager in Severn, Maryland. The caps aren't available in pet stores, but you can find them on the Internet.

Give them a mother substitute. Cats don't necessarily need live skin in order for nursing and kneading to feel good. Smith recommends putting a pillow between you and your cat. There's a good chance that she'll accept the swap and will happily knead away.

Take a lesson from Mom. "If Momma can say no to nursing simply by standing up and walking away, why can't people?" says Leslie Larson Cooper, D.V.M., a board-certified veterinary behaviorist in Davis, California. "Don't bother yelling," she adds. "Just put her on the floor and go away." If you do this every time your cat begins to suck, she'll probably give it up within a few weeks.

Give her something better. Cats who nurse people do it as a show of love. Rather than putting up with it, Dr. Cooper recommends showing love in another, more comfortable way by tossing a ball, pulling a string, or otherwise diverting your cat's attention. As long as she's getting the attention she's after, she'll be less likely to put on the kitten act, she says.

Plan ahead. Since it's so difficult to stop cats from nursing once they have the habit, you may want to consider getting an older cat the next time. Dr. Hibbs recommends adopting only cats who were weaned after they were 8 weeks old. This is especially important if you're getting a Siamese, who are more likely to nurse than other breeds. Siamese should stay with their mothers until they're 10 to 14 weeks old, she says.

CHAPTER 63

Leash Pulling

Dogs have very strong independent streaks. As much as they enjoy getting close to people, they want to do it on their terms. They certainly have no natural interest in being bound to your side by a strip of leather. This is why a puppy's first reaction is to pull away when a leash is clipped on his collar.

"If you haven't taken the time to train your dog not to pull on a leash, you can't blame him for jerking you around," says John Fioramonti, D.V.M., a veterinarian in Towson, Maryland.

Training isn't the whole story, however. Even dogs who are accustomed to leashes and who more or less heel most of the time will sometimes start pulling. Partly this is because their desire to sniff and explore is stronger than their desire to walk by your side. And sometimes it's because they think that pulling is what *you* want them to do, even if you haven't said it in so many words.

Serve and Protect

You would think that dogs would view each other in the kind light of kinship, just as an American expatriate living in France enjoys seeing someone from home. Over the millennia, however, dogs have come to feel much closer to people than to other dogs. In fact, unless your dog spent a long, leisurely puppyhood in close companionship with his littermates, he may not even recognize other dogs as kin.

This confusion about the family tree is most apparent when dogs, out in public and on their leashes, start straining or growling when they see other dogs. They're not sure who these strangers are and whether or not they're friendly. So they put on quite a display—not because they're scared, but because they want to make sure that the dogs know that you're being pro-

MESSAGES AND MEANINGS

Born to Pull

Macko had a serious attitude problem, which meant that his owner, Diane Perks, also had a problem. Macko, a 77-pound pit bull terrier, had too much energy. He was aggressive and hard to control. Putting him on a leash only made him worse. He would lunge and snap at people, and more than once he yanked Diane, a personal trainer in Portland, Oregon, off her feet.

"This dog was your worst nightmare," Diane says.

In an effort to get Macko under control, she experimented with every type of collar and leash, with no real improvement. "Trying to walk him was like trying to hold on to a freight train. Just impossible," she says.

Diane was about ready to give up on Macko when she heard something interesting. Pit bulls, like most terriers, love the challenge of pulling heavy loads. Diane had an idea. She harnessed Macko to her bicycle and let him run.

It didn't work. "He loved it, but in the end, I was the only one worn out," she says. "I had to stay on the brakes the entire time."

Still, she felt she was onto something. A trainer she'd been talking to told her about a type of dog cart for sale in Alberta, Canada. The $1,200 price tag was daunting, but Diane was committed. She sold her hot tub, bought the cart, and hitched Macko up.

He took off like he was pulling a feather. It was obvious that he needed a bigger load, so Diane talked a friend into riding with her. The weight of two people plus the cart was just shy of 400 pounds.

Macko loved it. He pulled like crazy, hitting 17 miles an hour. Now, Diane takes him out all the time, and even after he's finished running 1½ miles, Macko's tail is wagging. And the long-term results were impressive.

He quit pulling on the leash. He quit snapping at strangers. He was better behaved at home. The problem, Diane realized, hadn't been a bad attitude at all. Macko just needed a challenge—and a chance to pull in the right direction.

tected, says Joanne Hibbs, D.V.M., a veterinarian in Knoxville, Tennessee.

Pulling on the leash in this situation isn't likely to calm them down, Dr. Hibbs adds. In fact, it can send the opposite message. Your dog may interpret tension on the leash as meaning "I'm scared." Being a good dog, he'll throw herself against the leash even harder in an attempt to confront the threat head-on.

Too Excited for Words

Unless you live in the country and your dog spends his days chasing sheep, he probably doesn't get anywhere near the mental and physical stimulation that he's designed for. Until dogs master the "doorknob principle," they depend on us to let them out. After a day indoors with nothing to do, they nearly boil over with excitement when the leash comes out—and then pull like crazy in order to see and sniff all the exciting stuff out there.

This happens even with well-behaved dogs, Dr. Fioramonti adds. They're not deliberately ignoring your tugs and commands. They're just so caught up in the moment that they've forgotten you're attached to the other end of the leash. "They're doing what comes naturally," he says. "They see something cool, so they go for it."

Dogs who only pull when they're over-the-top excited are pretty easy to rein in, says Ken Nagler, a trainer in Beltsville, Maryland. "If you can keep their attention focused on you, they'll have no time to notice all the stuff going on around them."

Just pulling on the leash won't help because dogs will pull back without even thinking about it, he adds. If, however, you vary your pace when you're out on walks by suddenly speeding up, slowing down, or making a tight turn, your dog will keep watching you just to see what's going to happen next.

Easy Walking

Think of the leash as being a telephone wire that carries messages back and forth. The smallest messages get through, even the ones you didn't know you were sending. Your dog may not notice another dog approaching, but the slight tension in the leash as you grip it more tightly comes through loud and clear. By paying attention to your own signals and also reading your

Different Dogs, Different Collars

Collars do more than hold a rabies tag and anchor a leash. They're designed to encourage dogs to wait for and respond to the slightest pressure from the leash. Dogs who heel perfectly all the time don't need anything more than flat leather or nylon buckle-up collars. Those who are persistent pullers, however, may need training collars. Here are the options.

Choke collars. These act like fast-release nooses. When you give a sharp tug, the collar quickly tightens and gets a dog's attention. The pressure instantly releases when you relax your hold on the leash. Choke collars tell dogs, "Pay attention *now*."

Pinch collars. These act in the same way as choke collars, with a difference: They're equipped with flat-tipped prongs that normally lie flat so dogs don't feel them. When you pull on the leash, however, the prongs come together and pinch and poke the skin around the neck. The pinch is hard to ignore, and even headstrong dogs will quit pulling in order to avoid it.

Head halters. There are several brands of head halters, such as the Gentle Leader. Unlike collars, which encircle the neck, head halters have straps that slip over the muzzle and across the back of the neck, then fasten with a ring under the chin. Since the pressure is distributed over the entire head, it's much easier to guide your dog than it would be with a regular collar. In addition, the halters put pressure on the back of the neck and on the muzzle—the same spots that mother dogs grab when their puppies misbehave. Pressure on the halter tells dogs, "Straighten up—Mom doesn't like what you're doing."

You can get these halters from veterinarians, trainers, and behaviorists. They need to be professionally fitted, and you'll get instructions on how to use them properly.

dog's, you can make the leash act more as a communications device than as a restraint.

Check the distance. Unless you're training your dog for the showring, it probably doesn't matter if he walks in perfect heeling position. Every dog, however, tends to walk a certain distance away from his owner. You can tell your dog's mind is wandering when he's walking farther ahead or farther behind than usual. This is the time to change direction, call his name, or pat your leg, says Nagler. As long as your dog is interacting with and focusing on you, he won't be looking for distractions.

Reward a loose leash. Dogs don't do anything for free. At the very least, they expect to be rewarded with approval; food is even better. So put a few biscuits in your pocket when you go for walks. As long as your dog is walking nicely and the leash is slack, stop now and then and give him something to eat, Nagler suggests. He won't think about it, but unconsciously, he'll start to associate his behavior and your respective body positions with nice treats. After a while, he'll automatically walk with less pulling.

Pull fast, not slow. The message you send while pulling on the leash depends on how you pull it. Consider standard-bred racehorses. The harder their riders pull, the faster they trot. Dogs think a lot like racehorses. They tend to interpret hard, steady pulls as meaning, "It's time for me to pull back as hard as I can."

To prevent a tug-of-war with the leash, it's better to give a sharp, fast pull, then immediately let the leash go slack. "Pulling slowly sometimes makes dogs gag, which sounds terrible, but they couldn't care less," Nagler says. "They just ignore it and pull harder." A sharp tug, by contrast, instantly gets their attention and lets them know there's something you want, he explains.

Consider the breed. Every dog can learn to walk without pulling, but some breeds have a bit more baggage to overcome. Samoyeds, huskies, and malamutes were bred to be sled dogs long before they landed in your living room. Rottweilers and giant schnauzers are the descendants of carting dogs. And terriers, well, they just enjoy challenges, and pulling things gives them a real kick. You can't change dogs' natures, but you can give them a chance to get the pulling urge out of their systems, Nagler says.

You can buy dog carts and harnesses from some specialty catalogs, such as Dog Works in Stewartstown, Pennsylvania. Some people even hook their canine Clydesdales to child-size push scooters and let them pull them up the sidewalk. Once they've burned off some of that energy and satisfied their instincts, they'll be much less likely to pull the leash, Nagler says.

Start early. "I like to clip a leash on a puppy almost as soon as I bring him home," says Nagler. You don't even have to hold the leash at first. Just let it drag as your puppy gets used to it.

Encourage him to come to you. Puppies don't always do what people want, and coming when they're called isn't necessarily as interesting as going the other way. When you're ready to start leash training your puppy, and he's dragging the leash behind him, crouch down low, then pick up the leash as you call his name. The tug will get his attention, and your low position and pleasant tone will invite him to play, says Dr. Hibbs.

Your pup should run toward you, tail wagging. If he balks, resist the urge to reel him in like a fish. That will just get him used to feeling a tight leash, Dr. Hibbs says.

People first. "If you always go through the door or into the car before your puppy, you'll set the stage for obedience on the leash," says Nagler. Puppies who run ahead of people when they're off-leash are going to do the same thing when they're on one, he explains.

CHAPTER 64

Licking

For pets, the tongue is more than an eating utensil. It's a handy tool for grooming, cleaning wounds, and expressing affection and social ties. They spend so much time licking, in fact, that any decrease in tongue action usually means that they're sick, says Benjamin Hart, D.V.M., Ph.D., professor of physiology and behavior at the University of California, Davis, School of Veterinary Medicine and author of *The Perfect Puppy: How to Choose Your Dog by Its Behavior*. Researchers believe that some of the same changes in the body that accompany a fever, for example, may temporarily reduce the licking instinct.

Just as it's possible to know something about people by watching how they use their hands, you can tell quite a bit about pets by noticing where, what, and how much they lick. Dogs and cats use their tongues in slightly different ways, however, and they lick to express different emotions.

Always Clean

Cats spend enormous amounts of time licking their fur. Thanks to the papillae—tiny hairlike spines on the surface of the tongue that give it its sandpaper feel—cats are never caught without a hairbrush. The papillae act as bristles, keeping the hair neat and removing dirt, bits of food, or parasites such as fleas. A few minutes of licking is their way of giving themselves a rinse and comb.

Cats periodically give their owners (or other cats) a few licks, too. They use the same long, dragging strokes they use on themselves, which suggests that they enjoy grooming others, says Kimberly Barry, Ph.D., a certified applied animal behaviorist in Austin, Texas. "Cats often groom each other when they have good relations," she says. Cats who groom people are simply treating them as members of the family.

Cats also groom themselves as a way of dispelling anxiety. People sometimes get annoyed when their cats respond to a

WHAT'S MY PET SAYING?

Behavior
Indifference to Hygiene

What It Means
"I'm a Dog—I Have Better Things to Do"

When it comes to grooming, dogs and cats couldn't be more different. Dogs will happily spend 10 minutes rolling in dirt—then jump in bed with you. Cats, on the other hand, will spend 10 minutes cleaning their fur at the mere thought of dirt. Why the difference in basic hygiene?

It's probably because of their respective sizes, says Benjamin Hart, D.V.M., Ph.D., professor of physiology and behavior at the University of California, Davis, School of Veterinary Medicine and author of *The Perfect Puppy: How to Choose Your Dog by Its Behavior*. In eons past, your dog's ancestors were quite large. This means that their skin had a fairly small surface area compared to the total size of their bodies. "Their fur wasn't as important for insulation as it was for cats," he says. Cats needed to keep their fur lofty and well-groomed to stay warm and to keep their parasite population down, while for dogs, it was less of an issue.

It's not that dogs don't groom themselves, adds Myrna Milani, D.V.M., a veterinarian in Charlestown, New Hampshire, and author of *DogSmart* and *CatSmart*. But unlike cats, who spend a lot of time grooming their coats, dogs tend to limit their attention to the anal or vaginal areas. "Both areas have mucous membranes, and anywhere there's a mucous membrane, there's a potential for infection," she explains. "It's to the animal's advantage to keep them scrupulously clean."

scolding—for pilfering a chicken thigh, for example—by just licking their paws. They may look nonchalant, but the cats are probably just trying to deal with the stress, says Dr. Hart.

LOVE AND DEVOTION

While cats tend to use their tongues for grooming, dogs are renowned for how much they lick others. People often suspect that salty skin is what draws their dogs closer, but licking isn't about taste, says Dr. Hart. They do it because they like us. "When we want to show dogs that we're attached to them, we use our hands to pet them," he says. "The only part of their bodies that dogs can move that much is their tongues, so they lick us."

Licking is more than just a sign of affection, he adds. Dogs use their tongues to communicate a variety of messages, both to other dogs and to the humans in their lives.

"Give me something to eat." Puppies who lick their mothers' muzzles are politely asking Mom if she'd be kind enough to regurgitate a little food. Some experts believe this is why dogs seem almost compelled to lick people's faces. It's not that they expect you to deliver a meal on demand. They just associate this behavior with feelings of warmth and security.

"I'm friendly and submissive." Both puppies and adult dogs lick the muzzle of another dog when they want to acknowledge his superior status in the group. Dogs who lick their owners are saying that they recognize they're the "top dogs" in the family pack.

"Hi, what's up?" Just as humans shake hands or wave when they meet, dogs give a welcoming lick. It's a polite way of signaling their interest.

The amount of face- or hand-licking that dogs indulge in depends to a certain extent on the breed. Dogs such as Labrador retrievers are very expressive and do a lot of licking, while Chihuahuas and Alaskan huskies are typically more reserved. From the human end of things, of course, all this well-meaning slobbering isn't always welcome. Dogs can be trained not to lick people, but this behavior is such an intricate part of their personality that it takes quite a commitment to teach them to stop, says Dr. Hart.

TOO MUCH OF A GOOD THING

Veterinarians aren't sure why they do it, but some dogs and cats get almost compulsive about licking. They'll groom themselves so often that their fur is perpetually damp. Or they'll lick so long and vigorously that they develop painful, slow-to-heal sores called lick granulomas, says Myrna Milani, D.V.M., a veterinarian in Charlestown, New Hampshire, and author of *DogSmart* and *CatSmart*.

Natural Autoclaves

People cringe when they think of all the things—dirt, mucky water, or other bits of nastiness—that dogs and cats lick from their coats every day. While a tongueful of dirt isn't very hygienic, nature made sure that dogs and cats are up to the task. Their saliva and digestive systems can handle just about anything they lick up. "They have pretty powerful systems that can get rid of nasty things we might think twice about consuming," says Benjamin Hart, D.V.M., Ph.D., professor of physiology and behavior at the University of California, Davis, School of Veterinary Medicine and author of *The Perfect Puppy: How to Choose Your Dog by Its Behavior*.

Parasites, bacteria, or fungi don't have much chance of surviving, he explains. And because dogs and cats have saliva that acts as a mild disinfectant, their habit of licking their wounds can help prevent infection-causing germs from multiplying.

Stress almost certainly plays a role in over-the-top licking, says Dr. Hart. Pets respond to stress by licking their fur, just as people sometimes respond to stress by biting their nails or twirling their hair. Even when the original source of stress is long gone, they may keep licking just because it has become a habit. There's also a theory that pets have an internal grooming clock. "It tells them to deliver some grooming to their bodies every so often," he says. It's possible that this internal mechanism may become overactive, stimulating cats and dogs to lick more than they usually would.

Compulsive licking is always a problem, not only because it can damage the skin but also because it's a sign that something in their lives is out of balance, says Dr. Hart. Veterinarians usually recommend a four-step program to stop excessive licking.

1. Try to figure out what's setting them off. Dogs and cats don't adjust to change very well, and licking is often their response to something new or different. Getting a new pet may trigger licking in the resident pet, says Dr. Hart. So will making an outdoor cat become an indoor cat. Even changes in your routine, such as spending more time away from home, can result in nervous licking. Helping pets adjust to change, which often involves nothing more than time, patience, and a little extra attention, may be enough to stop the problem.

2. Keep them occupied. "Some people find that it helps to add some structure to the animal's environment," says Dr. Hart. This can be as simple as scheduling exercise once or twice a day. Better yet, do a little training or teach your pets some tricks. Interacting with people and the mental stimulation of learning new things is usually enough to take their minds off their coats.

3. Break the habit by redirecting their attention. Even when dogs and cats are feeling calm and happy, they'll sometimes continue licking because at some time in the past they got accustomed to calming themselves with this behavior. Habits are hard to break, and pets often need some help redirecting their attention to other, less harmful activities, says Dr. Barry. As soon as you notice your pet licking, distract her by making a noise, then give her a toy or play with her for a while, she advises. The fewer opportunities she has to lick herself, the easier it will be for her to give up the habit.

4. Ask about drug therapy. It isn't always needed, but drug therapy can be very helpful for pets who are constantly licking. Drugs help adjust the balance of chemicals in the brain, which can stop repetitive behavior, says Dr. Milani. Some pets will need to stay on medications, but most of the time they're only needed for a month or two and are used to supplement behavior therapy, she explains.

CHAPTER 65

Nighttime Activity

Dogs are the Dagwood Bumsteads of the animal world. They fall asleep in an instant and sleep through the night—and a hefty part of the day as well. They may keep *you* awake when they snore or hog the bed, but they sleep just fine.

Cats, on the other hand, have more in common with Andy Capp—they do their best prowling after hours. It wouldn't be so bad if they spent the wee hours knitting or catching up on their reading. But third-shift cats have a lot of energy and often pass the time in creative ways, like swinging from drapes, walking on the piano, knocking glasses off the counter, or taking swipes at your toes.

"Every animal has a natural waxing and waning of chemicals in the body that regulate activity levels," says Nicholas Dodman, B.V.M.S. (a British equivalent of D.V.M.), professor of behavioral pharmacology and director of the behavior clinic at Tufts University School of Veterinary Medicine in North Grafton, Massachusetts, and author of *The Cat Who Cried for Help* and *Dogs Behaving Badly*. Humans are most alert during the day, while cats get revved up in the late evening and very early in the morning—and when a cat's revved up, the game is definitely afoot.

This after-dark orientation explains why cats don't have the color vision that humans do, adds Pam Johnson-Bennett, a feline-behavior consultant in Nashville and author of *Twisted Whiskers* and *Psycho Kitty?* "But they have great focusing ability—they do their best work in the dark." In fact, all of a cat's senses are most intense at dawn and dusk. Even cats who live indoors feel the urge to hunt or do *something* during their peak sensory times.

WAKEFUL HOURS

Despite their propensity to be night owls, cats do sleep at night, says Dr. Dodman. Here are some of the reasons they occasionally go bump in the night.

They're not tired. Many cats spend their days alone with nothing to do except sleep—and that's what they do, often logging 18 hours in a 24-hour period. Cats who sleep all day, however, tend to be rested and ready for action at night.

They're lonely. Cats are generally low-maintenance pets who get along fine without playmates. But even an independent-minded house cat may start feeling lonesome now and then—and he'll want you to keep him company, regardless of the hour.

They're hungry. If you feed your cat once a day in the morning, he may try to adjust your sleeping habits in order to get an earlier meal. If he succeeds at coaxing you out of bed even once at 3:00 A.M., you can be sure he'll remember that for many 3:00 A.M.'s to come.

They have a wanderlust. Cats who aren't neutered spend a substantial part of their lives looking for love. Females meow to be let out, and traveling toms may hurl themselves against the door. All of this noisy behavior is due to predictable, natural urges that aren't limited to banker's hours.

They're on the defensive. Cats don't appreciate it when other cats enter what they perceive as their territory, which may extend to the farthest reaches of the yard. Even when visiting cats make their incursions in broad daylight, their unwelcome visits may keep your cat awake—and angry—at night, Johnson-Bennett says.

They have a bad habit. Whether it started as a sudden burst of energy, the hope of finding a playmate, or a hankering for a midnight snack, some cats stay up at night simply because they've gotten in the habit of doing it.

They're feeling sick. Cats who aren't feeling well sometimes sleep less soundly than usual. In addition, older cats occasionally develop an illness in which they produce too much thyroid hormone. This causes the metabolism to run faster than it should, giving them extra energy, says Dr. Dodman. Any sudden change in cats' sleeping habits should be checked by a veterinarian, especially if they're under the weather generally.

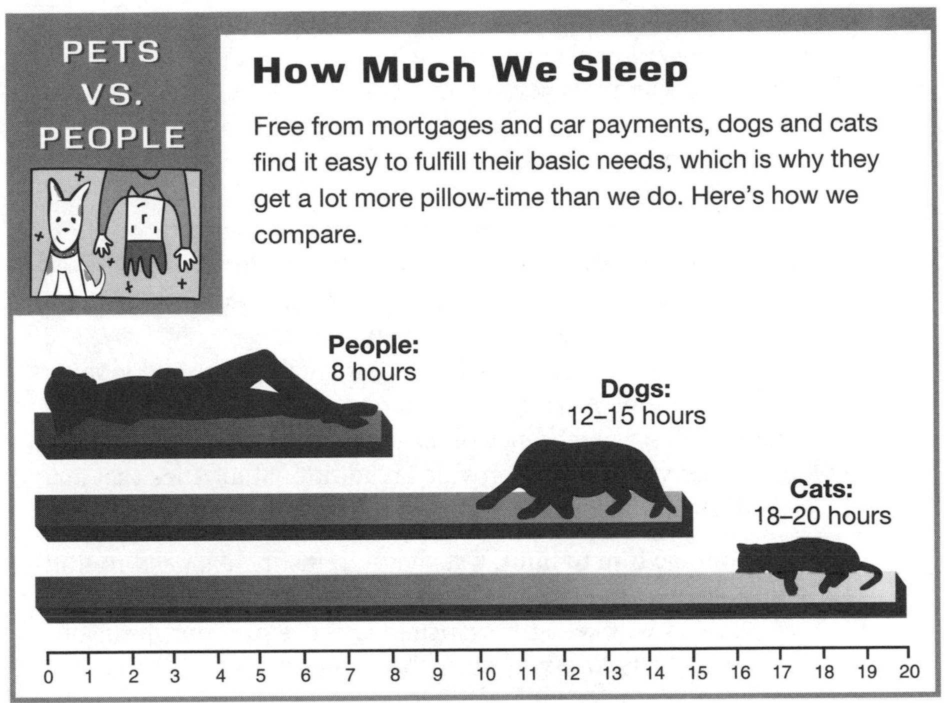

THE ROAD TO REST

The easiest way to cope with night-owl cats is to shut your bedroom door. As long as your cat's out of earshot, you're unlikely to be disturbed by his shenanigans.

It's not always that easy, of course. Some cats make so much noise that a closed door doesn't help. And many people don't want to ban their cats from the bedroom. Cats don't like it either, Johnson-Bennett adds. "If you push the cat out of the bedroom, he may begin to dig under the door."

It's worth checking with your vet to make sure that your cat's healthy and that his nighttime antics aren't signaling a physical problem. As long as he gets a clean bill of health—and in most cases he will—you can begin looking for ways to reset his little internal kitty clock.

Cut back on the catnaps. Since lazy days almost guarantee wakeful nights, it's worth looking for ways to keep your cat entertained during regular hours so that he's more tuckered out later on. For example:

• Get him some new toys, or at least toys he hasn't seen for a while. Cats enjoy playing with new things, and the novelty will often keep them busy even when you're gone, Johnson-Bennett says. Before you go to work in the morning, bring out a few "new" toys and put the old ones away. The next day, swap them again, she suggests.
• Putting the television or radio on a timer will add a note of excitement to an otherwise somnolent day. Even cats who don't seem to notice the TV or radio will be stimulated when the sound suddenly comes on, Johnson-Bennett says.
• Two of the things that cats like best are high places and looking out the window. A window perch or a cat tree positioned by a window will strike the fancy of many felines. Putting a bird feeder outside the window will provide an additional matinee that any cat will stay awake for, says Dr. Dodman.

Encourage him to hunt. Cats have an instinctive need to find and capture prey. Encouraging your cat to duplicate these activities indoors will keep him satisfied and tire him out, Johnson-Bennett says. Before you go to bed, spend 15 to 20 minutes tantalizing him with a movable toy—a cloth mouse attached to a string is ideal. He'll get some exercise and feel as if he's done a good day's work, which will help you both get a good night's sleep.

Put some food in his bowl. Cats don't sleep well when they're hungry, so you may want to try feeding your cat before you go to bed, Johnson-Bennett says. It doesn't have to be a huge meal—just enough to hold him over until morning.

Ignore his pleas. Cats who are hungry and wakeful can be very persistent, and it's tempting to get up and feed them just to get a little peace. "The hardest part comes at five in the morning, when the cat comes in and sits on your chest to wake you up," says Johnson-Bennett. But you have to be strong and not give in. "If you're meeting his needs on the other end by playing with him and giving him a late meal, before long he'll realize that he's not going to get what he's looking for from you in the middle of the night," she says.

CHAPTER 66

Overexcitement

It sometimes seems as though dogs and cats have split personalities. In the evening when you're all settled in, they're calm, happy, and relaxed. But the minute you stand up or someone comes to the door, they start running around, knocking glasses off the counter, or bowling people over with their mad-dash excitement.

"Healthy young animals often have more energy than they need, and they explode with exuberance just like little kids do," says Patricia McConnell, Ph.D., a certified applied animal behaviorist and assistant adjunct professor in the department of zoology at the University of Wisconsin at Madison. Some breeds, such as terriers and collies, continue to seethe with energy as adults. They were bred that way because they were meant to run around for 8 to 10 hours, not to sit balled up on the couch all day.

You're My Mouse

Although cats spend a lot of time sleeping, they also have tremendous amounts of energy, says Jeff Nichol, D.V.M., a veterinarian in Albuquerque, New Mexico. Cats evolved as hunters. Short of their occasional drunken forays with catnip, most feline excitement centers on the thrill of the chase, and modern life doesn't give them a lot of opportunities to indulge. Cats who spend their time running up window screens and drapes and generally tearing around the house are trying to tell you either that they're bored or in need of hunting practice.

"Even cats with abundant amounts of food spend a lot of their time hunting," says Dr. Nichol. Indoor cats don't have a lot of mice to chase, so they settle for stalking their owners. This type of "hunting" is called playful aggression. "They watch your movements as you walk through the house. They may grab for you or swat at you. It might seem like they are playing, but in many ways, they are deadly serious," he says.

You don't want to discourage your cat's hunting instincts, because chasing "prey" helps cats dispel energy and keeps their minds and bodies sharp. But you do want to redirect the energy so that you don't wind up catching an ankleful of claws, says Margaret Thompson, D.V.M., a veterinarian in Colleyville, Texas. She recommends tying a fishing line to a stick and attaching a fuzzy ball to the other end. When you cast the ball, your cat will bat it in midair or scramble after it on the floor. This will give her what she wants: hunting practice. And it will give you what you want: a tired cat and skin without scratch marks.

Play with Me

Dogs crave human contact and dislike being alone. When you come home after work or other people come to visit, they feel as if it's a once-in-a-lifetime homecoming, and they can hardly contain themselves. Their excitement gets even more pronounced when there's more than one dog in the family, because they'll compete for attention, says Dr. Thompson.

A common reason that dogs get overly excited is that someone in the family, usually one of the children, is surreptitiously encouraging them to jump, run, and romp. Dogs have a hard time distinguishing the messages they get from different people. If one human in the family encourages rough play, dogs assume that everyone likes it—and then get confused when they get scolded for doing what they thought they were supposed to do, says Dr. Thompson.

Dogs are a lot like people in that they periodically need a chance to blow off steam, adds Judith Kaufman, a trainer in Norwalk, Connecticut. "They race around to let off tension or to have fun," she says. "My own dog does that after she's been concentrating a lot. She'll just start winging about. It's her release time."

Taking the Edge Off

Most dogs need 30 to 40 minutes of vigorous exercise a day, and breeds like Border collies need a lot more. Giving your dog some stimulating exercise once or twice a day will make her much less likely to get worked up the rest of the time, says Dr.

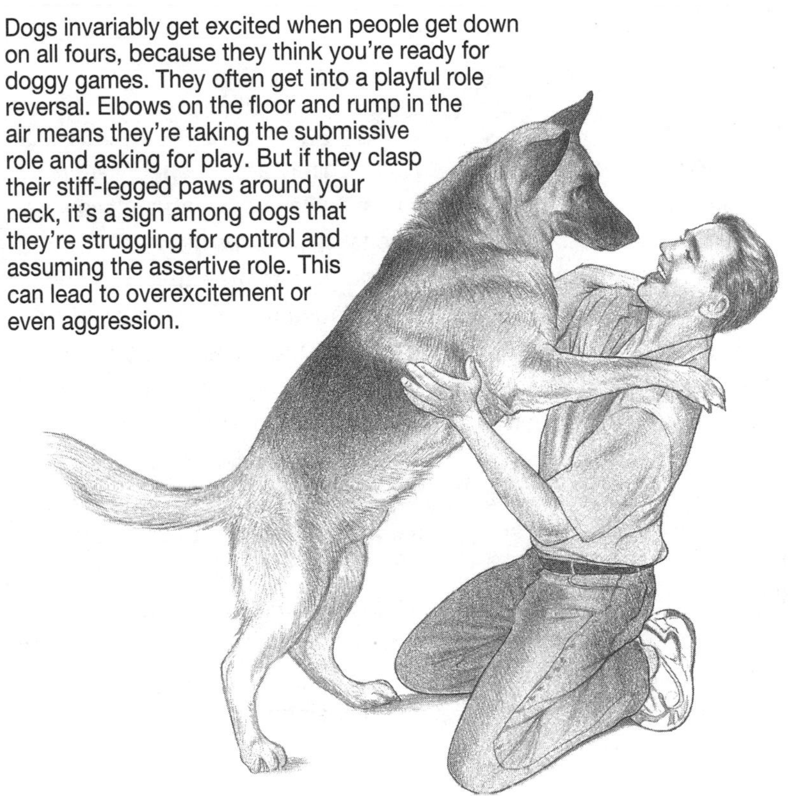

Dogs invariably get excited when people get down on all fours, because they think you're ready for doggy games. They often get into a playful role reversal. Elbows on the floor and rump in the air means they're taking the submissive role and asking for play. But if they clasp their stiff-legged paws around your neck, it's a sign among dogs that they're struggling for control and assuming the assertive role. This can lead to overexcitement or even aggression.

Thompson. But you have to choose the right exercise, she adds. Some kinds of play are too stimulating for dogs who get excited easily.

Dogs love it, for example, when people get down on the floor with them, especially when the people are on all fours. That's exactly how dogs play, and this position stimulates all of their ancient instincts to tumble around. It also stimulates their instincts to get overly excited or even aggressive, Dr. Thompson explains. Dogs are very conscious of size. When you're standing up, they know you're higher in the social hierarchy than they are. When you're on your knees, they may think of you as being just another dog and play accordingly.

Rough-and-tumble play inside the house also causes problems because dogs get the idea that the house is an acceptable venue for blowing off steam. That's why veterinarians recommend giving dogs exercise away from home or in the backyard.

Wearing dogs out is one way to take the edge off their excite-

Comfort in a Crate

This is a tale of two Labrador retrievers, Hershey and Quick.

Hershey and Quick started life as rambunctious puppies with over-the-top energy, which is how young Labradors usually are. Their original owner, finding them too much to handle, gave them away to different homes. Hershey went to Barbara and Tony Bowman in Melbourne, Florida, and Quick went to Tony's sister, Katriina Bowman in Orlando.

Four years later, the two dogs couldn't have been more different. Quick's exuberance only seemed to increase. She raced around, panted constantly, and was always jumping up on people. Hershey, on the other hand, calmly approached visitors with a smile and a wag and was calm whenever she was indoors. Why did two dogs from the same litter and background turn out so differently?

"It was the crate," Tony explains. "Every time we went somewhere, we put Hershey in a crate until she learned to stay calm." Hershey learned that showing overly exuberant behavior invariably resulted in being sent to her crate. After a while, she discovered that acting calmly allowed her to stay with her family, and that's what's motivated her ever since.

ment, but you also have to keep them mentally stimulated, says Dr. Thompson. At the same time, you need to make it clear that unruly behavior, whatever the occasion, isn't appreciated. Here are a few tips you may want to try.

Make them work for their food. Dogs don't play by themselves very well, which is why they get so worked up when their owners come home at night, Kaufman says. One way to help them entertain themselves is to give them a Buster Cube. This is a hollow toy that you can fill with kibble or bits of biscuit. Dogs smell the food and respond by nudging, batting, or tossing the cube. Periodically, they're rewarded when a little piece of food falls out. So they nudge it and bat it some more. Buster Cubes will keep some dogs entertained for hours, she says.

Communicate clearly. Dogs don't make pests of themselves deliberately to annoy you. Quite the opposite: They're so eager to interact that they can hardly control themselves. You can take advantage of their eagerness to please by consistently and firmly telling them no as soon as they start running around. A little firm discipline will help them understand that their eagerness isn't having its intended effect, and they'll look for other, calmer ways to get your approval, says Dr. Thompson.

For discipline to be effective, however, you have to sound like you mean it, she adds. Dogs learn to ignore halfhearted commands that aren't enforced. Saying no in a firm, no-nonsense voice and then ignoring them entirely or leaving the room if they don't listen will drive home the message that you mean what you say.

Be nonchalant. Since dogs are inherently social animals, they get a bit uneasy when they're left alone. Most dogs learn to adjust to modern life, but some get extremely uncomfortable when their owners are gone. Eventually, they settle down, but for the first few minutes after their owners leave, they feel abandoned, and they sometimes cope with their feelings by knocking over trash cans or tearing up pillows. At the very least, they store up all of that anxiety, then release it with a startling burst of energy the minute you come home.

"People unwittingly promote their anxiety by making an emotional fuss when they leave," says Dr. Nichol. Dogs pick up on their owners' anxiety, and this makes them even more desperate for reassurance. Veterinarians recommend acting utterly nonchalant when you leave the house and again when you come home. It's a way of teaching dogs that it's safe to be alone. The less anxiety they sense from you, the less likely they are to feel abandoned, he explains.

Give them a quiet place. Unlike people, who revel in wide-open spaces, dogs feel most comfortable when they're in slightly confined quarters. Dogs in the wild, in fact, instinctively gravitate to denlike spaces when they need a little rest and relaxation. You can get a similar effect by creating a "den" in the house by using a crate, for example, or even putting your dog's bed in a corner. Enclosed spaces make them feel more secure, and dogs who are secure are more likely to do what comes naturally—go to sleep—and less likely to rush around.

CHAPTER 67

Possessiveness with Toys

Rhea, a 10-year-old golden retriever in Central City, Pennsylvania, loves golf balls. She loves them so much, in fact, that she has dedicated most of her life to collecting them. Her owner, Jeanne Holman, started walking Rhea at the Indian Lake Golf Course when the dog was a puppy. Since then, Rhea has collected more than 14,000 balls.

The amazing thing is that she has returned every one. As much as she loves them, Rhea is always willing to give up her golf balls. Many of her canine peers could take a lesson in such gracious remittance. Dogs who are overly possessive with toys are frequent clients of trainers and behaviorists, many of whom believe possessive behavior indicates that a dog needs a refresher course in doggy etiquette.

A Line in the Sand

What's your dog trying to tell you when she snatches up a soggy stuffed animal or a ratty piece of rubber cheese and gives you that "don't touch this" look? Three simple things: "Mine. Mine. Mine."

It's not surprising that dogs love their toys, but it's important to make a distinction between a dog who enjoys a toy and one who is overly possessive. "It's like asking at what point is it appropriate for your child to kick you over a soccer ball," says Sarah Wilson, a trainer in Gardiner, New York, and coauthor of *Tails from the Bark Side*. "The ball *does* belong to the child, but that's not the point." Dogs who growl, snarl, or physically try to protect a toy have gone too far, whether it's theirs or not.

Dogs who are possessive about food, toys, or anything else are telling you two things: one, that they're very fond of the resource in question; and two, that it's up to them, not you, to make the rules, says Nicholas Dodman, B.V.M.S. (a British equivalent of D.V.M.), professor of behavioral pharmacology and director of the behavior clinic at Tufts University School of Veterinary Medicine in North Grafton, Massachusetts, and author of *Dogs Behaving Badly*, *The Dog Who Loved Too Much*, and *The Cat Who Cried for Help*.

In the distant past, when dogs lived in small societies called packs, everyone knew who was the leader—and who wasn't. Dogs who didn't want to get flattened learned quickly who they had to respect. Dogs don't live in packs anymore, but from their point of view, the same rules apply in the family. A dog who growls when you approach her food bowl or refuses to give up a toy is telling you, in no uncertain terms, that she's calling the shots.

This type of dominant behavior is rarely absolute, Dr. Dodman adds. A dog may be protective of a tennis ball or a bone but willingly give up her favorite perch on the bed. And a dog who is meek and mild most of the time may get more forceful when she feels that it's warranted or she can get away with it. "It's like someone coming along and getting in your car without permission," says Dr. Dodman. "If it's your mother or your boss, what are you going to do? But if it's a subordinate or a stranger, reactions vary from saying, 'Excuse me, but what are you doing?' to chasing the intruder with a bat."

KITTY CONFUSION

Unlike dogs, your cat's ancestors didn't live in packs. Then, as now, cats were solitary creatures, and things like leadership and dominance weren't really issues. Even though cats often have favorite toys or perches, they don't get as fiercely protective as some dogs. So possessive behavior is unlikely to be a problem.

This isn't to say that your cat won't snag your hand if you try to slip a catnip mouse out from under her paws. But it's not because she's feeling possessive. It's because she believes the mouse is her prey and that it's trying to escape, says Pam Johnson-Bennett, a feline-behavior consultant in Nashville and author of *Twisted Whiskers* and *Psycho Kitty?*

"What might appear to be possessiveness is usually a case of miscommunication," says Johnson-Bennett. "When you try to

Bonkers for Balls

Thanks to hundreds of years of selective breeding, teaching Labrador retrievers to retrieve a ball is about as hard as teaching them to breathe. Giving a ball back, however, is another story. Dogs who joyfully race across the backyard, falling over their own feet to capture a ball, may have serious reservations about handing it over, no matter how much they want you to throw it again.

Because of their go-get-it pasts, Labradors, golden retrievers, and retriever mixes seem to have the most trouble giving up their favorite balls, says Robin Downing, D.V.M., a veterinarian in Windsor, Colorado. It's not that they have a hidden agenda. It's just that they love their balls so much that they want to share them with you—and their idea of sharing is to make a game of it by running around the yard, with you in hot pursuit. It's exactly the way they would play with another dog, Dr. Downing explains.

It's nearly impossible to cool retrievers' ardor for balls, but you can take advantage of their passion to create a game that's a little more fun to play. Rather than throwing one ball at a time, put a second ball in play, Dr. Downing suggests. As soon as your dog comes tearing back with one ball, show her the second ball and tell her to "give." Being a dog, she'll decide that "your" ball is better than the one she already has, and she'll drop it at your feet. When she does, throw the second ball and scoop up the first one. It won't take your dog long to learn that "give" means extra play for her. She'll also be reminded that it's the retrieving, not the keeping, that makes the game worth playing.

take the toy away, your cat may interpret that as the prey struggling to escape. So she may bite down harder or clamp her paw down—and nip or scratch you in the process. But it's not possessiveness. It's the cat acting like a predator."

SETTING LIMITS

It's easy to ignore possessive behavior because most of the time you really don't want your dog's breakfast or soggy tennis ball. But your dog won't interpret your looking away as a lack of interest. Rather, she'll assume that her tenacity—or her growl or bite—paid off. Her thinking probably goes something like this:

"I told her to go away, and she did. I like this, and I'm going to do it again next time."

Even though possessive behavior isn't always scary, it is always inappropriate. "There shouldn't be anything that belongs to the dog and not to you," Wilson says. To get your dog used to sharing, here's what experts advise.

Take away her excuse. While some dogs are extremely possessive and will defend a tennis ball or their place on the bed as aggressively as they guard food, most have one or two objects that they have strong feelings for. The easiest solution is often to get rid of temptation, says Wilson. Toss the tennis ball in the trash while your dog is sleeping, or cover "her" place on the couch with a load of books. This won't change her personality, but it may eliminate the problem.

Give her something better. If there's one thing that dogs like better than praise, it's bribery, and you can often stop possessive behavior with a few well-timed, preferably tasty rewards, says Robin Downing, D.V.M., a veterinarian in Windsor, Colorado. Suppose your dog is holding on to something and won't give it back. Call her to you and use your usual "give" command—and offer a treat at the same time. She can't hold on to the object and take the treat at the same time, and she'll probably opt for the treat, at which point you take away the object, says Dr. Downing. Bribery can be a win-win situation. You get the object back, and your dog has to work for a treat, which is the essence of good training. If you do this consistently, she'll begin to associate the command "give" with getting treats, which will make her more likely to obey you later on.

Take the fun out of it. Dogs aren't always possessive because they love an object and can't bear to give it up. Sometimes they get grabby because they think *you* want it—and are willing to chase them in a rollicking game of tag. As you reach for the object, they're off like a shot, downright tickled that you're willing to play.

The only solution to this type of behavior is not to play the game. When your dog takes off with something you'd like to get back, ignore her, Wilson suggests. Turn your back, go inside, read a book, or do some gardening. Do anything except give her attention, which is what she really wanted in the first place. Keep-away is a pretty lame game with just one player, and she'll probably lose interest and drop the object on her own.

NAME: Scooter

OCCUPATION: Frisbee Dog

Scooter loves his toys, more specifically, his Frisbees. He loves them so much, in fact, that he's spent thousands of hours chasing, chewing, catching, and returning Frisbees to his owner, Lou McCammon of Las Vegas.

Lou admits that Scooter, a 12-year-old Australian shepherd, is a dog obsessed. But it's hardly a problem. Scooter's single-minded dedication has made him one of the country's top Frisbee dogs, with admirers around the world. His résumé includes two Canine Flying Disc World Championship titles, a 7-year stint as the mascot for the San Francisco 49ers, and gigs on talk shows and television commercials. He's even been on MTV.

Scooter showed an interest in Frisbees almost from the time he was born, and he really started showing promise by the time he was 4 months old. "I used to take Scooter to the park at three or four in the morning, and we'd practice in front of the headlights," Lou says. Scooter wasn't the best Frisbee dog at first, but Lou admits that he wasn't that good at throwing, either, so they both had a lot to learn.

It didn't take long. Lou discovered that Scooter had natural intelligence and athleticism, along with plenty of canine charm. And he has never once complained about his work—he basically lives to sink his teeth into Frisbees. And passion is the one thing a superior Frisbee dog needs, Lou says. Even today, after thousands of throws, leaps, and catches, Scooter still gets so excited when he sees the Frisbee that he can hardly stand still.

Take away her privileges. Dogs who hover over their toys and eye you suspiciously have somehow gotten the idea that it's acceptable to warn you away. You have to remind them that you make the rules—always and in all circumstances, Wilson says. "Taking control is not difficult," she says. "You just need to direct your pet's behavior in a way that makes sense to her." What this means is making sure that your dog understands that all of her rewards—things such as meals, attention, and treats—are directly tied to her behavior. When she acts properly, she gets good things. When she acts possessively, she doesn't.

Dogs instinctively understand that every family has leaders and followers, Wilson explains. To make sure that your dog understands she's second fiddle, make her do something every time she gets something. Before you feed her, have her sit first. Make her lie down before you let her out the door. Don't give her a treat unless she drops her toy first. When she does what you want, she gets her rewards. When she doesn't behave, she pays for it.

"Your dog will see that when she does things for you, good things happen," Wilson says. "She gets fed, the door opens, the ball gets thrown." Over time, her possessiveness—and her underlying questions about your leadership—will begin to disappear.

CHAPTER 68

Rolling in Smelly Things

Sometimes pets seem just like little people: clever, adaptable, resourceful, and intelligent.

Then there are those other times.

Like when your dog comes home smelling like a 2-week-old possum-and-cheese sandwich. Or smears his fur with Eau de Bunny Dung on his daily romp through the woods. Or makes a sharp right turn into a pool of swamp muck and proceeds to do the backstroke. The bizarre, unexplained urge to cover one's hide in stink is a powerful reminder that pets remain a little closer to their wild roots than do humans.

"The truth is, I can't figure out why dogs love to roll in smelly things," says Toni Beninger, editor of the dog Web site WorldClassDogs.com and a former Saint Bernard breeder in Victoria, British Columbia, Canada. "This is one of those occasions when I just can't comprehend why animals do the things they do."

There are a few theories about why dogs like to cover themselves in smelly stuff. (Incidentally, this is not a habit in which cats indulge. "In fact, they get really annoyed at dogs who do it," Beninger says.) Dogs' thinking probably goes something like this:

"There's no one here but us deer droppings." This once-popular theory holds that dogs, wolves, and other canines cover themselves in stink because they want to hide their own scent from predators and prey. It's easier to hide if you smell like your surroundings. And it's easier to hunt when smaller animals don't catch a whiff of you until it's too late.

The problem with this theory is that canines don't really have enemies, says Benjamin Hart, D.V.M., Ph.D., professor of physiology and behavior at the University of California, Davis,

The Clean Routine

Dogs aren't fussy about what they roll in. They like deer droppings just as much as horse manure, skunk carcasses, or pond scum. As long as it smells, they'll find an excuse to drop to the ground and roll with delight.

Since you can't persuade dogs that freshly mown grass is just as nice to roll in as manure, you'll invariably find yourself with a hose in one hand and a container of shampoo in the other. Except for skunk smell, which is almost impossible to eradicate, most substances dogs roll in will wash off with any commercial pet shampoo, says Toni Beninger, editor of the dog Web site WorldClassDogs.com and a former Saint Bernard breeder in Victoria, British Columbia, Canada.

Whichever shampoo you use, make sure to work up a good lather and let it soak into the coat for a few minutes before rinsing it off, she adds. It's also a good idea to stay away from strongly scented shampoos. Even though they help mask the original odor, your dog may decide that flowery scents aren't for him—and immediately find something else to roll in to disguise that awful smell.

School of Veterinary Medicine and author of *The Perfect Puppy: How to Choose Your Dog by Its Behavior*. And since canines openly pursue prey instead of stalking, it's not likely that they need to hide their presence.

"Sure, it stinks—but it's home." Another theory is that dogs roll in things in order to identify with their home turf. Smelling like the stuff on your territory is a powerful signal to others who would like to claim the area for themselves. It's almost as though a dog is telling potential challengers, "I own the territory down to the dead raccoon over the hill, and back up to the sheep pasture by the road. Keep off!"

"A rose by any other name still smells sweet." "Dogs smell things in ways that are completely foreign to us," Beninger says. "So it's not fair for us to say that things stink when a dog may find them appealing." Stuff that smells completely repulsive to people may, in fact, be quite tantalizing to dogs. It makes sense that dogs want to roll in interesting odors, just as people like to splash on aftershave or perfume.

Controlling the Rolling

Not all dogs are rollers, and researchers have yet to figure out what triggers the behavior in some pets and not in others. If you happen to be blessed with a stink-loving dog, you don't have to worry that discouraging the habit will make him any less happy. It's just an age-old instinct that your pet can do just fine without. "I think it's pretty safe to say that rolling has no benefit to domestic dogs," Dr. Hart says. And it certainly has no benefit to owners who have to smell the residue or clean up the carpets afterward.

Unfortunately, the urge to roll is powerful in some pets. "You're dealing with a real strong tendency. It could be tough to handle," Dr. Hart says. Since you may never completely rid a pet of his desire to roll, your only real option is to take preventive action.

Go on a scavenger hunt. It's worth taking a few minutes now and then to patrol the yard and pick up the types of odoriferous things dogs love, such as dung or fallen birds. "You need to get to them before your dog has a chance to indulge himself," Beninger says.

Keep him close. Dogs don't limit their rolling just to their own territory. No matter where you go, whether it's a neighborhood park or a forest preserve, dogs have an unerring nose for stench. Let them out of your sight for a second, and they're sure to come back with an odor that's not their own. Keeping your dog on a leash will eliminate this problem, says Andy Bunn, a trainer in Charlotte, North Carolina. Walking your dog on a leash has the additional benefits of helping you bond more closely with your pet while giving both of you a little extra exercise, he adds.

Take away the fun. Veterinarians and behaviorists don't worry about dogs' odoriferous tendencies because rolling in cow dung and other smelly things usually doesn't cause health problems, and dogs seem to enjoy it. But if your dog perpetually smells like something unmentionable, you may want to try a technique called aversion therapy to break the habit.

One type of aversion therapy involves using a collar that sprays citronella. It gives your dog an immediate, unpleasant sensation when you press a button on a remote control. Every time you see your dog rolling in something, you can press the button, which will make him stop what he's doing—and, in theory, think twice about doing it again.

For aversion therapy to be effective, however, you have to use the device *every* time he rolls. Otherwise, he'll never make the connection between the unpleasant sensation and the behavior that "causes" it. Yelling doesn't work, Dr. Hart adds, because your dog won't make the connection between the yelling and the behavior. He'll just wonder why you're so cross.

All in all, the simplest controls are also the most effective in this case. First, don't let your roll-happy dog outside unsupervised and unleashed. Second, go on "yard patrol" daily to pick up anything that's irresistibly smelly.

CHAPTER 69

Rubbing

For cats, rubbing is serious business, and they do it every chance they get. They'll swerve off course in order to brush against a coatrack or chair leg. They pause next to bookcases or coffee tables and rub them with their faces. Put something unfamiliar on the floor, and most cats will spend a little time rubbing it with their cheeks, chins, and the sides of their mouths.

There's a reason for all of this body work. Cats are fiercely territorial, and rubbing against objects is their way of saying, "This is mine."

Cats have more than 20 glands just beneath the surface of their skin. Located mainly on the head and face and around the lips, the glands are filled with an oily fluid. Like miniature atomizers, the glands release chemical scents whenever cats rub. Humans can't smell the scents, but to cats they're familiar, comforting odors that reassure them that they're on familiar ground. At the same time, the scents alert other cats that the area is "taken," says Benjamin Hart, D.V.M., Ph.D., professor of physiology and behavior at the University of California, Davis, School of Veterinary Medicine and author of *The Perfect Puppy: How to Choose Your Dog by Its Behavior*.

Cats mark more than just furniture. They also mark people—their legs, faces, hands, and any other part they can reach. "We're part of their environment, too," says Dr. Hart. "So we get marked."

A Rub to Say "I Love You"

Rubbing isn't only about chemistry, and it isn't limited to cats. There's an emotional component as well. Just as we pet dogs and cats because we enjoy the contact, they rub against us for pleasure. "Having contact with cats and dogs lowers our heart rates

WHAT'S MY PET SAYING?

Behavior
Rubbing against Edges

What It Means
"It Helps Me 'See' at Night"

Cats are nocturnal animals, and they do most of their exploring after dark, says Myrna Milani, D.V.M., a veterinarian in Charlestown, New Hampshire, and author of *DogSmart* and *CatSmart*. Cats see better in the dark than people do, but their vision isn't perfect. So they compensate with their sense of smell. "They use their scent glands to mark prominent objects," she explains. Afterward, they can navigate the area in pitch darkness without running into things.

and blood pressures," adds Myrna Milani, D.V.M., a veterinarian in Charlestown, New Hampshire, and author of *DogSmart* and *CatSmart*. "And there's been research that shows we have the same effect on dogs. I see no reason why it wouldn't be true for cats as well."

Dogs and cats have been domesticated for a long time, which means that people are their families. Their instinct for intimacy is strong, and rubbing helps them stay close and bonded. Just as pets rub against their mothers, they also rub against people. "It's their way of reassuring themselves that there's still a relationship," explains Dr. Hart.

Cats often begin by rubbing with their faces or heads to lay down a scent, then they follow that with a body rub as a way of saying, "We're family." Additional rubs are merely to tell you, "Pet me some more, I like that." Dogs don't share cats' abilities to leave scent markings by rubbing, but they also enjoy contact with their human packmates. "If you watch a group of dogs, they often rub against each other, and they particularly like to rub against the dominant animal," says Dr. Hart. "It reinforces the social bond."

Cries for Help

If there's one complaint people have about rubbing, it's that their pets don't do enough of it. But a sudden increase in hand nudging or face rubbing is worth paying attention to. Your pet is probably just feeling unusually affectionate, but there may be something else that he's trying to tell you.

"I'm feeling pushy today." It's natural for dogs to rub against people (or dogs) who they perceive as being dominant. It's just as natural for them to nudge and rub when *they're* being dominant. It's a way of demanding attention, and if you don't give it right away, they'll keep pushing and rubbing and nudging.

"If you have a nice dog who's well-behaved, responds well to commands, and doesn't harass anyone, maybe a little leaning and nudging is fine," says Dr. Milani. "But if the dog is acting aggressively by licking, jumping up, leaning against, or nudging you, you'll want to stop it."

You can curtail incessant demands for attention by ignoring them, Dr. Milani advises. Your dog wants something, and if you don't deliver, he'll realize that he's wasting his time. Don't yell or push him away, she adds. Even though it's negative, it will still give your dog the attention he's seeking.

"I'm insecure." Cats do a lot of rubbing when they encounter unfamiliar objects. When you get a new couch, for example, your cat will probably spend a lot of time putting his mark on it. Once he's used to it, he'll rub it less often. An exception is when cats aren't feeling very confident, says Dr. Milani. Cats who are insecure often feel as though they constantly have to mark their territory, including their people. This type of insecurity often leads to other problems, such as spraying, she says.

"Set up a little cat carrier in your bedroom and leave one of your old shirts in it," suggests Dr. Milani. Cats who are nervous often feel more secure when they have a small, safe place to retire to. It becomes their private getaway, while the rest of the house will seem more like neutral territory that doesn't need to be marked quite as thoroughly.

"I'm itchy." Dogs and cats tend to be itchier than people, especially when they have hay fever or other kinds of allergies. They usually use their teeth or claws for scratching, but sometimes a quick rub is a suitable substitute. Pets with allergies usually rub a spot, walk away, then rub the same spot some more, says Dr. Milani. Their skin may look irritated as well.

"I'm hooked." What begins as a convenient way to scratch an itch sometimes becomes a habit. In dogs especially, rubbing can become habitual when they realize that they get attention from their owners for doing it. "I've seen dogs who rub their faces or heads only in the owner's presence," says Dr. Milani. The only way to stop this type of rubbing is to ignore it, she explains.

CHAPTER 70

Scratching Furniture

Once it was an elegant, overstuffed chair. Then it was a ratty overstuffed chair, with tufts of cotton and gold threads hanging from the frame. Kate Gamble, a feline-behavior consultant in Auburn, California, wasn't surprised when her client said, "I think my cats have a scratching problem."

Everyone who lives with cats probably has a similar chair—or couch or set of drapes—that has fallen victim to merciless claws. But what's bad for owners is very good for cats (as well as upholsterers). Scratching helps cats keep their claws in shape. It's one of life's necessities, like using the litter box. Cats also like to stretch—and there's no better way to stretch than to reach high and hook their claws into something.

The main reason cats scratch has nothing to do with comfort or hygiene, however. It's about power. Scratching sends visual and olfactory messages to other cats as well as people. It tells the world, "This is mine, and here's my mark to prove it."

Eminent Domain

Dogs rarely scratch furniture unless their favorite ball happens to be stuck under a cushion. They will scratch doors and sometimes carpets, but for the most part, they use their mouths to explore and take possession of the world. They'd much rather chew on a chair leg than scratch it.

But for cats, scratching is central to their identity. Apart from the visual marks it leaves, scratching deposits scent molecules from the sweat glands between the toes and in the paw pads. People can't smell this scent, but cats can. They're constantly marking the house with their scents.

"Scratches and the scent are important for cats," says John C.

Wright, Ph.D., a certified applied animal behaviorist; professor of psychology at Mercer University in Macon, Georgia; and author of *The Dog Who Would Be King* and *Is Your Cat Crazy?* "Together, they advertise the cat's presence to others and provide the cat doing the marking with a familiar scent."

And for cats, smelling their own familiar scent is just as important as leaving their scent for others, Dr. Wright adds. Cats are intensely connected to places. Their scent is no less a part of a place than the furniture, the backyard, or the windowsills they perch on.

It's not that cats don't get connected to people. They do. That is why they mark them just as thoroughly as they mark the furniture, not with scratches but with head and body rubs, says Anitra Frazier, a holistic animal-behavior consultant in New York City and author of *The New Natural Cat* and *It's a Cat's Life*. Cats who rub against your shin are depositing their scent just as surely as if they were scratching at the drapes. And, in fact, the two activities may go together, she adds. Many cats will rush to their favorite scratching spot and give it a workout as soon as their owners come home. "They seem to be saying, 'Oh, you're home! Let's redo these marks so we can keep you safe,'" she explains.

A Scratch for All Occasions

At about the time that they're weaned, cats make the amazing discovery that they have the power to retract their claws. That's about when they begin their scratching explorations. Experts have identified a number of reasons that cats scratch. Here are some examples.

Claw maintenance. Wild cats, from tigers to bobcats, rely on their claws to survive in the wilderness. Sharp claws help them hold on to prey, fight when attacked, and climb out of reach when predators arrive. Trees and branches are nature's scratching posts. Domesticated cats spend most of their time inside, but they still need to keep their claws in good shape. Couches and chairs take the place of woody stalks and stems. Scratching carpets and other rough surfaces helps remove the dead outer layer, or sheath, which exposes the new sharp nail underneath.

Stretching. Anything that feels good makes sense to cats, and scratching feels very good. It stretches the toes in the front paws and tones muscles in the legs, shoulders, and back. "Scratching is a natural cat fitness move," Frazier says. "It's exercise that feels good."

Mindless movement. We tend to assume that there are good reasons for everything that cats do, but sometimes things are simpler than they appear. The instinct to scratch may be rooted in such necessities as territoriality and defense, but cats today don't face anything riskier than chasing catnip mice down a flight of stairs. But they scratch just the same. Sometimes it seems more of an unconscious behavior than a conscious form of communicating with another cat. They often stop in the middle of doing something just to scratch, just as they may stop to wash themselves.

SAVING THE SOFAS

Scratching is part of who cats are. The urge is in their genes, and it would be cruel, even if it were possible, to make them stop. But there are ways for cats and furniture to peacefully coexist. Basically, you have two choices: Make their usual scratching places less interesting, and give them more exciting ones to scratch, like a board or post.

Make furniture unscratchable. As anyone who has tried to give up smoking or nail biting can attest, habits are mighty difficult to stop. Imagine how hard it would be for cats to give up a habit that's eons old. Mere persuasion won't do it, but chicken wire might. Frazier recommends molding chicken wire, which is easily bendable, over furniture arms, corners, or other places that cats scratch. The wire is ugly, but cats hate the feel of it, so it works quickly. Once the wire comes down, many cats will continue to avoid the spot.

If wire-covered furniture isn't to your liking, you may want to protect vulnerable places by applying bubble wrap. Or use a hard, plasticlike covering, available through the classifieds section of any cat magazine. It's rugged and entirely unscratchable, says Allen M. Schoen, D.V.M., director of the Veterinary Institute for Therapeutic Alternatives in Sherman, Connecticut, and author of *Love, Miracles, and Animal Healing*.

Discourage them with oil. Most cats prefer scratching soft fabrics, but some go for wood, especially dresser legs, closet doors, and even pine floors. Rubbing wood with cinnamon, lemon, or eucalyptus oils will impregnate them with odors that some cats

Customized Scratching

Many scratching posts look as though they were designed by interior decorators who never owned a cat. Beautiful fabrics and expensive woods don't fill feline hearts with desire. What they want is something rough and scratchy, and long enough to give their claws a good drag. And the tattier it gets, the more they like it. Scratching posts are expensive, but they're very easy to make at home. Here's how.

Buy a 30-inch length of 4 × 4 lumber, preferably redwood (or pine as a second choice) for the post, and a 16-inch square of ¾- or 1-inch plywood for the base. (You can substitute a small log, with the bark in place, for the post.) Roughen the redwood using a wire brush. Then screw or nail the base to the post, and stand back while your cat has some fun.

may dislike, says Christina Chambreau, D.V.M., a holistic veterinarian in Sparks, Maryland, and educational chairperson for the Academy of Veterinary Homeopathy. The smell doesn't last forever, so you'll need to reapply it once a week. And be sure to test the oil first on a small area that's out of sight to make sure that it won't stain.

Give them something better. "People inadvertently teach their cats to scratch the furniture by not providing an alternative—a scratching post that is irresistible to them," Frazier says. It's not quite that easy, of course. Nearly everyone has paid good money for a scratching post—and then watched it attract dust as their cats gleefully ripped the couch.

The problem is that many commercial scratching posts are designed for human rather than cat tastes. A post that looks nice in the living room isn't necessarily one that's attractive to cats.

• Scratching posts should have long, rough, scratchy surfaces that provide good claw traction. The colors and patterns don't matter at all as long as the fibers run vertically. The best posts are covered with sisal, a strong fiber with a rough, ropy texture. The worst are covered with fluffy materials like carpeting.
• The post should be tall enough so that your cat has to stretch to reach the top. And since cats like to stand up and lean when they scratch, the post needs to be very solid and secure. Look for one with a wide base and enough weight that it won't easily tip or wobble.
• Most cats like vertical posts, but some scratch horizontally—a throwback to the days when they stretched out on branches for their daily claw routines. For those cats, you can buy corrugated cardboard at shipping centers. It's inexpensive, and cats love it, especially if you wedge it in a corner where it won't slide around too much. "You'll probably have pieces of cardboard all over the floor and will need to replace it often, but it works well," Frazier says. A neater alternative is to buy a scratching post and lay it on its side, she adds.
• Cats are fussy about where they scratch, which is why putting a post in the basement or near the litter box guarantees that it won't get a lot of action. Cats do their scratching in areas where they spend the most time, like in the living room or bedroom. You can't go wrong if you put the post near a place where your cat has been scratching. You can always move it, a little at a time, to an area you like better. As long as you move it slowly, your cat will follow it to the new place and won't even notice that it has been moved, Frazier says.
• To encourage your cat to use the post, show some enthusiasm. Run to it periodically, especially when you come home in the evening, and scratch it yourself. If you accompany your scratching with sounds of satisfaction and happiness, your cat will want to join the fun.

A Serious Operation

Declawing is a simple surgical procedure in which the tips of the bones that contain the claws are removed. For a long time, it was considered the best way to stop expensive damage.

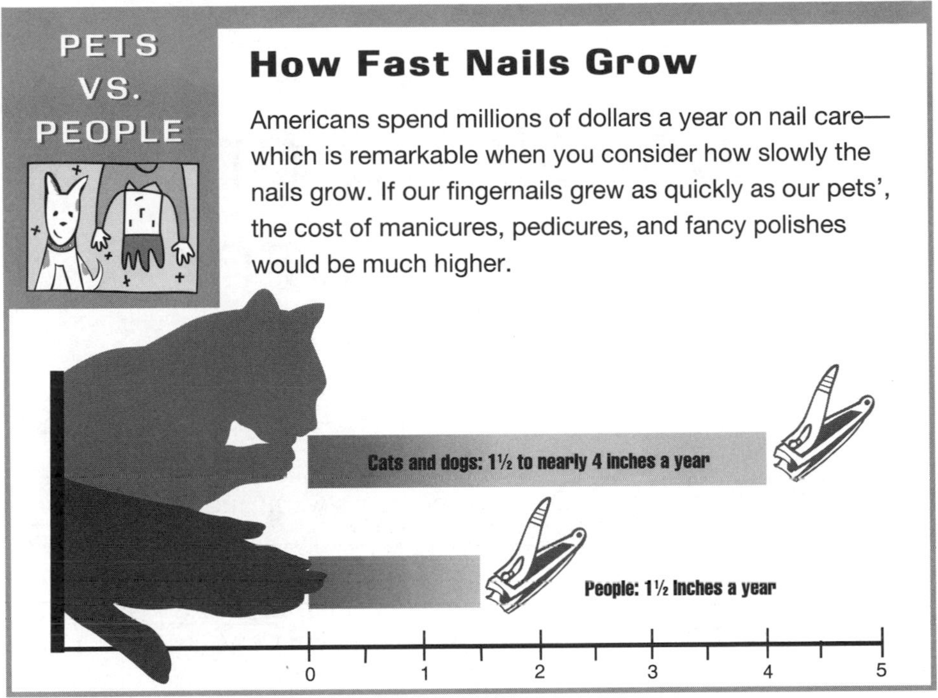

There's no question that declawing is effective. And for people who have tried everything else and are out of patience (and out of furniture), it's a kinder alternative to putting their cats up for adoption, says Dr. Schoen.

Some veterinarians are a bit squeamish about doing the procedure because of the slight risk that's involved in any surgery and because declawing may reduce a cat's natural ability to climb and defend herself.

In any event, declawing usually isn't necessary because there are easier ways to prevent damage—by giving cats quality scratching posts, for example, or by keeping the claws clipped, says Dr. Schoen. Another possibility is apply plastic claw caps, such as Soft Paws, he says. These are temporary caps that fit over the claws and keep the sharp tips covered. The caps aren't available in pet stores, but you can find them on the Internet.

CHAPTER 71

Sneaking onto Furniture

The next time your pet leaps up next to you on the couch, think twice about his intentions. Quality time may be part of it, but mainly he's taking over some of the real estate that you take for granted—a spot that's warm and soft and provides a great view of the room.

"Try sitting on the floor and compare that to getting on a couch or a bed. It's obviously less comfortable," says Nicholas Dodman, B.V.M.S. (a British equivalent of D.V.M.), professor of behavioral pharmacology and director of the behavior clinic at Tufts University School of Veterinary Medicine in North Grafton, Massachusetts, and author of *Dogs Behaving Badly* and *The Cat Who Cried for Help*.

Grabbing the best seat in the house isn't entirely about comfort. Dogs and cats have different reasons for getting off the floor and onto the sofa, and their reasons aren't the same as people's. Ultimately, it's about feeling good, emotionally as well as physically.

Safety First

Despite their speed and impressive fighting abilities, cats are still small animals. In their distant ancestral pasts, cats discovered that climbing high was the best way to avoid becoming lunch for larger, more aggressive animals. "For a cat, higher is safer," says Dr. Dodman. "When they encounter a dog they're not quite sure of, for example, they'll often choose to get to a high place, just as a cat who's outside will go up a tree."

Because of this instinct to go higher, cats feel more relaxed on the couch than on the floor, and the top of a bookcase may be even better. They don't do it because they're frightened, necessarily. It's just their way of feeling comfortable in their surroundings.

There's another reason cats prefer being off the floor and on the furniture. Just as a hunter will scramble to the top of a ridge to take a look around, cats climb on furniture to give themselves a bird's-eye view of what's going on beneath them. As hunters themselves, they take advantage of elevation to spot potential prey.

KING OF THE HILL

When two or more dogs get together, there are usually a few tense moments as they establish their respective positions in the canine scheme of things. Bigger dogs generally have more status than smaller ones, and they aren't at all shy about using their size to get what they want. Essentially, stature is status. A dog who's trying to assert his superiority over another dog will stand close and stretch his body upward, making himself look bigger. Getting on furniture, of course, makes dogs look larger still.

"Even though the primary reason for getting onto furniture may be its comfort value, dogs who are up high feel as though they're in control of everything beneath them," says Dr. Dodman.

It's not all about elevation, however. Dogs recognize that people are the dominant members in the family. People sit on sofas and lie on beds. Dogs want some of that same status for themselves, so they clamber up next to you. It's their way of saying, "We may not be equal, but we're close—and hey, this cushion feels pretty good."

A PLACE TO FEEL SECURE

The main reason pets are attracted to furniture has nothing to do with instincts, hunting, or status. They do it because they love us—or at least they love our smells. Dogs and cats take a lot of comfort from familiar smells, especially the smells of their owners. The carpet may be thick pile and made from wool, but unless it's imbued with human scents, the pets in the family won't love it.

Furniture is another story. That's where we spend most of our time, and dogs and cats know this instantly just from the smells we leave behind. For dogs especially, who tend to get nervous

WHAT'S MY PET SAYING?

Behavior
Grumbling in Bed

What It Means
"Hey, I'm Trying to Sleep"

Whether you have a tiny Pekingese who curls into a tight ball at the foot of the bed or a strapping Labrador who likes to spread out, you've probably heard a low-pitched, barely audible *grrr* as you shift your feet or pull away some covers. It's not a growl, exactly, more like a grumble, and it sounds as though your pet is having a bad dream.

"He's not having a bad dream," says Nicholas Dodman, B.V.M.S. (a British equivalent of D.V.M.), professor of behavioral pharmacology and director of the behavior clinic at Tufts University School of Veterinary Medicine in North Grafton, Massachusetts, and author of *Dogs Behaving Badly* and *The Cat Who Cried for Help*. "He's telling you 'Lie still and shut up because I'm trying to get to sleep.'"

For dogs, sleeping in the bed is the pinnacle of social success. It means they're high off the ground where lowlier pets prowl. It means they're sleeping right beside the people, which means they have status and standing. Sometimes this goes to their heads. That grumbly growl isn't as innocent as it sounds. It's your dog's way of telling you that he expects certain courtesies, and if you're going to dare to disturb his sleep, he's going to warn you not to do it again.

when they're alone, getting on the furniture allows them to bask in human scents, which they find very comforting, says Wayne Hunthausen, D.V.M., an animal-behavior consultant in Westwood, Kansas, and coauthor of *Handbook of Behaviour Problems of the Dog and Cat*.

Hard to Stop

Even if you don't mind the thousands of tiny, impossible-to-vacuum pet hairs on your favorite fabrics, pets who make themselves at home on the furniture can be a bother in other ways. They take up space. They lose their toys between the cushions. And they have a way of getting resentful when people assert their natural rights and try to push them off.

It's almost impossible to keep cats off furniture, if only because they're harder to train than dogs. But most dogs don't mind sleeping elsewhere—not that they won't get a little sneaky, especially during their adolescent years, says Amy Ammen, a trainer in Milwaukee and author of *Training in No Time*.

These early explorations don't have to turn into lifetime habits, Dr. Hunthausen adds. "Right from the beginning, you have to have rules," he says. "So don't hold your puppy in your lap when you're on the couch. Play with him on the floor instead."

Once dogs get a taste of the good life, however, they're extremely loathe to give it up. It's not that they don't know the rules. They do. That's why they may not climb up on the couch next to you, but instead will stealthily make their moves once you've gone to bed.

It's very hard to teach dogs not to do things when you aren't around to catch them doing them. You'll have to find other ways to let them know you're watching even when you're not there.

Make couches less comfortable. Probably the easiest way to discourage dogs from climbing on furniture is to pile it high with things dogs don't like. Plastic coat hangers are good because they're too uncomfortable to lie on, and they make a horrific clatter when dogs try to shove them aside, Ammen says.

Dogs aren't stupid, of course. A pile of coat hangers may keep them off the couch one day, but the minute you put them back in the closet, your dog will climb right back up. The only way this trick will work is if you keep it up for a few weeks. If every time your dog goes exploring, he finds the same clattery business, eventually he'll forget that the couch was ever an option. Once that happens, you can put the hangers away, and there's a good chance he'll never try it again.

Buzz them off. Making surfaces uncomfortable with things like plastic coat hangers and aluminum foil will deter many pets, but others are so attracted to furniture that they'll put up with a little discomfort in order to stake their claims. If you find yourself forced to choose between your pet's habits and an expensive piece of furniture, you may want to invest in a Scat Mat, says Benjamin Hart, D.V.M., Ph.D., professor of physiology and behavior at the University of California, Davis, School of Veterinary Medicine and author of *The Perfect Puppy: How to Choose Your Dog by Its Behavior*. Available in pet supply stores and catalogs, this is a small mat that gives a mild electrical shock when pets come into contact with it. The shock isn't harmful, but it's a creepy sensation, and dogs and cats will give it a wide berth once they've been buzzed a few times.

"For pets who are easily intimidated, a Scat Mat might be a little too intense," says Dr. Hart. "You might try a motion-sensor alarm, sold as a home-security device. These alarms can be set to go off when pets jump on the furniture. The loud sound may be enough to drive them away."

CHAPTER 72

Sniffing

Since dogs smell so many things and they smell them so clearly, it makes sense that they want to use their sniffing skills all the time. "Smell is the primary way that dogs get information about the world," says Ken Nagler, a trainer in Beltsville, Maryland.

It's pretty amazing what they can pick up. A dog can sniff a windowpane, for example, and catch the scent of a fingerprint that was deposited weeks before. She may be able to tell if it's your fingerprint or someone else's. Some experts speculate that she might even be able to tell if the fingerprint came from someone who was happy, angry, or sad.

Sniffing is a marvelous gift for pets, but it can be a nuisance for people. Dogs—and, to a lesser extent, cats—aren't content to put their noses only in patches of grass or against outstretched hands. They want to smell *everything*, including things and places you'd just as soon they left alone.

In Another World

Dogs' obsessions for scents often become an issue when you take them for walks. It's no fun getting yanked across the sidewalk because your dog feels compelled to lunge after every scent that gets her attention. Her nose gets so busy that she forgets she's supposed to be listening to you. "If she's really into a scent, a dog literally goes deaf," says Nagler. "You can yell at her all day, and she won't hear you."

"Dogs have a real thing for crotches," adds Joanne Hibbs, D.V.M., a veterinarian in Knoxville, Tennessee. "It's a natural habit, but it sure feels awfully rude."

Dogs simply don't have the zones of privacy that people do. And crotches are filled with scents that they find intriguing—so they shove their noses right in. They're trying to be friendly. It's a way of saying, "I want to get to know you."

Crotch sniffing isn't motivated only by the quest for scents. Dogs have learned from experience that it's a great way to get their heads rubbed. "When a dog sticks her nose in your privates, you drop your hand instinctively, just to protect yourself," says Dr. Hibbs. Once your hand is at head level, the natural next step is to pet her. "She gets a big reward," she says.

Cats can detect many of the same scents dogs do, but they're much more circumspect, Dr. Hibbs adds. For one thing, they can't reach the same places. And when they do come in to sniff, they do it gently. They don't shove hard, strong, cold noses into private places.

A Time to Sniff

You can't expect pets to ignore the gift that nature gave them. You would never ask someone to stop seeing, and you can't expect dogs to stop sniffing. What you can do, however, is fulfill their daily sniff quota in such a way that the people in their lives get a little peace.

Set aside sniff time. Dogs who have been cooped up all day are going to be eager to fill their noses with exciting smells when you take them out. Your walks will go much more smoothly if you let them run around in the yard for a few minutes before you take to the streets. "Let your dog have a little free time," says Nagler. Give her a chance to sniff and explore. This will take the edge off her excitement. Once she has filled her nose with scents, she'll be less frantic when she's on the leash, he explains.

Feed the other senses. Dogs who are determined to sniff are all but oblivious to the person at the other end of the leash. The only way you're going to make any progress on walks is to keep your dog's attention focused on you. This means that you have to make yourself more interesting than all those scents that are clamoring for her attention. Nagler recommends putting a few dog snacks in your pocket before you set out. When her nose starts to drift, twitch her collar with the leash and say, "Watch me!" When she looks at you, give her one of the treats. The smell of food in your pockets will become much more intriguing than the miscellaneous smells on the ground, and she'll be strongly motivated to keep up with you.

Protect your privates. Dogs should never be allowed to bury their noses in people's crotches. This type of greeting may be ac-

MESSAGES AND MEANINGS

Anything for a Laugh

Despite her name, Princess, a beautiful Great Pyrenees, had none of the aloofness of the aristocracy. Quite the opposite. She loved getting personal with people. Her approach wasn't subtle: She'd simply shove her nose into unguarded crotches.

"I always kept her on a short lead and watched her closely," says Barb Bowes of Point Pleasant Beach, New Jersey. "She knew better, but she wasn't reliable." On the show circuit, an owner's reputation hinges on her dog's behavior in and out of the ring. For the most part, Princess behaved impeccably. But one day, her nosy good nature got the best of her.

Barb and Princess were standing near the shoeshine area, where an industrious young woman was hard at work, her mind on her job and her rear in the air. Barb turned away to greet a friend and absentmindedly loosened her grip on the leash. Princess, who had been eyeing the shoeshine girl with great interest, saw her moment. She instantly lunged across the corridor and gleefully pushed her large, moist nose where it wasn't meant to go.

"The poor woman leaped about 4 feet into the air," says Barb, who remembers turning beet red as she apologized for Princess's impertinent behavior.

The shoeshine girl recovered in a moment, but the laughter spread. Doors flew open as people left the showring to check out the disturbance. Within minutes, everyone knew what Princess had done. "Afterward, everywhere we went, people would say, 'Oh, there's the Goose,'" Barb says.

Princess thoroughly enjoyed the attention—and what she clearly thought had been a very clever joke. "She looked at the woman and smiled. Her whole face scrunched up, her eyes closed, and she just beamed," says Barb. For Princess, it turned out, the entertainment value was worth a lot more than just a quick sniff.

ceptable among dogs, but it's not among people. Dr. Hibbs recommends raising a knee every time your dog goes in for a sniff. You don't want to bash her, but you do want to block the sniff before it gets under way. This sends an unmistakable message that attention and head rubbing aren't going to be forthcoming. Most dogs will then start looking for other ways to get attention, she explains.

Don't capitulate. It's almost an instinct to reach down and pet dogs who are persistently nosing for attention. That physical contact is what keeps them coming back. "Petting encourages them and guarantees that they'll chase crotches forever," says Dr. Hibbs.

Reduce their reach. Since dogs do most of their crotch sniffing when they're meeting someone new, Nagler recommends teaching them a new style of greeting. When people come over to your house, or when your dog is meeting people in public, have her sit right away. Your dog is still going to angle her nose forward, but she won't have the mobility to actually put it where she shouldn't. If you do this every time your dog meets someone, she'll realize that she only gets attention when she's sitting and people come to her.

CHAPTER 73

Spraying and Marking

Dogs have a way of turning even short walks into time-consuming marathons, especially when they insist on pausing at every tree, bush, and light pole to empty their bladders a teaspoonful at a time.

Why the amazing interest in all things upright? People aren't aware of it, but these spots—along with just about every patch of grass and spot of dirt—are like community bulletin boards for dogs. They're crammed with interesting olfactory information about all the other pets in the neighborhood.

"When a dog lifts his leg against a tree, he's not just relieving himself," says Liz Palika, a trainer in Oceanside, California. "He's also marking the tree with his scent, leaving his calling card for every dog who passes by after him."

Cats do things a little differently. Unlike dogs, who urinate and post a notice in one efficient motion, cats keep these activities separate. In fact, cats go to great lengths to conceal their personal scents by burying urine and stools. Occasionally, however, cats—typically unneutered toms—decide to leave their calling cards, too, either by leaving stools unburied or by backing up against a wall or other vertical surface and unleashing a powerful jet of urine in a diagonal, upward sweep.

No one would complain too much if cats and dogs did their marking outside. But sometimes they bring this habit indoors or right around the house and begin marking decks, porches, doors, and garage doors. Cat urine is especially pungent, and the stench—produced by an odorific soup of chemical compounds, including uric acid and pheromones—can linger for weeks.

A CHEMICAL MESSAGE

Humans can't appreciate the complex messages encoded in urine—not only because the smell overpowers our patience but also because we're oblivious to what our pets are trying to say. Their urine is rife with meanings. "They can tell if it was left by a male or a female, whether the animal is sexually mature or altered, whether he's young or old, and if he's healthy or sick," says Bonnie Beaver, D.V.M., a board-certified veterinary behaviorist, certified applied animal behaviorist, professor of animal behavior at Texas A&M University College of Veterinary Medicine in College Station, and author of *Feline Behavior: A Guide for Veterinarians*.

Nearly all male dogs mark and nearly all cats occasionally spray as long as they're mature and haven't been neutered, says Larry Lachman, Ph.D., an animal-behavior consultant based in Carmel, California, and author of *Dogs on the Couch* and *Cats on the Counter*. They don't do it to be malicious, and it doesn't mean they're angry. Here's what marking and spraying usually mean.

"This is mine." Just as people surround their homes with tight little fences, dogs and cats surround their territory—which can be as small as a patio or as expansive as several city blocks—with their personal scents. It's essentially canine and feline graffiti, says Palika. It proclaims to the world, "I was here; this is mine."

"I'm sexy." Female cats will occasionally spray, but it's mainly a guy thing spurred by the hormone testosterone, which impels them to proclaim their sexual availability, Dr. Lachman says. Neutered pets are less likely to spray because they produce very little of this hormone, and there's little point in advertising for a mate when they aren't able to reproduce. Still, they do it often enough that it's among the most common reasons people take their cats—females as well as males—to the veterinarian.

"Let me tell you about myself." Dogs and cats use urine as a scent marker that announces their presence to the world. Pets who smell their markings know all about them. And they know about all the other pets in the neighborhood by smelling their marks. A quick sniff tells them things like "You're that

Smells Like Home

Cats produce natural chemicals called pheromones that have been shown to stimulate a variety of moods. A group of researchers has claimed to have identified and isolated a particular fraction of the facial pheromones, called F3's, which are the scents that cats spread when they rub their cheeks against furniture or your legs. F3 is the chemical scent that gives cats the message, "This is home."

Since cats don't urine-mark in their favorite places, this particular pheromone scent might be helpful for keeping them from marking. A product called Feliway, available from veterinarians, contains a synthetic form of F3. A preliminary study has shown that about 65 percent of cats who were urinating or spraying indoors stopped completely after the areas were treated with the scent. And about 30 percent did it much less often.

The scent, which is applied as a spray, stays active for about 30 days. Even when it wears off, however, cats are unlikely to resume spraying because they probably spent many of the 30 days laying down their own scent—their way of matching one comforting smell with another.

poodle who lives around the corner, and you walk by this very tree every day just a few minutes before me."

WHO'S ON TOP?

The messages in scent markings are just as complex and interesting to dogs and cats as the stories in newspapers are to us. But it's not a perfect method of communicating. For one thing, the scents fade over time, which means they have to be reapplied often. In addition, there's an amazing amount of competition out there. As soon as a dog or cat leaves his mark, another pet is sure to come along and "erase" it.

"One way cats and dogs establish dominance over their rivals is by covering the rival's scent mark with their own," Palika says. This perpetual urge for one-upmanship has some comical consequences. Like most males, dogs aren't above a bit of exaggeration when it comes to size. "The higher up their mark is, the bigger and badder they'll seem to the competition," Palika explains. A big dog who's secure in his superiority will casually lift his leg without a second thought. Smaller dogs like Chihuahuas have more to prove. They've been seen arching their backs and stretching their legs to the limit in order to mark a higher spot.

In addition to spraying, cats do their share of sniffing and marking, too. But because they're rarely on leashes, we don't see them doing it, says Dr. Beaver. "Their noses are much closer to the ground so they don't have to hunch over to sniff the scent like most dogs," she adds.

Removing the Mark

It's not always easy to tell if spots in the house are the result of inevitable accidents or if they're deliberate marks. "Once housebroken, dogs will rarely revert unless it's an emergency," says Sara Etkin, a dog trainer and animal-behavior consultant in New Rochelle, New York. "A puddle near the back door is probably an accident. A puddle on a sofa cushion may mean something else entirely."

Cats are more deliberate and fastidious than dogs in their bathroom habits, so true accidents are rare. The occasional damp spot on a carpet or in a pile of laundry may mean that the litter box was full and uninviting. And dampness on the walls is certainly no accident. Cats usually spray vertical surfaces, such as chairs, walls, doorjambs, and windowsills.

Marking and spraying are often difficult to stop because it's a natural behavior, no matter how unnatural it smells to you. And once dogs and cats start doing it, they're often reluctant to give it up. Here are a few tips you may want to try.

Get rid of the smell. Because dogs and cats like to freshen up their scents from time to time, and because their sense of smell is so much better than ours, a perfunctory cleaning isn't going to help. Any lingering scent—and for pets, just a few scent molecules are as strong as cheap cologne—is sure to draw them back. Palika recommends scouring the area with a liberal shot of white vinegar. More effective are enzymatic cleaners, available at pet supply stores, which break down odor-producing compounds in urine.

One cleaner to avoid is ammonia. "Ammonia is a chief ingre-

A Nervous Habit

Cats tend to do the most spraying when there's a lot of stress in their lives. It's hard to imagine, especially when you watch them snoozing on the carpet all day, but cats have anxieties that people are hardly aware of. Here are some examples.

Unwanted animal visitors. Even cats who spend their time indoors are aware of what's going on outside. Visits to the yard by neighboring cats and dogs can trigger a rash of spraying, often around doors or windows. Some people resort to fencing their yards. Others keep the blinds drawn or rearrange furniture to keep their cats away from the windows and the troublesome sights outside.

Unwanted human visitors. It's not the epitome of hospitality, but cats sometimes feel threatened when visitors come to *their* house. A guest who gets up one morning and discovers his shoes have been anointed is probably the target of a little power play.

Noise and disruption. "Cats are very sensitive to changes in their physical environments," says Larry Lachman, Ph.D., an animal-behavior consultant based in Carmel, California, and author of *Dogs on the Couch* and *Cats on the Counter*. "Getting new furniture or having a team of construction workers knocking down walls to remodel the kitchen are very stressful events for a cat and may cause him to spray indoors."

Overcrowding. "Show me a house with six or more cats, and I'll show you a house where at least one of those cats is spraying," says Sara Etkin, a dog trainer and animal-behavior consultant in New Rochelle, New York.

dient in urine, and the smell can actually encourage your pet to cover the scent with his own," Palika explains.

Keep them moving. It's normal for dogs to mark trees and bushes, and except for the inconvenience of prolonged walks, most people don't mind when they do it. For dogs with somewhat dominant personalities, however, the freedom to mark at will can make them more dominant and harder to handle. "Being allowed to mark the entire neighborhood as his home turf can make a dog even more aggressive," Dr. Lachman says. He recommends picking one or two spots along your usual route where you'll always let your dog stop. The rest of the time, keep him moving, he says.

Tell them what you think. Pets are eager to please their people, which means they'll often quit doing things that they know make you unhappy. It doesn't do any good to punish them after they've made a mess, says Dr. Beaver. Dogs and cats have short memories and probably won't know what you're mad about, even if you lead them to the spot. In addition, punishment will make them anxious and afraid—emotions that cause some pets to spray or mark in the first place.

"The best way to help pets understand that you don't like their behavior is to catch them in the act and firmly tell them no," says Wayne Hunthausen, D.V.M., an animal-behavior consultant in Westwood, Kansas, and coauthor of *Handbook of Behaviour Problems of the Dog and Cat*. If that doesn't get your pet's attention and make him stop what he's doing, clap your hands or slap your palm against a table. As soon as he looks at you, put him to work. Tell him to lie down or sit for a while. For cats, hold them for a minute. You don't want to praise or reward them, but it's important not to let them finish what they started, he says. Dogs and cats are creatures of habit, and the longer you can keep them from marking, the less likely they'll be to continue doing it.

Incidentally, don't let your cat see you when you're making a sharp sound. "Cats don't recover from verbal discipline as quickly as dogs," Dr. Hunthausen says. You don't want your cat to blame you for scaring him.

Take away the opportunity. Since cats often spray in the same place, you can discourage them by rearranging the room so that the area is out of reach—behind a piece of furniture, for example. Better yet, Palika recommends putting your cat's food and water bowls near where he's spraying. Cats are very reluctant to make messes in places they associate with food and good times.

"If your dog is prone to marking indoors, don't allow him free run of the house when you're not around to watch him," suggests Palika. "Confine him to a kennel or crate when you're gone, and keep him in the same room with you at other times." Dogs who aren't used to crates don't always take to them easily, she adds, so talk to your veterinarian before shutting your dog in for the first time.

Work on their confidence. It's not much of an issue with cats, but dogs who are perpetually marking are sometimes anxious because they feel they have a lot to prove. Marking tells the world that they're bigger than they feel inside. Urinating in the house—

or, better yet, in your favorite chair—serves another purpose as well. Dogs are comforted by their own scents, especially when they mingle their scents with yours.

Probably the best way to help dogs feel more secure is to regularly practice obedience lessons, Dr. Lachman says. It's a bit of a bother, but practicing simple commands like "sit," "stay," and "down" gives dogs a sense of mission and purpose. They'll feel calmer generally and will be less likely to depend on marking to establish their place in the world, he explains.

Ask about neutering. Pets who are spayed or neutered—veterinarians usually recommend doing it when they're less than 6 months old—are much less likely to spray or mark than their intact counterparts, says Dr. Hunthausen. Neutering is more effective in cats than in dogs. About 50 percent of male dogs will continue to mark after neutering, says Dr. Hunthausen. Only about 10 percent of male cats, however, will continue to mark and spray after neutering.

CHAPTER 74

Throwing Up

People don't vomit very often, and when they do, it's usually because they're sick. Dogs and cats throw up all the time, whether they're sick or not. And they barely seem to notice. They heave a few times, deposit their breakfast on the living room carpet, then go back to whatever they were doing before.

Veterinarians get lots of calls from people who are worried because their pets are throwing up. Their advice is simple: As long as the vomiting is sporadic and the pets seem chipper and don't have diarrhea, it probably doesn't mean much of anything. They're just doing what dogs and cats have always done, says Holly Cheever, D.V.M., a veterinarian in Guilderland, New York.

Ancient dogs used to feed their puppies by regurgitating recently consumed game. Cats threw up when they swallowed gamey bits that they couldn't digest, such as fur. And today, dogs and cats throw up for some of the same reasons people do: They ate tainted food, they're feeling stressed, or they ate too much too fast, says Dr. Cheever.

I'll Eat Anything

Cats are more particular about food than dogs are, and for the most part, they don't have as many opportunities to indulge in mousy snacks as their ancestors did. Vomiting is rarely a sign that they ate something bad. Dogs, on the other hand, eat like pigs. They're neither finicky nor restrained, which helps explain how they've managed to survive for all these thousands of years. While cats can achieve astonishing bursts of speed, dogs are relative slowpokes. Their prey was often faster than they were, which meant their success at hunting wasn't very impressive. Since they couldn't grab an elk burger whenever their stomachs started grumbling, they learned to compensate by eating anything and everything.

MESSAGES AND MEANINGS

Time Change Troubles

Springer spaniels are intelligent, cheerful dogs who enjoy making their owners happy. But they also tend to be excitable, which is why Michael Lopez of Troy, New York, wasn't surprised when Jasper did things like drag toilet paper around the house or even hide the mail.

But he wasn't prepared for the vomiting. Jasper had always had a hardy constitution, but suddenly he was upchucking nearly every day. "Sometimes he did it right when I got home after work," Michael says.

At first he thought it was a temporary problem, but the days turned into weeks, and Jasper kept throwing up. Michael's veterinarian said that Jasper was fine physically, and she asked Michael if anything had changed recently. At first Michael said no, but then he thought of something. The problem started right about when daylight saving time ended. He began to wonder if Jasper, who had always been high-strung, was fretful because he thought his owner wasn't coming home until much later, when, in fact, it was the same time as always, only darker.

With this hunch in mind, Michael put it to the test: He came home earlier the following night. Jasper didn't throw up. So he did it again the next night, and the night after that. He occasionally came home at lunch as well. Jasper wagged his tail and ran around each time, but his stomach stayed calm. Which goes to show that the best way to a dog's stomach is through his heart.

"Dogs have no class," says Dr. Cheever. "They will eat anything." And they do. Week-old carrion is just as appetizing as fresh meat—or last night's trash. And if it happens to make them sick, well, they throw up—and eat that as well.

Better Be Quick

It's not only what dogs eat that makes them throw up so readily but also how fast they eat it. Once again, this tendency harkens back to the days when they lived in packs. Dogs who daintily picked at their food didn't get a lot to eat because their greedier packmates would beat them to it. The only dogs who thrived were those who adhered to the gobble-and-swallow school of etiquette. "Their thinking was, 'I have to eat this before someone else comes along,'" says Fred Oehme, D.V.M., Ph.D., professor of toxicology, pathobiology, medicine, and physiology at Kansas State University College of Veterinary Medicine in Manhattan.

With the possible exception of dogs who live in multidog families, the competition for meals is much less intense than it used to be. Yet old habits linger, which is why most dogs bury their faces in their food and leave them there until the bowl is licked clean. It's also why leaving a trash can in the open is an invitation to mayhem.

Dogs tend to be such incorrigible food hounds—and so indifferent to vomiting—that even professional trainers have a hard time teaching them restraint. About all you can do to protect the carpets is make it more difficult for them to scavenge, while at the same time limiting how much they eat at a time.

People customarily feed their dogs once a day because it's convenient and the dogs don't complain. But the hungrier dogs are when breakfast rolls around, the faster they're going to eat. Dr. Cheever recommends feeding them at least twice a day, and three or four times is probably better. You're not increasing the total amount they eat, she adds. You're just spreading out the servings so that they don't overwhelm their stomachs by stuffing it in.

Unlike humans, who can switch easily from Ragu to Prego, dogs are surprisingly sensitive to changes in their diets. Switching to a different brand of food, or even a different flavor of the same brand, will often make them sick for a day or two. Dogs don't need variety in their diets, which is why veterinarians usually recommend giving them the same food all the time. If you do change foods, make the change slowly by mixing in a little bit of the new food with a lot of the old, then adding a greater proportion of the new stuff every day. After about 5 days, they'll be ready to make the change entirely and probably won't get sick—at least, any more than they usually do, says Richard Levine, V.M.D., a veterinarian in Toms River, New Jersey.

ANYTHING TO LOOK GOOD

Since cats aren't as voracious as dogs, and because they're less likely to raid the trash, food usually isn't what makes them sick.

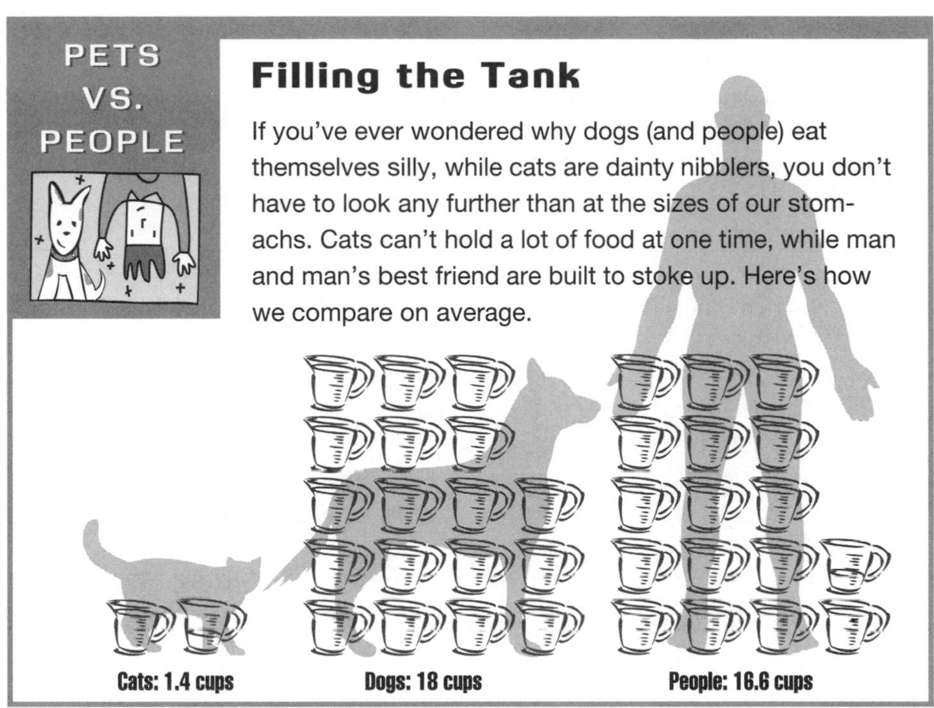

Filling the Tank

If you've ever wondered why dogs (and people) eat themselves silly, while cats are dainty nibblers, you don't have to look any further than at the sizes of our stomachs. Cats can't hold a lot of food at one time, while man and man's best friend are built to stoke up. Here's how we compare on average.

Hair is. It's one of nature's paradoxes that the same urge that accounts for their impeccable appearance is also the urge that makes them throw up. Cats will happily spend hours grooming their coats, and when they've covered every inch, they'll go back and start again. The tough little bristles on their tongues act like miniature hairbrushes, slicking the fur back and removing shed hairs at the same time.

Cats don't swallow all the hair they remove from their coats, but quite a bit of it does go into the stomach. The hairs aren't digested, however. Some pass out of the body in the stools, but large amounts stay in the stomach. As more and more hair accumulates, it begins forming an uncomfortable wad, which cats periodically hack up.

Hair balls are hardly ever a health threat, but they're ugly and messy. And it sometimes seems as though cats only hack them up, noisily, in the middle of the night. To stop the wretched retching, here's what veterinarians recommend.

Switch to a high-fiber food. The indigestible dietary fiber in pet foods accelerates the movement of food—and hair—through the digestive tract. Cats who are hacking up a lot of hair balls will often improve when they switch to a food that's high in dietary fiber—one that contains between 3½ and 10 percent fiber. "I like Vetasyl, which comes as a gelatin capsule filled with powdered fiber," says Jane Brunt, D.V.M., a veterinarian in Towson, Maryland. Available from veterinarians, Vetasyl helps keep the stomach full and calm and helps hair balls move through the system more quickly.

Dab petroleum jelly on the roof of the mouth. Cats don't like the taste, but putting a dab of petroleum jelly on the roof of their mouths every few days will lubricate the digestive tract and help swallowed hairs pass smoothly through, rather than jamming up in the stomach. Putting your finger in a cat's mouth isn't always the safest move, which is why veterinarians sometimes recommend putting the petroleum jelly—or a commercial hair-ball remedy—under the nose. Cats don't like the taste, but they like the sticky sensation even less and will lick it off, says Karen L. Campbell, D.V.M., professor of dermatology and endocrinology at the University of Illinois College of Veterinary Medicine at Urbana-Champaign.

Brush the heck out of them. Cats are always shedding, and brushing them once a day will remove loose hairs before they get swallowed, says J. M. Tibbs, D.V.M., a veterinarian in District Heights, Maryland. You can follow this up by giving them a wipe with a moist washcloth, which will remove even more loose hairs. Even cats who are always hacking hair balls may stop entirely once they're getting the spit-and-polish routine.

CHAPTER 75

Travel Phobia

With plush seats, climate control, and convenient cup holders, today's cars make going for a drive almost as cozy as relaxing at home. Cats, however, have a different perspective. For them, getting in the car is about as relaxing as getting their temperature taken—which is why they often start panting the minute they get in the car. Or they cling to the undersides of the seats while emitting spooky, otherworldly growls. Or paste themselves like Scotch tape against the upholstery, shivering like there's a windchill of 32 below.

Many dogs enjoy going for rides, but cats have a harder time getting used to it, says Melissa R. Shyan, Ph.D., a certified applied animal behaviorist, associate professor of psychology at Butler University in Indianapolis, and president of Companion Animal Problem Solvers.

Cats dislike changes in their routines, and the strangeness of riding in a car may make them extremely stressed. "They often cope by using the undersides of the seats as dens or safety caves," Dr. Shyan says.

Some dogs are equally reluctant to ride, she adds. The motion of the car and the strange environment can make them nervous or even panicky. And many pets get carsick, which makes their feelings of alarm even worse.

What's Driving Them?

Cars are such basic parts of our environment that it's a little hard for us to understand why dogs and cats get so nervous. But look at it from their point of view. They don't go for rides very often. Cars are big and strange. They make odd noises and smell funny, and they take pets to places they would rather not go. "Most people only put their pets in the car to take them to the veterinarian or groomer, which is not what pets think of as a really good time," says Carin Smith, D.V.M., a veterinary consultant in Leavenworth, Washington, and author of *101 Training Tips for Your Cat*. "All animals create routines, and any change from these routines creates stress."

Even when dogs and cats aren't terrified the first time they climb into a car, they often get that way when they realize that this rolling, rocking thing upsets their stomachs. Riding in a car causes imbalances in the inner ear, stimulating the part of the brain that causes nausea. A few experiences with car sickness can make them permanently nervous about traveling. And fear invariably makes their nausea even worse, which is why some pets throw up when they're sitting in a parked car.

A New Way of Thinking

A little bit of travel anxiety isn't a big deal, if only because dogs and cats don't travel very much, and when they do, it's usually for short distances. It's more of a problem when they're going to be logging a lot of miles because you're making a cross-country move, for example, or because you're living in two places and carting them back and forth.

Behaviorists have found that a technique called desensitization, in which pets are gradually exposed to whatever makes them nervous, can reduce and sometimes eliminate travel anxiety. "The key is to move very slowly from one procedure to the next," says Dr. Shyan. Here's how it works.

1. "Begin by sitting in the car once a day with your pet, with the engine off and the windows cracked," says Dr. Shyan. It's fine for dogs to be free in the car when it is not in motion, but cats usually feel more secure when they're in a carrier or crate. (It helps to let cats get used to being in a crate before putting them in a car.) Either way, they aren't going to enjoy this little interlude. Hand-feed your pet his favorite treats as a distraction. He should calm down within a few minutes, and then you can end the session.

Don't stop when they're acting nervous, because this will reinforce their original fears, says Dr. Shyan. Repeat this exercise once or twice a day for several days—or longer if it's taking time for your pet to get used to it. The goal is to get him used to the car before actually going for a drive.

2. The next step is to sit in the car with your pet, this time with the engine running, says Dr. Shyan. Again, give him lots of at-

NAME: Classic

OCCUPATION: Trucker

Sundee Myers hauls cargo all over the southeastern United States in her 70-foot tractor-trailer. As a big-rig driver, she spends a lot of time away from home, and what starts as an afternoon's work has a way of turning into several days on the road. It's a lonely job, fraught with pressure and feelings of isolation—which is why Sundee depends on her copilot, a 2½-year-old German shepherd-beagle mix named Classic.

Classic's job description is a little vague, Sundee admits. "He's pretty darn worthless in the guarding department," she says. "And he won't shift the gears or drop the landing gear of the trailer. But when I'm going to bed in my cab at night and Classic lies down next to me asking for a tummy rub, I feel connected to another soul."

Classic helps in other ways as well. As a self-described workaholic, Sundee has a natural inclination to drive farther and longer than she should. Classic puts the brakes on her ambitions because he needs regular rest stops, whether she does or not. "Even if it's only for 10 minutes at a time, Classic slows me down," Sundee says.

Classic isn't the perfect partner, she adds. He may be a great companion, but he isn't always on his best behavior. "He's eaten seven pairs of my sunglasses," she says. "I can't leave anything out on the dashboard. And he thinks the garbage pail is a really large food bowl."

tention and try to make him feel secure. Once he's acting calm and relaxed, you can shut off the engine and call it a day. Some pets get used to this fairly quickly, while others may need weeks of practice.

3. Go for a short drive—and for some pets, you'll need to make it very short, maybe to the end of the driveway and back. If he doesn't get upset, stop the drive on a good note. The next day, go a little farther. Then stop somewhere and take a break, says Emily Weiss, Ph.D., curator of behavior and research at the Sedgwick County Zoo in Wichita, Kansas. "That gives him an opportunity to have a special time with you. You can talk to him and take him for a short walk."

Desensitization is a very effective process. Some cats will never learn to love the car, but nearly every pet will learn to be a little more comfortable about traveling, says Dr. Shyan. It doesn't always work quickly, however. Some dogs and cats will start getting noticeably more relaxed within a week or two. Others may take months, and some will never get used to it, no matter how much you practice. Pets who don't show progress fairly quickly probably need to see a professional behaviorist, she says.

Fun on Four Wheels

A complete desensitization program is the best approach, but it takes a tremendous amount of time, effort, and dedication. Since most people only take their pets for occasional rides, it's not the kind of energy everyone wants to invest. That's why veterinarians often recommend other, quicker ways to help pets adjust.

Make the car seem like fun. Most dogs and cats associate cars with places and activities they don't like. You can turn this around by only taking them places where they'll have some fun. "If car rides are paired with things that feel good, chances are your dog will gleefully hop into the car with you," Dr. Weiss says.

Of course, while a game of Frisbee is a treat for dogs, it won't make your cat purr with excitement. An alternative is to take your cat with you to the store and slip him a few treats before you run inside, says Dr. Weiss. (Take someone with you so you don't have to leave your pet in the car alone while you go into the store.) Cats who get this feel-good treatment while they're kittens may grow up loving the car.

Drive slower than usual. Treats go a long way, but they won't overcome the discomfort pets feel if they happen to tumble off the seat when you take a hard turn. You have to drive slower than usual and avoid sharp turns or stops—not only for safety's sake but also to prevent car sickness, says Dr. Weiss.

Travel hungry. An empty stomach doesn't make car trips fun, but it will stay calm. "Don't give your pet food or water for about 4 hours before riding in the car," says Dr. Weiss.

If that doesn't help, your veterinarian may recommend giving him medicines for motion sickness, says Dr. Smith.

Keep them anchored. One reason dogs and cats dislike car rides is the feeling of being buffeted back and forth. You may help them feel safer by securing them in a crate or strapping them into a harness designed to work in conjunction with the car's seat belts. Crates are really the best choice, says Dr. Smith. As long as they've had a chance to get used to them, pets like crates because they help them feel safe and enclosed. They're also good for your safety because pets who wander loose in the car have a way of showing up in the worst places—like underneath the brake pedal.

CHAPTER 76

Wool Sucking

The psychoanalyst Sigmund Freud had a theory that most of the things people put in their mouths, like fingernails, toothpicks, or bucketfuls of butter-drenched popcorn, had less to do with satisfying hunger than with satisfying deep urges caused by premature weaning.

Freud didn't talk about feline fixations, but a similar impulse may send some cats in search of sweaters or socks, which they knead, suck, and chew with abandon. Some experts believe that this behavior, called wool sucking, may be a cat's way of returning to the comforts of Mom. But since wool sucking is most common in Asian breeds, such as Siamese, Burmese, and Himalayans, it may be genetic urges rather than longings for their mothers that put their mouths in motion. Dogs will chew just about anything, but they don't focus on fabrics, so wool sucking is mainly a feline problem.

If cats stuck to sucking their fabrics of fancy (they like wool, but anything that has a rough, nubby texture will do), veterinarians wouldn't worry about it. But sucking often turns to chewing, and chewing to swallowing—and the digestive tract isn't designed to handle thick wads of material. And cats who begin with fabrics sometimes graduate to cardboard, shower curtains, or extension cords.

Hidden Needs

Experts have a lot of theories to explain wool sucking, but no one's really sure why cats do it. Vint Virga, D.V.M., a veterinarian at the behavior clinic at Cornell University College of Veterinary Medicine in Ithaca, New York, suspects that the act of chewing releases a chemical in the brain that gives cats feelings of pleasure. Once they receive a few jolts of feel-good chemistry, it may be hard for them to stop. Some cats actually get addicted to chewing, at which point veterinarians sometimes recommend treating them with fluoxetine (Prozac) or other drugs.

The interesting thing is that cats who view fabrics as food items rarely show an interest in other types of chewables. There may be something about the crunch of chewing through fabrics that keeps them satisfied, says Barbara S. Simpson, D.V.M., Ph.D., a board-certified veterinary behaviorist and a certified applied animal behaviorist in Southern Pines, North Carolina. "If all that your cat eats is canned food, he may just miss the crunch of dry food," she says.

Eating fabrics could also be your cat's way of saying that he's missing something in his diet, says Alex Casuccio, D.V.M., a veterinarian in Morgantown, West Virginia. Cats with a thiamin deficiency will sometimes take to chewing fabrics, he explains. Thiamin deficiencies are especially common in cats who eat a lot of tuna, because fish is filled with an enzyme called thiaminase, which destroys thiamin.

Just as humans sometimes eat or chew their fingernails when they're bored, some cats may turn to fabrics as a way of passing the time, says Dr. Simpson. Chewing could also be their way of saying that they're anxious or stressed. They may view a bedspread or pair of socks as a personal security blanket that they can chew on until they feel better.

FABRICS ANONYMOUS

Wool sucking is a little bit like drinking: While some cats are satisfied with the occasional indulgence, others can't leave it alone. Even moderate chewers, once they start the habit, are likely to get more intense about it sooner or later. So it's worth stopping the habit before they get hooked.

Satisfy the craving. Since cats who chew wool are thought to crave crunch, you may be able to break the habit by giving them a crunchy substitute such as lettuce, says John C. Wright, Ph.D., a certified applied animal behaviorist; professor of psychology at Mercer University in Macon, Georgia; and author of *The Dog Who Would Be King* and *Is Your Cat Crazy?* Feeding pets lettuce, carrots, or dry kibble may satisfy their need for an *al dente* diet, making them less likely to go after the bedspread.

Give them a garden of their own. Another way to keep cats out of the closets is to put up a window box filled with catnip or grass. Cats love natural greenery, and the extra dietary fiber may decrease the urge to chew wool. "Cats tend to go through kitty gardens like lawn mowers," Dr. Virga adds. You can buy cat-specific window gardens in pet supply stores and some garden stores.

Keep them busy. People often forget that cats are high-octane animals who evolved as hunters, jumpers, and climbers. They need a lot of exercise, and if they don't get it, they look for other ways to blow off steam, such as gnawing their way through the wedding linens, says Kimberly Barry, Ph.D., a certified applied animal behaviorist in Austin, Texas.

Most cats don't go for walks the way dogs do, but they love to sprint—after a dragged piece of string, for example, or the light from a laser pointer. (Laser light is intense, so keep it away from their eyes.) And nearly every cat loves batting balled-up pieces of paper. You can make the crumpled paper even more exciting by hiding some food inside, says Dr. Barry.

Make life predictable. Humans adapt quickly to change, but cats don't, says Linda Goodloe, Ph.D., a certified applied animal behaviorist in New York City. Even small changes in routines, like moving the litter box to another room, can make cats anxious, and anxious cats sometimes start chewing.

You can't put your life on hold just to keep your cat happy, but you can try to minimize the types of disruptions that make them upset. The two things that cats care most about, apart from the house they live in, are regular meals and a clean litter box, Dr. Goodloe says. Keeping these two things predictable will help them weather most other changes that come their way.

Distract them with something better. You can train cats to leave your belongings alone as long as you distract them right away, says Dr. Goodloe. Whenever you see your cat chewing, clap your hands or make some other noise to get his attention. Then flick a ball or a length of string across his peripheral vision—an area cats closely watch because that's where mice and other prey appear. Once he starts playing, give him a reward—either a food treat or simply more play. He'll learn that he'll have more fun playing with you than chewing in private, she explains.

Change the taste. Cats don't chew fabrics because they taste good, but they may quit chewing them when they taste bad. Pet supply stores sell products such as Grannick's Bitter Apple, which you can spray on areas your cat is chewing. The repellents are fabric-safe and have tastes cats dislike. You can't coat your entire wardrobe, but most cats have a few favorite items that they return to again and again. Treating these items may convince your cat that *all* fabrics now have that yucky taste.

Another taste technique is to pour rubbing alcohol or Bitter Apple, along with a splash of your usual cologne, on a piece of clothing or linen that your cat has already destroyed. Then lightly scent other articles of clothing, using the cologne alone. The idea is for your cat to chew on his usual item and get a bad taste along with a noseful of cologne. He may connect the two and assume that anything that smells like cologne is not for him, says Dr. Wright.

CHAPTER 77

Yawning

We all have relatives like Uncle Peter. When he comes to visit, he settles into the cozy armchair in front of the fireplace and starts talking: about the 6 months he spent in France in World War II or the time he almost sold a Cadillac to Elvis Presley. By the time he gets to the one about the great little restaurant in Cincinnati, you can barely keep your eyes open. Even your dog is yawning.

Even though it's tempting, you really can't blame Uncle Peter for your dog's sleepy appearance. People yawn when they're bored, but your dog is probably communicating a different message—like the fact that the armchair is her favorite perch, and she's expressing her dissatisfaction at having to lie on the floor.

All animals, from alligators to zebras, let loose with long, languorous gapes from time to time. "Basically, if it has a backbone, it yawns," says Robert Provine, Ph.D., professor of psychology and neuroscience at the University of Maryland, Baltimore County, in Baltimore. Yawning is universal, but the reasons for doing it vary. Elephants, for example, only yawn when they're in the mood to charge—an important piece of trivia for your next safari. People yawn when they're sleepy or bored, or because the person next to them just did it. Dogs and cats don't yawn as often as people. When they do, they probably have a specific reason.

They need to signal distress. You'll often see dogs yawn when they're worried or anxious. In the waiting rooms of vets' offices, for example, you'll often hear a chorus of yawns.

They want to relax. Yawning briefly lowers blood pressure, and dogs may yawn because it helps them stay calm. In fact, one dog can relax just by watching another dog yawn, says Lisa Smith, a pet-behavior consultant and veterinary hospital manager in Severn, Maryland. "When a mother dog wants her puppies to settle down, she'll yawn at them. They quickly get the message and quiet down."

PETS VS. PEOPLE

How Often We Yawn

We think our lives are exciting, but the frequency of our yawns tells a different story. Researchers have counted how often dogs, cats, and people yawn in different situations. Here's what they found.

College students (taking calculus):
23.6 yawns an hour

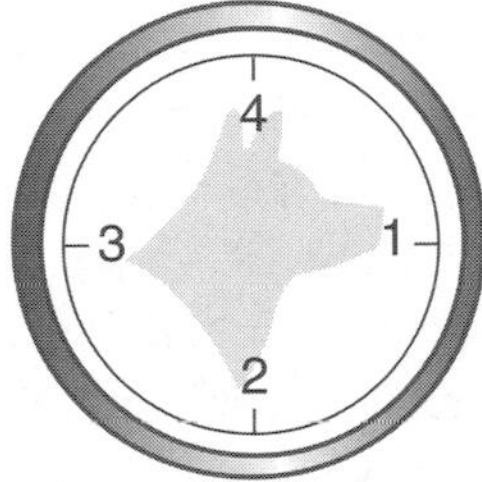

Dogs in a vet's office:
4 yawns an hour

Cats in a vet's office:
0 yawns an hour

Yawning feels good. When pets wake up, they invariably stretch and yawn, for no other reason than it feels good to do it, says David McMillan, a trainer and owner of Worldwide Movie Animals in Canyon Country, California.

With all this yawning going on, you would think that scientists would be able to explain why it happens, but they really don't know yet. All they're sure of is that yawns start somewhere inside the brain and appear to signal an emotional transition. "When the body is calming down from stress, waking up from sleep, or getting itself ready for action, a yawn often results," Dr. Provine says.

YAWNING BACK

Since cats sleep 12 or more hours a day, they spend a lot of time in transition between being awake and being asleep. They yawn quite a bit, but it doesn't mean very much. But dogs who yawn a lot are telling you something. Very rarely, yawning can indicate physical problems, such as an infected tooth or a problem in the brain. More often, it means that your dog is ner-

MESSAGES AND MEANINGS

How Aslan Got in Line

Aslan is the Turkish word for "lion," and Janice Frasche's 125-pound Anatolian shepherd looks as fierce as his name. But beneath his rusty red coat and black mask is the heart of a pussycat, says Janice, who for more than 6 years has literally leaned on Aslan for support.

Janice, who lives in Carmichael, California, has a neurological disease, and Aslan helps her walk and keep her balance when all the muscles in her body seem to be working against her. Without Aslan, she says, it would be almost impossible to get out and about. So when Aslan started yawning, Janice got a little worried.

Aslan had always been a slow-moving, laid-back dog, and the yawns didn't seem unusual at first. As time went by, however, Janice noticed he was yawning more and more frequently, especially when they went shopping. More specifically, he would yawn three or four times before he approached the checkout line, but not at all when they were in the frozen-food or canned-goods section.

Janice was sufficiently concerned that she made an appointment with a consultant specializing in pet behavior—who instantly knew what was going on.

Aslan didn't like the checkout line, she told Janice, because carts are jammed together, space is tight, and Aslan was sensing that Janice felt pressured and uncomfortable. He was experiencing a lot of stress, and yawning was his way of coping.

Once Janice understood why Aslan was yawning, the remedy was obvious. She made sure to position him out of the way of customers (and their noisy carts) in the checkout line. That way, he wouldn't be standing amidst all the bustling. She also learned that one of the cashiers kept a box of dog cookies by the register, and that, she figured, was a soothing payback for all of Aslan's hard work.

vous and would appreciate some reassurance—or at least a calming yawn in return.

Yawn like Mom used to. For dogs as well as people, the memory of Mom gives a lot of comfort. You can rekindle this memory in dogs by giving a big yawn whenever they're feeling stressed—after a confrontation with another dog, for example, or in the waiting room at the vet's. "It's best to start doing it when your dog is still young, before she forgets her native dog language," Smith adds.

Recognize the signs. Since dogs can't say when they're upset or why they're worried, you can use your knowledge of yawns to tell when something's up. Even minor issues can cause a spate of yawning, says Kay Cox, a pet counselor in Gilbert, Arizona. Suppose, for example, you usually forbid your dog to get on the couch, but in a moment of weakness, you ask her up. She'd love to get on the couch, but the idea of breaking the rules may make her uneasy, and she'll yawn to express her discomfort. Or maybe the cat just jumped on the kitchen table, and your dog expects you to shoo her away—and yawns when you don't. "She's probably saying, 'Someone needs to be in control here, and I sure hope it's not me,'" Cox says.

Give a little comfort. Dogs handle stress as well (or, in some cases, as badly) as people do, and yawning may be your cue that they need some relief—a walk around the block or a quick tummy rub, says Arthur Young, D.V.M., a veterinarian in Stuart, Florida.

Index

UNDERSCORED PAGE REFERENCES INDICATE BOXED TEXT.
BOLDFACE PAGE REFERENCES INDICATE ILLUSTRATIONS.

A

Actors, animal, 106, 204, 218, 365
Addictions, food, 334, 335–36
Adolph's Meat Tenderizer, to prevent dung eating, 296
Adoption, of older pets, 189–95
Affection
  breed differences and, 172
  expressions of, 168–70 (*see also* Petting)
    cooing, 169
    differences between pets and people, 169
    eye contact, 16, 146
    hugs, 137, 169
    praise, 170–71
    rambunctiousness, 170
    spoiling, 169
    touching, 39–40
  using, 170–73
    for behavior modification, 170–71
Afghan, 13
Aftershave scent, effect of, 162
Aggression. *See also* Dominance
  communicating, by
    ear position, 68, 70, **71**, 240
    eye contact, 7, 15, 16, 62–63, 126, 144
    eye position and movement, 61–62, **62**, **63**, 64
    facial expressions, 76–77, **76**
    posture, **98**, 99–100, 240, 264, 405, **405**
    staring, 64, 240
    tail position and movement, 84, **85**, **87**, 88, **89**, 91, 240, 264
    vocalizations, 105, 107–8
    whisker position and movement, 57, **57**, 58
  display of
    in animal shelter, 192
    by biting, 263–66
    in play situations, 227, 228, 234
    toward other dogs, 239
    on walks, 239
  gender and, 181
  playful, 403–4
  reasons for, 237–39
    food protection, 266
    instinct, 237–38
    jealousy, 327, 369
    testosterone effects, 238, 241
  redirected, 239
  signs of, 240
  toward people
    attacking feet or hands, 243–47
    in play situations, 234
    preventing, 240–42
    reasons for, 237–39
Airedale, 178, 196
Akita, 178
Alcohol
  colognes and aftershaves containing, 162
  using, to prevent
    chewing and digging, 164
    scratching, 166
    urination, inappropriate, 167
    wool sucking, 457
Allergies, rubbing as sign of, 421
Alpha dog, 230. *See also* Dominance
Aluminum foil, as deterrent, 431
Amaryllis, toxicity of, 303
American Eskimo dog, 250
American shorthair, 188
Ammonia, avoiding as cleaner, 167, 440–41
Anal glands, humping and, 364
Anatolian shepherd, 460

Anger. *See* Aggression
Anger at pets, controlling, 314, 357
Animal shelters. *See* Older pets
Antifreeze poisoning, 46
Anxiety. *See also* Fears and phobias; Separation anxiety
  behavior associated with
    barking, 258
    chewing, 273–74
    crowding, 279
    digging, 282, 284
    house soiling, 355
    licking, 394
    spraying and marking, 441, 442
    wool sucking, 455, 456
  reducing, 258
Appetite. *See also* Eating; Food
  finicky eating, 331–37
  influences on, 42
    boredom, 46
    exercise, 336
    illness, 42
    smell, 34
    stress, 42
Approach, to pets, types of
  body language, 127–28, **128**, 131, 245
  hand position and movement, 154–56
Aromatherapy, 31
Attack posture, 99–100
Attacks
  on feet or hands
    preventing, 246–47
    reasons for, 243–46
  on paper
    preventing, 249–51
    reasons for, 248–49
Attention
  getting, by using name, 203
  negative, 281
  redirecting, 398
  using, to prevent
    attacking paper, 250
    crowding, 281
    licking, compulsive, 397, 398
Attention-seeking behavior
  awakening early, 299
  barking, 105, 254–56
  begging, 259–62
  crotch sniffing, 435–36
  crowding, 281
  dung eating, 294, 295–96
  jealousy, 368–70
  jumping up, 376, 377–78
  meowing, 252–56, 253
  nursing, 387
  rubbing, 420
  yowling, 360
Australian shepherd, 412
Aversion therapy, to prevent rolling in smelly things, 416–17
Awakening, early-morning
  preventing, 298–99
  reasons for, 297–98

B

Bags, as cat toys, 187
Balance
  tail and, 82
  vestibular apparatus for, 72
Barking
  as behavior problem, 6, 253–58
  breed differences and, 178, 180, 231
  development of, 104
  at mail carriers, 325
  reasons for, 6, 252–55
    attention seeking, 105, 254–55
    boredom, 254, 256
    communication, 104
    excitement, 147
    fear, 253
    separation anxiety, 258, 311
    submissiveness, 105
    territorial defense, 105, 254
    training, as watchdog, 252–3
  stopping, 255–58
    with "down" command, 209
    with "quiet" command, 214
  at strangers, 321, 323
  types of, 105
Basenji, 109
Basset hound, 178

Bathroom cleaner scent, as deterrent, 166
Beagle
chasing cats by, 268
chewing by, 275
digging by, 282
smell, sense of, 231
Bearded collie, 23
Beds
hogging, by pets
preventing, 350–51
reasons for, 348–50
for pets, 350
Begging
finicky eating and, 331, 335
preventing, 260–62
reasons for, 260, 261
Behavior modification tools. *See also specific behaviors*
affection, 170–71
scent, 162–64, 166–67
smell, sense of, 32–33
Behavior problems. *See specific problems*
Bells, for cat collars, 383
Belly-up posture, meaning of, 94, **95**, 128–29
Bending over dogs, dominance and, 245
Bite a Bone dog toy, 223
Biting
by cats
while being petted, 157
hands or feet, 243–47
by kittens, 263, 265
preventing, 265, 266
teeth chattering and, 113
warning signs of, 264
by dogs
chin, 180
hands or feet, 244, 246–47
movement and, 132
during play, 228, 263, 265
preventing, 265–66
by puppies, 180, 263, 265, 328, 330
warning signs of, 264
inhibiting
in older pets, 244
in puppies, 263, 328, 330
Bitter Apple, to prevent
chewing, 164, 276
digging, 164
wool sucking, 456
Bladder infections, inappropriate urination and, 354
Blinking, meaning of, 62
Bloat, plant eating and, 303
Bloodhound
ear shape of, 67
exercise needs of, 178
howling by, 361
tracking by, 163
Body language, of people, 123–24
extrasensory abilities of pets and, 48
eye contact, 140–46
facial expressions
eyebrows, raised, 126
smiling, 126–27
staring, 124–26
yawning, 126
hand movements
by children, 158
when greeting pets, 153–56
in love and play, 156–58
height
of children, 139
downsizing tips, 135–39
pet's response to, 16–19
posture
for approaching pets, 127–28, **128**, 131
belly up, 128–29, **129**
bending, 129, **135**
crouching, 129–30, **130**, 154
vocal communication and, 118–19
Body language, of pets, 5
ear position and movement, 65–72
eye position and movement, 59–64
facial expressions, 73–81
posture, 91–100
as signal of intention to fight, 328–29
tail position and movement, 82–90
whisker position and movement, 55–58

Body temperature, digging to regulate, 283, 286
Bonding, touch as means of, 38
Bones, burying, 287
Border collie
- attacking hands or feet by, 243
- attack posture of, **247**
- chasing cats by, 269
- exercise needs of, 178, 404
- eye contact by, 12
- intelligence of, 180

Boredom, behavior associated with
- attacking paper, 249
- awakening early, 298
- barking, 254, 256
- chewing, 273
- digging, 285, 286–88
- dung eating, 294, 296
- eating objects, 307, 308–9
- finicky eating, 332
- food refusal, 46
- howling, 361
- wool sucking, 455
- yowling, 359

Bottom wagging, meaning of, 94, **95**
Bowing
- by dogs, 75–76, **75**, 92–93, **95**, 261, 329
- by people, 130–31, **130**, 158

Boxer, 60
Bubble wrap, as deterrent, 424
Bulldog, 60
Bull mastiff, 268
Burmese cat, 454
Burns, preventing, 36
Burying bones, 287
Buster Cube dog toy, 287, 406
"Bye-bye" command, 220–21

C

Calling pets
- "come" command, 212–13
- posture for, 129–30, **130**
- with rustling sounds, 151
- tone of voice and, 151
- voice modulation and, 149–50

Calmness
- crate training and, 406
- modeling, 319
- raising a dog with, 314–15
- rewarding, 318–19
- signals of
  - blinking, 62
  - standing still, 327
  - yawning, 143, 145, 458

Calories, recommended daily, 343, 344
Carpet runners, plastic, as deterrent, 375
Cars, fear of riding in, 449–53
Car sickness, 449–50
Carts, dog, for exercise, 389, 392
Cataracts, aging and, 19
Cat breeds, differences in
- affection, desire for, 172
- temperament, 187–88
- vision, 14
- vocalization, 111, 149, 359
- wool sucking, 454

Catch, playing, 224–26
Cat Dancer toy, 223
Caterwauls, 114
Catnip
- rolling in, 301
- toys, 34, 246, 301, 382

Chasing
- cats
  - breed differences and, 268–69
  - preventing, 271
  - reasons for, 267–69
- by owners, 295–6
- people, as game, 227
- tail, 83

Chewing. *See also* Wool sucking
- jaw strength and, 277
- by older pets, 190
- preventing, 274–77
- by puppies, 177, 183, 273
- reasons for, 273–74
  - habit, 274, 276
  - natural urge, 272–73
  - separation anxiety, 310, 311
- teething period and, 182

Chihuahua
  assertiveness of, 227
  choosing, 191
  energy level of, 178
  height of, 134
  licking by, 396
  urine marking by, 440
Children
  dog breed choice and, 180
  fast movements by, 322
  hand movements by, 158
  height of, 139
  households with, percentage of, 7
  tone of voice and, 150
Chin biting, by dogs, 180
Choke collars, 391
Choosing pets
  kittens, 184–88
  older pets, 189–95
  puppies, 177–83
Chow Chow, 7, 172, 178
Citronella, as deterrent, 416
Claws, cat
  caps for, 386, 427
  declawing, 426–27
  maintenance, by scratching, 423
  rate of growth, 427
  trimming, 385–86
Clinging. *See* Crowding
Collars
  for aversion therapy, 416–17
  for cats, bells on, 383
  choke, 391
  head halters, 391
  pinch, 391
Collie
  ear shape of, 66
  energy level of, 403
  hearing acuity of, 67, 317
  vocalization by, 109
Cologne
  alcohol in, 162
  to prevent wool sucking, 4
Color vision, 13, 14, 15
"Come" command
  for cats, 219
  for dogs, 212–13
Commands. *See also* Training
  for cats
    "come," 219
    "freeze," 219–20
    "sit," 217–19
    "wave," 220–21
  for dogs
    "come, 212–13
    "dead," 207–8, **208**
    "down," 208–9, **209**
    "get your toy," 215
    "give," 410, 411
    "go to your place," 214
    "leave it," 271
    "out," 210–12, **212**
    "quiet," 214, 361
    "sit," 155, 210
    "stay," 117, 210, 312–14
    "take it nice," 209–10
    "watch me," 142
  signals for, hand and verbal combined, 117, 119, 142
  teaching, 200–205
    how pets learn, 201
    how to give commands, 203–5
    rewards and, 201–3
Communication. *See also* Body language; Training; Vocal communication
  breed differences and, 7
  misunderstandings, 2, 3, 6
Companions, for dogs, 362
Competition
  jealousy and, 368–71
  for meals, 446
  during play, 226–28
Confusion, communicating, by facial expression, **78**, 78–79
Consistency, importance of, 234, 262
Contentment, communicating, by
  eye position and movement, 62
  facial expressions, 80–81, **80**, **81**
  posture, 94–96, 97
  purring, 113
  whisker position, 56
Cooing, as sign of affection, 169
Coprophagia. *See* Dung eating
Cornish rex cat, 111

- Counterconditioning therapy, for fear of strangers, 323–25
- Counters, jumping on. *See* Jumping on counters
- Crates, using for
  - car travel, 450, 453
  - training for
    - calmness, 406
    - fear of being alone, 314
    - house soiling, 353
    - marking, 442
- Crazy Circle cat toy, 223
- Cropping ears, 67
- Crotch sniffing, 433–36, 435
- Crouching
  - to prevent jumping up, 378
  - when calling pets, 129–30, **130**
  - when greeting pets, 154
  - when interacting with pets, 136, 245
- Crowding
  - preventing, 280–81
  - reasons for, 278–80
- Crown of thorns, toxicity of, 303
- Curiosity
  - facial expression and, 78
  - in kittens, 185
  - whisker position and movement and, 57, **57**
- Customs dogs, 341
- Cyanide, in fruit pits, 304
- Cycads, toxicity of, 304

D

- Dachshund, 282
- Daffodils, toxicity of, 304
- Dalmatian, 196
- Dead, playing, 207–8, **208**
- Deafness, eye color and, 60
- Declawing, 426–27
- Defensive behavior
  - defensive threat posture, 99–100
  - facial expression, 77–78, **77**
- Denning instinct, 314, 344
- Departure, of owner
  - affection, expressing, 173
  - managing, 407
  - pets' anxiety about, reducing, 258, 312
  - rituals with, 312
  - separation anxiety and, 311–14
- Desensitization
  - to departure rituals, 312
  - principles of, 318
  - using, to manage
    - fear of noises, 318
    - fear of strangers, 323–25
    - travel phobia, 450–52
- Destructive behavior
  - chewing, 272–77
  - digging, 282–88
  - house soiling, 352–57
  - jumping on counters, 372
  - scratching furniture, 422–27
  - separation anxiety and, 310–11
- Devon rex cat, 188
- Diarrhea, from diet change, 46
- Dieffenbachia, toxicity of, 304
- Diet, changing, 46, 446
- Digestive enzymes, to prevent dung eating, 296
- Digging
  - breed differences and, 282, 283
  - preventing, 284–88
  - reasons for, 8, 282–84
- Distraction, to prevent
  - house soiling, 357
  - wool sucking, 456
  - yowling, 360
- Doberman, 47, 67
  - ears of, 67
  - as watchdog, 180
- Dog breeds
  - choosing a puppy and, 178–80
  - differences in
    - affection, desire for, 172
    - chasing cats, 268–69
    - communication, 7
    - digging, 282, 283
    - ear shape, 66–67
    - eyes, 60
    - facial expressiveness, 75
    - fear of noises, 317
    - hearing, 21, 317

height, 134
howling, 358
interaction with people, 231
language comprehension, 115–16
leash pulling, 392
older pets and, 191
tail position and movement, 84–86, 90
vision, 13, 14
vocalization, 109, 137, 358
water consumption, 291
rescue programs for, 193
Dominance. *See also* Leadership, by owner
behavior associated with
aggression toward people, 238, 241
bed hogging, 349, 350
fighting to establish social status, 327, 330
food stealing, 338, 340, 352
getting onto furniture, 429
humping, 363–67
jealousy, 370–71
jumping up, 376
marking, 439–40
possessiveness, 409, 413
rubbing, 420
breed differences and, 178–80
communicating, by
crowding, 280
eye contact, 15, 140, 143–44
hand placement, 153–54
height, 134, 136–37
posture, 96–99, **98**, 129, 134, **135**, 136
tail position and movement, 84, **85**, 88, **89**, 90
eating order and, 340
play situations and, 226–28
puppies and, 182
Doorbell, barking and, 324–25
"Down" command, 208–9, **209**
Drinking from toilet
preventing, 290–92
reasons for, 289–90
Dumbcane, toxicity of, 303
Dung eating
preventing, 294–95
reasons for, 293–94

E

Ears. *See also* Hearing
communicating with
by cats, 70–72, **71**
by dogs, 67–70, **69**
cropping, 67
evolution and, 65, 66–67
mobility of, 22, 65, 71–72
vestibular apparatus, balance and, 72
Earthquakes, detected by pets, 35, 51
Easter lily, toxicity of, 304
Eating. *See also* Appetite; Food
behavior associated with
begging, 259–62, 261, 331, 335
dung eating, 293–96
fighting over food, 327–28
finicky eating, 34, 331–37
grass and plant eating, 300–305
swallowing or eating objects, 306–9
vomiting, 444–46
style
of cats, 332, 334
of dogs, 331–32
Egypt, ancient, cats in, 1, 47, 59
Elbows, bent, meaning of, 329
Endorphins, chewing and, 307
Energy level, breed differences and, 178
English ivy, toxicity of, 303
Enzymatic cleaners, to eliminate odors, 440
Epilepsy. *See* Seizures, predicted by dogs
Eukanuba pet foods, 334
Evolution. *See also* Instincts
dog's ears and, 65, 66–67
hearing and, 22–23
Excitement, excessive, 403–7
behavior associated with
aggression, playful, 403–4
barking, 147

Excitement, excessive (*cont.*)
  behavior associated with (*cont.*)
    jumping up, 379
    leash pulling, 390
    separation anxiety, 311, 407
    tail chasing, 83
  managing, with
    exercise, 404–6
    owner's behavior, 407
    security, providing, 407
  reasons for
    in cats, 403–4
    in dogs, 404
Excrement, eating. *See* Dung eating
Exercise
  appetite stimulated by, 336
  lack of
    chewing and, 277
    digging and, 285
  needs for, 232–33
  using, to prevent
    attacking feet or hands, 246
    digging, 286
    overexcitement, 404
    separation anxiety, 314
    wool sucking, 456
Extrasensory abilities, of pets, 47–52
Eyebrows, raised, meaning of, 126
Eye contact, 124–26. *See also* Eyes, communicating with; Staring
  breaking for time-out, 144–45
  choosing puppies by, 182
  communicating with pet and, 119
  emotions conveyed by, 146
  encouraging in pets, 142
  interpretation of
    by cats, 16, 140–41
    by dogs, 7, 15–16, 140, 245
  using for
    discipline, **256**
    giving commands, 205
    herding dogs, 12, 145
    training, 142, 143, 144
Eyes. *See also* Vision
  breed differences and, 60
  cataracts, 19
  color of, deafness and, 60
  communicating with, 14–19, 59–64
    blinking, 62
    direction of gaze, 62–64, **63**
    eye contact (*see* Eye contact)
    by herding dogs, 12
    openness, 61–62, **62**
    staring (*see* Staring)
  cornea, shape of, 11
  hypnotism and, 61
  nuclear sclerosis of the lenses, 19
  protection of, by whiskers, 37, 55, 56
  pupils, dilated, 5, 14, 60–62, **62**, 78
  reflections from, 14
  tapetum fibrosum, 14

F

Fabric chewing. *See* Wool sucking
Face licking, 170, 171
Face-to-face interaction, 136, 138–39, 378
Facial expressions
  of people
    crouching to exhibit, 135–36
    eyebrows, raised, 126
    smiling, 126–27
    staring, 124–26
    yawning, 126
  of pets (*See also* Eyes, communicating with)
    aggressive, 76–77, **76**
    in art, 4
    confused, 78–79, **78**
    defensive, 77–78, **77**
    happy, **79**, 80–81, **81**
    playful, 75–76, **75**
    sad, 79–80, **79**
    smiling, 4, 74
Fear
  behavior associated with
    barking, 253
    crowding, 279
    hiding, 316, 317, 321, 323
  communicating, by
    ear position, 68, **69**, 70, **71**
    eye position, 60
    facial expression, 77–78
    scent, 160
    tail position, 88, **89**

whisker position, 57, **57**
yowling, 360
Fears and phobias
men, fear of, 322, 323, 324
noises, fear of, 316–20
separation anxiety, 310–15
strangers, fear of
managing, 322–25
reasons for, 322
travel phobia
managing, 450–53
reasons for, 449–50
Feces, eating. *See* Dung eating
Feeders, automatic, 299
Feeding, 446. *See also* Appetite, influences on
Feet
owner's, attacking, 243–47
dog's, handling, as temperament test, 182
Feliway, to prevent marking, 439
Feral cats, facial espression of, 185
Fertilizers, toxicity of, 304
Fetching, 181
Fiber
using, to prevent
dung eating, 296
hair balls, 447–48
plant eating, 305
wool sucking, 456
sources of
human foods, 305, 337
pet foods, 301, 343
Field of view, 13, 14, 16
Fighting, with other pets. *See also* Aggression
gender and, 329
preventing, 329–30
reasons for, 327–28
signaling intention of, 328–29
Finicky eating
example of, 333
reasons for, 34, 332–34
Fireworks, fear of. *See* Noise, fear of
Flehmen, by cats, 30
Fluoxetine. *See* Prozac
Food. *See also* Appetite; Eating
amounts, 344
behavior associated with
addictions, 334, 335–36
aggression, 266
begging, 259–62, 261, 331, 335
fighting, 327–28
stealing (*see* Food stealing)
vomiting, 446
calorie requirements, 343, 344
canned versus dry, 344
human, 335, 337
refusal, reasons for, 42
as reward, 201–3
spoilage, 44, 334
stomach capacity and, 447
treats (*see* Treats)
warming, 34, 46, 336
Food stealing
example of, 339
as nutritional signal, 343–44
preventing, 340–43
reasons for, 338–40
For-Bid, to prevent dung eating, 296
"Freeze" command, 218–19
Frisbees, 18, 223, 225–26, 412
Furniture
scratching
preventing, 424–27
reasons for, 422–24
sneaking onto
preventing, 430–32
reasons for, 428–30

G

Games, 18, 224–28. *See also* Play; Toys
Gentle Leader halter, 391
German shepherd
aggressive reputation of, 238
ear shape of, 66
eye contact and, 7
intelligence of, 180
police use of, 257
training, 138
Giant schnauzer, 392
"Give" command, 410, 411
Golden retriever, 50, 211, 308, 408
affection, desire for, 172
possessiveness of, 410

Golden retriever (*cont.*)
 barking by, 252
 ear shape of, 67
 eye contact and, 7
 as guide dog, 125
"Go to your place" command, 214
Grannick's Bitter Apple. *See* Bitter Apple
Grass and plant eating
 preventing, 302–5
 reasons for, 300–302
Great Dane, 67
Great Pyrenees, 23, 435
Greeting pets
 crouching and, 154
 eye contact and, 143
 face-to-face, 138–39
 hand movements and, 153–56
 height adjustment and, 129–30, 138–39
 nose greetings, 154–55
 with pencil, 155
 sniffing and, 32
 tips for, 245
Greyhound
 adopting, 189, 193
 bed hogging by, 348
 breed rescue for, 193
 chase instinct of, 231, 268
 tail position of, 90
Grinning, meaning of, 74, 76
Grooming
 by cats, 394–95, 395, 447
 by dogs, 395
Growling
 by cats, 114, 148
 meaning of, 107–8, 147, 388, 430
  dominance signal, 350
  possessiveness, 409, 410
 rewarding, 330
Guard hairs, purpose of, 37
Guide dogs, 125

H

Habits, undesirable
 bed hogging, 350–51
 chewing, 274, 276
 licking, 398
 marking, 442
 nighttime activity, 400
 rubbing, 421
 scratching furniture, 424
 wool sucking, 454–55
Hackles, raised, meaning of, 27, 98, 99, 134, 240
Hair. *See also* Whiskers
 brushing, to prevent hair balls, 448
 raised, 27, 98, 99, 134, 240
 touch and, 37
Hair balls, preventing, with
 brushing, 447
 fiber, 305, 447–48
 petroleum jelly, 447
Hand movements
 by children, 158
 greeting pets and, 153–56, 245
 in love and play, 156–58
Hands, attacking
 preventing, 246–47
 reasons for, 243–46
Hand signals, for training
 "sit" command, 155
 with verbal commands, 117, 119, 142
 visibility of, 16, 137
 "watch me" command, **142**
Happiness, communicating, by
 ear position, 68, **69**, 70, **71**
 eye position, 62
 facial expressions, 80–81, **80**, **81**
 posture, 94–96
 purring, 113
 tail position and movement, 84, **85**, 86, **87**, 88, **89**
Head butting, meaning of, 96, 129, 138, 154, 211
Head cocking, meaning of, 202
Head halters, 391
Hearing
 acuity of, 21, 49–51, 148, 317
 breed differences and, 21
 communication and, 26–27 (*see also* Vocal communication)
 deafness, eye color and, 60
 distance and, 22, 23

ear mobility and, 22, 71–72
ear shape and, 67
evolution of, 22–23
frequency range of, 317, 319
head cocking and, 202
learning and, 24–25
mechanism of, 24
visual impairment and, 19–20
Hearing dogs, 378
Height, 133–39
altering, for communication, 134–35
breed differences and, 134
of children, 139
dominance and, 134, 136–37
downsizing tips for, 135–39
giving commands and, 205
Herding dogs
attacking hands or feet by, 243–44
attack posture of, **247**
barking by, 231
chasing cats by, 269
eyes, communicating with, 12
hearing acuity of, 317
tail movement, decreased and, 86
vision of, 13
vocalization by, 109
Hiding
in dangerous places, 347
food, 336
reasons for, 345–47
fear of noises, 316, 317
fear of strangers, 321, 323
in small spaces, 346, 347
Hiding places, creating, 317
High places, cats and, 72, 138, 349
Himalayan cat, 111, 454
Hissing, meaning of, 114, 247
Holly, toxicity of, 304
Homecoming, jumping up and, 376, 379
Hormones
behavior associated with
food stealing, 344
humping, 364, 366
yowling, 359, 360
testosterone, 238, 241, 438
Hot-sauce, to prevent
chewing, 276
food stealing, 342
Hounds
barking by, 231
ear shape of, 67
howling by, 358
Houseplants, eating. *See* Grass and plant eating
House soiling
preventing, 355–57
reasons for, 353–56
separation anxiety and, 311
Howling
breed differences and, 358
reasons for, 6, 358–59
cat mating, 111
long-distance communication, 104, 108
separation anxiety, 108–9
stopping, 361–62
Hugs, as signs of affection, 137, 169
Humping
preventing, 364–67
reasons for, 363–64
training and, 365
Hunger
behavior associated with
dung eating, 294, 296
nighttime activity, 100, 102
speed of eating and, 146
Hunting
by cats
encouraging, 402
hearing and, 23, 27
killing mice and, 380–83
vision and, 13–14
by dogs
hearing and, 23
tail movement and, 84–86
vision and, 11
Husky
assertiveness of, 178
digging by, 283
ear shape of, 66
howling by, 358
leash pulling by, 392
licking by, 396

Hydrogen peroxide, to induce vomiting, 303
Hyperactivity, separation anxiety and, 311
Hypnotism, 61

I

Ice cubes, to encourage water bowl use, 291–92
Illness. *See* Medical conditions
Insects, detected by cats, 27
Instincts, behavioral, 8
- awakening early, 297, 298
- chasing cats, 267, 271
- climbing, 428–29
- denning, 314, 344
- digging, 8
- humping, 363
- hunting, 404
- killing mice, 380–81, 383
- kneading, 385
- licking, 394

Intelligence, breed differences and, 180
Intestinal parasites. *See* Parasites, intestinal
Introduction, of new animals
- cat's reaction to, 166
- jealousy and, 369, 371

Intruder, detected by dog, 26–27
Irish setter, 268, 313
Irish wolfhound, 134
Italian greyhound, 90

J

Jack Russell terrier, 178
Jacobson's organ, smell and, 30, 165
Javanese cat, 111
Jaw strength, of dogs, 277
Jealousy
- aggression and, 327, 369
- managing, 369–71
- reasons for, 368–67

Jonquil, toxicity of, 303
Jumping abilities, 374
Jumping on counters
- discouraging, with
  - alternatives, 373
  - carpet runners, plastic, 375
  - noise, 234, 373–74
  - spraying with air, 375
  - spraying with water, 16, 374–75
  - tape, double-sided, 375
  - traps, **373**, 373–74
  - visual cues, 375
- yelling at cats for, 16, 234, 372–73

Jumping up
- excitement and, 379
- by hearing dogs, 378
- preventing, with
  - crouching, 378
  - ignoring, 377
  - knee raising, 377
- reasons for
  - dominance, 170
  - face-to-face interaction, 136, 138–39

K

Kelpie, 25
Kidney stones, 354
Killing mice
- benefits of, 381–82
- display of kills, 382
- managing, 383
- reasons for, 380–82

Kittens
- biting by, 263, 265
- calorie requirements of, 344
- choosing, 184–88
  - breeds and temperament of, 187–88
  - personality of, testing for, 185–86
- kneading and nursing by, 384
- new, introducing, 369
- weaning age of, 385

Kneading
- managing, with
  - claw caps, 386
  - medication, 385
  - redirection, 386–87
  - trimming claws, 385–86
- reasons for, 384–85

Kong dog toy, 223, 309, 361

L

Labrador retriever
- affection, desire for, 172
- possessiveness of, 410
- chasing cats by, 267, 268
- chewing by, 272
- digging by, 285
- ear shape of, 67
- eating objects by, 306
- energy level of, 177, 178, 406
- licking by, 396
- smell, sense of, 231
- temperament of, 191
- as working dog, 179, 341, 365

Language, pets' comprehension of, 2, 115–18
- breed differences and, 115–16
- consonants and, 26
- name recognition and, 117–18, 197–99, 203
- voice tone and, 116, 118
- word associations and, 116

Laser pointer, as cat toy, 456
Lavender oil, soothing effect of, 31
Lawn chemicals, toxicity of, 304
Leadership, by owners
- aggression and, 241
- tips for, 232–34
- what cats want, 230–31
- what dogs want, 229–30

Learning, rate of, 213
Leash pulling, 388–93
- breed differences and, 392
- example of, 389
- preventing, with
  - collars, 391
  - leash training, 390–93
- reasons for, 388–90

"Leave it" command, 271
Lhasa apso, 178
Licking
- breed differences and, 396
- compulsive, managing, 396–98
- faces, 170, 171
- reasons for
  - by cats, 394–95, 395, 397
  - by dogs, 395, 395–96, 397

Listening
- rewarding, 151
- teaching pets, 119

Litter boxes
- accessibility of, 354
- cleanliness of, 353, 354, 440
- dogs eating from, 295
- multiple, 354
- smells and, 166–67
- urinating outside of, 356

Loneliness, behavior associated with
- finicky eating, 332
- getting onto furniture, 430
- howling, 359, 361–62
- nighttime activity, 400
- separation anxiety (*see* Separation anxiety)

M

Mail carrier, barking at, 325
Malamute
- assertiveness of, 178
- digging by, 283
- howling by, 358
- leash pulling by, 392
- tail position of, 90

Maltese, 333
Marking
- meaning of, 438
- of owners, 165, 350
- preventing, with
  - cleaning, 166–67, 440–41
  - communication, 442
  - confinement, 442
  - Feliway, 439
  - neutering, 165, 443
  - training, 443
- reasons for, 439–40, 441
- territorial, by
  - rubbing, 165, 418–19, 419, 420, 423
  - scratching, 166, 422–23
  - urinating, 165–66, 356, 437–41

Massage, therapeutic, 38
Mastiff, 178
Mating, vocalizations for, 111, 114
Medical conditions, behavior associated with
  finicky eating, 334
  food refusal, 42
  food stealing, 343–44
  house soiling, 354
  humping, 364
  licking, decrease in, 394
  nighttime activity, 400, 401
  wool sucking, 455
  yawning, 459
  yowling, 360
Men, fear of, 322, 323, 324
Meowing
  meaning of, 111–12, 148
  as problem behavior
    preventing, 255–58
    reasons for, 253, 254–55
    waking owner by, 298, 299
  silent, 114
  types of, 112
Mice, cats and
  detecting, 27, 151
  killing, 380–83
Miscommunication, 2, 3, 6
Mistletoe, toxicity of, 304
Mooching, 233, 259, 261. *See also* Begging
Motion-sensor alarm, as deterrent, 432
Mousetrap trainers, as deterrent, 373, 374
Mouthing, 311. *See also* Biting; Chewing
Movement
  attack induced by, 132, 244, 266
  children and, 132, 158, 322
  of hands, 152–58
  importance, to pets, 131–32
  of tail, communicating with
    by cats, 86, **87**
    by dogs, 84–86, **85**, 91, 94

N

Name
  choosing, 196–98
  learning, by pet, 198–99
  popularity of, 198
  using, for commands, 203
Nausea. *See* Car sickness; Vomiting
Negative attention, 281
Neoteny, dog behavior and, 222
Neutering, to prevent
  aggression toward people, 241
  digging, 288
  fighting, 330
  house soiling, 356
  humping, 366
  nighttime activity, 400
  spraying and marking, 443
  yowling, 360
New pets, introducing, 369, 371
Nighttime activity
  managing, 401–2
  reasons for, 399–400
Noise
  behavior associated with
    barking and meowing, 253–58
    howling and yowling, 358–62
  fear of
    breed differences and, 317
    managing, 317–20
  using, to prevent
    anxiety, 258
    attacking feet or hands, 246
    awakening early, 299
    jumping on counters, 234, 373–74
    nighttime activity, 402
Nose. *See also* Smell, sense of
  structure of, 29–30
  wet, reasons for, 30
Nose greeting, 154
Nuclear sclerosis, aging and, 19
Nursing
  reasons for, 384
  preventing, with
    distraction, 87
    mother substitute, 386–87
    Prozac, 385
  weaning age and, 385, 387
Nutro pet foods, 344

O

Obedience training. *See also* Training
marking, preventing with, 443
"stay" command, 117
vocal communication, 117
Odors. *See also* Scent
eliminating
skunk, 415
urine, 440
litter box, 166, 354
Oils
for aromatherapy, 31
to prevent scratching, 424–25
Old English sheepdog, 60, 75, 178
Older pets
advantages of, 189–90
breed differences and, 191
breed rescue for, 193
dogs versus cats, 190–91
health of, 193–94
homecoming for, 194–95
personality of, testing for, 192
Olfaction. *See* Smell, sense of
Organ of Corti, hearing and, 24
"Out" command, 210–12, **212**
Overexcitement, 403–7
managing, with
exercise, 404–6
owner's behavior, 407
security, providing, 407
reasons for
by cats, 403–4
by dogs, 311, 404
Oxalic acid crystals, in plant leaves, 304

P

Pacinian corpuscles, touch and, 36
Pain, vocalizations with
by cats, 113
by dogs, 107
Paper, attacking, 248–51
Paper bags, as cat toys, 187
Parasites, intestinal
dung eating and, 293
food stealing and, 344
grass eating, as remedy for, 301–2
Pekingese
energy level of, 178
grooming needs of, 191
Perfumes
cats and, 34
visually impaired pet, guiding and, 20
Persian cat, 172, 187
Personality, predicting
for kittens, 185–86
for puppies, 180–83
Pesticides
in catnip, 301
on lawns, 304
Petroleum jelly, to prevent hair balls, 448
Petting, 158
areas of pet's body, acceptability of, 156, 172–73
attacks during, 157
cats, 38–39, 58
dogs, 39–40
people's response to, 168
limitations on, 157
Pheromones, in cat urine, 437, 439
Philodendrons, toxicity of, 304
Phobias. *See* Fears and phobias
Picking up
to facilitate communication, 137–38
as greeting, 153
to test kitten personality, 186
Pig ears, for dogs, 275
Pinch collars, 391
Pit bull terrier, 270, 388
Plants, eating. *See* Grass and plant eating
Play
biting during, 263, 265
as cause of overexcitement, 405
choosing pet and
kitten, 186
puppy, 181, 183
communicating, by
belly-up posture, **128**, 129
bowing, 92–93, **95**
hand movements, 157–58
play bow, 130–31, **130**

Play (*cont.*)
communicating, by (*cont.*)
posture, 92–94, **95**
pouncing, 93–94, **95**
competitive, 226–28
as exercise (*see* Exercise)
facial expressions in, 75–76, **75**
getting into shape for, 225–26
inappropriate
aggression, 241
attacking feet or hands, 243–47
need for, 232–33
to prevent thunderstorm anxiety, 319–20
safe, 224–26
signals for
"get your toy" command, 215
posture, 92–94, **95**
tail wagging, 84–94
toys (*see* Toys)
Play bow, <u>268</u>
by dogs, 75–76, **75**, 92–93, **95**, <u>268</u>, 329
by people, 130–31, **130**, 158
Playful aggression, 403–4
Poinsettias, toxicity of, 304
Poisons
antifreeze, 46
plants, 303–4
Pomeranian
barking by, 109
energy level of, 178
hearing of, 21
Poodle
howling by, 358
intelligence of, 180
temperament of, 227
Positive reinforcement, training and, 201
Possessiveness, with toys
preventing, 410–13
reasons for
by cats, 409–10
by dogs, 408–9
Posture, 91–92. *See also* Body language
to communicate
attack intentions, 99–100
contentment, 94–96, <u>97</u>
dominance, 96–99, **98**
happiness, 94–96
play signals, 92–94, **95**
submission, 94, **95**, 100
of people, 127–31
for approaching pets, 127–28, **128**, <u>131</u>
belly up, 128–29, **129**
bending, 129, **135**
crouching, 129–30, **130**, 154
when giving commands, 205
rolling and, <u>93</u>
during sleep, <u>97</u>
T-posture, 97–99, **98**, 129, 135
Pouncing, 93–94, **95**
Praise, as reward, 170–71, 217
Prozac, to treat
fear of noises, 320
kneading and nursing, 385
wool sucking, 455
Prozyme, to prevent dung eating, 296
Pug, 60
Pupils, dilated
communicating with, 5, 60–62, **62**, 72
as light reaction, 14
Puppies
barking by, 252–53
biting by
chin, <u>180</u>
inhibiting, 263, 328, 330
during play, 265
calm temperament in, encouraging, 314–15
calorie requirements of, 344
chewing by, 273
choosing, 177–83
breed differences and, 178–80
personality of, predicting, 180–83
crate training and, 314
dung eating by, 294
eating objects by, 306
face licking by, <u>171</u>
food for, types of, 337
grass eating by, 301–2
humping by, 363–64

leash and
pulling, 388
training, 392–93
new, introducing, 369
socializing, 329–30
weaning age of, 385
Puppy mills, 183
Purring, meaning of, 112–13

Q

"Quiet" command, 214, 361

R

Ragdoll cat, 187
Rain, playing in, 319–20
Regurgitating. *See* Vomiting
Reinforcement, training and
intermittent, 292
positive, 201
Relaxation, communicating, by
blinking, 62
ear position, 68, **69**
sleep posture, 97
whisker position, **57**
Repellents, to prevent chewing, 276
Rescue programs, 193
Retriever. *See also* Golden retriever; Labrador retriever
chewing by, 272–73
toy preferences of, 225
Rewards, types of
affection, 170–71
positive reinforcement, 201
praise, 202–3, 217
treats, 46, 171–72, 201–3
Rhodesian Ridgeback, 109
Rolling in smelly things, 93
controlling, 416–17
reasons for, 414–15
shampooing after, 415
Rottweiler
assertiveness of, 180, 227
leash pulling by, 392
size of, 376
tug-of-war games with, 227
Routine, dogs and, 315
Rubbing, reasons for
dominance, 420
habit, 421
insecurity, 420
itching or allergies, 420–21
scent marking, 165, 418–20, 419, 423

S

Sadness, facial expression for, 79–80, **79**
Saint Bernard, 21
Saliva, disinfectant qualities of, 397
Saluki, 83, 317
Samoyed, 66, 392
Scat Mat, as deterrent, 431–32
Scent. *See also* Smell, sense of
for behavior modification, 162–64, 166–67
to communicate
fear, 160
stress, 164
human, 160–62, 163
marking, 350
of owner, 419, 423
reasons for, 438–39
by rubbing, 418–19, 419, 423
by scratching, 422–23
in toys, 34
using, to prevent
chewing, 164
digging, 164
scratching, 166
separation anxiety, 162
urination, inappropriate, 166–67, 439
Schnauzer, 49, 261
Science Diet pet foods, 344
Scolding dogs, inadvisability of, 280–81
Scottish terrier, 193
Scratching
discouraging, with scent, 166
as marking behavior, 166

Scratching furniture
  preventing, with
    furniture covers, 424
    declawing, 426–27
    oiling wood furniture, 424–25
    scratching posts, 425–26, 425
  reasons for, 6
    claw maintenance, 423
    scent marking, 422–23
    stretching, 423–24
    unconscious behavior, 424
Scratching posts, 425–26, 425
Screams, cat, 114
Seasonal affective disorder, dogs and, 279
Sebaceous glands, marking and, 166
Seizures, predicted by dogs, 48, 50, 51
Senses, of pets. *See specific senses*
Separation anxiety, 310–15, 407
  behavior associated with
    chewing, 274, 311
    digging, 285
    house soiling, 311
    howling, 108–9, 311, 361–62
  example of, 313
  preventing, 311–15
  recognizing, 310–11
Shampoo, odors and, 415
Shetland sheepdogs
  attacking hands or feet by, 243
  barking by, 231
  chasing cats by, 269
Shoes, destroyed by pets, 5, 6
Shyness, fear and, 321, 322
Siamese cat
  affectionate nature of, 172
  eye color of, 60
  nursing by, 387
  temperament of, 188
  vision of, 14
  vocalization by, 111, 252, 359
  wool sucking by, 454
Siberian husky. *See* Husky
Sierra antifreeze, 46
"Sit" command
  for cats, 217–19
  for dogs, 155, 208
Sixth sense, of pets, 47–52
Skunk smell, eliminating, 415
Sleep
  amount of, 401
  bed hogging during, 348–51
  body posture during, 97, 349
Smell, sense of
  acuity of, 28, 29, 43, 49, 159, 160, 161, 433
  appetite and, 34
  aromatherapy and, 31
  communicating with
    by cats, 164–67
    by dogs, 160–64
  encouraging pet's use of, 31–34
  flehmen, by cats, 30
  human scent and, 160–62, 163
  importance of, 29
  Jacobson's organ and, 30, 165
  perfumes and, 34
  rolling by dogs and, 93, 414–17
  toy preference and, 274–75
  tracking dogs and, 33, 163
  using, for
    behavior management, 32–33, 162–64, 166–67
    social interaction, 31–34
    teaching tracking, 33
  visual impairment and, 19–20
Smiling
  by dogs, 4, 74
  by people, 126–27, 143
Snappy Trainers, as deterrent, **373**, 374
Sniffing
  reasons for, 433–34
  undesirable, managing, 434–36
Social status, fighting to establish, 327, 330
Soft Paws, to manage scratching by cats, 386, 427
Sounds. *See also* Hearing
  fear of
    breed differences and, 317
    managing, 317–20
  frequency range of, 21, 317, 319
  startling pets with, 234, 246, 299, 373–74
Space, personal, crowding and, 278, 280

Spaying. *See also* Neutering
  digging and, 288
  humping and, 366
Speeds, running, 225
Sphynx cat, 111, 188
Spinal anatomy, sleeping position and, 349
Spoiling
  finicky eating and, 334
  play and, 228
  with unearned affection, 169
Spraying, 437–43. *See also* House soiling; Marking
  meaning of, 438
  preventing, with
    cleaning, 166–67, 440–41
    communication, 442
    confinement, 442
    Feliway, 439
    neutering, 165, 356, 443
    training, 443
  reasons for, 165–66, 268, 439–40, 441
Springer spaniel, 445
Staring, 124–26. *See also* Eye contact
  by cats, 64, 79, 99
  duration of, 141
  by herding dogs, 145
  at pets, 15–16, 126
  by puppies, 182
  as sign of
    aggression, **63**, 64, 99, 240, **247**
    alertness, **63**
    authority, 64, 143–44
    concentration, 64
  stopping, 143
Startling pets
  barking response to, 253
  by using
    compressed air, 375
    noise, 234, 246, 299, 432
    Snappy Trainers, **373**, 374
    verbal noises, 150
    water, 16, 246, 299, 374–75
  using, to prevent
    food stealing, 342
    jumping on counters, 373–74, **373**
"Stay" command
  separation anxiety and, 312–14
  teaching, 117, 210
  voice tone for, 117
Stealing food. *See* Food stealing
Stereotypy, boredom and, 307
Stomach capacity, eating habits and, 447
Strangers, fear of
  managing, 322–25
  reasons for, 322
Stress
  in animal shelter, 192
  appetite and, 42
  behavior associated with
    food refusal, 42
    house soiling, 311, 355
    hyperactivity, 311
    licking, 397
    separation anxiety, 311
    wool sucking, 455
  communicating, by
    blinking, 62
    scent, 164
    vocalizations, 109
    yawning, 126, 458–61, 460
Stretching and scratching, by cats, 423–24
String swallowing, by cats, 226, 307
Submission, communicating, by
  ear position, 68
  eye position and movement, 59, 62–63, **63**
  facial expression, 74, 79–80
  licking, 396
  posture, 94, **95**, 100, 144, 405, **405**
  tail position and movement, 84, **85**, 88, 90
  vocalizations, 104, 107, 148
Submissive urination, 355–56
Sunburn, preventing, 188
Swallowing objects
  preventing, 308–9
  reasons for, 307–8

T

Tag, playing, 411
Tail chasing, 83
Tails
  balance and, 82
  communicating with
    by cats, 86, **87**
    by dogs, 84–86, **85**, 91, 94
    position of, 86–88, **89**
  to communicate
    biting intention, 264
    dominance, 84, **85**, 88, **89**, 90
    happiness, 84, **85**, 86, **87**, 88, **89**
    submissiveness, 84, **85**, 88, 90
  docked, 83, 90
  rubbing, 39–40
"Take it nice" command, 209–10
Talking back, by cats, 149
Tape, double-sided, as deterrent, 375
Tapetum fibrosum, vision and, 14
Tapeworms, dung eating and, 293
Taste, sense of
  acuity of, 43, 43, 308
  feeding and, 42, 44–46
  importance of, 43–44
  mechanics of, 42–43
  unpleasant, as repellent, 276
Tastebuds, 42, 43
Teeth chattering, meaning of, 113
Teething, chewing and, 182, 183
Telepathy, of pets, 52
Temperament
  breed differences, in cats, 187–88
  communication and, 7–8
  of kitten, testing for, 186
  of older pets, 190–91, 192
  play and, 227, 228
Temperature, body, digging to regulate, 283, 286
Termites, detected by cats, 27
Terriers
  affection, desire for, 172
  barking by, 180
  chasing cats by, 268
  digging by, 282, 285
  ear shape of, 66
  energy level of, 178, 181, 285, 403
  field of vision of, 13
  leash pulling by, 392
  toy preferences of, 225
  as watchdogs, 180
Territory
  defending, by
    barking, 105, 254
    nighttime activity, 400
  marking, by
    rolling in smelly things, 415
    rubbing, 165, 418–19, 419, 420, 423
    scratching, 166, 422–23
    urinating, 165–66, 356, 437–41
Testosterone
  aggression and, 238, 241
  spraying and, 438
Thiamin deficiency, wool sucking and, 455
Thirst
  breed differences and 291
  reducing, with wet food, 291
Throwing up. *See* Vomiting
Thunderstorms, fear of, 316–20
Thyroid hormone, nighttime activity and, 400
Toilet, drinking from
  preventing, 290–92
  reasons for, 289–90
Toilet paper, attacking, 248–49, 251
Tone of voice
  for calling pets, 151
  of children, 150
  for giving commands, 203–5
  modulating, 148–50, 169
  for startling pets, 150
  volume of, 150, 205
Tonkinese cat, 111
Touch, sense of
  bonding and, 38
  communicating with, 278
  heat and, 36

importance of, 20, 35
mechanisms of
guard hairs, 37
nerve endings in nose, 36–37
whiskers, 35, 37
petting
cats, 38–39
dogs, 39–40
Toxic materials. *See* Poisons
Toys
for cats, 15, 246
Cat Dancer, 223
catnip, 34, 246, 301, 382
Crazy Circle, 223
houseplants as, 300, 302
laser lights, 456
paper, 251
paper bags, 187
scented, 34
storing, 226
therapeutic use of, 383, 402
for dogs, 287
balls, 410
Bite a Bone, 223
breed preferences and, 225
Buster Cube, 287, 406
chew, 274–76, 275
Frisbees, 18, 412
Kong, 223, 309, 361
Number Needed, 223–24
Nylabone Gumabone Frisbee, 223
pig ears, 275
for redirection, 271
scented, 34
Soft Bite Floppy Disc, 223
to teach tracking, 33
fighting over, 327
possessiveness with
managing, 410–13
reasons for, 408–10
tails as, 83
using, to prevent
attacking feet or hands, 246–47
howling, 361
killing mice, 383
nighttime activity, 402
wool sucking, 456
T-posture, dominance and, 97–99, **98**, 129, 135
Tracking dogs
bloodhound, 163
German shepherd, 257
sniffing by, 231
teaching, 33
water consumption by, 291
Traction, on play surface, 224
Training
actors, animal, 204
benefits of, 206–7
hand signals
for "sit" command, 155
verbal commands and, combined, 117, 119, 142
eye contact and, 142, 143, 144
rate of learning, 213
with smell, 162–64, 166–67
teaching commands, 200–205
for tracking, 33
verbal commands
hand signals and, combined, 117, 119, 142
modulating voice for, 148–51
rewards, for listening to, 151
startling with, 150
"watch me" technique, 142
Training lessons
for cats
come, 219
freeze, 219–20
sit, 217–19
tips for, 217
waving, 220–21, **220**
for dogs
come, 212–13
dead, 207–8, **208**
down, 208–9, **209**
get your toy, 215
go to your place, 214
out, 210–12, **212**
quiet, 214
sit, 208
stay, 210
take it nice, 209–10

Travel phobia
  preventing, with
    crating, 453
    desensitization, 450–52
    rewards, 452
  reasons for, 449–50
Treats
  food stealing and, 340
  as rewards, 46, 171–72, 201–2
  tricks for giving, 201–3
  using, for counterconditioning, 324–25
Tug-of-war, playing, 227
Tulips, toxicity of, 304

U

Urinary tract infections, 354, 364
Urination
  inappropriate (*see also* Marking; Spraying)
    discouraging, with scent, 166–67
    reasons for, 165, 269
  submissive, 355–56
Urine, cat, pheromones in, 437, 439

V

Vestibular apparatus, balance and, 72
Vetasyl, for hair balls, 448
Vibrations, detected by pets, 26, 35, 36
Vibrissae. *See* Whiskers
Vinegar, to clean marked areas, 440
Vision. *See also* Eyes
  acuity of, 11
  binocular, 13, 14
  breed differences and, 13, 14
  of cats, 13–14
  color, 13, 14, 15
  communicating with, 12, 14–19
  of dogs, 11–13
  eye contact (*see* Eye Contact)
  field of view, 13, 14, 16
  at night, 14
  peripheral, 51
  staring (*see* Staring)
  toys for cats and, 15
Vocal communication
  behavior associated with
    barking and meowing, 253–58
    howling and yowling, 358–62
  by cats, 5, 92, 110–14, 148
    breed differences and, 111, 149, 188
    meowing, 111–12, 148
    purring, 112–13
    silent speech, 114
    strained-intensity sounds, 113–14
    talking back, 149
    vocabulary of, 5, 255
  by dogs, 92, 103–9, 147–48
    barking, 104, 147
    growling, 107–8, 147
    howling, 108–9
    individual differences in, 109, 137
    vocabulary of, 255
    whining, 104, 105–6
  by people to pets, 115–20
    body language and, 118–19
    calling pets, 151
    children and, 139
    comprehension, breed differences and, 115–16
    giving commands, 203–5
    imitating pets, 120
    pet names, 198–99
    startling pets, 150
    tips for, 116–18
    tone of voice and, 147–51
    visually impaired pet and, 20
    volume of, 150
Vomiting, 444–48
  example of, 445
  inducing, 303
  reasons for, 444–48
    car sickness, 449–50
    grass or plant eating, 300, 302, 303
    hair, swallowing, 446–48
    indiscriminate eating, 444–45
    speed of eating, 445–46

W

Walking dogs, behavior problems and
- aggression toward other dogs, 239
- marking, 437, 441
- sniffing, 433

Watchdogs, 180
"Watch me" command, 142
Water
- from toilets, drinking, 289–92
- using, to startle pets, 16, 246, 299, 374

Water bowls, 291
"Wave" command, 220–21
Weaning age, 385, 387
Weimaraner, 4
Whimpering, meaning of, 148
Whining, reasons for
- attention seeking, 254
- begging, 107
- learned behavior, 104, 105
- pain, 107
- submissiveness, 107

Whippet, 67, 231
Whiskers, 55–58
- locations of, 37, 56
- sensitivity of, 58
- using, for
  - communication, 56–58, **57**
  - eye protection, 37, 57
  - navigation, 49
  - touch, 35, 37
- waist-whisker ratio, 58

Wolves, dogs and, 1
Wool sucking
- preventing, 455–57
- reasons for, 454–55

Worms. *See* Parasites, intestinal

Y

Yawning, 458–61
- as calming signal, 143, 145, 458
- by cats, 126
- frequency of, 459
- by people, 126, 143, 145
- as stress signal, 4, 458–61, 460

Yelling, at pets, 16, 372–73, 417
Yelping, 265–66
Yowling
- breed differences and, 359
- reasons for, 359
- stopping, 359–60